THE SECOND ISAIAH

INTRODUCTION, TRANSLATION
AND COMMENTARY TO
CHAPTERS XL–LV

Oxford University Press, Amen House, London E.C.4

GLASGOW NEW YORK TORONTO MELBOURNE WELLINGTON
BOMBAY CALCUTTA MADRAS KARACHI LAHORE DACCA
CAPE TOWN SALISBURY NAIROBI IBADAN ACCRA
KUALA LUMPUR HONG KONG

THE SECOND ISAIAH

INTRODUCTION, TRANSLATION AND COMMENTARY TO CHAPTERS XL–LV

BY

CHRISTOPHER R. NORTH

Professor Emeritus of Hebrew
University College of North Wales
Bangor

OXFORD
AT THE CLARENDON PRESS
1964

PRINTED IN GREAT BRITAIN

TO MY WIFE

PREFACE

THIS book is intended as an all-purposes commentary and my hope is that it may be reasonably intelligible to preachers and teachers whose knowledge of Hebrew is limited, and even to those who know no Hebrew at all.

The Translation is fairly literal, so long as it is understood that the unit of translation is the 'stich' (usually a 3-beat line) and not the single word. Occasionally I have paraphrased, where the literal translation of the standard English Versions may convey a misleading sense, as at xl. 10*b*. Reasons for such paraphrases are given in the Commentary.

I have often been uncertain where to place quotation-marks in the Translation. The reason is that the Prophet speaks in the name of God and it is by no means always clear whether the words are his own or those of God, for whom he is speaking.

The Commentary is as objective and impersonal as I have been able to make it, and I have only used the first-person pronoun in a single paragraph, at the end of the Introduction. I have tried to convey the meaning of the Hebrew in current English, allowing the text to explain itself in the context of Scripture as a whole.

As much as any text in the Old Testament, Deutero-Isaiah raises ultimate questions, questions which are certain to be vigorously debated for the rest of this century. In the last two sections of the Introduction I have indicated what those questions are and the reader will no doubt gather what is my attitude to them. But the answers to them must be left to theologians more expert than myself.

I have not cluttered the book with references to everything that everybody has ever written on the subject. To do so would only confuse the kind of reader I have in mind. Where an author is quoted with only a page reference, the title of his work will be found in the Bibliography. Where an author is mentioned without any page reference, the reference is to his Commentary *in loc.*

Each section of the Commentary proper begins with notes

on the text, printed in Hebrew, and the more difficult points of grammar. In the exegetical notes the text is transliterated and the transliterations of Hebrew and other Semitic words are as in *The Old Testament and Modern Study*, ed. H. H. Rowley, 1951, except that the distinction between (say) *ô* and *ō* is that between vowels pure-long and tone-long, not between long vowels written *plene* and defectively. Chapter and verse references are to the English Bible, and where the Hebrew numeration differs, Hebrew references are in italics and bracketed: e.g. Joel ii. 28 f. (*iii. 1 f.*).

The Index of Semitic Words is selective. To have listed every transliterated Hebrew word might have made the book appear more pretentious than (I hope) it is.

Two articles which would at least have been included in the Bibliography reached me only after my typescript had gone to the printer. Both are in *Supplements to Vetus Testamentum* IX, Leiden, 1963. They are A. Lauha: 'Das Schilfmeermotiv im Alten Testament', pp. 32–46, and M. Haran: 'The literary structure and chronological framework of the Prophecies in Is. xl–xlviii', pp. 127–55.

I owe much, as indeed do all contemporary Hebraists, to the lexicographical researches of Professor G. R. Driver. My thanks are also due to the Rev. Islwyn Blythin, M.A., a former pupil, now my colleague, who has compiled the Index of Scripture References.

Some few passages in the book are taken, by courtesy of the SCM Press, from my 'Torch' Commentary on Isaiah xl–lv.

Finally, I wish again to express my gratitude to the Delegates of the Oxford University Press for their acceptance of the book for publication, and to the readers of the Press for the skill and courtesy with which they have handled the proofs.

C. R. N.

Bangor
Easter, 1963

CONTENTS

ABBREVIATIONS

A	Aquila (Greek Version).
ANET	J. B. Pritchard, *Ancient Near Eastern Texts relating to the Old Testament*, 1950, ^{2}1955.
AOTB	H. Gressmann, *Altorientalische Texte und Bilder zum Alten Testament*, 2. Band, Bilder, ^{2}1927.
BDB	Brown–Driver–Briggs, *A Hebrew and English Lexicon of the Old Testament*, 1952.
BH	*Biblia Hebraica*, Edidit Rud. Kittel, ^{3}1937.
BJRL	*Bulletin of the John Rylands Library.*
BL	Bauer–Leander, *Historische Grammatik der hebräischen Sprache*, Erster Band, 1922.
BSOAS	*Bulletin of the School of Oriental and African Studies.*
BWANT	Beiträge zur Wissenschaft vom Alten und Neuen Testament.
BZAW	Beihefte zur *Zeitschrift für die alttestamentliche Wissenschaft.*
DI	Deutero-Isaiah (Prophet or Book).
EVV	The Standard English Versions (AV, RV, RSV) where they substantially agree.
GK	Gesenius–Kautzsch, *Hebrew Grammar*, Engl. Trans. A. E. Cowley, ^{28}1910.
HUCA	*Hebrew Union College Annual.*
JBL	*Journal of Biblical Literature.*
JTS	*Journal of Theological Studies.*
KB	Köhler–Baumgartner, *Lexicon in Veteris Testamenti Libros*, 1953.
MT	Massoretic Text.
NEB	*The New English Bible, New Testament*, 1961.
OL	The Old Latin Version.
P	Peshitta Syriac (occasionally the P Code).
PEQ	*Palestine Exploration Quarterly.*
Q^{a}	The First Isaiah Scroll from Qumran (1QIs^{a}).
Σ	Symmachus (Greek Version).
SOED	*The Shorter Oxford English Dictionary*, 2 vols., ^{3}1944.
SS	C. R. North, *The Suffering Servant in Deutero-Isaiah*, 1948, ^{2}1956.
Syn.	A. B. Davidson, *Hebrew Syntax*, ^{3}1902.
T	Targum.
Tens.	S. R. Driver, *A Treatise on the Use of the Tenses in Hebrew*, ^{3}1892.
TLZ	*Theologische Literaturzeitung.*
V	Vulgate.
ZAW	*Zeitschrift für die alttestamentliche Wissenschaft.*

I · INTRODUCTION

HISTORICAL BACKGROUND

It is all but unanimously agreed that the historical background of Isa. xl–lv is the closing years of the Babylonian exile. (For the contrary opinion of C. C. Torrey see *infra*, pp. 23 f.) The Persian conqueror Cyrus II (the Great), who died in 529 B.C., is twice named in the prophecy (xliv. 28, xlv. 1) and the general opinion is that he is also referred to in xli. 2, 25, xlv. 13, xlvi. 11, xlviii. 14 f. He rose to prominence some years before 550, and after a series of spectacular victories, first over the Medes, then over Croesus of Lydia (547), and finally over the Babylonians, he entered Babylon in 538 and gave permission to the peoples who had been deported there to return to their own countries.

During the ministry of Isaiah, in the second half of the eighth century B.C., the world power was Assyria, and the Prophet described Assyria as a rod with which Yahweh would chastise his own people (x. 5–15). In 612 Nineveh, the Assyrian capital, fell before a joint attack of Medes and Babylonians. In 605 the Egyptian Pharaoh Necho II was defeated at Carchemish on the upper Euphrates by the Babylonian Nebuchadrezzar, and the greater part of the Assyrian Empire came under the control of a revived Babylonian (sometimes called Chaldean) Empire. In 586 Jerusalem fell to the Babylonians; the Temple was destroyed and the more influential of the inhabitants of Judah were deported to Babylonia. (There had already been a first deportation, which included King Jehoiachin, in 597.)

In Isa. xl–lv Assyria is not mentioned except as an oppressor in the undefined past (lii. 4). The Jews—if we may now call them so—are in exile (xlii. 22–25, xlviii. 20) in the land of the Chaldeans (xlvii. 5 f.). Jerusalem and the cities of Judah are in ruins but are going to be rebuilt (xliv. 26, xlv. 13, lii. 2, 9), likewise the Temple (xliv. 28). Babylon is herself to be conquered (xliii. 14, xlvi. 1 f., xlvii) and the Jews are to return to their homeland (xl. 9–11, li. 3). Even, therefore, if xl–lv was written by the eighth-century Isaiah, it is against this sixth-century background (*circa* 550–538) that it must be interpreted.

DATE AND AUTHORSHIP

The Qumran Scrolls of Isaiah are tangible evidence that by the beginning of the Christian era *Isaiah* existed in the form in which we have it, and—this especially on the evidence of Scroll B—that its text was already substantially that of the present MT. That Isaiah was believed to be the author of the whole book is clear from the NT (Matt. xii. 17; Acts viii. 30), but as if to indicate that NT writers could be mistaken, or, it may be, casual about such matters, in Mark i. 2—according to the best manuscripts—a passage from Mal. iii. 1 is quoted as from 'Isaiah the prophet'.

Belief in the unity of *Isaiah* was already current early in the second century B.C. In Ecclesiasticus (*circa* 180 B.C.) there is a passage which reads: 'In his (Isaiah's) days the sun went backward; and he added life to the king. He saw by an excellent spirit what should come to pass at the last; and he comforted them that mourned in Zion. He shewed the things that should be to the end of time, and hidden things or ever they came' (Ecclus. xlviii. 23 f.). This is evidence that the story of Hezekiah's sickness (Isa. xxxviii) and what we now call DI (cf. xl. 1, lxi. 3) were believed to be by Isaiah. It may be remarked that in the Qumran Scroll A there are three ruled but empty lines at the foot of the column containing ch. xxxiii. This *may* indicate some recollection or tradition that there was a change of author at that point. (It is sometimes argued that DI begins at xxxiv.) But too much should not be made of this, since xl. 1–2*a* is written on the last line of the column containing xxxix.

OT prophecy is largely prediction. Isa. xl–lv (lxvi) is prediction. But is it prediction two centuries in advance? There is no denying that prophets sometimes ventured on 'long-range' prophecy, but when they did it was briefly and in general terms, as in Isa. ii. 1–4, xi. 6–9. The predictions of a prophet were always related to the circumstances of his own time and it is difficult to see the relevance for Isaiah's time of a corpus of sixteen chapters containing descriptions of events and persons two centuries later. What is predicted in Isa. xl–lv is the rapidly approaching overthrow of Babylon and the return of the Jews to their homeland. The exile is not predicted (as in xxxix. 5 ff., whoever the author of those verses may be) but has already taken place, and the oppressor is not Assyria in the eighth century but Babylon in the sixth.

There is one passage in the prophecy which is unintelligible if it was written by the eighth-century Isaiah:

> From now on I announce to you new things,
> things hidden, which you have not known.
> They are created now, not long ago,
> and until now you have never heard of them,
> lest you should say, 'Of course I knew them'
> (xlviii. 6 f.)

If, as those who defend the Isaianic authorship agree, the 'new things' were not to happen for two centuries, it could not be said in the eighth century that 'they are created now'. Nor could sixth-century readers be told that they had never heard of them. They might fairly retort that they had, unless it be that xl–lv was hidden for two centuries, and the defenders of Isaianic authorship do not allege that it was. The conception of 'hidden things' as 'sealed apocrypha' (cf. Dan. viii. 26, xii. 4, 9; Rev. x. 4, xxii. 10) is apocalyptic and was not current in Isaiah's time. Isa. xl–lv is not an apocalypse, and viii. 16 has to do with oral teaching, not with a sealed 'book'. Another 'now' which is meaningless if the prophecy was written in the eighth century is that in xliii. 19. Indeed, the overwhelming impression left by xl–lv is that its predictions are soon to be fulfilled. That this raises serious problems for the interpreter is not to be denied (see *infra*, pp. 23 ff.), but the problems are the same no matter whether the author was Proto- or a presumed Deutero-Isaiah.

There is much else in xl–lv besides the historical background which points to a later date than the eighth century, but there is no need to enter into details at this stage. Even Roman Catholic scholars, notwithstanding the findings of the Biblical Commission (1908) that it was inadmissible to say that Isa. xl–lxvi was *not* the work of Isaiah, now appear to be free to say that the chapters are by an anonymous author (or authors) contemporary with the situations described (see Steinmann, pp. 7–11). In short, apart from Torrey and the one or two scholars who have shared his views, and ultra-conservative scholars who feel bound to take the NT quotations of Deutero-Isaianic passages from 'Isaiah' as final for the discussion, it is agreed on all hands that xl–lv is by an anonymous prophet of the exile. In the closing verses of the prophecy (lv. 12 f.) the release from Babylon is still future and the *terminus ad quem* of the chapter should be earlier than the liberation edict of Cyrus. The beginning of the Prophet's ministry almost certainly dates from about the time when Cyrus began his career of conquest. The earliest of his poems which can be fairly accurately dated is xli. 1 ff., and it fits in well with the early victories of Cyrus, up to the fall of Sardis in the autumn of 547. Nothing is known of the person and work of the Prophet except what little may be inferred from his poems. He remains 'the great unknown'.

LITERARY STRUCTURE

For some twenty years after the publication of Duhm's *Commentary on Isaiah* (first edition 1892) it was still usual to regard Isa. xl–lv as a *book* written to a definite plan, though there was already general agreement that the pre-exilic prophets were speakers rather than writers. Budde, in particular, fought a vigorous rearguard action in which he maintained the unity (*Bucheinheit*) of DI (*Das Buch Jesaia*, 1909). His argument was largely determined by the exegetical premiss that the Servant of lii. 13–liii. 12 must be the Servant = Israel of the rest of the prophecy, this against Duhm, who had asserted that the 'Servant Songs' were from a later author than DI and that the Servant in them was an individual. Budde divided xl–lv into six parts: an Introduction (xl–xli), four main sections (xlii–xliv. 23, xliv. 24–xlviii, xlix–li. 8, li. 9–liii) and a Conclusion (liv–lv). He allowed that the sixteen chapters were not published together. The several parts were circulated anonymously, and secretly, very much as flysheets. This, he admitted, necessitated some overlapping and repetition, and the whole was not a composition of which each part was neatly joined to what preceded it.

In 1914 Gressmann opened the flood-gates in his article 'The Literary Analysis of DI'. He seized upon Budde's qualificatory admissions. It is characteristic of flysheets, he argued, that each is a unit in itself; but none of them necessarily presupposes another, and there can therefore be no question of one large composition. A unit of sixteen chapters would be unique in the prophetical literature. Moreover, a writer who sets out to compose an artistic whole does not repeat himself, as Budde allowed that DI had done. An answer to that might be that a modern author would not repeat himself, but it does not follow that a Hebrew writer would not. His persuasion would be by repetitive emphasis—poetic parallelism shows that—rather than by logical argument. Be that as it may, Gressmann proceeded, largely on the basis of introductory and concluding formulae, to divide the sixteen chapters into 49 independent pieces or *Sprüche* of an average length of six or seven verses. This started a critical fashion which has since been followed by most writers on the subject. The largest number of units is Köhler's 70. Other estimates vary, but 50 is about the average.

The form-critics might have been more cautious if they had drawn the logical conclusion from Gressmann's thesis. Gressmann, whether he realized it or not, was in some ways begging the question. In his final paragraph he wrote: 'If DI is to be assigned a place in the literary history of Israelite prophecy it must be said that what characterizes him is that the dissolution of the prophetic types begins with him. The fixed forms that had prevailed until then break up. While the types of utterance employed by the pre-exilic prophets are mostly very sharply distinguished from one another, in DI exact separation is often impossible; the supplementary reflexions with which the oracles are surrounded have overgrown everything, so that the boundary lines between the word of God and the word of the Prophet cannot always be clearly recognized' ('Die literarische Analyse Deuterojesajas', p. 295). In other words, while Gressmann said that DI was much like Amos, Proto-Isaiah, and Jeremiah, he also said that he was different from them. His individual units are more complex than theirs—Köhler shows this very convincingly (p. 103 f.)—and if DI is not a writing prophet he comes near to being one. (Even a quite long modern poem may be in the poet's mind in very much its finished form before he puts pen to paper.)

We may now proceed to reduce Köhler's seventy units to something like the usual fifty. Thus, Köhler has three units in xlvi, not including vv. 5–8 which he thinks are not genuine. He has five in xlvii, the taunt-song against Babylon. Each of these chapters is surely a unit, and Köhler's units correspond roughly, though not exactly, to the paragraphs of the RSV.

He has four units in xl. 1–11. So has Mowinckel, though he calls vv. 1–11 an introductory statement (*programmatiske utsagn*), i.e. a prelude or overture to the whole. It is likely enough that the overture contains what were originally four separate poems; but even Eissfeldt, who can fragmentize with anybody, after saying that xl. 1–8 consists of three 'at least relatively independent pieces', goes on to say: 'All the same, the three passages are to be thought of as from the outset parts of the higher unity vv. 1–8' (*Einleitung in das AT*, pp. 379 f.). That is surely so, not because two of the pieces begin with a catchword (*ḳôl*, 'voice') and in a third Zion-Jerusalem is bidden to lift up her voice, but because the three (Eissfeldt) or four (Mowinckel) themes keep recurring in the main body of the prophecy as pervasively as do the themes of the overture to *Die Meistersinger*.

Again, Köhler makes a separate poem of xli. 8–10, 'But you, Israel my servant, Jacob whom I have chosen . . . fear not', having removed vv. 6–7, the fragment about idol manufacture, and attached them to xl. 19. Mowinckel removes vv. 5–7 and makes a unit of 1–4, 8–10, this presumably because ver. 8 begins with a conjunction ('but') and conjunctions normally join what follows to what precedes them. Surely Mowinckel is right, whether or not we remove 5 (6)–7, especially if, with Begrich, we point the verbs as imperatives: 'See, you far shores, and fear . . . but you, Israel my servant . . . fear not!' Köhler then takes xli. 11–13 as a separate poem, perhaps because of the metre, which is 3:2, not 3:3 as in the preceding verses. Mowinckel also takes it as a separate poem but says it is possibly a continuation of what precedes, notwithstanding the change of metre. (We should hesitate to cut up Ps. xcviii because it begins in 3:2 rhythm and then changes to 3:3.) Again, Köhler and most form-critics treat xli. 14–16 as a separate unit, partly no doubt because of the change of figure, and partly because Israel is now addressed in the 2nd pers. sing. fem. (*'al-tîr^{e}'î*). But we may easily overlook that in vv. 15*b*–16 the verbs are once more masculine. This may be because the poet forgot that he had started with the feminine form and changed to the masculine, though one would judge from the rest of his work that he was too skilful an artist to nod like that. Is it not rather that the figure of the worm (*tôla'aṯ*, fem.) required the feminine in the preceding imperative and that thereafter he could revert to the masculine? (The feminine suffixes in 14*b*–15 can be pointed as masculines without altering the MT.) This is not to say that vv. 1–16 were composed during one period of pacing to and fro along a Babylonian canal. It may well consist of four poems composed at intervals. It is easy enough to relate them to one another by catchwords, though catchwords are not mere sounds but convey related ideas. In xli. 1–16 there are, if we choose to read them so, four short poems. They may or may not be consecutive in time, but together they make up a unit of extraordinary impressiveness, and they stand almost inevitably together, and exactly where they are.

Another example that may be adduced is the 'New Song' in xlii. 10–17. Köhler, but not Mowinckel, takes this as two pieces, the first ending with the description of Yahweh as a berserk warrior (metre 3:3) and the second beginning with the figure of Yahweh as a woman in childbirth (metre very appropriately irregular, but mainly 2:2 and 3:2). For an analysis of the passage see the Commentary *in loc.* in which it is argued that the passage is a single unit. It may even be a subsidiary unit in a larger whole. Engnell, for example, would argue so. According to him, DI is a prophetic collection of the type he calls 'liturgy'. By this he does not mean that it was intended for use as a liturgy, but that it is a prophetic imitation of such a liturgy, and specifically of a New Year festival-liturgy. This idea was first suggested by Rafael Gyllenberg in the *Svensk Exegetisk Årsbok*, v, 1940, pp. 83–94, but it has not been worked out in detail. It may be doubted whether it can be worked out in detail, since we have little knowledge of the form a full liturgy would take in ancient Israel. A major reason why Engnell takes Isa. xl–lv as a liturgical whole is that he wants to relate his Messiah-Servant of lii. 13–liii. 12 to the comparatively near context lv. 3 f., the passage about 'the sure mercies of David', a passage which cannot without further ado be given an individual messianic reference. Besides, if we are going to interpret the Servant from the proximate or general context, there is a case, as Budde insisted, for making the Servant = Israel.

Even Mowinckel, for whom Isa. xl–lv is a prophecy of what Engnell would call the *diwan*—not the liturgy—type, has no hesitation in saying that the influence of the Psalms, particularly of the enthronement psalms and liturgies, is very marked in DI.

As to Mowinckel's 'catchword' theory, no one has ever been wholly satisfied with it. Volz (p. xxxv) remarked that if pressed too hard it became 'an artificial and external scheme', and Eissfeldt that 'it is hardly right, at least not everywhere . . . rather would it appear that, at all events here and there, a grouping according to subject-matter is to be recognized' (*Der Gottesknecht bei DJ*, p. 10). Indeed, Mowinckel himself admitted community of subject-matter as a secondary principle of association. That was putting the cart before the horse. On the whole, community of subject-matter is the first, and catchwords a secondary principle of association. In *Det Gamle Testamente III* (1944) Mowinckel goes some way towards acknowledging this. He says that the chapters appear to be made up of three complexes of tradition: (1) xl–xliv. 23, words of comfort to Jacob-Israel, prefaced by xl. 1–11 and concluding with a short hymn, xliv. 23; (2) xliv. 24–xlviii, dealing mainly with Cyrus and the conquest of Babylon; (3) xlix–lv, words of comfort to Zion-Jerusalem, with a conclusion similar to the introduction to part 1. But having said so much, Mowinckel holds to his original theory in so far as he says that within the three main complexes catchwords are the first and similarities of subject-matter a secondary principle of association.

It seems likely, then, that many small units should be linked together, just where they stand, into larger complexes. For example, xl. 27–31 is related to the cosmological vv. 12–26 both by catchwords and as their proper sequel. (Gressmann treated xl. 12–31 as a unit.) The man who is in despair (*'ên 'ônîm*, 'powerless') is not to be comforted by the most impressive argument that Yahweh has 'omnipotent might' (*rō*ḇ *'ônîm*) at his disposal; he needs to be assured that 'those who wait for Yahweh renew their strength'. Or take the 'Awake, awake!' and 'Rouse yourself!' passages beginning at li. 9, 17 and li. 1, and the 'Listen to me' and 'Attend to me' passages at li. 1, 4, 7: if association is to be by catchwords they stand inevitably together. Equally inevitably they stand together if the associative principle is community of subject-matter.

Viewed as a whole, then, DI is a shapely and orderly document, more orderly indeed than any block of materials of comparable length in the prophetical writings. The main features of this shapeliness have long been remarked: Jacob-Israel in xl–xlviii, never in xliv–lv; Zion-Jerusalem in xlix–lv, not (except in the overture and xli. 27) in xl–xlviii; Cyrus and Babylon in xl–xlviii, never in xlix–lv; polemic against the idol-gods, summonses to assize-inquests, and the appeal to prophecy, in xl–xlviii, never in xlix–lv. Or if we take the references, implicit and explicit, to Cyrus: Cyrus, very appropriately, is not named until he is directly addressed, more than half-way through xl–xlviii, as if by that time there was no further need for anonymity and half-veiled allusions. This and much else points to the prophecies being in approximately chronological order. There is, notwithstanding much that may strike us as verbiage, a broad continuity in the Prophet's thinking. Following the prelude the theme is that of Yahweh as Creator; next Yahweh as Lord of history; and finally, Yahweh as Redeemer of Israel and Zion.

And now, if we can no longer be entirely content with the detached units theory, what is to be said of attempts to discover in the sixteen chapters a perfectly integrated, architectonic whole, as though what has come down to us is, exactly as it stands, the finished work of DI himself? That appears to be the view of Torrey, Kissane, and Muilenburg.

Torrey regarded xxxiv–xxxv, xl–lxvi as a unity of twenty-seven poems in all, with no break at the end of lv. He took lvi. 1, 7–8 (vv. 2–6 being a later insertion) as the continuative conclusion of lv, and there are sixteen poems in xl–lvi. 8. Kissane also regarded xl–lxvi as a unity, consisting of ten poems, each with a conclusion or 'tail-piece'. Each of these longish poems is further subdivided into three, and the whole is made up of ten triads on a logically developing theme. Like Torrey, he made no break at the end of lv. His seventh section ends at lvi. 2, of all places—it looks as if we must take liberties with ch. lvi if we are to join it to lv—while lvi. 3–8 is a later insertion. Torrey and Kissane had much in common; each thought of DI as a poet rather than a prophet. But although each proposed to analyse the poem into its several units, hardly ever do the beginnings and endings of their sections and sub-sections correspond. This does not inspire confidence in the methods or results of detailed analysis. It is plain that subjective considerations must largely determine the literary analysis of a poem so long and so repetitive as Isa. xl–lv.

This brings us to Muilenburg, who divides xl–lv into twenty-one poems in all; fourteen in xl–xlviii under the general heading 'The Imminent Coming of God', and seven in xlix–lv, under the heading 'The Redemption of Israel'. The twenty-one poems are subdivided into a total of 127 strophes, not including a dozen or so short pieces variously labelled as proems, codas, lyrical interludes, and insertions. The strophes average six to a poem. The smallest number in a poem is three, the largest twelve. They vary in length from a single verse to as many as seven; the majority consist of either two or three verses. The principles on which they are recognized and delimited are similar, though rather more numerous and detailed, to those employed by Gressmann for his *Sprüche*. 'Second Isaiah uses a large number of devices to begin and end his strophes. Notable among these, of course, is the emphatic personal pronoun ("I", "thou", &c.) the oracular formula, exclamations like "Behold", imperatives like the call to hear, transitional devices like "But now", rhetorical questions, impressive vocatives like "O afflicted one, storm-tossed and not comforted", particles like "for" (*kî*), and shifts in speaker or those addressed. Perhaps the most common and in many ways the most impressive among these is the use of the imperative' (Muilenburg, p. 391).

Muilenburg's work on the poetic form, structure, and style of DI is as fine as anything in his Commentary; but how far he believes that he has accurately divined the intentions of the Prophet, or whether his analysis is his way of making the prophecy intelligible and assimilable to himself, it is difficult to say. Let it be said without reserve that the second of these alternatives is exegetically permissible and fair, on the principle that Scripture may well contain more than the original writers were consciously aware of, and that it is the task of successive generations to make explicit what may only have been implicit in the original texts. But it seems unlikely that Muilenburg supposes his detailed analysis to be absolute and final. It is certain that if we start from the assumption that in DI we have a series of poems from one author, and roughly in logical and chronological order, and then set ourselves the task of analysing them as Muilenburg has done, no two scholars will agree either with one another or with Muilenburg.

Most students will probably feel more happy about

Muilenburg's strophic divisions than about his larger units. For example, he makes xlii. 1–4 (the first Servant Song) the concluding strophe of his third poem (xli–xlii. 4), entitled 'The Trial of the Nations'. xlii. 5 is the 'Oracular Introduction' to a fresh poem (xlii. 5–17) entitled 'The New Event of the Divine Intervention'. It is surely more probable that xlii. 1–4 is the beginning, not the end, of a section, and that vv. 4–9 are explicative of it and not to be disjoined from it. There seems no justification for taking xlix. 1–6 (13) as the beginning of a single poem, 'The Servant of the Lord: Called, Commissioned, and Comforted', which extends to the end of xlix. Verses 14 ff., beginning 'And Zion said, Yahweh has forsaken me and the LORD has forgotten me', seem to have no thematic relation to the Servant. Neither have vv. 1–3 of ch. l, 'This is the word of the LORD, where is your mother's writ of divorce . . .', any connexion with vv. 4–9 (11), the third Servant Song, so obvious that ch. l should be taken as a unit of four strophes. Muilenburg takes lii. 13–liii. 12 to be a separate poem with five strophes. This is obviously right. But it is difficult to see what connexion it has with either the preceding or the following context. It is of course where it is, and if we take the prophecy as a whole it is proper to say that it is in harmony with the major context. But the Servant Songs read like separate pieces, and it is difficult to believe that they were contemporary with the main prophecy in the sense that they appeared in a first and definitive edition of his work by DI himself. This is not to say that the Songs are not from the Prophet; indeed, the present writer has been at considerable pains to try to show that they are (*SS*, ch. IX). But if they are, the likelihood is that they made their first appearance in what we may call a second edition of the book, whether issued by the Prophet or by his disciples. There is no hint of the Suffering Servant in ch. lv, the happy ending which recapitulates the beginning, with its fulfilment in (say) ten years from the time it was uttered. As to the relationship of the Servant to Cyrus, two possibilities have been suggested: (i) That Cyrus is the agent of the political, and the Servant the agent of the spiritual rehabilitation of Israel, in which case they might be expected to be contemporaries; (ii) the more satisfying suggestion that the revelation of the Suffering Servant came to the Prophet when he had found reason to be disappointed in Cyrus, or—and this is more likely—disappointed in the empirical Israel. His final vision is not of the political rehabilitation of Israel but of the salvation of mankind. There is no political background to the first, third, and fourth Songs, and only a diminishing little in the second.

In conclusion, as between the small-units theory on the one hand, and an elaborately constructed, perfectly integrated edition of 'developed literary compositions' (Muilenburg, p. 391*a*) on the other, it is difficult to decide exactly where we should stand. The truth lies somewhere between these extremes, it matters little where. It must be sufficient to say that DI's theology may be one thing if his work is a reasonably well-ordered whole; it may be rather another if we have to deduce it from a random assortment of small pieces arranged on a purely mechanical principle. And as between these alternatives we need have no hesitation in opting for the former.

THEOLOGY OF DEUTERO-ISAIAH

It is a homiletical and liturgical commonplace that the arch of the biblical revelation rests upon two piers, the Egyptian Oppression and Exodus in the OT, and the Cross and Resurrection in the New (cf. John Mason Neale's Easter hymn, 'The foe behind, the deep before'). If we need a middle pier between two spans, none is stronger than Isa. xl–lv, which, more than any part of the OT, looks back to the Exodus, and, as the NT understood it, forward to the Advent.

From what has been said in the preceding section (*supra*, p. 11) it is convenient, indeed necessary, to deal with the Servant Songs separately from the main prophecy. This is done even by von Rad (*Theologie des ATs*, ii, pp. 264 f.). Von Rad does not doubt that the Songs are from DI, but he volunteers to say that we cannot without more ado co-ordinate them with the Prophet's general circle of ideas, and that they stand in a certain isolation from his message, besides being attended by problems of their own.

It is difficult to write an outline of DI's message without seeming to be, or, indeed, without being, in some measure dependent upon von Rad's summary of it. He reminds us that the Prophet, like all his predecessors, was heir to the three constituent traditions concerning Yahweh's election of Israel. These were the Exodus, the David, and the Zion traditions. Of them DI elaborated the first and the third, but the second he mentions only once (lv. 3 f.), where he seems to say that Yahweh's covenant with, and the evidential manifestations of his love for, David, are now to be transferred to Zion-Israel (see on lv. 3). The Davidic monarchy had deservedly come to an end (xliii. 28) and there is no suggestion that it will be revived, no hint of a David *redivivus*, or whatever we are to understand by 'my servant David' in Ezek. xxxiv. 23 f., xxxvii. 25. The conception of David as 'witness' (*'ēḏ*) to and 'leader' (*nāḡîḏ*, lv. 4) of the peoples has been 'democratized'. Yahweh's witnesses are now his people Israel (cf. xliii. 10), and DI knows no individual Messiah, unless he be Cyrus. But when Yahweh calls Cyrus 'his messiah' (xlv. 1) this must be rhetorical. Cyrus is Yahweh's tool in much the same way as the Assyrians (x. 5 f.) and Nebuchadrezzar (Jer. xxv. 9) had been, the difference being that Cyrus is agent for the deliverance, not the chastisement of Israel.

1. *Yahweh the Creator of the World*

DI's emphasis on Yahweh as Creator of the world is something new in prophecy. (Amos iv. 13 is an unrelated fragment and its genuineness is open to question; the same applies to Isa. iv. 5.) The fact that the great cosmological passage xl. 12–26 comes immediately after the overture to the prophecy should not mislead us into assuming that OT religion, or even DI's theology, began with a doctrine of Yahweh as Creator. The Hebrews first knew Yahweh as their deliverer from Egypt and the doctrine of creation was something in the nature of an afterthought. xl. 12–26 is not so much a cosmological argument as a series of rhetorical questions and affirmations. Nor does DI think of Yahweh's original creation of the world as a finished work, complete in itself and separate from his saving activity in history. Not, of course, that we are to think of 'continuous creation' in our contemporary meaning of the expression. But von Rad is right when he says that for DI 'create' (*bārā'*) and 'redeem' (*gā'al*) are almost synonyms. Yahweh created and has redeemed Israel (xliii. 1, 14 f.), and the 'new things' he announces are 'created now, not long ago' (xlviii. 6 f.).

What DI would have replied to any suggestion that the original creation was the best of all possible worlds (Gen. i. 31; cf. Isa. xlv. 18) and that only after things had gone wrong did Yahweh decide to 'redeem' it, we can only conjecture. He probably knew nothing of a doctrine of the 'fall'. In any case he would have said that Yahweh's saving work was entirely in keeping with his character. The Creator God is Saviour and the Saviour is Creator. Salvation is a work of (new) creation (cf. Ps. li. 10 [*12*]) and creation was the first act in the drama of history.

Most readers of the Bible take the doctrine of creation for granted, without pausing to reflect on how singular, unique, and, indeed, well-nigh incredible a doctrine it is. Nowhere, except in a few psalms such as the *Venite* (xcv; cf. civ), is it extolled as part of the *kerygma*—if the word may be used of the OT recital of Yahweh's 'Saving deeds'—and yet without it there could be no *kerygma*. That is why the first verse in the Bible begins with it, likewise the first clause in the Creeds. Outside the Bible it has no parallel, except in the Qur'ān, which is Judaism and Christianity at second hand. The concept of creation is not obvious, nor does it come naturally to mankind. Everywhere except in the Bible, interpretation of the universe is naturalistic, and worship is, in one form or another, worship of 'the great god Pan'. This is true of the religion of classical Greece, of 'polymorphic' Hinduism, of humanism in its various forms, of the current concept of 'one single branching metabolizing protoplasm', and of the popular idea of 'the life force' as the creative agent in the universe. Outside biblical theism all interpretations of the universe are so many more or less refined forms of what the OT stigmatizes as the worship of Baal, Baal being conceived as the personification of the life process. Once man is left to his unaided reason for an explanation of the universe, he invariably seeks to explain it *from the inside*, and the resultant philosophy or religion—call it what we will—is some form of naturalism, and worship is worship of 'the creative process', rather than of God the Creator of the process.

It should, perhaps, be said that outside biblical theism, even in crude polytheisms, there are stories of creator-gods, like Marduk in the Babylonian epic of creation. But Marduk did not originate the universe: he and all the gods of the Babylonian pantheon were so many aspects of the universal process. Gods and men were all, in their different orders of precedence, parts of the universal process.

It is generally agreed that creation in the OT is not creation *ex nihilo*. This is certainly true for Gen. i, which is approximately contemporary with DI. It is probably true also for DI. But no one coming across xl. 12–26 for the first time would need to conclude so. The passage is mythological in the sense that it is an imaginative description of something that took place before there was any recorded history, but, except perhaps in 'the (primeval) ocean' (*mayim*) of xl. 12 (cf. Gen. i. 2) it contains no echoes of dependence on the Babylonian creation myth, as does Gen. i. True, there are echoes of the Babylonian myth in li. 9 f. ('Rahab' and 'the sea-monster'), but there, as in xliii. 16 f., the myth has been 'historicized' and is only so much embroidery in an impassioned reference to the saving deed at the Exodus. Creation *ex nihilo* or not, imagination reels at the picture of Yahweh, alone, *vis-à-vis* his created work (xliv. 24, 'no one was with me!'). No part of the creation, nor all of it together, bears any comparison with him who created it (xl. 17 f.). How the doctrine of creation is to be communicated or expounded in the context of a universe so vast as we now know the universe to be, is the business of the systematic rather than of the biblical theologian. All that the biblical theologian can be expected to contribute to the discussion is his testimony that he cannot fit biblical history—and by that he means not just biblical *salvation history* but biblical *history* from the Exodus to the Resurrection—into any purely naturalistic interpretation of the universe.

2. *Yahweh the Only God*

The *Nichtigkeit* ('nothingness') of idols and of the 'gods' they are supposed to represent and embody, follows as a logical consequence. Idolatry excited the Prophet to indignation and ridicule (xl. 19 f., xli. 6 f., xliv. 9–20—this last passage *may* not be from DI). There is little doubt that idols were forbidden to the Hebrews before the doctrine of creation came into prominence (Exod. xx. 4 f.). There can be no place for objects so tawdry and lifeless alongside Yahweh 'the Holy One of Israel'. It is difficult for us to-day to feel moral indignation, at least against anything cultic. We are suspicious of absolute moral standards or imperatives. But we are more at sea than we need be, largely because the concept of God lacks definition and is often 'a faceless blur'. Briefly, idolatry is worship of the creature instead of the Creator, the substitution of the creative process for him who created and sustains the process.

The pretensions which their devotees make for the idol-gods are brusquely denied by the Prophet. In a series of vivid pictures (see on xli. 1–7) he has Yahweh summon now the idolators (xli. 1–4), now the gods themselves (xli. 21–29), to assize-inquests to substantiate the claims made for them. Is it they who have stirred up Cyrus? Had they any premonition of his rise to power, or even a glimmer of understanding of what it portends? A question still harder to answer: do they know what the future still holds? No answer is forthcoming. None is expected. It is as if to wait for an answer would be a waste of the court's time. Judgement is passed against the gods by default. Yahweh it is who has acted and wrought, calling the generations of men from the very first. 'I, Yahweh, am the first, and, with the last, I am He' (i.e. 'I am God', see on xli. 4). This is explicit monotheism. Yahweh alone is God: he is God because in times past he predicted events which have now happened, God because he is ready now with announcements of 'new things' still to come. And the reason why he, and he alone, knows the future, is that he in fact controls history. For the 'new things' see below, p. 18. To define what the 'former things' are is not always easy. But prophecy had already a long history in Israel and there could be no gainsaying that the exile had been predicted over and over again (see on xlviii. 3). It is also possible that DI took the events of his own time as the fulfilment of the predictions, now extant in xiii. 17–20, xxi. 1–10, of the overthrow of Babylon by the Medes (see on xlv. 21).

3. *The New Salvation*

DI describes the salvation of Israel in terms of a new and more wonderful Exodus. This new Exodus is imminent. After the brief initial 'Comfort' to Jerusalem (xl. 1 f.) the Prophet hears a proclamation addressed to angelic agents bidding them prepare a highway directly across the desert from Babylon to the Holy City. Yahweh is returning, accompanied by his people whom he has freed from exile, and his glory (*kāḇôḏ*) is to be revealed to all mankind simultaneously (xl. 3–11). The triumphal procession will be preceded by a runner heralding the glad tidings of its approach (a *m*^e^*ḇaśśēr*, LXX εὐαγγελιζόμενος, lii. 7). Shouts of jubilation will ring out from the city's watchmen, who are to have, if it is not irreverent to put it so, a 'close-up' of Yahweh's return to Zion. The desert highway is to be transformed into an oasis; there will be abundance of water and the route will be planted with forest trees (xli. 17–20). Subhuman ('the wolves and the owls', xliii. 20; cf. xlii. 11) and even inanimate nature (mountains and hills, lv. 12) will join in the universal rejoicing, and 'all the trees of the countryside will clap their hands'. The preparations for the first Exodus had been made 'in haste' (*b*^e^*ḥippāzôn*, Exod. xii. 11; Deut. xvi. 3). Not so in this second and even more signal deliverance: there will be no haste and nothing is to be done to put the sanctity of the temple vessels in jeopardy (lii. 11 f.). Finally, the last verse in the prophecy seems to say that the sacred way across the desert will be kept in perpetuity as a commemorative park (lv. 13).

The immediate occasion of the deliverance from Babylon is to be the conquest of the city and the overthrow of the Babylonian power by Cyrus. It is Yahweh who has stirred him to activity and is prospering all his enterprises. Yahweh has summoned him by name, has grasped his right hand in confirmation of the legitimacy of his kingly authority, and is going before him, smoothing his passage through the mountains, shattering the gate-bars of the tyrant city and giving him access to its closely guarded treasures (xlv. 1–3; cf. xliii. 3). (Notwithstanding, in xlv. 13 Cyrus is to carry out his commission 'not for anything by way of payment or a bribe'.) Cyrus does not 'know' Yahweh (xlv. 4), but Yahweh's purpose is that he shall know that it is Yahweh who has summoned him, and in xli. 25 (assuming that the text is right—see *in loc.*) Cyrus is to invoke Yahweh, i.e. acknowledge that it is Yahweh who has commissioned him. He is Yahweh's 'shepherd', who shall execute the divine will by ordering Jerusalem to be rebuilt and the temple foundations relaid (xliv. 28).

In xliii. 18 f. 'the new thing' (*ḥ*^a^*ḏāšāh*) which Yahweh is 'about to do', and which clearly refers to the new Exodus, is contrasted with 'the former things' (*rî'šônôṯ*), which equally clearly refer to the first Exodus (cf. vv. 16 f.). Israel is bidden not to let memory linger over the past nor dwell on happenings of long ago. Von Rad takes this to mean that Israel is from now on to turn away from the hallowed tradition of the past. 'What can this mean except that the first period of Yahweh's dealings with Israel is closed? The exile was an end to history as the prophets had understood it. . . . But for DI there now begins the 'new', the first signs of which can already be discerned. 'The first is ended' and has no longer validity except as a type of the new' (p. 262). This is a large conclusion if it is based on a single passage, but it is true of DI's thought as a whole. In two passages (xlii. 9, xlviii. 6) there is mention of 'new things' (*ḥᵃḏāšôṯ*) but what they are is not defined. There is in DI no mention of a 'new covenant', as in Jer. xxxi. 31–34, but lv. 3 speaks of 'a lasting covenant' (*bᵉrîṯ 'ôlām*), the covenant made with David (2 Sam. xxiii. 5; Ps. lxxxix. 28 f.) and now to be renewed with all Israel. Volz had it that 'DI is eschatological through and through' (p. 31). This is hardly true if it means that his eschatology is the dualistic cosmological eschatology of the later apocalyptists. We are still on the plane of history. 'It is true that the Prophet sees a great and glorious change; the new things, however, do not mean *the end* of history but a continuation of the present historical order in ideal forms. Future history will develop on this earth, as history has done hitherto, though under better conditions' (Lindblom, *The Servant Songs in DI*, ch. 5; see also his article 'Gibt es eine Eschatologie bei den alttestamentlichen Propheten?' in *Studia Theologica*, vi. 2, 1952, pp. 79–114; also Th. C. Vriezen, 'Prophecy and Eschatology', in *Supplements to Vetus Testamentum*, i, 1953, pp. 199–229).

4. *The Restoration of Zion*

To have any idea of the utter dejection of the scanty populace of Jerusalem a generation after 586 B.C., we need only read the book of Lamentations, much of which was composed while the city was still reeling under the shock of the disaster that had overtaken it. 'Hear how I groan; there is none to comfort me' (Lam. i. 21). And nothing, so far as we know, had been done to alleviate her misery. It had been a mistake to elevate into a dogma Isaiah's doctrine of the inviolability of Zion (xxviii. 16, xxxvii. 33–35). The lesson, if belatedly, was now thoroughly taken to heart: the judgement was the consequence of the city's grievous sin (Lam. i. 8 f.); Yahweh was in the right (i. 18). But looking back over forty years, DI could hear Yahweh say that Jerusalem had received from his hand 'twice-over for all her sins' (xl. 2). She had drained to the dregs the cup of his wrath (li. 17). N. K. Gottwald is right to say that 'the Book of Lamentations was one of the major sources of Deutero- and Trito-Isaiah' (*Studies in the Book of Lamentations*, p. 115).

Jerusalem thought that Yahweh had 'divorced' her. This was not so. There had been a temporary separation, indeed, but no decent husband could disown the bride of his youth (liv. 6). Still less could Yahweh abandon the city he still loved. A woman might forget the child she bore and suckled, but Yahweh would never forget Zion. He has engraved a model of her upon the palms of his hands; her walls are never out of his sight (xlix. 15 f.). She is to be rebuilt in greater splendour than before (liv. 11–14). Her children are to return to her from all the places to which they have been exiled, and in such numbers that her boundaries will have to be extended to take them all in (xlix. 14–21). At Yahweh's signal the nations, led by their kings and queens, will bring the exiles home with all ceremony (xlix. 22 f.). The city will be a place of pilgrimage even for African peoples, who will volunteer to confess that there is only one God and that he is with Israel (xlv. 14). All who dwell at the farthest ends of the earth are invited to turn to Yahweh and be saved; to him every knee shall bend and every tongue swear fealty (xlv. 22 f.). But no 'world-mission' of Israel appears to be contemplated. It is rather that Israel is Yahweh's witness in his controversy with the idol-gods. The nations will see what Yahweh has done for her and will consequently acknowledge his sole Deity. Nor does it appear that there is to be any mass conversion of the heathen. Instead, by ones and twos they will join themselves to Israel (xliv. 5).

No clear distinction is drawn between the city of God and the people of God. Even in the opening verses of the prophecy 'Jerusalem' and 'my people' are parallel expressions, and in xlix–lv the emphasis is equally upon Zion and upon its inhabitants. Zion is already on its way to become a symbol for the household of God (see on xl. 2 and cf. N. W. Porteous,

'Jerusalem-Zion: the Growth of a Symbol', in *Verbannung und Verkehr*, Rudolph *Festschrift*, ed. A. Kuschke, 1961, pp. 235–52).

5. *The Suffering Servant*

So much has been written about the Suffering Servant that it seems an impertinence to write anything more, unless one has something new to say. In the subsequent Commentary full notes are given on the Servant Songs (xlii. 1–4, xlix. 1–6, l. 4–9, lii. 13–liii. 12); here it must suffice briefly to summarize the history of interpretation, to indicate the contemporary 'lie' of the discussion, and to offer a postscript.

Until almost the end of the eighteenth century Christians were practically unanimous in regarding lii. 13–liii. 12 as a prophecy pointing directly to Christ. Jews were equally emphatic that the Servant was the Jewish people persecuted by Christians during the Middle Ages. During the nineteenth century most Christian scholars abandoned the messianic interpretation and saw in the Servant the Jewish people during the Babylonian exile. In 1892 Duhm separated the 'Servant Songs' from their contexts and conjectured that the Servant was an individual, otherwise unknown to history, who lived about a century after DI. Since then some ten or a dozen 'historical individual' theories have been proposed, including one which would see in the Servant the prophet DI himself. None of these theories has any considerable following, or, indeed, any following at all, today.

The majority opinion is that the Songs are from DI but it is no longer taken for granted that because in some passages of the prophecy (cf. xli. 8) Israel is called Yahweh's servant, the Servant in lii. 13–liii. 12 must therefore be the empirical Israel. Consistency is no longer demanded of the Prophet. That collective Israel should be called Yahweh's servant is a startling conception (see on xli. 8). Hitherto only individuals had been accorded the title. There are still scholars who stand by the collective interpretation but they agree that no nation, not even Israel, ever did, or perhaps ever will or can, measure up to the stature of the Servant in the Songs. Only Christ has done that. We must therefore begin with DI's equation of the Servant with Israel, but for Christians the Servant in the last resort can be none other than Christ. The Prophet may have intended to describe Israel but his final portrait is that of the perfect Israelite.

Von Rad has made the suggestion that the Servant the Prophet expected was to be, not indeed 'a second Moses' or a Moses *redivivus*, but a prophet 'like Moses' (cf. Deut. xviii. 18). Moses is called 'the servant of Yahweh' some forty times, and several times in Deuteronomy (iii. 23 ff., iv. 21, ix. 9, 18 ff., 25 ff.) he is represented as standing between Israel and Yahweh much as the Servant 'stood in the place of the transgressors' in Isa. liii. 12, and finally as having died vicariously for Israel's sins. Put thus, this is a more attractive suggestion than that of Aage Bentzen, who concluded that 'The "Ebed Yahweh" is Deutero-Isaiah and Israel, the new Moses ("Messias" in radically changed form) and the congregation for which he is ready to die, in one single person' (*King and Messiah*, p. 64). Concerning such 'all-in' theories W. Zimmerli rightly says that they 'serve only to befog the whole problem' (*The Servant of God*, note 68 on p. 25).

Another reason why von Rad thinks that the Servant was to be 'a prophet like Moses' is that part of his mission was 'to raise up the tribes of Jacob and to bring the saved ones home' (op. cit., p. 273; cf. Isa. xlix. 6), thus linking the Servant's work with the main theme of DI. In other words the new Exodus, like the first Exodus, needed its Moses. But it is doubtful whether there is much, or indeed any, cogency in this. There is no hint of a mission to Israel in the first Song—on the contrary—nor yet in the third and fourth, unless we are to take 'my people' in liii. 8 (so EVV, but see the Commentary *in loc.*) as meaning Israel. Even so it is no political mission to Israel that the Servant has in liii. 8. In the main prophecy it is Yahweh himself who is to lead the exiles home, though perhaps we should not take the words 'Yahweh himself is going before you, the God of Israel is your rear-guard' (lii. 12) too literally, but regard them as reminiscent of passages like Exod. xiv. 19, xxxiii. 14, xl. 34–38. However that may be, the last Song moves on a higher plane than that of any political restoration. As to xlix. 5 f., the meaning appears to be 'It is little matter that you should be my servant to re-establish the tribes of Jacob . . .', and Yahweh goes on to tell the Servant where his real task lies, namely in being a light to the nations. All the same, we need not doubt that there are features of Moses, of Jeremiah, and indeed of DI himself, in the portrait of the Servant.

Yet when we have said that in the last resort the Servant is Christ, it still remains true that collective Israel has good claims to the title of the Suffering Servant. Unreflecting Christians may think of Christ as a Christian crucified by the Jews. In fact it was a Jew who hung on the cross. Paul Winter (in *The Trial of Jesus*, Berlin, 1962) may or may not be right when he argues that in the NT Gospels the load of guilt for the crucifixion has been laid too heavily upon the Jews. But thinking Christians are constrained to admit that in the last resort responsibility for the crucifixion rests upon corporate humanity and not upon any one race or community. In a BBC 'Meeting Point' programme in 1961 the Chairman, himself an Irish Catholic, told how he had attended some sessions of the Eichmann trial and that he had come away feeling, much to his own surprise, a sense of personal guilt for the horrors of the Nazi gas-chambers. In very truth Israel, alike in the Babylonian exile, and within the memories of people who are still young, 'has received from the LORD's hand twice-over for all her sins' (xl. 2). And if suffering is the great cathartic, perhaps we should say that 'at the cost of his wounds there is healing for us' (liii. 5).

POET OR PROPHET? THE PROBLEM OF SALVATION HISTORY

According to R. H. Pfeiffer 'the conciseness, variety, and concreteness of Isaiah's poetry contrast sharply with the eloquent verbosity, repetitiousness, and vagueness of Isa. 40–55. Isaiah belongs to the golden age of Hebrew literature, Isa. 40–55 to its silver age. The difference is that between naïve, unconscious art, and deliberate striving for majestic eloquence by means of rhetorical devices . . . It should perhaps be said that we are here concerned with the original Hebrew text and not with the English versions. The magnificent grandeur of Isa. 40–55 and of Deuteronomy lent itself well to rendition into superb Elizabethan prose. Accordingly, Isa. 40–55 and Deuteronomy are more impressive literary masterpieces in the Authorized Version than in the original Hebrew' (*Introduction to the OT*, pp. 462 f.).

That is as it may be, though few will deny that DI could write poetry. Pfeiffer, indeed, concedes so much: 'The Second Isaiah was a theologian and a poet rather than a prophet . . . (but) more important as a thinker than as a poet. But he was unquestionably a genuine poet, though hardly, even in his own sphere, "supreme and unrivalled among the great poets of the world"' (quoting from C. C. Torrey, *The Second Isaiah*, p. 91).

Torrey, like Pfeiffer, thought of DI as a poet rather than as a prophet: 'It may be doubted whether the Second Isaiah ever thought of himself as a prophet, but it is beyond question that he knew himself to be a master poet. There is in the book no intimation that its author was conscious of a divine election other than that which any devout man of letters may claim' (op. cit., p. 90). The prevailing critical view that Isa. xl–lv is from a 'prophet of the exile' makes its author a 'spineless and morally deficient sky-gazer' (ibid., p. 18). Similarly U. E. Simon says that if it was written during the exile its author must have been 'a fantastic lunatic' (*A Theology of Salvation: A Commentary on Isaiah 40–55*, p. 108).

Accordingly, Torrey denied that Isa. xl–lv (lxvi) had anything to do with the Babylonian exile—he had long maintained that the traditional account of the exile and restoration was a fiction of the Chronicler anyhow. By the simple expedient of deleting 'Cyrus' (xliv. 28, xlv. 1), 'Babylon', and 'Chaldea' (xliii. 14, xlviii. 14, 20), on metrical grounds, as explanatory additions to the text by someone who had learned his history from the Chronicler, he declared that Isa. xxxiv–xxxv, xl–lxvi is a unity dating from about 400 B.C. And since the author was a 'poet' rather than a prophet, Torrey felt free to treat as purely figurative his exuberant descriptions of rivers flowing in a desert now planted with forest trees.

Torrey's *The Second Isaiah* was published in 1928. Few scholars of any standing have accepted his theory. It therefore looks as if we must make the best we can of the exilic date and the fantastic lunacy of the Prophet. For a prophet is what he considered himself to be. His conviction that he too was uttering the word of God is sufficient evidence of that (cf. von Rad, pp. 256 f.). It is not as if a lowering of the date by a century and a half would make any material difference, even after the deletions of 'Cyrus' and 'Babylon'. The new Exodus would still be a leading theme in the 'poem' and it is wholly improbable that the author, who presumably believed that the first Exodus was an historical event, was only allegorizing about the second, or imagining anything so remote from the thought of his own time as that, for example, the desert would one day be transformed into oasis by Israeli irrigation of the Negev (cf. Simon, op. cit., p. 78).

No problem is presented, in this connexion, by the Servant Songs. No terminus attaches to their fulfilment and, notwithstanding differences of detail as between them and their fulfilment in Christ, their verisimilitude is astonishing. If any parts of the Bible are inspired, they are.

The processional highway across the desert and the imminent coming of Yahweh in 'glory', accompanied by his redeemed people, and the wonders of Zion rebuilt, are another matter. Was the Prophet 'mistaken'? Before we write him down as a fantastic lunatic we should consider whether there is not sufficient to be set on the credit side for us to think of him as a man with at least some measure of political sanity. The sixth century B.C. was a remarkable century. Cyrus may by modern standards have been a first-class ruffian, but he did found a new kind of empire, an empire which had some conscience about the welfare of its subjects. Jews and others were allowed to return to their ancestral homes. They were free in the exercise of their religion. The temple, albeit tardily, was rebuilt and became the centre of a monotheistic faith to which many of the best spirits in the ancient world began to look with wistful eyes.

On the other hand it must be admitted that the high expectations of the Prophet were only very imperfectly realized. As the decree of Cyrus is reported in the OT (2 Chron. xxxvi. 23 f.; Ezra i. 2 ff.) it reads as if he acknowledged Yahweh as the only God and the giver of victory to him. But since there is extant an inscription in which he attributes his victories to Marduk (*ANET*, pp. 315 f.), it would seem that the Chronicler's version of his decree has been coloured by the patriotic monotheism of the Jews, perhaps even by DI's expectations of him. Certainly he did not become a convert to the Jewish faith. The evidence is overwhelming that the century following the first meagre 'return' was a time of disillusionment and hopes deferred. The Jerusalem Jews were poor and dispirited and they had much ado to keep their faith alive amid the semi-heathenism which surrounded them.

Perhaps the Prophet did not intend his descriptions of a speedy return across the desert-turned-oasis to be taken literally? This is a difficult question to answer. Austin Farrer, writing on the demythicization controversy raised by Bultmann, says: 'How far symbol is taken for literal fact in the New Testament is a subtle question'. His own opinion is that 'On the whole it is truer to say that the relation of mythical expression to literal belief is left undecided, than to say that it is decided in the sense of literalism' (*Kerygma and Myth*, ed. H. W. Bartsch, Engl. trans. R. H. Fuller, 1953, p. 215). The same applies to the OT in general and to DI in particular. His Yahweh has all the bodily parts of a man (hands, &c.) but no one supposes that his conception of Yahweh was crudely anthropomorphic. His descriptions of the new Exodus are a kind of Salvation History (*Heilsgeschichte*) in prospect instead of in retrospect. There is much of the kind in the prophets, e.g. messianic prophecy and Isa. ii. 2–4, though as a rule its *terminus ad quem* is 'in the latter days', not in the imminent future. Salvation History is usually interpretation of history *after the event*. In DI the relation between Salvation History and history is in reverse, so to speak, and his prophecy raises in an acute form the problem of the credibility of the biblical Salvation History. We know in what terms DI anticipated history. We know enough about the century following the liberation edict of Cyrus to say that nothing happened commensurate with his glowing expectations, even allowing that he may not have intended them to be taken quite literally. We also know how the early Hebrews interpreted the saving deed of the Exodus. But we do not know exactly what happened, or when or where or how it happened. No doubt by the time of DI it was taken for granted that the salvation history of the first Exodus was history, and it was natural enough that the Prophet should base his anticipations of the new Exodus upon that assumption. But in point of fact the Exodus from Egypt was probably a comparatively trivial incident capable of a naturalistic explanation. Must we then say that OT salvation history was born of the Hebrews' patriotic enthusiasm for Yahweh and that its doctrine of election is no more than a pious fiction? There may be times when the theologian is inclined to feel that the traditional relation between Christianity and history is a liability rather than an asset. But if the biblical theologian is going to abandon the doctrine of God's involvement in history, he may as well go out of business. For that matter, so long as Christianity is committed to the doctrine of the Incarnation, Christian theologians, whatever their specialized fields, have no option but to relate Christianity to history. And presumably, if in Christ the Word became flesh, God did not begin to be active in history in the first century A.D. We should expect him to reveal himself in history before that, as the OT affirms he did, if only to prepare man for some understanding of his full revelation in Christ.

Martin Noth is generally regarded as sceptical in his attitude towards much of what has passed for early Hebrew history. In the Introduction to his *History of Israel* he says: 'Inevitably . . . there is an element of mystery, of the "unhistorical"—("metahistorical" would perhaps better convey his meaning in English) —in all human history which makes its presence felt on the frontiers of all historical knowledge' (p. 2). And a little further on: '"Israel" . . . appears a stranger in the world of its own time, a stranger wearing the garments and behaving in the manner of its age, yet separate from the world it lived in, not merely in the sense that any historical reality has its own individual character, and therefore an element of uniqueness, but rather that at the very centre of the history of "Israel" we encounter phenomena for which there is no parallel at all elsewhere, not because the material for comparison has not yet come to light but because, so far as we know, such things have simply never happened elsewhere' (ibid., pp. 2 f.).

It is not only the credibility of early Hebrew history (and salvation history) that is in question. The historian, if he interrogates the Gospels, may have to admit that we cannot always be certain that what is reported as a dominical saying is something that Jesus actually said, as what is reported in Hansard is a verbatim report of proceedings in Parliament. He may have his doubts about the historical accuracy of much that Jesus is said to have done, especially in the miracle stories. He may have his doubts about the Virgin Birth and even of the Resurrection. He may say that such knowledge as we have about Jesus is what the early Church, for the purposes of its evangelism, said that Jesus said and did, and that we cannot get behind the apostolic *kerygma* to the authentic words and works of Jesus. We may take bits and pieces from anywhere in the Bible and have our doubts about them. We may have to admit that at every point we must rely upon historical probability rather than upon historical demonstration, and that the 'truth' of Bible history is in the last resort accessible only to faith. But when we take it all together, from Abraham and/or Moses to Jesus and the apostolic Church, it does cohere together; there is a consistency about it, and as *history*—not simply some imaginary salvation history—it is without parallel anywhere or at any time in the history of this planet. It is incredible that a fictional salvation history was kept up, in spite of disasters like the exile, and tragedies, humanly speaking, like the crucifixion, and even gathered momentum over a period of some fifteen hundred years, if the real Author of it was not the living God, who created the world and created Israel to be the vehicle of his purpose in history, as the Prophet of the exile proclaimed. Here lies the paradox: the 'history', such as it was, gave birth to the salvation history; but by and large it was the salvation history that shaped the history. Biblical history *is* salvation history.

I remember, as if it were yesterday, my first sight of the high Himalayas, now fifty years ago. A colleague and I had travelled all night from Lucknow, arriving at Kathgodam, the rail-head at the foot of the hills, on the morning of Maundy Thursday. From there to the hill-station at Ranikhet was a walk of some fifty miles, which would take us three days. (Nowadays, of course, one goes by car in two hours.) We toiled up some four thousand feet to Bhimtal, 'Dark hollow' (Sanskrit–Hindi 'tal' = hollow, valley, cf. German *Tal*, English 'dale'). The air resounded with the calls of the cuckoo, but we could see nothing beyond. The next day, Good Friday, we walked for the most part downhill, looking down through the wooded *khud* to a brawling stream. On the Saturday another fifteen miles, uphill to Ranikhet. There was no visibility that evening. At daybreak next morning, Easter Day, we looked out. We were facing Trisul and Nanda Devi. They appeared almost to tower above us, though they were sixty or more miles away. (On any clear night they might be seen in the Indian moonlight.) The terrain immediately beyond Ranikhet slopes downwards and it was as if we were on the rim of a gigantic saucer, with a semicircle of glittering peaks on its far side. To reach even the lower limit of the snow-line would have meant organizing a twelve-day expedition, with porters to carry our gear and provisions, including a sheep to be slaughtered on the way.

The comparison may be whimsical, but I never relive that exhilarating but at times fatiguing tramp to Ranikhet without being reminded of the spiritual pilgrimage of Israel. That pilgrimage began with deliverance from the night of Egyptian oppression, and after centuries of alternating modest achievement and (more often) depressing failure, it looked as if all was lost in the tragedy of the exile. And then, after fifty years, a voice rang out: 'Make ready in the wilderness the way of the LORD!' Deutero-Isaiah may or may not be the greatest prophet of them all, but with him prophecy had delivered itself of its essential message. It is as if, with him, OT revelation reached a point from which, over another intervening five hundred years, 'the revelation of the glory of God in the face of Jesus Christ' (*NEB* at 2 Cor. iv. 6) could be discerned. His vision was foreshortened, as prophetic visions always are. But his vision of the Suffering Servant was astonishingly clear. For the rest, he expressed himself in 'mythological' language based on the traditional salvation history of his people. It was the only language available to him for describing a reality which in some ways exceeded his grasp. Without him it is difficult to see how Israel could have recovered herself from, or even survived, the disaster of the exile. He may have expected too much in the immediate future but his expectations were astonishingly widespread and persistent (cf. Isa. xxxv, lx–lxii; Zech. viii); in fact they never died. And when, half a millennium later, Christ came, the NT evangelists saw in his coming the realization of the vision of the εὐαγγελιζόμενος of the exile.

THE TEXT

It is generally recognized that the text of Isa. xl–lv has been well preserved and this conclusion is confirmed by both the Qumran Scrolls, the second of which (1QIs[b]), dating probably from the first century A.D., agrees almost word for word with the MT. The first Scroll (1QIs[a], abbreviated to Q[a] in this Commentary) agrees with the MT more closely than anyone would have imagined possible before such a document came to light. Sometimes it confirms emendations based on the LXX (as at xlix. 24), and, very occasionally, emendations previously conjectural (as at xliv. 21). But for the most part MT readings are to be preferred to those of Q[a], and no one, if he had to choose one of the two texts, would dream of choosing Q[a]. Occasionally the MT may be corrected from LXX, even where MT and Q[a] agree (as at xliv. 7*a*), but where MT makes no sense the LXX is likely to be equally unintelligible (as at xl. 19 f., xliv. 7*b*). It would therefore seem that such corruptions as there may be in the Hebrew text are earlier than the LXX and the Scrolls. In the comparatively few places in this commentary where the MT has been emended, the differences are indicated by *. . .* in the translation. Reasons for the emendations are given in the textual notes in the Commentary.

SELECTED BIBLIOGRAPHY

(For a fuller bibliography see C. R. North, *The Suffering Servant in Deutero-Isaiah*, second ed., Oxford, 1956 = *SS*.)

ANDERSON, B. W.: 'Exodus Typology in Second Isaiah', in *Israel's Prophetic Heritage*, ed. B. W. Anderson and W. Harrelson, New York, 1962, pp. 177–95.

BEGRICH, J.: *Studien zu Deuterojesaja*, BWANT, 4 Folge, Heft 25, 1938.

BENTZEN, A.: *Jesaja fortolket, Bind II, Jes. 40–66*, Copenhagen, 1943.

—— *Messias, Moses redivivus, Menschensohn*, Zürich, 1948; Engl. trans. *King and Messiah*, London, 1955.

BLANK, S. H.: 'Studies in Deutero-Isaiah', *HUCA* 15, 1940, pp. 1–46.

BUDDE, K.: 'The so-called "Ebed-Jahweh-Songs" and the Meaning of the Term "Servant of Yahweh" in Isaiah Chaps. 40–55', *The American Journal of Theology*, July 1899, pp. 499–540.

—— *Das Buch Jesaia Kap. 40–66*, in *Die Heilige Schrift des Alten Testaments, übersetzt und herausgegeben von E. Kautzsch*, 3 Aufl., I, Bd., Tübingen, 1909, pp. 609–71.

CASPARI, W.: *Lieder und Gottessprüche der Rückwanderer* (*Jesaja 40–55*), BZAW 65, 1934.

CONDAMIN, A.: *Le Livre d'Isaïe: Traduction critique avec notes et commentaires*, Paris, 1905.

DE BOER, P. A. H.: *Second-Isaiah's Message*, *Oudtestamentische Studiën*, XI, Leiden, 1956.

DE LEEUW, V.: *De Ebed Jahweh-Profetieen*, Assen, 1956 (Summary in French).

DUHM, B.: *Das Buch Jesaia übersetzt und erklärt*, Göttingen, 1892, 4th ed., 1922.

ELLIGER, K.: *Deuterojesaja in seinem Verhältnis zu Tritojesaja*, BWANT, 4 Folge, Heft 11, 1933.

ENGNELL, I.: 'The 'Ebed Yahweh Songs and the Suffering Messiah in "Deutero-Isaiah"', *BJRL* 31, 1948.

FELDMANN, FR.: *Das Buch Isaias übersetzt und erklärt*, *Exegetisches Handbuch zum Alten Testament*, 14 Bd., Zweiter Teil, Münster i. W., 1925–6.

FISCHER, J.: *Das Buch Isaias übersetzt und erklärt, II Teil: Kapitel 40–66*, Bonn, 1939.

GLAHN, L., and KÖHLER, L.: *Der Prophet der Heimkehr*, Giessen, 1934.

GRESSMANN, H.: 'Die literarische Analyse Deuterojesajas', *ZAW* 34, 1914, pp. 254–97.

HAAG, H.: 'Ebed Jahwe-Forschung 1948–1958', *Biblische Zeitschrift*, Neue Folge, Heft 2, 1959, Paderborn, pp. 174–204.

HOONACKER, A. VAN: *Het Boek Isaias*, Brugge, 1932.

JONES, D. R.: 'Isaiah—II and III.', in *Peake's Commentary on the Bible*, revised ed., 1962, pp. 516–36.

KISSANE, E. J.: *The Book of Isaiah: Translated from a Critically Revised Hebrew Text with Commentary, vol. ii* (*XL–LXVI*), Dublin, 1943.

Köhler, L.: *Deuterojesaja (Jesaja 40–55) stilkritisch untersucht*, BZAW 37, 1923.
König, Ed.: *Das Buch Jesaja eingeleitet, übersetzt und erklärt*, Gütersloh, 1926.
Levy, R.: *Deutero-Isaiah: A Commentary*, Oxford, 1925.
Lindblom, J.: *The Servant Songs in Deutero-Isaiah: A New Attempt to Solve an Old Problem*, Lund, 1951.
Mowinckel, S.: 'Die Komposition des deuterojesajanischen Buches', *ZAW* 49, 1931, pp. 87–112, 242–60.
—— 'Jesajaboken, II. Kap. 40–66', in *Det Gamle Testamente, oversatt av S. Michelet, Sigmund Mowinckel og N. Messel, III. De Senere Profeter*, Oslo, 1944, pp. 185–283.
Muilenburg, J.: 'The Book of Isaiah, Chapters 40–66', *The Interpreter's Bible*, vol. v, 1956, pp. 381–773.
North, C. R.: *The Suffering Servant in Deutero-Isaiah*, second ed., Oxford, 1956.
—— 'The "Former Things" and the "New Things" in Deutero-Isaiah', in *Studies in Old Testament Prophecy*, ed. H. H. Rowley, Edinburgh, 1950, pp. 111–26.
Nyberg, H. S.: 'Smärtornas man. En studie till Jes. 52, 13–53, 12', *Svensk Exegetisk Årsbok* 7, 1942, pp. 5–82.
Ploeg, J. S. van der: *Les Chants du Serviteur de Jahvé dans la seconde partie du livre d'Isaïe*, Paris, 1936.
Porúbčan, Š.: *Il Patto nuovo in Is. 40–66*, Rome, 1958.
Rignell, L. G.: *A Study of Isaiah, ch. 40–55*, Lund, 1956.
Robinson, H. W.: *The Cross of the Servant: A Study in Deutero-Isaiah*, London, 1926.
Rowley, H. H.: *The Servant of the Lord and other Essays on the Old Testament*, London, 1952.
Simon, U. E.: *A Theology of Salvation: A Commentary on Isaiah 40–55*, London, 1953.
Skinner, J.: *The Book of the Prophet Isaiah Chapters XL–LXVI*, Cambridge, revised ed., 1917.
Smith, G. A.: *The Book of Isaiah*, Vol. II, second ed., London, 1927.
Smith, Sidney: *Isaiah Chapters XL–LV: Literary Criticism and History* (Schweich Lectures, 1940), London, 1944.
Steinmann, J.: *Le Livre de la consolation d'Israël*, Paris, 1960.
Torrey, C. C.: *The Second Isaiah: A New Interpretation* Edinburgh, 1928.
Volz, P.: *Jesaia II übersetzt und erklärt*, Leipzig, 1932.
Wolff, H. W.: *Jesaja 53 im Urchristentum*², Berlin, 1950.
Young, E. J.: *Studies in Isaiah*, London, 1954.
Zimmerli, H., and Jeremias, J.: *The Servant of God*, London, 1957.

For the theological concepts of DI the reader may consult recent works on the Theology of the Old Testament:

Jacob, E.: *Theology of the Old Testament*, translated by A. W. Heathcote and P. J. Allcock (London, 1958).
Vriezen, Th. C.: *An Outline of Old Testament Theology*, Oxford, 1960.
von Rad, G.: *Theologie des Alten Testaments*, Band ,II München, 1960.
Eichrodt, W.: *Theology of the Old Testament*, vol. i, translated by J. Baker from the sixth German Edition, 1959 (London, 1961).

II · TRANSLATION

CHAPTER XL

1. Comfort my people, comfort them,
   says your God.
2. Tell Jerusalem to be of good heart,
   and proclaim to her
   that she has served her sentence,
   that her penalty is discharged,
   that she has received from the LORD's hand
   twice-over for all her sins.

3. A voice proclaims!
   'Make ready in the wilderness
   the way of the LORD,
   make through the desert
   a level highway for our God.
4. Every deep cleft is to be filled in,
   every mountain and hill become lowland,
   steeps be turned to level surface,
   and tangled hillocks to open plain.
5. And the glorious majesty of the LORD shall be revealed,
   and all mankind shall see it together,
   for the mouth of the LORD has spoken.'

6. A voice says, 'Proclaim!'
   and answer comes back, 'What shall I proclaim?'
   'All flesh is grass,
   and all its constancy like the flower of the field'—
7. 'Grass withers, flower fades,
   when the breath of the LORD blows upon it;
   —surely mankind is grass.'
8. 'Grass withers, flower fades,
   but the word of our God shall endure for ever.'

9. O Zion, herald of glad tidings,
   go up with all speed to the high mountain;

Jerusalem, herald of glad tidings,
lift up your voice with strength,
lift it up, have no fear;
say to the townships of Judah,
'Your God is at hand!'
10. Know that the Lord God is coming in might,
with regal arm outstretched;
and that with him are the sheep he has earned;
they are his prize and they march in his vanguard.
11. He will tend his flock like a shepherd,
gather up the lambs with his arm,
carry them in his bosom
and lead the ewes to their resting-places.

12. Who is it that held the primeval ocean in his palm,
that marked out the bounds of the skies with his span,
measured earth's soil in a quart container,
weighed the mountains from the arm of a balance,
and the hills in scale pans?
13. Did anyone gauge the mind of the Lord,
or proffer him advice on equal terms?
14. To whom did he turn for advice and instruction,
who taught him to make right decisions,
[taught him knowledge]
and endowed him with all-penetrating insight?
15. Indeed, the nations are like a drip from a bucket,
as little to be reckoned as the moisture on scales;
the shorelands of the western sea are light as fine dust.
16. Even Lebanon would not be fuel enough,
nor its wild life suffice for a holocaust.
17. All the nations are as nought in his presence;
they count for him as empty nothings.

18. Then to whom will you liken God,
or what form will you compare with him?
19. An idol? A craftsman casts it,
and a goldsmith overlays it with beaten gold,
and forges silver fence-chains.
20. **Choice is made of a durable wood,
and they look for a joiner skilled to work it,
to fix the image securely so that it will not fall down.

21. Do you not know? Have you never heard?
    Has it not been told you from the very beginning?
    Is it not clear to you from the creation of the world?
22. He it is enthroned upon the rounded vault of the earth
    (its inhabitants look like grasshoppers),
who stretched out the skies like gauze,
    and opened them out to be a habitable tent;
23. who brings potentates to nought
    and reduces the rulers of the earth to chaos.
24. No sooner are they planted, no sooner sown,
    no sooner has their stem taken firm root in the earth,
than he blows upon them and they wither,
    and the storm-wind carries them off like chaff.

25. 'Then to whom will you liken me or whom do I resemble?',
    says the Most Holy.
26. Lift up your eyes on high
    and see: Who created these?
He that leads out their host by number
    and marshals them all by name;
because of his omnipotent might
    not one lags behind.

27. Why do you ask, O Jacob,
    and keep saying, O Israel,
'The path I tread is hidden from the LORD,
    and my plea for justice is disregarded by my God'?
28. Do you not know? Have you never heard?
The LORD is the eternal God,
    Creator of the ends of the earth.
He faints not, neither grows weary,
    his understanding is unfathomable.
29. He gives strength to the faint,
    increase of vigour to those who are powerless.
30. Though youths faint and grow weary,
    and young men fall exhausted;
31. those who wait for the LORD renew their strength,
    they soar on eagle pinions,
they run and do not grow weary,
    they march but do not faint.

CHAPTER XLI

1. Silence, you far shores, for me:
and let the peoples *draw near and come*!
First let them approach, then let them speak;
let us go into court together.
2. Who is it that has stirred up out of the east
the man whom victory greets wherever he goes?
that surrenders nations before him
and beats down kings *beneath him*?
He pulverizes them with his sword,
his arrows scatter them like wind-driven chaff.
3. He pursues them and passes on unscathed,
not treading the highway with his feet.
4. Who has acted and wrought,
calling the generations from the very first?
I, the LORD, am the first,
and, with the last, I am He.

5. See, you far shores, and fear,
let the ends of the earth tremble!
6. Each man of them helps his mate,
and says to his companion, 'Courage!'
7. The craftsman encourages the goldsmith,
he that wields the forge-hammer him that strikes with the nail-hammer,
saying of the solder, 'That's fine!'
and they strengthen it with nails so that it will not fall down.

8. 'But you, Israel my servant,
Jacob whom I have chosen,
the children of Abraham my friend;
9. I took hold of you from the ends of the earth,
and called you from its far corners,
and said to you, "You are my servant,
I chose you and have not rejected you."
10. Have no fear, for I am with you,
do not be alarmed, I am your God;
I strengthen you and I will come to your aid,
I support you with my victorious right hand.

11. 'Verily, all who rage at you
 will be disappointed and mortified;
those who arraign you
 will vanish as if they no longer existed.
12. You will seek your assailants
 but you will not find them;
those who war against you
 will be as nothing at all.
13. For I, the LORD your God,
 hold you by your right hand,
saying to you, "Have no fear,
 it is I who help you."

14. 'Have no fear, you worm Jacob,
 you contemptible Israel!
I it is who help you—this is the word of the LORD—
 and your Redeemer is the Holy One of Israel.
15. I am resolved to make you a threshing-board,
 new, studded with teeth;
you will thresh mountains and crush them,
 and reduce the hills to chaff;
16. you will winnow them and the wind will take them up,
 and tempest scatter them;
but you will rejoice in the LORD,
 and glory in the Holy One of Israel.'

17. The poor and the needy go in search of water and there is none,
 their tongues are parched with thirst;
I the LORD will answer them,
 I who am Israel's God will not desert them.
18. I will open up rivers on the sand belts,
 springs in the valley beds;
I will transform the wilderness with reedy pools,
 the arid land with bubbling waters.
19. I will place in the wilderness the cedar,
 the acacia, myrtle, and oleander:
I will put in the desert the juniper,
 the plane and cypress together:

20. that it may be seen and known,
    and men give heed and understand once for all,
that the hand of the LORD has done this
    the Holy One of Israel created it.

21. Present your case, says the LORD;
    advance your arguments, says the King of Jacob.
22. Let them *come forward* and tell us
    the course of events.
Of events already happened, tell us what they signify,
    that we may apply our minds to them
    and know their outcome;
    or inform us of happenings still to come.
23. Tell us what the future holds,
    that we may know you are gods;
do anything at all, be it good or ill,
    that we may be gripped by fear and alarm.
24. It is clear, you are nothing at all,
    and your work has no existence;
    who chooses you is loathsome as you are!

25. I stirred up one from the north and he came,
    from the land of the sunrise one who will invoke me;
and he *trampled* on rulers as if they were mortar,
    like a potter treading clay.
26. Who foretold this from the first, that we might know it,
    and beforehand, that we should say, 'Just so!'?
No one foretold, no one informed,
    still less did anyone hear words of yours.
27. *I appoint* leading counsel for Zion,
    and send a herald of glad tidings to Jerusalem.
28. But when I looked, there was no man,
    and among *their gods* no counsellor
    to answer a word to anything I might ask them.
29. Look at them all!
    Their deeds are null and nothing,
    their effigies wind and emptiness.

CHAPTER XLII

1. See here my servant, whom I support,
    my chosen, on whom my favour rests;

I have endowed him with my spirit,
   he shall reveal my law to the nations.
2. He will not shout or cry aloud,
   nor make his voice heard in the street.
3. He will not snap off the broken reed,
   nor snuff out the smouldering wick.
He will faithfully reveal my law.
4. With faith undimmed and spirit unbroken
   he will establish my law in the world,
   and for his teaching the shorelands are waiting.

5. This is what the LORD says—he is God—
   who created the heavens and stretched them out,
who spread out the earth with its teeming life,
   who gives breath to the peoples upon it,
   and life to whatever moves about in it:
6. I the LORD have called you for a saving purpose,
   I take you by the hand and will protect you,
and make you the mediator of my covenant with the peoples,
   a light to the nations;
7. to open the eyes that are blind,
   to bring the captives out of the dungeon,
   those that sit in darkness out of the prison.
8. I am the LORD, that is my name;
   the honour due to me I surrender to no other,
   nor my praise to idols.
9. The former prophecies have clearly been fulfilled,
   and I will declare new things;
before they begin to show themselves
   I tell you of them.

10. Sing to the LORD a new song,
   let the whole earth sound his praise.
Let the sea *roar* and all that fills it,
   the shorelands and their inhabitants.
11. Let the wilderness and its cities shout,
   the settlements where Kedar dwells;
let the denizens of the rocks cry aloud,
   let their cries resound from the tops of the mountains.

12. Let them ascribe glory to the LORD,
 and declare his praise in the far coastlands.

13. The LORD is marching out like a warrior,
 like the hero of many battles he will rouse himself to fury;
he will utter a warcry, he will roar aloud,
 he will show himself mighty against his foes.
14. 'I have long been inactive,
 keeping silence and restraining myself;
I will groan like a woman in her pangs,
 I will gasp and pant with all my might.
15. I will lay waste mountains and hills,
 and dry up all their herbage;
I will turn river-beds into *deserts*,
 and dry up all the pools.
16. And I will lead the blind on their journey**,
 guiding them by paths they know not.
I will turn their darkness into light,
 and make crooked paths straight before them.
These are the things I will do,
 and I will not leave them undone.
17. Those who put their trust in idols
 will be turned back, utterly ashamed,
those who say to molten images,
 "You are our gods".'

18. Listen, you deaf;
 and look, you blind, that you may see!
19. Who is blind but my servant,
 and deaf as my messenger whom I send?
Who so blind as he who has been granted my covenant of peace,
 and *deaf*, as the LORD's servant?
20. You see much, but you pay no heed to it;
 though your ears are open, *you* do not hear.
21. It pleased the LORD, for his righteousness' sake,
 to make his law surpassing in grandeur.
22. But they are a people despoiled and plundered,
 all of them trapped in holes,
 hidden away in prisons,

carried off as spoil without hope of rescue,
as plunder, and no one says, 'Release them!'
23. Would that among you someone would listen to this,
pay attention and hear from now on!
24. Who was it that gave Jacob to be plundered,
and Israel to the spoilers?
Was it not the LORD, against whom we sinned,
[and they were not willing to walk in his ways]
and would not obey his law?
25. And so he poured out over them his burning anger,
and the fury of battle;
and it wrapped him in flames, but he did not understand,
and scorched him, but he did not take it to heart.

CHAPTER XLIII

1. Yet now
This is what the LORD says,
he that created you, Jacob,
and formed you, Israel:
'Fear not, I have redeemed you;
I have called you by name, you are mine.
2. When you pass through the waters I will be with you,
and through the rivers, they shall not overwhelm you;
when you walk through fire you shall not be burned,
nor shall its flames scorch you.
3. For I am the LORD your God,
the Holy One of Israel, your deliverer;
I give Egypt as your ransom,
Nubia and Seba in exchange for you.
4. Because you are precious to me,
honoured, and I love you,
I give *lands* in exchange for you,
and peoples as the price of your life.
5. Fear not, for I am with you;
I will bring your children from the east,
and gather you from the west;
6. I will say to the north, "Release!"
and to the south, "Do not withhold them!
bring my sons from far,
and my daughters from the end of the earth,

7. everyone who belongs to me,
whom I created so that my majesty might be clearly seen,
and formed him, in short, I made him".'

8. Bring in the people who are blind, yet have eyes,
and deaf, although they have ears!
9. All the nations have been convened,
the peoples assemble.
Who among them foretold this,
or *announced* past events in advance?
Let them bring their witnesses and so win the verdict,
that the court may say, 'It is true!'
10. 'You are my witnesses'—this is the word of the LORD—
'and my servant whom I have chosen,
that you may know and trust in me,
and understand that I am God.
Before me no god was formed,
nor shall be any after me.
11. I, I alone, am the LORD,
and besides me there is no Saviour.
12. I it was who foretold ** and announced,
not some foreign god you fancied;
and your part is to be my witnesses'—this is the word of the LORD
13. 'I am God and shall be ever the same;
none can release from my grasp.
I act, and who can reverse it?'

14. This is the word of the LORD,
your Redeemer, the Holy One of Israel:
'For your sakes I send against Babylon,
and I will drive the Chaldeans downstream,
fugitives all, in their proud ships.
15. I am the LORD, your Holy One,
Israel's Creator, your King.'

16. This is the word of the LORD,
who made a way through the sea,
a path through the surging waters,

17. who led out chariots and horse,
a whole army in mass formation;
they sink down, nevermore to rise,
they are extinguished, quenched like a wick:
18. 'Let not memory linger over the past,
or dwell on happenings of long ago.
19. I am about to do a new thing;
now shall it spring up—surely you must know it!—
I will even make a way through the wilderness,
paths in the desolate waste.
20. The creatures of the wild will honour me,
the wolves and the owls;
when I supply water in the wilderness,
rivers in the desolate waste,
to give drink to my chosen people,
21. the people I formed for myself
that they might rehearse my praises.'

22. 'Do not imagine, O Jacob, that it was me you invited to your feastings,
or that you, Israel, went so far as to weary yourself on my account!
23. You did not offer me your holocausts of sheep,
or do me honour with your sacrifices.
I did not make you slave at preparing grain-offerings,
or weary you by demanding frankincense.
24. You did not buy me fragrant cane with your money,
or soak me with the fat of your sacrifices.
On the contrary, you made a slave of me with your sins,
you wearied me with your iniquities.

25. 'I, in very truth I, do wipe out your transgressions because I am what I am,
and your sins I will remember *no more*.
26. Recall the past to my memory, let us get at the truth together;
say what you have to say, that you may be judged innocent.
27. Your first father sinned,
and those who should have been my spokesmen to you flagrantly disobeyed me.

28. That is why I deprived the consecrated princes of their sanctity,
and abandoned Jacob to destruction,
and Israel to those who reviled him.'

CHAPTER XLIV

1. 'But now
Hear, Jacob my servant,
Israel whom I have chosen!
2. This is the word of the LORD who made you,
who formed you in the womb and will help you:
Have no fear, my servant Jacob,
Jeshurun whom I have chosen.
3. For I will pour water on the thirsty,
copious rains upon the dry ground;
I will pour my spirit on your children,
my blessing on your children's children.
4. They will grow apace *like* the verdant poplar,
like willows alongside watercourses.
5. One here will say, "I am the LORD's",
and another there will call himself Jacob.
Yet another will sign himself as "The LORD's",
and add to his name the surname Israel.'

6. This is the word of ** Israel's King
and Redeemer, the LORD of hosts:
'I am the first and I am the last;
there is no God but me.
7. If anyone thinks he is like me, let him *stand up and* say so,
and make his declaration and state his case to me.
Those who ages ago announced coming events
should be able to tell *us* what the future still holds.
8. Do not dread or be alarmed;
did I not announce and tell you long ago?
and you are my witnesses.
There is no other God to my knowledge,
nor any Rock. I know none.'

9. Those who fashion idols are all of them empty-heads,
and their darlings are utterly worthless;

their devotees are blind and ignorant,
    or they would be ashamed.
10. The man who fashions a god
    has but cast an image to no purpose or use.
11. See! All his accomplices look sheepish
    (even smiths are but men),
they gather, all of them stand,
    in a mixture of dread and confusion.
12. The ironsmith ** works in the forge
    and shapes it with hammers;
he works at it with his brawny arm;
    he is famished, his strength deserts him,
    he drinks no water, he is faint.
13. The woodworker stretches his tape-line,
    makes a crayon sketch,
sets to work with chisels,
    and traces it out by compass;
he gives it the shape of a man,
    of a fine-looking man,
    to settle down in his house.
14. He goes out to fell cedars,
    selects cypress or oak,
    makes his choice among the forest trees;
or he plants a laurel
    and the rain makes it grow.
15. And when a man is in need of fuel,
    he takes bits and pieces and warms himself;
while he is about it he stirs up the fire and bakes bread;
nay more, he makes a god and goes down on his hands and knees,
    makes it into an idol and prostrates himself before it.
16. Half of it he burns as firewood,
    on the other half he *roasts meat*;
he eats his fill of the roast;
    meanwhile he is warm and laughs 'Ha ha!
    I am warm, I can see the firelight!'
17. And what is left over he makes into a god, his idol;
    he prostrates himself full length before it,
and prays to it and says,
    'Save me, for you are my god!'

18. They have neither sense nor perception,
for their eyes are so smeared over that they cannot see,
and their minds that they cannot understand.
19. And it never occurs to him to reflect,
nor has he the sense or perception to say,
'Half of it I burned in the fire,
on its embers I baked bread,
I have roasted meat and eaten,
and am I to make what is left into a loathsome thing,
and prostrate myself to a block of wood?'
20. He is like a sheep grazing on an ash-heap,
a deluded mind has led him astray,
so that he cannot set himself free,
or ask himself, 'Am I not clutching a lie?'

21. 'Remember all this, O Jacob,
and you, Israel, for you are my servant;
I formed you to be my servant;
you must not *play false with* me, Israel!
22. I have wiped out your rebellious past as the sky is cleared of clouds,
and your sins as if they were cloud-drift.
Come back to me, for I have redeemed you!'
23. Ring out, you heavens, for the LORD has acted;
raise shouts of joy, you deep abysses of the earth;
break forth, you mountains, into ringing cries;
forest and every tree in it;
for the LORD has redeemed Jacob
and points to Israel as his crowning achievement.

24. This is the word of the LORD your Redeemer,
who formed you in the womb:
'I am the LORD, Maker of all that is,
who stretched out the heavens, I alone.
who spread out the earth—no one was with me!—
25. who nullifies the omens of *wordy prognosticators*
and makes the diviners crazed;
who refutes the wise
and turns their knowledge to foolishness;

26. who carries out the word of his servant
    and executes the purpose announced through his envoys;
who says of Jerusalem, "She shall be inhabited**
    and I will rebuild her ruins";
27. who says to the ocean-deep, "Run dry!
    I will make your currents vanish away";
28. who says of Cyrus, "My shepherd!
    and he shall execute all my will,
by ordering Jerusalem to be rebuilt
    and the temple foundations relaid".'

CHAPTER XLV

1. This is the word of the LORD:
'To his anointed prince, Cyrus,
    whose right hand I grasp,
in token that I will beat down nations before him
    and strip kings of their weapons,
that I will open doors before him
    and that gates shall not be shut:
2. I myself will go before you
    and smooth your passage through the mountains;
I will shatter the doors of bronze
    and hew in pieces the iron gate-bars.
3. I will give you treasures hidden away in darkness,
    buried in secret hiding places,
that you may know that I am the LORD,
    who summon you by name,
    the God of Israel.
4. I do this because of my servant Jacob,
    Israel whom I have chosen,
and to this end I address you by name,
    I give you a title of honour, although you do not know me.
5. I am the LORD, than whom there is no other;
    except me there is no God;
    I arm you, though you do not know me,
6. that it may be known,
    from where the sun rises to where it sets,
    that there is none besides me.
I am the LORD and there is no other God;

7. I form the light and create darkness,
   I make weal and create woe.
I am the LORD who does all these things.'

8. You skies above, distil moisture,
   and let the heavens rain victory;
let the earth open her womb,
   that prosperity may *blossom*
   and salvation burst into flower.
I the LORD have created it.

9. Who is he that would cavil at his Maker?
   What is he better than a piece of common earthenware?
Is the clay to say to the potter, 'What are you making?'
   or *the finished work*, 'He has no skill'?
10. As well might a son say to his father, 'What are you begetting?',
   or to his mother, 'To what are you giving birth?'
11. This is the word of the LORD,
   the Holy One of Israel,
   who shapes the future:
'Is it for you to take me to task about my children,
   or give me orders about what I do?
12. I it was who made the earth
   and created man upon it;
with my own hands I stretched out the heavens,
   and set all their host in motion.
13. I, too, have stirred him up for a saving purpose,
   and I will direct all his ways aright;
he shall build my city,
   and set my exiled people free,
not for anything by way of payment or a bribe',
   says the LORD of hosts.

14. This is the word of the LORD:
'The toilers of Egypt and the merchants of Nubia,
   and the tall Sabeans,
shall make pilgrimage to you and be yours;
   they will pay court to you,
   coming with manacled hands.

They will bow low to you
    and make supplication to you, saying,
"God is with you and there is no other,
    no God at all but he".'
15. In very truth, thou art a God who conceals himself,
    O God of Israel, Saviour.
16. All who *rage at him* are disappointed and mortified,
    those who carve idols are sunk in disgrace.
17. But Israel shall be saved by the LORD
    with a lasting deliverance;
you shall not be disappointed or mortified
    world without end.

18. For this is the word of the LORD,
    who created the heavens
    —he is God!—
    who formed the earth and made it;
    he established it firmly;
    he did not create it a chaos,
    he formed it to be inhabited:
    'I am the LORD, and there is no other.
19. I have never spoken in secrecy,
    in some place in the land of darkness;
I have never said to the children of Jacob,
    "Seek me in the void".
I, the LORD, speak the truth,
    I declare what is right.

20. 'Assemble yourselves and come,
    with one accord draw near,
    you survivors of the nations!
They are ignorant
    who carry about their wooden idols,
and keep praying to a god
    who cannot save.
21. State your case and advance your arguments
    —by all means let them confer together—
Who announced this long ago?
    in time past declared it?
Was it not I, the LORD?
    and there is no God besides me,

a victorious God and a Saviour;
there is none except me.

22. 'Turn to me and be saved,
all who dwell at the farthest ends of the earth!
For I am God and there is no other.
23. By myself I swear,
truth has gone forth from my mouth,
a word that shall not be recalled:
"To me every knee shall bend,
and every tongue swear fealty".'
24. 'Only in the LORD'—it shall be said—
'is there victory and might'.
To him shall come all who rage at him,
and they shall be ashamed.
25. To the LORD shall the whole family of Israel
sing their victory hallelujahs.

CHAPTER XLVI

1. Bel crouches, Nebo cowers;
their effigies have been made over to beasts and cattle,
carried like burdens
loaded on weary pack-animals.
2. They crumple up completely,
they cannot carry their burden to safety,
but themselves trudge into exile.

3. 'Hearken to me, O family of Jacob,
all you remnant of the family of Israel,
who have been borne from birth,
carried ever since you were parted from the womb;
4. even to your old age I remain the same,
and to grey hairs I will support you.
I have made a beginning,
and I myself will support
and carry you through to safety.

5. 'To whom will you liken or equal me,
or compare me, that we may be alike?

6. There are those who lavish gold out of a bag,
 and weigh out silver in a balance;
they hire a goldsmith to make it into a god,
 and then prostrate themselves full length before it.
7. They carry it laboriously on their shoulders,
 they set it down in its place and it stays there,
 not moving from where it stands.
Even if a man cries out to it, it does not answer,
 or deliver him from his distress.

8. 'Remember this and show yourselves obedient,
 recall it to mind, you rebels!
9. Remember what happened ages ago,
 for I am God and there is no other,
 very God, and there is none like me.
10. I announce the end from the beginning,
 from long ago things not yet done,
saying, "My purpose stands,
 and I will carry out all my will";
11. summoning out of the east a falcon,
 from a far country the man who shall carry out my purpose.
In short: I have spoken, and I will do as I have said;
 I have resolved, and I will bring it to pass.

12. 'Hearken to me, you stubborn-hearted,
 you who are far from deliverance!
13. I have brought near my deliverance,
 it is not far off,
 and my salvation shall not delay;
and I will give in Zion my gift of salvation,
 to Israel my pride.'

CHAPTER XLVII

1. Get down and sit among the rubble,
 virgin city of Babylon;
sit throneless on the bare earth,
 lady Chaldea;
for you are no more to be called
 dainty and voluptuous.

2. Bend to the millstones and grind meal,
uncover your tresses,
strip off your train,
bare your thighs,
wade through rivers.
3. You will suffer rape,
your shame will be plainly evident;
I will take vengeance
and I will parley with no man.
4. [Our Redeemer, his name is the LORD of hosts, the Holy One of Israel.]

5. Sit in silence and go into the dark,
lady Chaldea,
for you are no more to be called
the queen of kingdoms.
6. I was angry with my people,
I ceased to regard them as any longer mine;
I gave them into your power,
you showed them no pity,
on the aged you laid your yoke
most heavily.
7. You said, 'I shall go on being
a queen for ever';
you did not lay all this to heart,
you gave not a thought to how it would end.

8. And now, listen to this, you pampered jade,
you who sit free from care;
who say to yourself,
'I am, and there is none else beside.
I shall never sit a widow,
I shall never know loss of children'.
9. Yet both these shall come to you,
in a moment, in one single day:
loss of children and widowhood
shall come to you at one fell stroke,
in spite of your many incantations
and for all the great potency of your spells.

10. You felt secure in your wickedness,
    you said, 'No one sees me'.
Your very wisdom and knowledge
    misled you;
and you said to yourself,
    'I am, and there is none else beside'.
11. And so there shall come upon you disaster
    you will not know how to charm away;
ruin shall fall upon you,
    which you will not be able to appease,
and there shall come upon you suddenly
    such a crash as you never knew.
12. Stand your ground, by all means, with your spells
    and with your many incantations,
in which you have toiled from your youth;
    maybe you will be able to profit from them,
    maybe you will still strike terror.

13. You are worn out with your many consultations.
    Let them, if they can, stand to and save you,
those who divide up the heavens,
    who gaze at the stars,
who at every new moon announce
    the quarters which indicate what is to befall you.
14. They are nothing but so much chaff,
    fire consumes them;
they cannot save even themselves
    from the power of the flames.
It is no coal to warm at,
    no firelight to sit by!
15. Such is all they care about you,
    those on whom you have spent so much labour,
    with whom you have trafficked from your youth;
each goes his own random way,
    there is not one to save you.

CHAPTER XLVIII

1. Hear this, O family of Jacob,
    you who are called by the name Israel,
    and sprang from the *loins* of Judah;

who swear by the name of the LORD,
and invoke the God of Israel,
but neither in good faith nor sincerity.
2. For they style themselves as from the holy city,
and lean for support on the God of Israel,
the LORD of hosts is his name.

3. 'Long ago I foretold the events of times now past,
I declared and made known what they would be;
then suddenly I acted and they happened.
4. Because I knew how stubborn you are,
your neck rigid as iron,
and your brazen effrontery,
5. therefore I told you long ago,
before anything happened I gave you notice of it,
lest you should say, "My idol caused them,
my metal image set them in motion".

6. 'All that you have heard you are now to behold,
and it must be your part to make it known.
From now on I announce to you new things,
things hidden, which you have not known.
7. They are created now, not long ago,
and until now you have never heard of them,
lest you should say, "Of course I knew them!".
8. On the contrary, you neither heard nor knew;
what is more, your ear has long been firmly closed;
for I know how disloyal you are,
and that you are well called "A rebel from birth".

9. 'For my name's sake I am slow to anger,
and for the sake of my renown I restrain it,
otherwise I should destroy you.
10. I have assayed you, but not for silver;
I chose you in the furnace of affliction.
11. For my own sake, for my own sake, I act as I do
—for how should *my name* be profaned?—
and the honour due to me I surrender to no other.

12. 'Listen to me, Jacob,
Israel whom I called!

I am he, I am the first,
    I, too, am the last.
13. My own hand laid the foundations of the earth,
    and my right hand spread out the skies;
as I was summoning them,
    they sprang into being.

14. 'Assemble, all of you, and hear.
    Who among them predicted these things?
He whom I call "Friend" shall carry out *my* purpose
    against Babylon, and *his arm shall overpower the Chaldeans*.
15. It is I, I who have spoken, I who have called him;
    I have brought him, and his undertaking shall prosper.
16. Come near to me, hear this:
    Never from the beginning have I spoken in secrecy;
    ever since anything came to pass, there am I'
[and now the Lord God has sent me, and his spirit].

17. This is the word of the Lord your Redeemer,
    the Holy One of Israel:
'I am the Lord your God,
    who teaches you for your profit,
    who directs you in the way you should go.
18. Would that you had paid heed to my commands!
    Your peace would have been like a river,
    and your prosperity like the waves of the sea;
19. your children as numerous as the sand,
    and your descendants like its grains;
their name would never be obliterated
    or destroyed out of my sight.'

20. Go out from Babylon,
    haste away from Chaldea!
Proclaim with a shout of jubilation,
    let this be heard!
Tell it out
    to the end of the earth;
Say, 'The Lord has redeemed
    his servant Jacob!'

21. and that they thirsted not
    in the deserts through which he led them;
he made water flow
    out of the rock for them,
by splitting the rock
    so that water gushed out.

22. 'There is no peace', says the LORD, 'for the wicked'.

CHAPTER XLIX

1. Listen, you far shores, to me,
    and attend, you distant peoples!
The LORD called me before I was born,
    while I was yet in the womb he named my name.
2. He made my mouth like a sharp sword,
    in the shadow of his hand he hid me;
he made me a polished arrow,
    in his quiver he concealed me,
3. And he said to me, 'You are my servant,
    you Israel in whom I take pride'.
5*b*. So I was honoured in the sight of the LORD,
    and my God became my strength.
4. But I said, 'I have toiled to no purpose,
    I have exhausted my strength entirely in vain;
yet the LORD will assuredly declare his confidence in me,
    and my recompense is safe with my God'.

5*a*. And now, this is the word of the LORD,
    who formed me, before I was born, to be his servant,
to bring back Jacob to him,
    and that Israel might be gathered to him:
6. **'It is little matter that you should be my servant
    to re-establish the tribes of Jacob
    and to bring back the offshoots of Israel;
so I make you a light to the nations,
    that my salvation may reach
    to the end of the earth'.

7. This is the word of the LORD,
    Israel's Redeemer and Holy One,

to one deeply despised,
loathed by the nations,
the slave of tyrant rulers:
'Kings will see and stand to attention,
princes, and they will prostrate themselves,
because of the Lord, who is faithful to his word,
the Holy One of Israel, who has chosen you.'

8. This is the word of the Lord:
'In the hour of my favour I respond to your need,
in a day of deliverance I come to your aid;
and I will protect you and make you
the mediator of my covenant with the peoples;
that you may resettle the land,
and recover possessions now deserted;
9. saying to the prisoners, "Go out",
to those who are in darkness, "Show yourselves".
By *all* pathways they shall feed,
and on all sand-belts shall be their pasture.
10. They shall not hunger nor thirst,
neither scorching sand nor sun shall strike them;
for he who has compassion on them shall lead them,
and shall guide them by springs of water.
11. And I will make all my mountains a pathway,
and my highways shall be put in order.
12. See! These come from afar,
and these from the north and west,
and these from the land of Syene.'
13. Ring out, you heavens,
and exult, O earth;
break out, you mountains, into shouts of jubilation!
For the Lord has comforted his people,
and will have compassion on his afflicted.

14. But Zion says, 'The Lord has forsaken me,
my God has forgotten me'.
15. 'Can a woman forget the child she suckled,
a compassionate mother the son she bore?
Even these may forget,
but I will not forget you.

16. See! I have engraved you on the palms of my hands,
    your walls are never out of my sight.
17. Your builders make haste,
    those who destroyed and devastated you
    go out from you.

18. 'Lift up your eyes round about and see;
    all of them are gathered and come to you.
As I live—it is the word of the Lord—
    you shall put them all on as ornaments,
    and fasten them on as a bride does her finery.
19. As for your wastes and desolations
    and your devastated land—
you will not have room enough for your inhabitants,
    and those who swallowed you up will be far away.
20. The children born to you while you were bereaved
    will keep repeating in your ears,
"The place is too cramped for us,
    make room for us to live in".
21. And you will say to yourself,
    "Who has borne me these?
I was childless and barren
    exiled and turned away,
    and who has brought up these?
I was left quite alone;
    where, then, have these come from?"'

22. This is the word of ** the Lord:
'See! I will beckon with my hand to the nations,
    and hoist my signal to the peoples;
and they shall bring your sons in their arms,
    and your daughters shall be carried on their shoulders.
23. Kings will be your foster-fathers,
    and their queens your nursing-mothers.
With their faces to the ground they will bow low to you,
    and lick the dust on your feet;
and you will know that I am the Lord,
    who never disappoint those who wait for me.'

24. Can a tyrant be robbed of what he has seized,
    or the captives of the *bully* be rescued?

25. Surely, this is the word of the LORD:
'The tyrant shall be robbed of his captives,
and what the bully has seized shall be rescued.
Whoever contends with you will have to contend with me,
and I myself will liberate your children.
26. And I will make those who maltreat you devour their own kin,
and they shall be drunk with their own blood as with heady wine;
and all mankind shall know
that I am the LORD your Deliverer,
and your Redeemer, the Mighty One of Jacob.'

CHAPTER L

1. This is the word of the LORD:
'Where, pray, is your mother's writ of divorce,
with which I sent her away?
Or which of my creditors is it
to whom I sold you?
Nay! It was for your iniquities that you were sold,
and for your flagrant disobedience that your mother was sent away.
2. Why, when I came, did I find no man?
Called, and there was none to answer?
Is my hand so shortened that it cannot rescue?
Or am I powerless to set you at liberty?
Surely not! If I were to rebuke the sea, I should dry it up;
I should turn its ocean tides to desert!
Their fish would stink from lack of water,
and die of thirst.
3. I drape the skies with blackness
and make sackcloth their covering.'

4. The Lord GOD has given me
an expert tongue,
so that I am skilled to sustain
the weary with a word **.
Morning by morning he wakens in me an attentive ear,
to hear as those who are taught.

5. The Lord God has given me an open ear,
and I have not been disobedient,
nor have I turned back.
6. I laid bare my back to those who flogged me,
my cheeks to those who tore at my beard;
I have not *turned away* my face
from insults and spitting.

7. But the Lord God will come to my aid;
therefore I am not humiliated;
therefore I have set my face like flint,
and I know that I shall not be put to shame.
8. My Vindicator is near.
Who will impeach me?
Let us take our stand together!
Who is my opponent?
Let him come near to me!
9. The Lord God will surely come to my aid;
Who then can win a verdict against me?
Nay! They will all wear out like a garment
and become moth-eaten.

10. Who is there among you that fears the Lord,
obeying the word of his servant;
that gropes in darkness
and has no glimmer of light?
Let him trust in the name of the Lord
and firmly rely on his God!
11. All you who strike fire,
and surround yourselves with a girdle of sparks!
By all means walk by the flames of your fire
and among the sparks you have kindled!
This is what you may expect from me,
you shall die and go to a place of torment.

CHAPTER LI

1. 'Listen to me, you who endeavour after right,
who seek the Lord:
think of the rock from which you were hewn,
and of the quarry from which you were digged.

2. Think of Abraham your father,
   and of Sarah who gave you birth;
for he was but one when I called him,
   and I blessed him and made him many.
3. For the Lord will comfort Zion;
   he will comfort all her ruins,
and will make her wilderness like Eden,
   her desert like the garden of the Lord;
joy and rejoicing will be found in her,
   thanksgiving and the sounds of praise.

4. 'Attend to me, O *peoples*,
   and, you *nations*, give ear to me;
for from me there issues the voice of authority,
   and my ordinances, to bring light to the peoples.
5. My victory is immediately near,
   my triumph rises like the break of day,
   and my sovereign power shall rule the peoples.
The far shores look to me with longing,
   expectant of my rule.
6. Lift up your eyes to the heavens,
   and look at the earth beneath;
for the heavens will vanish like smoke,
   the earth wear out like a garment,
   and its inhabitants die like swarms of gnats;
but my victory shall be for ever,
   and my triumph shall never be annulled.

7. 'Listen to me, you who know and do what is right,
   the people in whose heart is my law;
Do not fear the taunts of men,
   or be dismayed at their revilings;
8. for moth will eat them like a garment,
   and the clothes-moth eat them like wool;
but my triumph shall be for ever,
   and my victory to all generations.'

9. Awake, awake, exert thy might,
   O arm of the Lord!
Awake as in bygone days,
   the generations of long ago!

Art thou not the arm that hewed Rahab in pieces,
  that pierced the sea-monster?
10. Art thou not the arm that dried up the sea,
  the waters of the great deep;
that made the ocean-depths a pathway,
  for the redeemed to pass over?
11. And the LORD's ransomed people shall return,
  and enter Zion with shouts of joy,
  crowned with never-fading gladness.
Gladness and rejoicing shall overtake them,
  and sorrow and sighing shall flee away.

12. 'I it is, I, who comfort you;
  how is it that you live in fear
  of man who is mortal,
  of man whose life is short-lived as grass;
13. that you have forgotten the LORD who made you,
  who stretched out the heavens
  and laid the foundations of the earth,
and live your days in hourly dread
  because of the rage of the oppressor,
when he sets about to destroy?
  And what is the rage of the oppressor?
14. The burdened slave is soon to be set free;
  he shall not die and go down to the pit,
  nor shall he even want for bread.
15. For I am the LORD your God,
  who stirs up the sea so that its waves roar,
  whose name is the LORD of hosts.
16. And I have put my words in your mouth
  and covered you with the shadow of my hand,
stretching out the heavens,
  laying the foundations of the earth,
  and saying to Zion, "You are my people".'

17. Rouse yourself, rouse yourself,
  stand erect, Jerusalem,
you who have drunk at the LORD's hand
  the cup of his wrath,

who have drained to the dregs
  the goblet of reeling.
18. Of all the sons she has borne
  there is not one to guide her;
of all the sons she has brought up
  there is none to take her hand.
19. These two disasters befell you—
  who is there to condole with you?—
devastation and destruction, famine and sword;
  who is there to console you?
20. Your sons swooned and lay prostrate
  at the top of every street,
  like antelopes in a net;
they were filled with the wrath of the LORD,
  the rebuke of your God.

21. Therefore
Hear this, you who are so afflicted,
  drunk, but not with wine.
22. This is the word of the LORD, your Lord,
  your God who champions the cause of his people:
'Know that I am taking out of your hand
  the cup of reeling,
  the goblet of my wrath:
you shall drink of it no more;
23. and I will put it into the hand of your tormentors
  and those who humiliated you,
who said to you,
  "Lie down for us to trample over you";
and you lay full length on the ground,
  to serve as a footpath for such as passed by.'

CHAPTER LII

1. Wake up, Zion, wake up,
  assume your proper might;
put on your sumptuous garments,
  Jerusalem, the holy city;
for no more shall there enter into you
  anyone uncircumcised and unclean.

2. Shake yourself from the dust, stand erect,
O *captive* Jerusalem;
free yourself from your neck-fetters,
O captive daughter of Zion.
3. For this is the word of the LORD: 'You were sold for
4. nothing, and you shall be redeemed without money.' For
this is the word of the Lord GOD: 'First, my people went
down to Egypt as guests; then the Assyrians oppressed them
5. for no reason at all. And now, what do I find here?'—
this is the word of the LORD—'My people have been
taken away for nothing; those who domineer over them are
braggarts'—it is the word of the LORD—'and all
6. the day long my name is derided. Therefore my people shall
know my name ** on that day, that it is I, in very truth I,
that speak.'

7. How welcome is the runner
coming over the hill-tops with news;
who announces, 'All is well!'
who brings good news,
who announces deliverance,
who says to Zion,
'Your God reigns!'
8. Hark! Your watchmen!
They raise their voices,
shouting together!
For theirs will be an immediate view
of the LORD's return to Zion.
9. Break out into one resounding shout of joy,
you ruins of Jerusalem;
for the LORD has comforted his people,
he has freed Jerusalem.
10. The LORD has bared his holy arm
in the sight of all the nations,
and all the ends of the earth shall see
the victory of our God.

11. Away! Away!
Go out from there,
touch nothing unclean;

march right away from her,
rid yourselves of all impurity,
you who carry the sacred vessels.
12. Yours shall be no hurried escape,
still less will you go in flight;
the LORD himself is going before you,
the God of Israel is your rear-guard.

13. Behold, my servant shall prosper,
he shall be high and lifted up and very exalted.
14. As many were horrified at him—
his appearance was unlike that of a man,
so disfigured that he did not seem human—
15. so shall many nations guard against contagion by him,
and kings shut their mouths against him;
because they have seen what had never been told them,
and become attentive to something of which they had never heard the like.

CHAPTER LIII

1. Who would have believed what we have heard?
And to whom has the arm of the LORD been revealed?
2. For he shot up like a sapling,
as from a root in an arid soil;
he had no presence or dignity that we should look at him,
no beauty that we should be drawn to him.
3. He was despised and shunned the company of men;
a man weighed down by sorrows and humbled by sickness;
and as one from whom men hide their faces,
he was despised, and we thought him of no account.

4. But ours were the sicknesses that he bore,
ours the sorrows he carried;
while we supposed him stricken,
smitten by God, and afflicted.
5. Yet he was pierced by our transgressions,
crushed by our iniquities;
his was the chastisement that brought us weal,
and at the cost of his wounds there is healing for us.

6. All we had gone astray like sheep,
each turned his own way;
and the LORD brought down upon him
the guilt of us all.

7. He was harshly treated, though he submitted humbly
and did not open his mouth.
As a sheep led away to be slaughtered,
and as a ewe before her shearers
is dumb,
so he did not open his mouth.
8. After arrest and sentence he was led away,
and none gave a thought to his fate;
for he was forcibly removed from the world of living men,
for the sin of peoples who deserved to be stricken themselves.
9. And they gave him burial among felons,
and with the dregs of men when he died;
although he had done no wrong,
or uttered so much as a word of deceit.

10. But it was the LORD's will that he should be broken by suffering.
If with his own life he makes restitution for the guilt of others,
he shall see his children enjoying long life,
and the LORD's purpose will prosper under his charge.
11. After his sorrowful labours he shall see *light*
and have fullness of knowledge;
my servant, himself righteous, shall bring righteousness to many,
and himself bear their iniquities.
12. Therefore I will give him the many as his victory award,
and he shall distribute countless spoil;
this because he gave himself utterly and to the death,
and was counted among transgressors,
by bearing the sin of many
and standing in the place of the transgressors.

CHAPTER LIV

1. 'Rejoice, O barren woman who have borne no child;
break out into shrill and joyous cries,
you who have not been in labour;
for she who now is deserted
shall have more children than when she lived with a husband,
says the LORD.
2. Enlarge your tent-space,
widen the curtains of your dwelling—
no need to be sparing!—
lengthen your cords and strengthen your stakes.
3. For you shall spread out on every hand;
your children will succeed to the nations,
and reoccupy cities now desolate.

4. 'Have no fear, you will not be abashed;
do not be intimidated, you will not be embarrassed;
for you will forget the shame of your youth
and remember no more the disgrace of your widowhood.
5. For your husband is your Maker,
his name, "The LORD of hosts";
and your Redeemer is the Holy One of Israel,
his title, "God of the whole earth".
6. For when ** he called you, you were a woman
outcast and utterly dejected—
yet who can disown the bride of his youth?
says *the LORD* your God.

7. 'For a brief moment I forsook you,
but with great compassion I will gather you home.
8. In a flush of anger I hid
my face from you for a moment;
but with undying devotion I will have compassion on you,
says the LORD, your Redeemer.
9. This is to me like the days of Noah over again,
when I declared on oath that the waters of the flood
should never again sweep over the earth;

so now I swear that never again
  will I be wroth with you or rebuke you.
10. For though the mountains should remove
  and the hills withdraw from sight,
my steadfast love shall never remove,
  or my covenanted peace be withdrawn from you,
  says the LORD, who has compassion on you.'

11. 'Poor tempest-driven, inconsolable city!
Listen!
I will lay your stones in black cosmetic,
  and bed your foundations in azure.
12. I will make your pinnacles of chalcedony,
  and your gates of carbuncle,
  and all your boundary wall of splendid stones.
13. All your masons shall be taught by the LORD
  and great shall be the prosperity of your children.
14. You shall be built on a foundation of righteousness,
  so far from oppression that you will not need to fear,
  and from terror, that it shall not come near you.
15. If anyone stirs up strife, he shall have no support from me;
  whoever picks a quarrel with you shall fall because of you.
16. I it is who have created the smith
  who fans the charcoal in the fire,
  and produces weapons of all kinds;
I, too, have created the ravager to destroy.
17. No weapon forged against you shall succeed,
  and if anyone brings an action against you, the verdict shall be yours.
This is the inheritance of the servants of the LORD
  and their right guaranteed by me.
This is the word of the LORD.'

CHAPTER LV

1. 'Attend! Attend!
All you who are thirsty, come for water;
  even if you have no money, come!
Buy grain and eat, without money,
  wine and milk without payment.

2. Why do you pay out money for what is not bread,
   and your riches for what does not satisfy?
If you listen to me, you will eat what is good,
   and your taste be delighted with rich food.
3. Give heed and come to me,
   listen, that you may have life in its fulness;
and I will make a lasting covenant with you,
   with the dependable manifestations of my love for David.
4. As I appointed him a witness to the peoples,
   a leader and commander of the peoples,
5. so you shall summon nations you do not know,
   and nations that do not know you shall come running to you,
because of the LORD your God,
   and because the Holy One of Israel has invested you with honour.'

6. 'Seek the LORD while he is to be found,
   call to him while he is near;
7. let the wicked man abandon his way of life,
   and the evil-doer his thoughts;
let him turn back to the LORD, that he may have mercy on him,
   and to our God, for he is always ready to forgive.
8. For my thoughts are not your thoughts,
   neither are your ways my ways,
   says the LORD.
9. For as high as heaven is high above the earth,
   so my ways are higher than your ways,
   and my thoughts than your thoughts.

10. 'For as the rain comes down,
   and the snow from heaven,
   and do not return there,
   but water the earth,
making it give birth and send out buds,
   and give seed to him that sows
   and bread to him that eats;

11. so shall my word be that goes out from my mouth;
    it shall not return to me unfruitful;
instead, it shall do what I purpose,
    and succeed in the mission on which I send it.

12. 'For you shall go out with rejoicing,
    and be led along in safety;
the mountains and hills will break out into cries of joy at
        your approach,
    and all the trees of the countryside will clap their hands.
13. Instead of the camel-thorn shall come up the juniper,
    instead of the nettle shall come up the myrtle;
and it shall be to the LORD for a memorial,
    for a lasting inscription which shall never be effaced.'

III · COMMENTARY

XL. 1–11. OVERTURE

1. יֹאמַר] Not the usual אָמַר (pf.) but imperfect for repeated action in the present (*GK* 107 *f*).

2. דַּבֵּר עַל and דַּבֵּר אֶל are interchangeable (cf. Jer. xi. 2, xxv. 2), the former being not common but more forcible (*GK* 119 *dd*). מָלְאָה צְבָאָהּ] Lit. 'she has ended her צָבָא, which is masculine and acc. obj. after מָלְאָה, the verb being sometimes transitive in *Qal* (*BDB* 570 *a*. 2). בְּכָל־] *Beth pretii*, 'in exchange for'.

3. קוֹל] Perhaps interjectional (*GK* 146b), 'Hark! One who proclaims'. This can be expressed without clumsiness by an exclamation mark after 'proclaims'. בָּעֲרָבָה] 'through the desert' (cf. Gen. xii. 6, xiii. 17).

6. וְאָמַר] LXX, V, read 'and I said' (וָאֹמַר), supported by Q[a]. Most moderns accept and remark that this is the only passage in which DI refers to himself. This would be singular. A continuative *waw consec. pf.* can follow a participle, e.g. vi. 2 f.; 2 Sam. xvii. 17. The Prophet overhears a dialogue between two speakers. חַסְדּוֹ] For variant readings and suggested emendations see *BH*, but MT gives a perfectly good sense (see below).

7. Omitted in LXX, OL, and in Q[a] has been inserted between the lines and in margin by another hand. This is not decisive evidence for deletion. It must have been easy for a translator or copyist to omit by homoioteleuton. The different verb (נָשְׁבָה not עָבְרָה) makes it improbable that the passage was filled out from Ps. ciii. 16. נָשְׁבָה] Expressing a common experience or recurrent natural phenomenon (*GK* 106 *k*). אָכֵן חָצִיר הָעָם. Usually regarded as a gloss. This is not conclusive on metrical grounds, since ver. 9 has a similar הָרִימִי אַל־תִּירָאִי, which no one proposes to delete. On the other hand, the phrase is vague (who are 'the people'?) and the sentiment commonplace. With it the poetry sags—unless this is intentional in a slow movement—instead of being heightened as in ver. 9, and the contrast between vv. 7 and 8 is blunted. It may be a (perfectly sound) gloss defining 'all flesh' to mean 'mankind' (cf. xlii. 5, xlix. 26).

9. עֲלִי־לָךְ] The so-called 'ethic dative' (*GK* 119 *s*); cf. 'Get thee to a nunnery', now obsolete. In Hebrew most frequently with verbs of motion, and with a note of immediacy. מְבַשֶּׂרֶת צִיּוֹן / יְרוּשָׁלָםִ] AV

and RSV take as appositional genitive, 'glad messenger (of) Zion' (cf. *GK* 128 *k*), Zion being personified in the feminine as the bearer of good news; cf. 'the virgin of Israel' = 'virgin Israel' (Amos v. 2), or Engl. 'the city of London'. RV, AV mg., RSV mg. take Zion as acc. obj. of מבשרת (cf. lxi. 1; Jer. xx. 5), which must then be a fem. sing. coll. (*GK* 122 *s*), 'those who tell good tidings'. Both translations are possible. The first is preferred (see below).

10. בְּחָזָק] A pointing בְּחֹזֶק, 'with might', based on versions, is supported by Q[a] בחוזק. The ב is *beth essentiae* (*GK* 119 *i*), 'in the capacity of (= as) a mighty one' (cf. Exod. vi. 3). This is more vivid and may stand, but is awkward to express in Engl. 'In might' may serve for בְּחָזָק.

11. Mass. punctuation gives a metre 3:3, 2:2. Most moderns read בְּחֵיקוֹ, with metre 3:2, 3:2. But since they would be lambs, not sheep, that the shepherd picks up, MT may stand. For a similar 3:3, 2:2 in a rallentando ending see xl. 31 (at least according to Köhler).

This passage contains what may originally have been four separate pieces, vv. 1–2, 3–5, 6–8, 9–11. The first three are 'auditions' and may be said to constitute the Prophet's 'call'. For a similar arrangement cf. Jer. i. 4–10, 11–12, 13–19. All four themes are taken up and expanded in the course of the prophecy. Except in these opening verses the fortunes of Zion-Jerusalem are not prominent in chs. xl–xlviii (only xli. 27, xliv. 26–28), but are one of the main themes in xlix–lv. For these reasons, and because the conclusion of the prophecy (lv. 12 f.) refers back to the beginning; it seems probable that xl. 1–11 was intended as the overture to the completed whole, rather than as detached pieces arranged on a 'catchword' or other mechanical principle. (This is not to deny that there are catchwords, e.g. 'voice', vv. 3, 6, 9; 'all flesh', vv. 5, 6).

Vv. 1–2. 'COMFORT MY PEOPLE'. The Prophet overhears an iterated divine summons to comfort Jerusalem with the tidings that her 'warfare' is ended. Those who are to convey the comfort are addressed in the plural, but it is not said who they are. There is something in Volz's comment that the emphasis is not so much on those who are bidden to comfort as upon the cumulative abundance of the comfort. The Prophet is to comfort by every means he can.

It has been said that 'It would be hard to find in any language words that more gently woo the broken heart of a people' (G. A. Smith in *The Legacy of Israel*, ed. E. R. Bevan and C. Singer, 1927, p. 13). This is true of both the form and the content of the passage.

As to its form, two elegiac lines 3:2 are followed by an accelerated 2:2, leading to a more leisurely 3:3. The structure is more elaborate than in earlier prophecy. DI inverts the normal order, 'Thus says Yahweh', and places first the repeated 'Comfort, comfort', followed by 'says your God' in parenthesis. Repetition for emphasis is characteristic of DI (xliii. 11, xlviii. 11, 15, li. 9, 17, lii. 1) and its use here sets the key for the whole prophecy. 'Your God' is more intimate than 'Yahweh' would have been, and is balanced by 'my people' preceding. Instead of 'Jerusalem' simply, we have the threefold 'my people . . . Jerusalem . . . her', with corresponding amplification in the verbs 'comfort . . . speak to the heart of . . . and proclaim'. Instead of the normal 'Yahweh said to me', the divine imperative is in the plural. Finally, the actual message to Jerusalem is in indirect speech. This is unusual in Hebrew and places the emphasis on the summons to comfort rather than on the content of the comfort (see Köhler, pp. 102–4 for this analysis). Yet it would be a mistake to suppose that the Prophet decided upon his metre and then filled out his lines with the requisite number of words. The form does not determine the content, the content determines the form. DI may often seem verbose, but he is an artist and means all he says.

As to content, the word for 'comfort' (*naḥḥ^{a}mû*) is charged with feeling and is closer to the psycho-physical bedrock of human emotions than the Latin words 'comfort' or 'console', which are the only expedients of the translator. Its middle consonant is the dry 'whispered' aspirate (Arab. *ḥ*, not *ḫ* as in 'loch'), which was doubled. The first and third consonants are 'liquids' and the alliteration on liquid and glottal sounds in ver. 1 is perfect. The Hebrews were well aware of the intimate relation between physical and mental states; their language alone is evidence of that. The root meaning of *nḥm* is 'breathe deeply' (D. W. Thomas in *Expository Times*, 44, 1932–3, pp. 191 f.; 51, 1939–40, p. 252). The *Niph.* and *Hithpa'ēl* are used of getting relief, easing one's self, physically and mentally, even by taking vengeance. 'Comfort' is always *Pi'ēl* (intensive) and such nouns as there are from the root are mostly intensive plurals. 'Console' in the sense of 'free from the sense of misery' (Johnson's *Dictionary*) expresses the meaning as well as 'comfort', but on the whole 'comfort' (so EVV) is to be preferred. Forty years had passed since a stricken Jerusalem had cried forlornly, 'None comforts me' (*'ên m^{e}naḥḥēm lî*, Lam. i. 2, 9, 16 f., 21).

1. *my people . . . your God*] The covenant formula, 'You shall be my people and I will be your God', with minor variations, goes back to the Exodus (cf. Jer. vii. 23), though it is most frequent in Jer., Ezek., and the Priestly writings. Even in the prophets of judgement Yahweh generally speaks of 'my people', though sometimes caustically 'this people' (e.g. Isa. vi. 9 f.; Jer. vi. 19). Hosea had been

bidden to call one of his children Lo-ammi ('No people of mine', Hos. i. 9), in token that Yahweh had rejected his people, though he had prophesied that the day would come when they would once more be called 'My people' (Hos. ii. 23 [*25*]). That time had now come.

2. *Tell Jerusalem to be of good heart*] Lit. 'Speak to the heart of Jerusalem'. The expression is found eight times (Gen. xxxiv. 3, l. 21; Judges xix. 3; Ruth ii. 13; 2 Sam. xix. 7 [*8*]; 2 Chr. xxx. 22; Hos. ii. 14 [*16*], and here). In Gen. l. 21 and Ruth it is preceded by 'comfort', as here. In Gen. xxxiv. 3; Judges; and Hos. it is used of a lover's endearments and it is tempting to take that as the sense here. The figure of Jerusalem as Yahweh's bride is clear in liv. 1–8. But the sexual metaphor is absent from Gen. l. 21 and 2 Sam. xix, and Ruth would hardly have suggested to Boaz so early in their acquaintance that he was making love to her. Some such meaning as 'reassure', 'encourage', with a note of affectionate concern, is common to all eight passages. *sentence*] Heb. *ṣāḇā'*, originally 'army', 'warfare', comes in Job vii. 1, xiv. 14; Dan. x. 1, to mean 'hard service' (cf. EVV mgs. here). *her penalty is discharged*] Or 'her punishment is accepted' (as sufficient), RV mg., accords better with the context than 'her iniquity is pardoned'. Heb. *'āwôn*, 'iniquity', serves also for the guilt which attaches to iniquity and the punishment which is its consequence (cf. Gen. iv. 13, RV mg.). The word 'discharged', 'accepted' is the same as is used in xlii. 1 of the Servant in whom Yahweh 'delights', and is cognate with an Arabic verb 'to be well pleased with'. *that she has received*] 'that' (not 'for', AV), as in the preceding clauses. On either rendering there is the suggestion that sin can, and must be, expiated by the bearing of its penalty. The prophets never thought of the exile as due to political misfortune, the fate of a small country doomed at the hands of aggressive empires, but as penalty for sin, 'received at Yahweh's hand'. *twice-over*] Heb. *kip̄layim* ('double') occurs elsewhere only in Job xi. 6, where RV and RSV render 'manifold'. It should not be taken as indicating exact measure, and it is reading too much into it to say that one half of the sufferings of Israel, the servant of Yahweh, is to go to the credit of the Gentiles. The Servant of ch. liii. did not deserve to suffer at all. The prophet of consolation is speaking to the grandchildren of those whom his predecessors had castigated so severely: in Lev. xxvi the refrain 'seven times for your sins' occurs four times. Jerusalem has suffered 'more than enough'.

The prophecy will have much to say of the city of Jerusalem, its temple and walls. But Jerusalem was hundreds of miles away and the comfort was as much for the exiles in Babylon as it was for the mother-city in the homeland. Here Jerusalem is personified and is parallel with 'my people'. We can speak of a city as 'she' but in the Bible such personifications are more vivid than with us. 'Jerusalem' in DI stands not only for a geographical location, but for an idea, the community of God's people. There is little difference between 'my people', 'Jerusalem', and 'Jacob-Israel'. Jerusalem is already on the way to becoming a symbol and has become a type in the NT (cf. Gal. iv. 26; Heb. xii. 22 f.; Rev. xxi. 2, 10). In the language of Christian devotion it has become almost synonymous with the Church.

Vv. 3–5. 'A HIGHWAY FOR OUR GOD'. The Prophet hears a herald bidding angelic ministers prepare a processional highway for Yahweh's return to Jerusalem. Valleys are to be raised, mountains levelled, and every hindrance removed. 'The majesty of Yahweh' is to be disclosed simultaneously to all mankind. Any doubts that may linger after the initial consolation are dispelled by the assurance 'for the mouth of Yahweh has spoken'.

The metre, taking 'A voice proclaims!' as anacrusis, is 2:2, 2:2, 3:3, 3:3:3. The initial orders are peremptory, and with the increasing emotion the poetry rises in a crescendo to a final tristich.

Ezekiel had witnessed the departure of 'the glory of Yahweh' from the doomed city of Jerusalem. Now Yahweh is to return in public triumph. The description is primarily of physical hindrances, but it goes without saying that moral hindrances, as well as physical, must give way to Yahweh. It will be 'a holy way' (cf. xxxv. 8–10). The returning exiles will be in the retinue of their Deliverer (vv. 10 f.) but they are not specifically mentioned here. The emphasis is on the divine theophany. All eyes will be upon Yahweh.

3. The punctuation should be as in RV, RSV. This gives perfect parallelism in what follows. The punctuation in Mark i. 3 and parallels follows LXX, which was taken as referring to John the Baptist, who appeared in the wilderness as the herald of Jesus. *Make ready*] Heb. *pannû*, used in Gen. xxiv. 31 of clearing away things scattered about, and in Zeph. iii. 18 of 'clearing out' an enemy: cf. also lvii. 14, lxii. 10; Mal. iii. 1; Ps. lxxx. 10. *wilderness*] Heb. *midbār*, as distinct from a desert, is properly 'a place for driving' (sheep or cattle). *a level highway*] Heb. *yaššerû* conveys the double sense 'straight and level'. The road will be 'as the crow flies'; that it will be without steep gradients is clear from what follows. *the desert*] 'the Arabah', in EVV Joshua xviii. 18 and sometimes a name for the Jordan valley and Dead Sea depression. Originally a common noun, 'desert plain', 'steppe', it is not infrequently || 'wilderness'; e.g. xxxv. 1, 6. Here it must be the Syrian Desert, as in xli. 19, with a central massif mostly over 2,000 ft., intersected by numerous wadis, mostly running east–west. *highway*] A 'raised highway' (*m^e^sillāh*, √'cast up', cf. xlix. 11) with supporting earthworks, corresponding to what we should call a trunk-road; cf. Num. xx. 19; Judges xx. 31 f.; also Moabite Stone, line 26; the word is never used of a city street. Its use here is the first hint in the prophecy of a comparison between the approaching exodus from Babylon and the Exodus from Egypt (cf. xi. 16). The highway is to be on the grand scale; the stars have their *m^e^sillôṯ*, from which they fought against Sisera (Judges v. 20).

4. *deep cleft*] Heb. *gai'* was a narrow 'gorge' or 'ravine' as distinct from the broader and more open 'valley' or 'plain' (cf. Gen. xi. 2; Ezek. xxxvii. 1 f.) at the end of the verse. *become lowland*] But not brought down to sea-level; the Hebrew verb is from the same √ as 'The Shephelah' (e.g. Joshua xi. 16), the foothills between the Mediterranean coastal plain and the central range of Palestine. *steeps*] The Hebrew word is similar to *'āḳēḇ* ('heel'), √'be protuberant' (?); cf. Arab. *'aḳabat*, 'a difficult mountain path'. *level surface*] *mîšôr*, cf. *supra* on ver. 3, whether 'plain' (1 Kings xx. 23, 25; Zech. iv. 7) or 'plateau' (Deut. iii. 10, iv. 43). *tangled hillocks*] *r^e^ḵāsîm*, only here. *KB* 892 *b* compares with Arab. *'arkasa*, 'become solid', 'round' (of a girl's breasts). This meaning is not attested by Lane, but see the Arabic dictionary of F. Steingass (p. 431 *b*) and A. Wahrmund, Giessen, 1877 (p. 290 *a*).

5. *all mankind*] Heb. 'all flesh' may mean (1) all living creatures, (2) animals as distinct from man, (3) mankind as distinct from God (e.g. Gen. vi. 12 f.; Num. xvi. 22). Here it must mean the last, as also in ver. 6, xlix. 26, lvi. 16, 23 f. *together*] *yaḥdāw* (√ 'be united'), a characteristic word of DI, who uses it more than any other writer. For the idea of 'all-of-a-suddenness' as well as simultaneity attaching to it, see on xli. 19 f.

These colossal preparations recall the martial triumphs of the kings of antiquity. But they are even more reminiscent of cultic rites in which gods were carried in festal procession, as in a cuneiform text addressed to Nabu (cf. xlvi. 1), which reads: 'Make haste to set out, thou son of Bel, who knowest the ways and art familiar with the ceremonies! Make his (Marduk's) way prosperous, put his road in repair, make his pathway straight, hew out a footpath for him' (E. Ebeling, *Keilschrifttexte aus Assur religiösen Inhalts*, No. 104, quoted by Volz). They may even be reminiscent of pre-exilic festivals in which the Ark of 'the King of glory' was carried in procession to the temple (cf. Ps. xxiv. 7–10). To say that DI used language similar to that of heathen rituals he scorned is not to derogate him. His whole prophecy is based on the principle of contrast: everywhere he insists that what the gods of Babylon made a show to do, but could not, Yahweh can do with omnipotent ease (cf. L. Dürr, *Ursprung und Ausbau der israelitisch-jüdischen Heilandserwartung*, 1925, pp. 147 ff.).

But the immediate inspiration of this and similar passages (e.g. xli. 17–20, xliii. 16–21) describing the way back from Babylon, is the saga of the Exodus and the wilderness wanderings. That DI was familiar with this, whether from written documents or from the free currency of oral tradition, is obvious. With the passage of time history had become 'salvation-history', with a liberal infusion of the miraculous. By the time of DI the salvation-history had in its turn become 'history'. God had acted in the past, and he could, and would, act again, and as marvellously.

THE GLORY (MAJESTY) OF YAHWEH. *SOED* defines 'the glory of God' as 'the majesty and splendour attendant upon a manifestation of God'. The standard EVV all have 'glory'. The Hebrew word (*kāḇôḏ*) is based on a √ 'to be heavy'. Man as well as God may have *kāḇôḏ*. A man's 'glory' consists of anything which is the outward evidence of his prosperity, such as his wealth (e.g. Gen. xxxi. 1; Isa. lxi. 6; Esth. v. 11) or his reputation (e.g. Ps. iv. 2 [3]; Job xix. 9). In poetry it can be almost equivalent to the 'self' (e.g. Gen. xlix. 6; Ps. xvi. 9), though the pointing in these passages should perhaps be *kᵉḇēḏî*, 'my liver', still in the sense of 'my self'.

A study of 'the glory/majesty of Yahweh' may begin with Exod. xxxiii. 18–23, in which Moses asks to see Yahweh's *kāḇôḏ*, which in the course of the narrative seems to be much the same as his *pānîm* ('face'), vv. 20, 23, i.e. his 'self' ('me', ver. 20), which no man can survive the seeing. The heavens are constantly declaring the divine *kāḇôḏ* (Ps. xix. 1 [2]), the earth is full of it (Isa. vi. 3), though in Isaiah's vision only the seraphim see it in its effulgence, and even they veil their faces. In stories of the Exodus the glory of Yahweh is associated with the 'signs' which he 'wrought' in Egypt and the wilderness (Num. xiv. 21 f.), and similarly in the Psalms (Ps. xcvi. 3). Much of this material in its present form is comparatively late, but there is no reason to doubt that it goes back to early traditions associated with phenomena like the pillar of cloud and fire. Ezekiel is the first to identify the glory with a specific physical phenomenon, a bright or fiery substance resembling the rainbow (Ezek. i. 27 f.). The circumlocution in which he describes it is remarkable: 'This was the appearance of the likeness of the glory of Yahweh', and its effect on him was such that he fell upon his face. He witnesses the departure of the 'glory' from Jerusalem (xi. 23) and in a final vision he sees its return to the new temple (xliii. 1–5). All this he sees in vision, not with the natural eye. In P the glory is similarly a fiery substance wrapped in cloud (in the wilderness, Exod. xvi. 7, 10, and on Sinai, Exod. xxiv. 16 f.), and in this tempered form it was visible to all Israel. In the subsequent wanderings the glory is always present in the tabernacle (Exod. xxix. 43, xl. 34 f.; Num. xiv. 10; cf. 1 Kings viii. 10 f.).

In Isa. xl. 5 it is probable that 'the glory of Yahweh' has some relation with Ezekiel's conception (cf. also lviii. 8, lx. 1 ff.), but it is something far more impressive than the cultic manifestation to which it has shrunk in P. Clearly what is anticipated is the coming of Yahweh himself, a theophany compelling in its majesty, which is to mark the beginning of a new era for all mankind (cf. Num. xvi. 22; Deut. v. 26). It is difficult to choose between 'glory' and 'majesty'. The translation *glorious majesty* is taken from the Collect for Advent. LXX, as usual, renders δόξα, which points forward to the ultimate sequel in Luke ii. 9; 2 Cor. iv. 6.

Vv. 6–8. CREATURELY TRANSIENCE AND DIVINE PERMANENCE. Two voices are heard, the one saying 'Proclaim!' to which the other answers, 'What shall I proclaim ?'. Verses 6*b*, 7, are perhaps antiphonal (cf. vi. 3), ver. 8 in unison. The burden of the proclamation is that all sentient life is as evanescent as the flower which fades. By contrast, the 'word' of God will endure for ever.

The metre is 3:3, 3:3, 4:4, (3?), 4:4. Verses 7–8 are adagio, appropriately to the theme. The repeated 'Grass withers, flower fades'—seven syllables in the Hebrew, all with long vowels, and four stresses, the last two a spondee—sound like a dirge. In 'blows upon it' (*nāšᵉḇābbô*, two stresses) the conjunctive *dagh. forte* acts as a brake, and the sound is like a wave beating on the shore and then dragging back over shingle. Contrast the final stich (8*b*), in which the pace quickens to allegro.

The proclamation begins with metaphor and then passes to simile. It is important to observe this if we are not to get into trouble with the word *ḥeseḏ* ('constancy'). The flowers (*ṣîṣ*, lit. 'shining' or 'sparkling' things) are wild flowers (cf. 'the lilies of the field'), gardens in ancient Palestine being mostly for utility (cf. 1 Kings xxi. 2; Isa. i. 8). All visitors to Palestine are struck by the wealth of its wild flowers. Volz keeps MT *ḥeseḏ* and renders *Anmut* ('grace' or 'charm'), on the basis of Aram. *ḥᵃsîḏā'*, 'charming' (of a bride or face). This would be analogous to Gr. χάρις in its Homeric sense of physical grace or charm. But the *ḥeseḏ* in the text is not the *ḥeseḏ* of flowers but of 'all flesh', which the gloss (?) interprets, rightly enough, of mankind. *ḥeseḏ* is 'constant love', 'devotion', 'loyalty', between relatives or friends, master and slave, king and subject, or those bound by covenant obligations. This is the meaning here: cf. Hos. vi. 4: 'Your *ḥesed* is like a morning cloud, or like the dew that quickly vanishes'. Man's constancy begins brightly, but languishes so quickly. Another passage which should be studied is Ps. ciii. 15–17. The short-lived frailty of flowers is a common theme in the Bible (Ps. xc. 5 f.; Job xiv. 2; Isa. xxviii. 1; Luke xii. 28) and in literature generally: most of Herrick's poems on flowers recur to it. But nowhere except in the Bible and in literature inspired by the Bible is reflection upon the impermanence of creaturely existence followed by the triumphant assurance of God's permanence and constant love. Though the contrast between human *bāśār* ('flesh') and the divine *rûaḥ* ('spirit') is not expressly drawn, as in Gen. vi. 3; Isa. xxxi. 3, it is not far from the thought of the passage—'the *rûaḥ* ('wind', RV and RSV 'breath') of Yahweh blows upon it'. But the main contrast is between the transitoriness of 'all flesh', which is 'grass', and 'the word of our God', which 'shall endure (cf. Job viii. 15, xiv. 2) for ever'. This contrast is expressed with shattering simplicity: lit. 'and the word of our God. . .'. The Hebrew adversative 'and' = 'but' is usual in antithetical propositions (so in Proverbs) and gives a lightness of touch to what might otherwise be cumbrous. Two contrasted ideas are joined by simple 'and', thus heightening the paradox: cf. again Ps. ciii. 15–17: 'as for man, his days are as grass . . . . *and* the *ḥesed* of Yahweh is from everlasting to everlasting'. The 'word' of God which is to endure for ever must neither be limited to the 'words' of this passage—the OT speaks relatively seldom of the 'words' of God—nor even to the words of this whole prophecy. It is rather the active will of God, his declared and all-embracing purpose (cf. lv. 11), the word by which the heavens were made (Ps. xxxiii. 6), by which all mankind shall come to the knowledge of God (xlv. 23), the word settled for ever in heaven (Ps. cxix. 89). The Word already was when all things began (John i. 1).

Vv. 9–11. THE EVANGEL OF THE GOOD SHEPHERD. A summons to Jerusalem to announce to the townships of Judah the near advent of Yahweh. He is coming as a ruler, accompanied by the captives he has liberated. His gentle care of them is described under the figure of a shepherd tending his flock.

In this passage the glad tidings are announced by human, not celestial voices. The LXX renders *m^ebaśśereṯ* ('bearer of glad tidings') by εὐαγγελιζόμενος, very appropriately in a translation of this 'evangelist of the OT', thus anticipating the NT evangel.

The metre is mainly 3:2, with extra beats (2 each) in 'Lift it up, have no fear' and 'with regal arm outstretched', which sustain the flight of the poetry.

9. *O Zion/Jerusalem, herald of glad tidings*] Cf. AV, RSV, and to be preferred to RV, though both translations are possible (see *supra*). AV is in keeping with the wider context: Zion-Jerusalem has already heard the glad tidings (vv. 1 f.) and is now to pass them on to her 'daughter' townships. As the triumphal procession (vv. 3–5) approaches the city, its inhabitants are to *go up with all speed to the high mountain*, somewhat hyperbolical for what must be the Mount of Olives; cf. xxii. 1 f., which speaks of the city as 'gone up, all of you, to the house-tops'. (Olivet lay to the east of Jerusalem and would afford the first view of a column approaching from the east.) There they are to lift up their voices, undeterred by fear of Babylonian espionage or by lingering want of faith. Voices in hill country travel far (cf. Judges ix. 7; 1 Sam. xxvi. 13 f.) and orientals can make their voices very penetrating. The cry is to go out *to the townships of Judah*, '*Your God is at hand!*' (See note below on *hinnēh*, 'Behold'.) The gaze of the beholders will be fixed, not upon the returning exiles but on Yahweh. *He* is still the centre of the picture. Two qualities he displays, the might of a ruler and the gentleness of a shepherd. The figure of the shepherd combines both. The king in the Ancient East was the 'shepherd' of his people, and wherever in the OT the word shepherd is used figuratively, it is always of a ruler (e.g. 2 Sam. v. 2; Ezek. xxxiv; the only exception is Jer. xvii. 16, where 'shepherd' is wrongly pointed).

10. The God who now leads his people in this second Exodus, *with regal arm outstretched*, is he who once led his people out of Egypt 'with mighty hand and outstretched arm' (Deut. iv. 34). *the sheep he has earned*] *śᵉḵārô*, lit. 'his wages' (Gen. xxx. 28, 32, xxxi. 8; Deut. xv. 18; Zech. xi. 12 f.). *prize*] *pᵉʿullāh*, orig. 'work', so AV, then by metonymy the 'wages' which are the reward or recompense (RV, RSV) of toil, as in Lev. xix. 13. Yahweh's *śāḵār* and *pᵉʿullāh* are not, as EVV may suggest, largesse he is going to distribute, but his people whom he has acquired by his labours in their behalf. The rendering of 'his wages' by *the sheep he has earned* is justified by the shepherd/sheep simile in ver. 11, and by Gen. xxx. 32, xxxi. 8, where Jacob takes his wages from Laban in sheep. Indeed, vv. 10 f. here seem more reminiscent of Jacob's return from exile in Paddan-aram, than of the Exodus from Egypt. It is not suggested that Yahweh has bought his people for a ransom price, as in xliii. 3 f. The thought is rather that underlying Jer. xxxi. 15 f., where Rachel's restored children are the reward of her long vigil of bitter weeping: 'your work shall be rewarded', lit. 'there shall be wages (*śāḵār*) for your work' (*pᵉʿullāh*).

11. The figure of the Good Shepherd is frequent in the Bible; cf. Ps. xxiii; Ezek. xxxiv; Luke xv. 3–7; John x. 1–18. The best commentary is Gen. xxxiii. 12 f., where Jacob says he must adjust his pace to that of the children, the ewes, and their lambs. The word *flock* (*‘ēḏer*) is from a √ ‘lag behind’ and the inverse alliterations in *k^{e}rô‘êh ‘eḏrô yir‘êh biz^{e}rô‘ô y^{e}ḳabbēṣ* picture, as well as language can, sheep milling round and round, and the patience of the shepherd as he keeps them together. *the lambs*] *ṭ^{e}lā’îm*. The metaphor is transparent; the lambs are the children. The word was, or became, in Aramaic an epithet for children (*ṭalyā’*, ‘boy’, *ṭ^{e}lîṯā’*, ‘girl’). Jesus addressed the daughter of Jairus as *Talitha!* (Mark v. 41). *the ewes*] *‘ālôṯ, Qal* ptc. fem. plur. of *‘ûl*, ‘suckle’. There is nothing to choose between AV, RSV, ‘those that are with young’, and RV ‘those that give suck’. Syr. *‘ûlâ* can mean either foetus or the new-born baby. In any case, ewes for most of the year are either pregnant or suckling their lambs. *and lead the ewes to their resting places*]. Only two words in Hebrew: ‘(and) lead (the) ewes’. The same impression of leisureliness can be conveyed by the longer sentence in English. EVV ‘gently’ is perhaps reminiscent of Jacob’s ‘I will lead on softly’ (Gen. xxxiii. 14). The √*nhl* properly means ‘to lead to a watering-place (Arab. *manhal*) and cause to rest there’ (cf. *BDB* 625*a*). The ‘place where’ is sometimes expressed by an adverbial expression, as in ‘beside waters of rest’ (Ps. xxiii. 2, cf. EVV mgs.), or ‘by springs of water’ (Isa. xlix. 10); cf. also Exod. xv. 13.

NOTE ON HEB. HINNĒH, ‘BEHOLD!’ Heb. *hinnēh*, whether alone or preceded by the conjunction *w^e* (‘and’), occurs nearly 800 times in the OT. In addition, it is found many times with pronominal suffixes. The shorter *hēn* occurs 100 times, twenty-one of them in Isa. xl–lxvi. In the EVV they are generally rendered ‘Behold!’, less frequently ‘Lo!’, and occasionally ‘See’. ‘Behold!’ and ‘Lo!’ are now archaic and the translator into modern English is often at a loss to know what to do with *hēn* and *hinnēh*. They are, of course, not verbs, but demonstrative interjections related to Arab. *’inna*, ‘surely’, ‘certainly’. They are frequent in prose and are one of the evidences that stories circulated orally before they were reduced to writing. They were part of the stock-in-trade of the story-teller. Speaking generally, they introduce an element of vividness or surprise, and call attention to the noun or phrase they precede. In poetry *hinnēh* is sometimes outside the metre (anacrusis), but where it occurs as one beat in a 2- (xl. 9) or 3-beat stich (xl. 10 *bis*) it must never be assumed that it was so much ‘stuffing’ to fill out the line. How it should be represented in modern translation is largely a matter of the ‘feel’ of any particular passage; e.g.:

Say to the townships of Judah,
'Your God is *at hand*!'
Know that the Lord God is coming in might,
with regal arm outstretched;
and that with him are the sheep he has earned,

There can be many variations, without striving after virtuosity.

XL. 12–26. THE INCOMPARABLE

12. בַּזֶּרֶת] Qᵃ בזרתו, balancing 'in his palm', probably rightly, though the sense is clear without the suffix. וְכָל . . . וְשָׁקַל] Perfects with simple *waw* (*Syn.*, § 58 *a*). כָּל is *Qal* perfect 3rd pers. sing. masc. from כול, 'to contain' (trans.). Greek versions wrongly construe as כֹּל, 'all'. עָפָר] Some would delete this and the ה following, claiming support of the Greek versions. The word may be an interpretative gloss on [הָ]אָרֶץ, but if so it is a perfectly sound one; see below.

13. The מִי of the first stich governs also the second: lit. 'and (who was) his counsellor (who—the relative particle being omitted, *GK* 155 *f*) gave him knowledge?' It is convenient to remark here that the difference between Hebrew perfect as past and the imperfect as present or future 'tense' cannot be sustained, especially in poetry (cf. *Syn.*, § 45 R. 3, 51 R. 5). For the reasons see G. R. Driver, *Problems of the Hebrew Verbal System*, (passim). The same applies in vv. 19 f. and elsewhere.

14. וַיְלַמְּדֵהוּ דַּעַת] Wanting in LXX. The words come in between the second and third members of what would be a tristich 3:3:3. Neither of these grounds is decisive for deletion, since DI sometimes uses extra 2-beat stichs (cf. vv. 9, 12 above). But the words do seem repetitive and may be later amplification.

15. יִטּוֹל] EVV 'He (Yahweh) takes up'. The verb (נטל) is found elsewhere only in 2 Sam. xxiv. 12 (where the || 1 Chron. xxi. 10 has נֹטֶה); Lam. iii. 28; and Isa. lxiii. 9 (*Piʿēl*). The noun נֵטֶל, 'weight', occurs in Prov. xxvii. 3; cf. נְטִילֵי, 'weighing' (Zeph. i. 11). In Syriac the verb means 'weigh', 'turn the scale', and none of the OT uses is inconsistent with this. Read יִטְּלוּ, 'the isles weigh like dust'. This fits the context better. The final *waw* may have been assimilated to לְבָנוֹן following.

17. מֵאֶפֶס] The hitherto conjectural כְּאֶפֶס now has the support of Qᵃ; cf. כְּאַיִן preceding, and כְּשַׁחַק . . . נֶחְשָׁבוּ, ver. 15.

18. תְּדַמְּיוּן] Cf. *GK* 47 *m*, 75 *dd*.

19–20. These verses are notoriously difficult. As they stand they appear to be an answer to the questions in ver. 18. The ה of הַפֶּסֶל is generally taken as generic, 'any idol' (*GK* 126 *m*), but it could be interrogative. The most serious difficulties are the use of צוֹרֵף as a verbal-participle so soon after the noun-participle צֹרֵף (Q[a] writes both *plene*) and the phrase הַמְסֻכָּן תְּרוּמָה. Some would emend to יִצְרֹף (impf.), with no difference in meaning. Torrey (pp. 199 ff.) points out that DI likes to use the same word in different senses in near contexts. הַמְסֻכָּן תְּרוּמָה] Lit. 'he that is poor (in respect of) a תרומה'. Although מְסֻכָּן is ἅπ. λεγ. the adj. noun מִסְכֵּן (4 times in Eccles.) is found in the cognate languages; cf. Fr. *mesquin*. תרומה could be verbal accusative of material (*GK* 117 *hh*), or specification (*GK* 118 *q*), or after a verb (here pass. ptc.) describing lack of something (*GK* 117 *z*). A תרומה is properly something 'lifted off' (√רום), 'contribution', often a technical sacrificial term (RV 'heave offering'), and therefore, it has been argued, inappropriate in this context. G. R. Driver (*JTS* 36, 1935, 396–406) relates with Akk. *tarimtu*, a 'sacred object' of great value, 'possibly an effigy'. Torrey (p. 308) emends to תְּמוּרָה and translates 'he who is poor in substance' (cf. Job xx. 18), i.e. reduced to poverty. But how, on these suppositions, should a poor man be able to employ a skilled joiner? Duhm's (*Jesaja*[3], 1914) הַמְּכֹנֵן תְּמוּנָה is based on LXX ὁμοίωμα κατεσκεύασεν. According to Jerome *amsuchan* was a kind of wood. Torrey dubs this 'fantastic Jewish exegesis' which 'does not deserve any serious attention'. But Sidney Smith (pp. 171 f.) treats it seriously, identifies *amsuchan* (following R. Campbell Thompson, *The Assyrian Herbal*, p. 181) with Akk. *musukkanu*, 'mulberry', and translates: 'The wise artificer chooses mulberry of the offering, a wood that will not rot; he seeks to secure it to the cast figure, so that it will not tumble', adding that 'there is no need to assume far-reaching corruption'. That may be, but it is extremely clumsy Hebrew. Why should the Hebrew be pointed מְסֻכָּן instead of the normal מִסְכֵּן? There is much to be said for deleting המסכן תרומה. It is wanting in V, was unintelligible to LXX, and in Q[a] has obviously been written in by a second hand. It makes an awkward subject to יִבְחָר and breaks in between two tristichs in vv. 19 and 20. המסכן will then be a gloss on עֵץ—the word cries out to be glossed—and תרומה either an attempt to explain מְסֻכָּן ('poor'), or a secondary gloss on עץ or המסכן, perhaps a mangling of תְּמֹרָה, 'palm' (cf. LXX ὁμοίωμα = תְּמוּנָה). H. Zimmern (*Zeitschrift für Assyriologie* 9, 1894, 111–12), the first modern to identify המסכן as a tree, thought it was a palm. T has *'ôran* (*Laurus nobilis*). Sa'adya (so Levy p. 123) thought it was the holm-oak.

20. יִבְחָר . . . יְבַקֶּשׁ] Both with indef. subj., translated by passives.

לוֹ] Probably 'for it' (the wood), not 'unto him(self)', as AV, RV. פֶּסֶל] Art. omitted in poetry. לֹא יִמּוֹט] A final clause (as in xli. 7; cf. Ps. xciii. 1, xcvi. 10, civ. 5), not adjectival.

21. מוֹסְדוֹת] Properly acc. obj., 'Have you not understood the foundations of' (RV mg.). Read probably מִיסֻּדַת, or the like, 'from the foundation of'. The meaning is much the same: see below.

26. וְאַמִּיץ] Read וְאֹמֶץ (Qª, LXX, T, P). כֹּחַ] Read כחו (Qª).

These verses are controversial in tone and ask a series of rhetorical questions. Yahweh is incomparable, the omnipotent (ver. 12) and omniscient (vv. 13 f.) Creator, sole Architect of the universe (vv. 12–14), Lord of the nations (vv. 15–22) and of history (vv. 22–24), and Marshal of the stars (vv. 25 f.). A striking feature of the passage is that although it is clearly implied that Yahweh is incomparable, he is nowhere described in negations. Instead—and this heightens the paradox—he is portrayed anthropomorphically.

12. The questions are not 'Who is able to measure this and weigh that?'—scientists today can do that with some accuracy—but 'Who measured this in his palm and weighed that in scales?'—this when he created the world. The answer, 'Yahweh' (= God, ver. 18) is implied in ver. 13. The general picture is similar to that in Ps. civ. 1–9. Yahweh is a colossal figure whose palm held 'the waters' and whose 'span' measured out the heavens. *the primeval ocean*] *mayim*, 'the waters'. There is no need to emend to *yammîm*, 'the seas' (*BH*) or to *mê yām*, 'the waters of the sea' (Qª). The reference is to 'the great deep' (*tᵉhôm rabbāh*, li. 10; Amos vii. 4), cf. Ps. civ. 3–6; Gen. i. 1–7. Note the assonance *mayim wᵉšāmayim*. The materials of which the earth is made up are its 'dust', i.e. its loose *soil* (cf. 1 Kings xviii. 38; Job v. 6, xiv. 8), its *mountains*, and *hills*. The first third was contained in a *šālîš* (a 'third' dry measure, 'terce'—*quart container* conveys the sense), the mountains *weighed . . . from the arm of a balance* (*peles*), *and the hills in scale pans* (*mô'zᵉnayim*).

13–14. These verses, besides answering the questions in 12, go on to ask questions to which the only answer can be 'No one!'. Yahweh is omniscient. *gauge*] *tikkēn*, the same word as *marked out* (RV 'meted out', RSV 'marked off') in ver. 12; cf. Job xxviii. 25 *b*. A possible translation in ver. 12 is 'adjusted' (cf. Ps. lxxv. 3 [*4*] 'I adjust its pillars') but the parallelism requires some equivalent of 'measured'. The sense is 'Who had the measure of the mind (*rûᵃḥ*) of Yahweh?'—cf. Prov. xvi. 2, xxi. 2, xxiv. 12, where it is said that Yahweh measures minds (*rûḥôṯ*) and hearts (*libbôṯ*). It is going beyond the thought of the passage to read into it the doctrine of the 'spirit' of

Yahweh as the agent in creation: *rûᵃḥ* here means *mind*, as a comparison of Ezek. xi. 5, xx. 32 (*rûᵃḥ*) with Isa. lxv. 17; Jer. iii. 16 (*lēḇ*) makes clear; cf. also Rom. xi. 34; 1 Cor. ii. 16, where the present passage is (*pace* Muilenburg) correctly interpreted. *or proffer him advice on equal terms*] Lit. 'or (who was) the man of his counsel (who) caused him to know?' It would be reading too much into the words to make them mean 'What *man* taught him?' Obviously no *man* was there.

14. *To whom did he turn for advice and instruction?*] Lit. 'With whom did he take mutual counsel (reciprocal *Niph.*) and he (i.e. who) gave him discernment?'—a more concentrated construction than is usual in Hebrew. *to make*] Lit. 'in the path of'; cf. Engl. 'put him in the way of'. *endowed him with*] Lit. 'caused him to know the way of'. *right decisions*] *mišpāṭ*; but the usual forensic sense is not prominent here (see on xl. 27, xli. 1). *all-penetrating insight*] *tᵉḇûnôṯ*, 'insights'; plural of intensification or amplification (*GK* 124 *e*).

15. Yahweh controls history with the same effortless economy of means as he employed in creation. *the nations are like a drip* (that falls) *from a bucket* (√ 'pull up') when it is drawn up from a well. *moisture*] *šaḥaḳ*, √ 'pulverize'; elsewhere always of clouds. But the meaning may be 'fine dust' (EVV, cf. Exod. xxx. 36; Job xiv. 19). Dust or moisture on scales in a market place would not need to be taken into reckoning, though scales in a modern laboratory would be a different matter. *the shorelands of the western sea*] *'iyyîm*, √ 'make for' (a place) and so 'be eager' to reach it; cf. *ta'ᵃwāh* (same √) 'desire'. Hence the 'desired haven' of the sailor, whether coastland or island proper; in OT generally of the Mediterranean (especially the Ionian?) coasts and islands, with some emphasis on their far distance (cf. xlix. 1).

16. If Lebanon were the altar and all its forest trees fuel for a holocaust of all the wild life upon it, even that would be a sacrifice inadequate to honour Yahweh. (The passage is not concerned to ask whether animal sacrifice has religious value, or whether wild animals are admissible as sacrifices.) Volz and Muilenburg think the verse may be a later addition. It certainly breaks the continuity between 15 and 17 and in Qᵃ appears to be by a later hand (the same applies to 14*b*–15, though—and this is perplexing—space appears to have been left for 14*b*–16).

17. *in his presence*] Cf. i. 7, *negdô*, stronger than the usual *lᵉpānâw*, 'before him'. It is almost as though all the nations, in Yahweh's presence, are *not there*! The Prophet was speaking of Egypt, Babylon, Greece, and the rest. He would doubtless have said the same of the 'great powers' of today. *empty nothings*] *'ep̱es wāṯôhû*, 'non-existence and chaos'. The vacuity of *tôhû* is clearly heard in the *tôhû wāḇôhû* (Carlyle's 'tohubohu') of Gen. i. 2. Versions render *tôhû* by *κενόν*, *οὐδέν*, *inane*, *vacuum*. The meaning is not that God is contemptuous of the nations but that *vis-à-vis* him, their pretensions and their towers of Babel are totally insignificant. There are thousands of millions of stars in the galaxy of which the sun is a member. If the diameter of the galaxy were reduced to the dimensions of the continent of Europe, the sun would be a tiny speck and the earth invisible. And no one knows how many millions of galaxies there are, at an average distance of two million light-years from one another.

18. *God*] *'ēl*. The use of this word, rather than the more frequent *'ᵉlôhîm*, calls for remark. *'ēl* was an early Semitic word (Ugaritic, Phoen., Akk.) for god, and could be used for any god (plur. *'ēlîm*), and especially for El, the old Semitic 'High God'. In conformity with this, DI uses *'ēl* six times of idols (xliv. 10, 15, 17 *bis*, xlv. 20, xlvi. 6) and in the other eight passages (xlii. 5, xliii. 10, 12, xlv. 14 f., 22, xlvi. 9 and here) there is strong monotheistic emphasis. Too much should not be made of this, since *'ᵉlôhîm* also occurs with monotheistic emphasis in xliv. 6, xlv. 5, 18, 21, liv. 5; but it is perhaps significant that *'ēl* is confined to chs. xl–xlvi., where polemic against idols and the monotheistic emphasis are strong. *'ēl* and *'ᵉlôhîm* are found together in xlv. 14 f., xlvi. 9, and it may be that DI used *'ēl* partly for the sake of variety, much as the author of Job used it together with *'ᵉlôah* and *šadday*. *form*] *dᵉmûṯ*, from the same √ as the vb. *liken* preceding, is an abstract noun, mostly of late usage, and was not an opprobious word. Indeed, man was made in the 'likeness' (*dᵉmûṯ*) of God (Gen. i. 26). The word is never used of an idol, but an idol might with some show of reason be said to be a *dᵉmûṯ*. Very well! 'What sort of a *dᵉmûṯ* will you compare with (lit. "arrange for") God?'

19–20. *An idol?*] *hᵃpesel*. A *pesel* (√ 'hew into shape') was originally a carved image as distinct from a *massēḵāh* (√*nāsaḵ*, 'pour out') or cast image. But already in the early story of Micah, a *pesel* is made by a *ṣôrēp̄*, a gold- or silversmith, from silver (Judges xvii. 3 f.). In MT, as now pointed, two idols are described, both of them domestic, the first made for a rich and the second for a poor man. The second, especially, seems a peddling thing in the context of 'all the nations'. The Prophet may have intended it so but, if he did, much of the dignity of the passage is lost. If, as is argued above, the intractable 'He that is too impoverished for *such* an oblation' is deleted, we are left with a picture of one imposing idol, similar to the image of gold which 'Nebuchadnezzar the king' set up and dedicated with due public ceremony (Dan. iii), or 'the statue of Sin made by the order of Nabonidus' (S. Smith, pp. 67, 173). The procedure would be much as follows: first *a craftsman casts it* from some common metal *and a goldsmith overlays it with beaten gold*. The *ṣôrēp̄* then *forges silver fence-chains*. The meaning of this is not immediately clear. If the chains were fixed to the sides of the image and then anchored in a base to keep it erect, they would be much weaker than struts. Smith speaks of 'pouring molten silver alloy into sockets to hold the figure upright' (p. 171). But in either case the setting up of the figure is the final operation, ver. 20*b*. Presumably the image would be fenced off in some way, rather like a 1914–18 war memorial. A cognate word *riṯḵā'* is used in Talmudic Aramaic for a 'chain-like fence'; in 1 Kings vi. 21 we read that Solomon 'drew chains (*rattûḵôṯ*) of gold across in front of the inner sanctuary' (*d*ᵉ*ḇîr*) of the temple. The next thing is to make a platform or base for the image. This must be of hard wood—that it was mulberry is a later fancy. To make the platform and *fix* (*hāḵîn*, 'make firm') *the image securely so that it will not fall down* is the work of another skilled craftsman, this time a *joiner* (*ḥāraš 'ēṣîm*, xliv. 13). And when all is finished, what a pitiable 'likeness' of the living God! This is not malicious caricature. Dürr (*Ursprung und Ausbau der israelitisch-jüdischen Heilandserwartung*, 1925, p. 147) quotes from the Babylonian New Year Festival liturgy a 'prescription' for making an idol: '(He summons) an engraver and gives him precious stones and gold from the treasury of Marduk to make two images for the sixth day (of the festival). He summons a joiner and gives him cedar and tamarisk-wood. He summons a goldsmith and gives him gold'. *overlays it . . . beaten*] *y*ᵉ*raḵḵ*ᵉ*'ennû*, lit. 'beats it out', cf. xlii. 5, xliv. 24; Exod. xxxix. 3; Num. xvii. 4; Jer. x. 9. A noun from the √ is *rāḵîa'*, 'firmament' (Gen. i. 6), conceived as a solid covering, 'beaten out', cf. Job xxxvii. 18, which speaks of 'beating out' the skies as a molten mirror. There are many similarities between DI and the Creation Story in P; cf. *tôhû*, ver. 17 above. Many scholars would transfer xli. 6 f. to this context. But surely enough has been said. To bring in all the ludicrous details of xli. 6 f. here would be to reduce the austere majesty of xl. 12–26 to something like farce.

21. *Is it not clear to you from the creation of the world?*] Lit. 'Have you not discerned from the foundation of the earth?' For the 'founding' and 'foundation(s)' of the earth see Ps. xxiv. 2, lxxxix. 11 (*12*), civ. 5; Prov. iii. 19 (vb.); Ps. xviii. 15 (*16*), lxxxii. 5; Isa. xxiv. 18; Mic. vi. 2 (noun). It is difficult to form a clear cosmological picture, nor, perhaps, should the attempt be made. In Ps. xxiv. 2 Yahweh is said to have founded (*yāsaḏ*) the world 'upon the seas', i.e. the primeval waters, and in Ps. civ. 5 he founded the earth on its bases (*m*ᵉ*ḵônêhā*), perhaps pillars driven down into the abyss (cf. ver. 3; Job xxxviii. 6).

the world] Heb. *'ereṣ*, 'the earth'. The Hebrews had no word for 'the universe' as we know it (though see on xliv. 24). In EVV a convenient distinction is made between 'the world' (*tēḇēl*) and 'the earth' (*'ereṣ*), but where the OT says 'the earth' we should often say 'the world'. *from*] Here temporal *min* ('since'), as in the preceding clause. But no man was present when Yahweh laid the foundations of the earth (Job xxxviii. 4). The meaning must be either that the heavens have always declared the glory of God (Ps. xix. 1 (*2*)), or, more probably, Hebrew thought by the time of DI had a *Weltanschauung* which began with an account of creation.

22. *enthroned*] For this sense of 'sits' cf. Ps. ii. 4, ix. 7 (*8*); xxix. 10 (Yahweh); and of an earthly king 'sitting upon his throne', 1 Kings i. 46, ii. 12. *upon*] *'al* can mean 'above' (RV mg.), but 'upon' is more natural and *enthroned upon* is dignified enough. *the rounded vault*] *ḥûg*, conceived as a dome-shaped cupola overarching the earth (Job xxii. 14, xxvi. 10). In Prov. viii. 27 it is said to be 'in front of the deep' (*teh̄ôm*), i.e. between the earth (as one looks up) and 'the waters above the firmament' (Gen. i. 6 f., 20). It was therefore the same as the firmament, whose function was to prevent the waters of the original chaos from breaking through to deluge the ordered cosmos (Ps. civ. 5–9; Job xxxviii. 8–11). From that height *the inhabitants* of the earth are as insignificant (cf. Num. xiii. 33) as *grasshoppers* (*ḥagāḇîm*). These are properly locusts, but since Engl. 'grasshopper' includes all orthopterous insects, it may be allowed to stand. Note the alliterations in 22*a*. *stretched out the skies*] Cf. xlii. 5, xliv. 24, xlv. 12, li. 13; Jer. x. 12, li. 15; Ps. civ. 2. *gauze*] *dōḳ* (√ 'pulverize'), ἅπ. λεγ., but similar to *daḳ*, 'fine dust', in ver. 15. *opened them out*] The verb is from the same √ as 'sack' (*'amtaḥaṯ*) in Gen. xlii–xliv. *a habitable tent*] Cf. xlv. 18.

23. *potentates*] *rôzenîm*, the 'rulers' of Ps. ii. 2. Always ‖ 'kings', except in this passage (see Judges v. 3; Hab. i. 10; Prov. viii. 15, xiv. 28, xxxi. 4). *chaos*] *tôhû*; see on ver. 17.

24. The successive perfects and the pausal forms sound like blows from a sledge-hammer (2:2:2:2). Or, to vary the figure, they convey the impression of 'bean-stalk' rapidity and evanescence (cf. vv. 7 f.) *taken firm root*] The form (*Po'ēl*, Arab. conj. III) conveys the suggestion of effort (*GK* 55 *c*).

25. At this point Yahweh intervenes *in propria persona*, as he does out of the storm-wind (*se'ārāh*) when the arguments of Job and his friends are exhausted (Job xxxviii. 1): *Then to whom will you liken me or whom do I resemble?*] The interrogative 'whom' governs the second as well as the first clause (*GK* 150 *m*, cf. AV). *the Most Holy*] *ḳāḏôš*.

Morgenstern's plea ('The Loss of Words at the Ends of Lines in Manuscripts of Biblical Poetry', *HUCA* 25, 1954, p. 54) that *ḳāḏôš* 'is here utterly impossible' and that the word 'is never used alone, unsupported by some additional word, anywhere in the entire Bible, as the title of the Deity', and that the original reading was 'the Holy One of Israel', thus giving a 3-beat stich, will not bear examination; see Hab. iii. 3; Job. vi. 10. The 2-beat stich is intentional and has all the force of the trisagion in vi. 3. Notwithstanding that Hebrew poetry is sparing of the article, the anarthrous form here is significant. 'Holy' is no longer simply an attribute of Deity but has become almost a proper name, 'The-Most-Holy'.

26. *created*] *bārā'*. Of the rather more than fifty occurrences of the word, nearly half are in Isa. xl–lxvi; otherwise it is most frequent in the P source of the Pentateuch. It is a theological word. It does not in itself carry the meaning of creation out of nothing, but it is never used except with God as subject. *these*] Muilenburg remarks that 'the word *these* is almost breathless in its awe'. In what follows the stars are described as the martial retinue of Yahweh (cf. Judges v. 20). The thought is not that when darkness falls the stars 'come out' and that not one fails to shine. Yahweh *leads* them *out* as a commander leads an army (*ṣāḇā'*, *host*). For this sense of the *Hiph.* of *yāṣā'* cf. xliii. 17; 2 Sam. v. 2, x. 16. The military figure is continued in *by number* (cf. 2 Sam. ii. 15, and 14 times in Num. i). Only God knows the number of the stars (Gen. xv. 5), let alone their names (Ps. cxlvii. 4; cf. *ANET*, p. 429). *his omnipotent might*] Lit. 'abundance of strength and his mighty power'. Hebrew had no one word for 'omnipotence' and had to express the idea, which is clear enough throughout this passage, by periphrasis. 'Omnipotent' may be allowed here, in view of AV at Rev. xix. 6. *lags behind*] or 'is missing (on parade)', cf. 2 Sam. xvii. 22. The √ is the same as for the laggard 'flock' (*'ēḏer*) which the Good Shepherd 'gently leads'.

Babylon was the home and centre of star-worship. The Babylonian gods were mostly star-gods. The Prophet of the exile makes bold to affirm that the God of his captive people 'created' the stars whom their captors worshipped as gods. *Astra regunt homines, sed Deus regit astra.* Never, except in the Cross, has there been such a victory over defeat and humiliation.

XL. 27–31. THE EAGLE WINGS OF HOPE

31. יַעֲלוּ] May be either *Qal* or *Hiph.* The verb can mean 'grow' (intrans.) in *Qal* (lv. 13; Gen. xl. 10) and presumably 'grow' (trans.) in *Hiph.*—'they shall grow wings' (obj. acc.); cf. LXX πτεροφυήσουσιν. Some have seen an allusion to the popular belief that the eagle renews (cf. יַחֲלִיפוּ כֹחַ preceding) his plumage in old age. This is rather fanciful: in Ps. ciii. 5 the reference is only to the longevity of the eagle. In any case the 'eagles' here are really griffon-vultures (see below). כַּנְּשָׁרִים] EVV take as modifying the verb, 'as eagles (do)'. But it can qualify אֵבֶר, 'eagle-(like) pinions'. There is little difference of meaning.

Israel has fallen a prey to self-pity. Does he not know that Yahweh is the eternal God, who faints not, neither grows weary? Natural strength becomes exhausted, but those who wait for God are renewed in strength that never fails.

xl. 12–26, more than any passage in the Bible, presents something like a cosmological argument. But no matter how persuasive the cosmological and teleological arguments might be, they would afford little comfort to the soul in anguish. The crucial question is whether God is concerned with human life and destiny. Israel had never doubted the existence or the creative power of Yahweh, but the argument from creation to the Creator might well seem more appropriate for idol-worshipping polytheists than to a people who had known God's goodness but were now, however deservedly, rejected by him. A man may acknowledge the justice of his sentence and yet, if the sentence is a long one, come to be consumed by self-pity. Even more so may a people come to labour under a sense of injustice, especially the relatively innocent among them, who suffer equally with the rest and feel the shame more keenly. That was Israel's situation after four decades of banishment.

27. *The path I tread*] Heb. *derek̲* is from a √'tread'. Here it has almost the sense of 'destiny', 'fate' (cf. Jer. x. 23; Ps. xxxvii. 5). *is hidden from the* LORD] 'In a universe so vast I am lost and he can no longer find me!' *my plea for justice*] Cf. Job xiii. 8, xxiii. 4; Ps. ix. 4 (5). *mišpāṭ* can be either a case presented to a judge (*šôp̄ēṭ*) or the sentence pronounced by him. *is disregarded*] For this sense of 'pass away' (*'āb̲ar*) cf. Amos vii. 8, viii. 2; Mic. vii. 18; Prov. xix. 11, and of 'vanishing (from sight)' xxix. 5; Jer. xiii. 24; Ps. cxliv. 4; Job vi. 15; Song v. 6. The complaint is 'He no longer concerns himself with me!' To this Yahweh's answer is '*Why* (a note of reproach here) do you *keep saying* so?' The interrogative brings the action into the present (*Syn.* § 45 R. 1) and the imperfects are frequentative.

28. The address is to Israel in the singular. There is nothing unusual in this but the contrast with ver. 21 is worth noting. *the eternal God*] *The*, not 'an', since the next clause is definite. The expression (*'elôhê 'ôlām*) is only found here and is not identical with the Heb. of Gen. xxi. 33; Deut. xxxiii. 27. Even if it were, those passages would not be decisive for its meaning here, which must be determined in its relation to the context and to DI's thought as a whole. The general sense of *'ôlām* is 'long duration'. Whether we translate *eternal* or 'everlasting'—it is difficult to choose, indeed impossible to find any one word for it—it may be taken as certain that the word does not convey an abstract or metaphysical concept of time, whether unending time or timelessness. Any such conception would be unhebraic. DI's thinking, for all his idealism, was firmly anchored in the history of his people, and the clue to the meaning must be sought in the parallel stich, in which Yahweh is described as *the Creator of the ends of the earth*. There the emphasis is upon Yahweh's sovereignty over nature. Here it is on his sovereignty in history, and, by implication, over all time. He controls the history of all peoples; how much more the *derek̲* and *mišpāṭ* of Israel? Ver. 28 is thus the answer to the sorry complainings of ver. 27. When DI wishes to be more explicit he makes Yahweh say, 'I am the first and I am the last' (xliv. 6; cf. xli. 4, xlviii. 12). See E. Jenni, *Das Wort 'ōlām im AT*, 1953, pp. 67–69. *the ends of the earth*] = 'the earth in its entirety', not only its extremities but all that is included within them (cf. Ps. xix. 7; Job xxviii. 24), an assurance that Yahweh controls the whole earth, not only the land where his people languish in exile. *his understanding is unfathomable*] cf. Ps. cxlvii. 5; Job v. 9, xi. 7; Rom. xi. 33.

29. *powerless*] *'ên 'ônîm* (intensive plur.), 'those who have no power at all'; this in contrast to ver. 26, in which Yahweh has 'abundance of *'ônîm*' at his disposal. Notice how the verbs *faint* and *weary*, with and without the negative, keep resounding in this passage; indeed, words like 'understanding' (*tᵉb̲ûnāh*), 'might' (*'ônîm*), and 'strength' or 'power' (*kōᵃḥ*), are woven into the texture of vv. 12–31. This is not due, as has been alleged, to DI's 'poverty of words' (*Wortarmut*), but to consummate literary art. *young men*] *baḥûrîm* (√ 'choose'), 'picked troops' (Judges xx. 15 f.; 1 Sam. xxiv. 3; 1 Kings xii. 21), though the word is used in the general sense of men in the prime of early manhood (1 Sam. ix. 2). It could be used of 'seeded' athletes, had there been any such in OT times (1 Macc. i. 14 is the first reference to anything resembling public games). *fall exhausted*] Lit. 'utterly stumble' (infin. abs.). The more usual expression is 'stumble and fall' (e.g. iii. 8, xxxi. 3; Ps. xxvii. 2). Is there the suggestion that young men fall exhausted because they are over-confident, and often insist on running when they should be content to walk?

31. *wait for*] AV, RV 'wait upon' has come to have almost the meaning of 'pray to'. It is not that, if we mean that we speak while God listens (see on xli. 1). It is not God, but we, who are at the receiving end. The verb (*ḳāwāh*, some 50 times) is, appropriately, *Pi'ēl* intensive, except for *Qal* ptc., as here, and there is always in it the suggestion of the tension, and hopeful expectancy, of waiting; cf. *ḳaw*, 'line' (drawn taut). Characteristic passages are v. 2, 4, 7; Job vii. 2; Ps. xxvii. 14, xl. 1 (*2*). Such 'waiting for Yahweh' in expectant hope is never 'ashamed', i.e. 'disappointed' (xlix. 23; Ps. xxv. 3; Rom. v. 5). From this point the passage rises to a splendid crescendo (3:3), and touches earth once more in a rallentando (2:2) movement. The timeless Hebrew imperfects ('future' in old lexicons) are best rendered by English present, not future, tense. The fulfilment of the promises is now, not in some undefined future. RV and RSV retain 'shall', perhaps to convey assurance, but there is no justification for it in ver. 30. *renew*] √'pass on'; cf. Arab. *ḫalîfa*, i.e. 'successor' (of Muhammad). In Ps. xc. 5 f. the *Qal* means 'come on afresh' (of grass). The *Hiph.* is used of 'changing' clothes (Gen. xxxv. 2) and wages (Gen. xxxi. 7, 41). Here 'obtain fresh strength' or 'exchange strength' (for better). *on eagle pinions*] *pinions*, *'ēḇer*, √ 'be strong', a word used only in poetry, as distinct from 'wing' (*kānāp̄*). *eagle*, *nešer*, properly the griffon-vulture (cf. Lev. xi. 13 RV mg.; Mic. i. 16 speaks of its baldness), Arab. *nisr*. But *nisr* is used of other raptores beside the griffon, and several species of eagles proper are known in Bible lands. In any case the emphasis is on the soaring flight of the *nešer* (cf. Job xxxix. 27; Prov. xxiii. 5; Obad. 4), which has a wing-span of some nine feet. *they run*, &c.] A perfect return to earth. For most of us the Christian life, and indeed our communion with God, is something we must keep alive, not by feats of extraordinary daring and adventure, but in the humdrum duties of our daily lives; cf. Wordsworth's *Ode to Duty*. There may also—though this is not actually said—be some comfort in the words for those who can no longer soar, nor even run, but only walk.

XLI. 1–7. THE VICTOR FROM THE EAST

1. יַחֲלִיפוּ כֹחַ] Comes oddly after xl. 31 and, if the text is right, must be ironical (so Torrey). Of conjectural emendations the most attractive is Volz's יִקְרְבוּ וְיֶאֱתָיוּן, 'let (the peoples) draw near and come'. This is based on the last two words of ver. 5, which hang loosely where they stand. They may have been displaced from ver. 1, either accidentally or as an appropriate introduction to vv. 6 f. (see below). We should then suppose that 'renew their strength' was supplied from xl. 31 to fill the gap.

2. יַרְדְּ] *Hiph.* juss. רדה, 'and makes (him) tread down' (cf. Joel iv. 13, RV, RSV). But the jussive is strange. This difficulty can be avoided by pointing יָרֹד (*Qal* רדד, cf. xlv. 1; Ps. cxliv. 2) or יָרֵד

(*Hiph.* ibid., cf. 1 Kings vi. 32), both meaning 'beats down', (רדה and רדד are closely related, 'trample', 'beat down'). Q[a] has יוריד (*Hiph.* ירד) 'brings down'. The stich has only two beats and this may be a case where it should be supplemented by some such word as תַּחְתָּיו, 'beneath him' (cf. Ps. cxliv. 2). The subject of the first יִתֵּן must be 'who' preceding, so also of ירד (*pace* RSV). יִתֵּן כֶּעָפָר חַרְבּוֹ וגו׳] A difficult sentence, but emendation unnecessary. The meaning cannot be that Yahweh makes the victor's sword like dust, unless we suppose a very strong ellipsis, 'he makes his sword (scatter them) like dust'. The sentence may be construed either (*a*) 'He (the victor) makes (them) like dust (with) his sword . . .' (instrumental accus.; so RSV, Torrey, cf. אֵבֶר, xl. 31; Ps. xvii. 13), or (*b*) 'His (the victor's) sword makes (them) like dust . . .'—for masc. pred. with fem. subj. when verb stands first see *GK* 145 *o*. For ellipsis of pron. obj. with יִתֵּן cf. Gen. xviii. 7, xxiv. 41. The picture is clear, even to details, no matter how we construe and whether or not we read תִּתְּנֵם/יִתְּנֵם. קַשְׁתּוֹ] Synecdoche for 'his arrows', probably for assonance with קַשׁ.

5. רָאוּ . . . וְיִירָאוּ . . . יֶחֱרָדוּ] Point רְאוּ . . . וִירְאוּ (imptv.)—note the alliterations—and take יחרדו as jussive; so Begrich (p. 29, n. 2), after 32 MSS[Kenn], cf. Q[a] ויראו. This gives a sharper contrast with אַל־תִּירָא (ver. 10) but is only justified if vv. 6 f. are secondary (see below). קָרְבוּ וַיֶּאֱתָיוּן] Transferred to ver. 1 (see *supra*).

Yahweh bids the nations assemble for a judicial inquiry. Can they say who it is that has set in motion the conqueror who is victorious wherever he goes? It is Yahweh, who has been active in the world since its beginning, and will be to its end. Well may the nations fear and (in the present text) set to work to make more potent idols.

The passage is one of several in DI (xli. 21–29, xliii. 8–13, 22–28, xliv. 6–8, xlviii. 1–11, l. 4–9) which must be interpreted against the background of ancient legal procedure (cf. Begrich, pp. 19–22). Litigants, if unable to come to an amicable settlement, would appeal to court for a 'judgement' (*mišpāṭ*) between them. *mišpāṭ*, a word with many nuances, can mean the court (lit. 'place of judgement') itself (xxviii. 6; Deut. xxv. 1; 1 Kings vii. 7; Eccl. iii. 16), or a judgement or decision pronounced by a judge sitting in court. Here it may have either meaning, with emphasis upon the former.

1. A *court* was held in the open air, 'in the gate'. Round the judges and principals a gathering would form of people interested. The litigants would vociferate and the crowd join in the babble: hence *let them approach, then let them speak*. There is here no mention of judges. The omission is significant and necessary, because Yahweh is one of the parties involved. Indeed, it is he who brings the action, and there can hardly be judges in a case where he is concerned, unless it be all heaven and earth, as in Mic. vi. 1 f. The theatre here is almost as wide, the summons being to the far coastlands and peoples. The proceedings open with a call for silence. It is Yahweh who calls for this as he opens his case. *Silence, you far shores, for me*] 'Keep silence before me' (AV, RV) is hardly strong enough. The verb is intensive *Hiph.*, 'exhibit silence' (*silentium facere*, *GK* 53 *d*) and the construction pregnant (*GK* 119 *gg*), 'exhibit silence unto me', cf. our 'Pray silence for so-and-so'. But here the convener of the court himself brings the action and his imperative is emphatic: 'Keep silence and listen to what I have to say': cf. Job xiii. 13.

2. The question to be decided is *Who has stirred up out of the east the man whom victory greets wherever he goes?*] AV, RV 'raised up' is not strong enough for *hēʿîr* (*Hiph.* *ʿûr*), a verb which means 'to impel into activity', as in Ezra i. 1. The second stich, the *man whom victory greets*, is a noun clause, acc. obj. of 'stirred up' (*GK* 120, 157—the relative particle being omitted before 'victory'.) *victory*] Heb. *ṣeḏeḵ* and *ṣᵉḏāḵāh*, 'righteousness', come, esp. in DI and Ps., to mean righteousness as vindicated, i.e. 'victory', 'prosperity' (xli. 10, xlv. 8, xlvi. 13, li. 5 f.). *greets*] *yiḵrāʾēhû*. Heb. has two verbs *ḵārāʾ*, (1) 'meet', (2) 'call', both transitive. AV and RV take as (2), RV mg. (second reading) and RSV as (1). The word can of course mean either and may have been intended to; *greets* is an attempt to catch both nuances. The passage comes as near to a personification of victory as Hebrew monotheism could ever get. *wherever he goes*] Lit. 'to/at his foot', exactly the same expression as in Gen. xxx. 30; cf. RV mg. there.

3. *He pursues them* (*and*) *passes on unscathed*] The asyndetic construction conveys an impression of speed and the picture is of rapid pursuit, bloodless victory, and a further advance, leaving the defeated enemy in the rear; cf. 2 Sam. xviii. 23. Herodotus (i. 78) says that Cyrus was his own messenger and that Croesus had no news that he was on the way. *not treading the highway with his feet*] Lit. 'a (*or* the) way with his feet he does not enter'. For this near-transitive sense of *bôʾ* ('come' = 'enter') cf. Judges xviii. 18; 2 Kings xi. 19; Ps. c. 4. The reference is still to the speed of the conqueror's advance but exactly how the words are to be understood is not immediately clear. They might mean that he does not keep to the highways but takes unfrequented by-ways; cf. Judges. v. 6. But why, if he was irresistible, should he deny himself this advantage? Sidney Smith's explanation, that 'the Persians were mounted' (p. 159), will hardly do. DI would not express himself so prosaically. And anyhow, Herodotus says that Cyrus feared the Lydian cavalry and therefore assembled a camel

corps. The meaning probably is that his advance was so swift that his feet seemed scarcely to touch the ground, like the he-goat (Alexander the Great) in Dan. viii. 5, where the phrase 'touched not the ground' is actually used. It is as if (cf. the preceding phrase) he leap-frogged over those who stood between him and his main objective. (In xlvi. 11 he is called 'a bird of prey'.) There may be a hint of the widespread belief in the levitation of supernatural beings (cf. Hocart, *Kingship*, 1927, ch. XIII) and we are reminded of the winged solar-discs which are a feature of Near Eastern art from Egypt to Persia (see *AOTB*, plates 308–11 and esp. 333).

4. *Who has acted and wrought?*] The Hebrew verbs mean much the same, the first being a poetical synonym of the second. Both are transitive, but are used here without object (as in xliii. 13, xliv. 23, xlvi. 4, xlviii. 11). Together they mean 'Who has acted decisively?' (cf. xliii. 13). To supply an object (AV, RV 'it', RSV 'this') is to lay the emphasis on the events already described, whereas in what follows the emphasis is on the divine activity throughout history. The stirring up of the victor from the east is only the latest of a series of initiatives which go back to the beginning (*rō'š*) of the world, i.e. to the creation; cf. xl. 21, xlviii. 16; Prov. viii. 23. The rendering *from the very first* is intended to call attention to the similarity in ver. 4*b*, *I, the* LORD, *am the first* (*rî'šôn*). *the generations*] From a √ 'to move around in a circle', is suggestive of the transitoriness of human life (cf. Eccles. i. 4). But that the OT does not think of history as 'cyclic' is everywhere clear, and nowhere more so than here. *I, the* LORD, *am the first ...*] A statement of fact, not, as in EVV, an answer to the questions in 2–4*a*, which are rhetorical and imply their own answers. The meaning is not exactly that Yahweh is 'eternal' (see on xl. 28) but that he is contemporary with all history, from its beginning to its *eschaton*. *I am He*] *'ănî hû'*. This 'monotheistic formula' recurs in xliii. 10, 13, 25, xlvi. 4, xlviii. 12; cf. Ps. cii. 27 (*28*), where 'Thou art the same' is lit., 'Thou art He'. Indeed, 'I am (one end) the same' would be a permissible rendering here (*GK* 135 *a*, N. 1); cf. Heb. xiii. 8: 'Jesus Christ is the same yesterday and today and for ever'. There is no copula in the Hebrew and Rev. i. 4, 8, 'Who is and who was and who is to come', is only drawing out the implications of these two equated personal pronouns. That 'personality' is attributed to Yahweh is clear from them both. Yet another translation could be 'I am God' (cf. Arab. *huwa*, of God). OT theism is in strong contrast with Hindu pantheism: the one has Yahweh say to man, 'I am He than whom there is none other'; the other bids man say to himself, 'thou art That One than which there is nought else'.

Who is the victor of vv. 2 f.? Jewish exegesis has almost unanimously referred the passage to Abraham's victory over the four kings (Gen. xiv.). The majority of Christian interpreters, until modern times, have been of the same opinion. The interpretation was probably suggested by ver. 8. The general view today is that the reference is to Cyrus, who is actually named in xliv. 28, xlv. 1. Torrey, followed, with some modifications in detail, by Kissane, has revived the Abraham interpretation. According to him, 2*a* refers to Abraham, 2*b*–4 to Israel, Abraham's descendants. It must be conceded that the Prophet includes the distant past in his purview. But Torrey (not Kissane) points *ṣeḏeḳ* (ver. 2) as *ṣaddîḳ*, 'righteous one'—AV 'the righteous *man*' is a mistranslation—saying that 'the massoretic division of the first half-verse is wrong'. This, to say the least, is disputable: 2*a*, as pointed and punctuated, is 3:3; as Torrey punctuates it, it looks like 4:2. He can only make it 3:3 by taking *mî hē'îr* as one beat and *yiḳrā'ēhû* as two, and it looks as if his 'Cyrus-interpolation' theory has determined his metrics. The description in 2 f. agrees well with the victories of Cyrus up to the fall of Sardis in the autumn of 547, and the passage gives the impression that it was composed while those victories were still the subject of wild surmise. It seems unrealistic, even academic, that the nations should be urgently summoned to debate who called Abraham more than 1,000 years previously.

5. *the ends of the earth*] See on xl. 28. But here the emphasis is on the far distances.

6–7. Many scholars regard these verses as a fragment displaced from xl. 19 f. But there are good reasons for rejecting this view (see *supra*) That they are a fragment is likely. The object of all the fuss is not stated except by the pron. sf. in *they strengthen it*. Sidney Smith (pp. 159 f.) thinks the passage describes the making of armour and says there is no reason to distinguish between *deḇeḳ* (lit. 'joining', generally rendered 'solder') here and the plural *deḇāḳîm* (RSV 'scale armor') in 1 Kings xxii. 34. But what should a worker in precious metals (*ṣôrēp̄*) be doing with armour? His craft, when described in any detail, has always to do with the making of idols (Judges xvii. 4; Isa. xl. 19, xlvi. 6; Jer. x. 9, 14, li. 17). The literary affinities of the present passage are with xl. 19 f.; Jer. x. 4, 9, where the meaning is not in doubt. Most of these 'idol-interludes' read like fugitive pieces (e.g. xliv. 9–20) which have been inserted into suitable contexts. That may be so here: the verses, with their unrelated pronoun, read like a commentary on xl. 19 f. If a context had to be found, none could be better than where they stand. And as the passage now stands the verbs in ver. 5 are pointed as indicatives and the nations feverishly set to work to make a more potent idol. They may well fear. They have reason enough to fear Cyrus; but the verses leave the impression that it is Yahweh, who has stirred up Cyrus, that they have most to fear.

7. *He that wields* (lit. 'smooths with', instrumental accusative) *the forge-hammer*, &c.] The sentence is clumsy, probably intentionally so, to describe the swink and sweat of the workmen. The word for *forge-hammer* (*paṭṭîš*) denotes a blunt (cf. Arab. *fiṭṭîsa*, 'swine's snout', Syr. *peṭaš* 'flat-nosed') and heavy (Jer. xxiii. 29) instrument. *nail-hammer*] *paʿam* ('stroke', 'beat', as in 1 Sam. xxvi. 8) nowhere else means 'anvil'. Here it is probably a small hammer (so T). The word is instrumental accusative and the phrase exactly parallel with the preceding: the craftsman who casts the image encourages the gold-plater; (the same) who smooths with the forge-hammer (encourages) the plater who strikes with the nail-hammer. It is Big John and Little John. There is irony too in '*Courage!*' ... *encourages* ... *strengthen*, all from the same Hebrew √. For the last Wyclif had 'comforted'!

XLI. 8–10. ISRAEL, YAHWEH'S SERVANT, IS NOT TO FEAR

10. תִּשְׁתָּע] Generally taken as *Hithpaʿēl* שעה, 'gaze', the sense 'gaze anxiously' (EVV 'be not dismayed', RV mg. 'look not around thee') being inferred from context. The *ḳāmeṣ*, also in xli. 23, indicates that the Massoretes understood it so. It is now certain that the word is *Qal* שתע, 'fear', which in Ugar. (*ṯṯʿ*) is ‖ *yrʾ* (C. H. Gordon, *Ugaritic Handbook*, ii, 1947, texts 49:VI:32 and 67:II:7). It is also found on the Karatepe Inscription (cf. Obermann, *Karatepe*, 1949, p. 12).

That this section is related to the preceding is clear from the adversative 'and' (= 'but') with which it begins. This connective contrast is evident also from the content of the passage: the nations have been bidden to fear (ver. 5), Israel is not to fear (ver. 10); and the play on '*Courage!*' ... *encourages* ... *strengthen* (as vv. 6 f. now stand) is continued by yet another nuance (*Hiph.*) of √*ḥzḳ*, *I took hold of you* (ver. 9). (This may be an argument for the originality of vv. 6 f. where they stand.)

The words *Have no fear* are the more impressive because they are the climax of a series of relative clauses in which Israel's unique status with Yahweh is defined. Indeed, the verses are as expansive as those in which Yahweh's own attributes are described (e.g. xlii. 5, xliii. 16). Israel is *my servant* (cf. xliv. 1 f., 21, xlv. 4, xlviii. 20, xlix. 3), *whom I have chosen* (similarly ‖ 'my servant' in xliv. 1 f., xlv. 4), *the children of Abraham* (cf. li. 2) *my friend* (cf. 2 Chr. xx. 7; James

ii. 23). *My friend* (*'ôhᵃḇî*, 'him whom I loved') implies a more intimate relationship than *rēʿî*, the usual word for 'my friend/companion'. *Servant* and *chosen* are repeated in ver. 9, making assurance doubly sure.

Servant (*ʿeḇeḏ*), lit. 'slave', could be anything but a term of reproach. It expressed the weaker partner's relation to the stronger in a covenant (*bᵉrîṯ*). As such the *servant* was privileged, and entitled, as of right, to look to his master for protection and even 'steadfast love' (*ḥeseḏ*, cf. Ps. cxxxvi. 22, RSV).

The calling of Israel *my servant* deserves more attention than it has generally received. DI was the first, as he is almost the only, writer, to call Israel so. Of the other two passages, Ps. cxxxvi. 22 is late, and Jer. xxx. 10 (not in LXX) = xlvi. 27 f. cannot with confidence be assigned to Jeremiah. (In Ezek. xxviii. 25, xxxvii. 25 'my servant Jacob' is the patriarch of the past, not the nation of the present.) How DI came to equate the servant with Israel can only be decided from the contexts in which the equation occurs. In them the leading motif is that Yahweh *chose* Israel. This brings the concept into relation with the doctrine of the 'election' of Israel, so prominent in Deuteronomy.

The doctrine of the choice or election of Israel is deeply rooted in the OT. Genesis is the story of how God gradually narrowed down the circle of his choice to the descendants of Noah's firstborn, Shem, 'the father of all the children of Eber' (i.e. the Hebrews, Gen. x. 21, cf. xi. 10, 16), Terah (xi. 27), Abraham, Isaac (xxi. 12, 'through Isaac [not Ishmael] shall your descendants be named'), and finally to Jacob and his descendants. This interpretation of history is doubtless a simplification of obscure and complicated tribal movements, but in the light of its sequel, Christianity, and on a broad view of history, it is not to be dismissed out of hand. Under the stress of exile the Jews might well conclude that Yahweh had cast them off, as he had every right to do, for their unfaithfulness to their part of the covenant. Yahweh reassures them, *I chose you and have not rejected you*. Never would he abandon the descendants of the man he had loved through toilsome journeyings in the hallowed past.

10. *I strengthen you*] The verbs in 10*b* are all in the perfect (*perfectum confidentiae*, *GK* 106 *n*). They may be translated as present, or future, the former being the more comprehensive. Indeed, the 'perfect' comes more naturally to God than the 'imperfect' (Engnell, *Gamla Testamentet*, i, 1945, pp. 21 f.). *and*] *'aḇ*, 'also'. DI uses this monosyllabic particle 25 times, twice in this verse, 3 times in xl. 24. The sense is 'nay more' but it is difficult to translate literally without being clumsy. *my victorious right hand*] Lit. 'the right hand of my victory' (see on ver. 2 above).

These verses are remarkable for the repetitions of the suffixed endings î (6 times) and *îkā* (9 times). This is as near to being rhyme as anything in Hebrew poetry. It may not be euphonic but it is nothing if not emphatic, as befits the theme.

XLI. 11–13. ISRAEL'S ENEMIES ARE POWERLESS

11. הַנֶּחֱרִים] As pointed is *Niph.* חרה, only here, xlv. 24, and Song i. 6, and with no distinctively *Niph.* sense. Point הַנֹּחֲרִים, *Qal* participle נחר, 'snort' (with indignation), a meaning attested by the cognates and by nouns in Jer. viii. 16; Job xxxix. 20 (Driver, *JTS* 36, 1935, pp. 398 f.).

The more violent Israel's enemies become, the less is their power to harm.

The thought continues that of vv. 8–10: *Have no fear, it is I who help you* is repeated and there are similar suffix endings, but attached to nouns, not verbs. Verses 8–13 may well be one poem, notwithstanding that the metre changes from 3:3 to 3:2 in vv. 11–13: cf. Ps. xcviii.

The violence of Israel's enemies is cumulative. First they *rage* (lit. 'snort') with indignation (11*a*); then they *arraign* (11*b*). *Those who arraign you*] Lit. 'the men of your *rîḇ*'. A *rîḇ* is commonly a suit in law: cf. 'my adversary', lit. 'the man of my suit', Job xxxi. 35. But the word may be used of a wordy quarrel, no doubt with some scuffle, as in Gen. xiii. 7. Next, there is resort to naked force: *your assailants*] Lit. 'the men of your striving' (*maṣṣûṯ*, from a √ always used of physical struggle: Exod. xxi. 22; Deut. xxv. 11; 2 Sam. xiv. 6). Finally, there is open war.

The power of Israel's enemies is in inverse proportion to their violence. For the sense *be disappointed and mortified* for 'be ashamed (disappointed) and humiliated', cf. Jer. xiv. 3. A final link-up with the sequence 'Courage! . . . encourage . . . strengthen . . . take hold' of vv. 6–9, is *I hold you by your right hand.* Abraham had no choice but to obey when Yahweh called him (Gen. xii. 1–4). Neither had his, as yet, unborn descendants when Yahweh took hold of them (ver. 9). Only the right hand of Yahweh had saved his people from falling prostrate (ver. 10). Now, erect, hand clasped by hand, what has Israel to fear?

XLI. 14–16. THE 'WORM' ISRAEL WILL BECOME A THRESHING-BOARD

14. מְתֵי] EVV 'men of' is a feeble ‖ to 'worm'. LXX ὀλιγοστὸς is certainly euphemism. The original may have been רִמַּת, some kind

of corrupting, anthropophagous worm, which is || תּוֹלַעַת in xiv. 11; Job xxv. 6, and may well have seemed objectionable as an epithet for Israel. Or מתי may be cognate with Akk. *mutu*, 'louse' (Driver, *JTS* 36, 1935, p. 399). For the translation *contemptible* cf. *SOED*, *sub voce*: 'So small and contemptible an animal (the Flea) 1664'.

15. חָרוּץ] Adj. 'sharp', used as a noun, 'threshing-board', in xxviii. 27; Amos i. 3; Job xli. 22. It looks metrically superfluous here and may be an explanatory gloss on מוֹרַג, which occurs otherwise only in 2 Sam. xxiv. 22 || 1 Chron. xxi. 23.

Again Israel is bidden not to fear. She is now a contemptible 'worm' but her 'Redeemer' is 'the Holy One of Israel'. He will make her a threshing-board capable of crushing mountains.

The thought is similar to that in vv. 8–10 and 11–13, but Israel is now addressed in the 2nd pers. sing. fem., not masculine, and the figures are different. But observe that the feminine reverts to the masculine in 15*b*, 16. In all probability the feminine 'Fear not' was required for agreement with 'worm' (fem.); and a threshing-board could hardly be other than masculine! The encouraging *have no fear* has become almost a refrain—10 times in DI: xl. 9, xli. 10, 13, xliii. 1, 5, xliv. 2, 8, li. 7, liv. 4, and here. The main emphasis is the contrast between the insignificant (cf. Job xxv. 6) and contemptible (cf. Ps. xxii. 6 (7)) worm that Israel now is in her own and her enemies' eyes, and the threshing-board, capable of dealing not only with corn, but with mountains (a figure for worldly powers), she shall become; cf. Thomas Olivers:

He calls a worm his friend,
He calls himself my God.

The figure *worm . . . threshing-board* is not incongruous: the worm is a 'thresher' of soil. A threshing-board was a heavy wooden board *studded with* metal *teeth* on its underside (cf. Amos i. 3). After it had been dragged round the threshing-floor, the grain and chaff were tossed into the air by shovel and/or pitchfork (xxx. 24; Jer. xv. 7) and the chaff was carried away by the wind. *teeth*] Lit. 'lots of mouths', a reduplicated form; cf. Ps. cxlix. 6, where 'a two-edged sword' is lit. 'a sword of mouths', i.e. edges.

The change in Israel's fortunes will be due to the help (cf. vv. 10, 13 preceding) of Yahweh *your Redeemer . . . the Holy One of Israel*. The conception of Yahweh as Israel's redeemer is more prominent in DI than anywhere else in the OT. The Heb. √ is *gā'al*, of which the noun-participle *gô'ēl*, 'redeemer', is used in xliii. 14, xliv. 6, 24, xlvii. 4, xlviii. 17, xlix. 7, 26, liv. 5, 8, and here (in TI lix. 20, lx. 16, lxiii. 16), the finite verb in xliii. 1, xliv. 22 f, xlviii. 20, lii. 3, 9 (in TI lxiii. 9), and the passive participle 'redeemed ones' in li. 10 (TI lxii. 12; lxiii. 4, cf. xxxv. 9). That Yahweh is 'Redeemer' is generally introduced by 'Thus says the LORD', but here, for the first time and emphatically, by *this is the word of the* LORD. We must not read back into 'Redeemer' all the meaning the word has acquired in Christian theology. Even so, it has a rich content and cannot be translated by any one word. The primary meaning of the √ may have been to 'cover' and so 'protect' (A. R. Johnson, 'The Primary Meaning of √גאל', in *Supplements to Vetus Testamentum*, i, 1953, pp. 67–77). In that case 'Protector' (or 'Champion'?) would be an adequate general translation. But in OT usage the √ has acquired the meaning 'buy back', 'redeem' (Lat. *redimere*). This may be illustrated from Lev. xxv. 25 f., 48 f. Among the words by which *gô'ēl* is rendered in EVV are '(near) kinsman' (9 times in Ruth), 'avenger (of blood)' (Num. xxxv. 12, 19–27; Deut. xix. 6, 12; Joshua xx. 3, 5, 9). These usages indicate that the redeemer-relationship depended upon ties of kinship. A *gô'ēl* was a kinsman upon whom devolved the responsibility of protecting the interests of his relative by every means in his power, whether by 'redeeming' him or his property during his lifetime, or by avenging his death if he had been murdered. Passages like lii. 3 and Ps. lxxiv 2 make it clear that the metaphor of 'buying back' must not always be rigorously pressed. Two points seem emphasized in the present passage: (1) Yahweh's covenant bonds with Israel are as close as those which bind members of the same human family, and he will never repudiate his self-imposed obligations; (2) Yahweh was Israel's Redeemer at the Exodus (Exod. vi. 6, xv. 13; Isa. li. 10; Ps. lxxiv. 2, cvi. 10); he will be the same in the approaching exodus from Babylon.

Of the 'Redeemer' passages in DI no less than 6 go on to describe Yahweh as *the Holy One of Israel*. This epithet, found 11 times in DI and twice (lx. 9, 14) in TI, is the most obvious external link with Proto-Isaiah (13 times). The expression is infrequent outside the book of Isaiah, and Isaiah was the first to use it. Its origin and the key to the understanding of it are to be found in the *trisagion* of the Temple-vision (Isa. vi). Yahweh's holiness denotes his perfect moral purity combined with his transcendent exaltation. In Isa. i–xxxix the major emphasis in 'the Holy One of Israel' is upon Yahweh as Judge (i. 4, v. 19, 24, xvii. 7, xxix. 23, xxx. 11 f., xxxi. 1). In DI it is always upon his saving power and protection. Accordingly, Israel will *glory* (lit. 'show themselves boastful') *in the Holy One of Israel*. The suggestion of arrogance or pretence, though usual, does not necessarily attach to the *Hithpa'ēl*, especially when the glorying is 'in Yahweh'; cf. Ps. xxxiv. 2 (*3*); Jer. iv. 2. See further on xlv. 25.

XLI. 17–20. THE DESERT WILL BE TRANSFORMED TO OASIS

17. הָעֲנִיִּים וְהָאֶבְיוֹנִים] Some would delete והאביונים (Q^a is without the conjunction). מְבַקְשִׁים] Some would shorten to מְבַקְשֵׁי, again *metri causa*. But note the four *îm* terminations and the forlorn ending to the search—וָאַיִן. The heavy stich may be intentional; it exactly describes a procession, weary and footsore. נָשָׁתָּה] The rare *d.f. affectuosum* (*GK* 20 *i*), with doubled *t*—note the five vowels *ḳāmeṣ*—describes, as well as sound can, the cleaving of the tongue to the roof of the mouth (cf. Job xxix. 10).

18. אֲגַם־מַיִם] The suggestion to read אֲגַמִּים is *metri causa* and to avoid reduplication with מַיִם in the || stich. This is unnecessary, cf. Ps. cvii. 35, cxiv. 8.

Yahweh will make provision for his people's comfort during their journey across the desert. There will be abundance of water and the route will be lined with trees.

The theme is developed more fully in xliii. 18–21, xlix. 9–11 (cf. xxxv). It has already been anticipated in xl. 10 f. and there are echoes of it in xlviii. 21 and lv. 13. The paragraph begins abruptly and pictures the exiles as though they have already set out on the journey home. It reads as if the Prophet is anticipating objections about the hardships of the journey.

17. *The poor and the needy*] In Hebrew these words are near synonyms: any distinction between them is that *the poor* are the 'poor in spirit' (cf. Matt. v. 3) and *the needy* the indigent poor. They occur frequently in parallelism and occasionally (Ps. xl. 17 (*18*), lxxxvi. 1, cix. 16, 22) together as here. There will be no need for the Massah and Meribah (Exod. xvii. 7) of the first Exodus. Any such untoward contingency is anticipated by the promise *I the* LORD *will answer them, I who am Israel's God will not desert them*—always this emphasis on the indissoluble bond between him and his people. Long ago, he had brought out water from the rock (xlviii. 21; Exod. xvii. 1–7; Num. xx. 1–3). He will do no less during this second Exodus. Indeed, he will do more: he will *open up rivers* (*nᵉhārôṯ* which 'flow', not *nᵉḥālîm*, 'torrent-wadis') *on the sand belts* (*šᵉpāyîm*). This word is from a √ 'sweep bare'. The conventional translation 'bare heights' is probably based on LXX ἐπὶ τῶν ὀρέων. The meaning is 'bare earth', 'sand-dune', cf. Arab. *sâfiyya* (so G. R. Driver, 'Confused Hebrew Roots', in *Gaster Anniversary Volume*, ed. Bruno Schindler, 1936, pp. 78–80; similarly *KB* 'bare ways formed without human work by the traffic of caravans').

18. *with reedy pools*] lit. 'into', but this must be hyperbole. For *reedy pools*, *'ᵃgam-mayim*, cf. Arab. *'aǧama*, 'marshy jungle', and Heb. *'agmōn*, 'bulrush'.

19. The desert highway will become a permanent oasis (see on lv. 13) in which sizeable trees will grow. What some of these were is obscure. The *acacia* (*šiṭṭāh*, AV transliterates) is probably an Egyptian loan-word (*šndt*), the *Acacia nilotica*; *myrtle* (*hᵃḏas*) *Myrtus communis L.* (*hadas* in Yemenite Arabic); the *oleander* (Heb. 'oil tree') the genus *Nerium* as distinct from *zayiṯ*, 'olive', genus *Olea*. The *juniper* (*bᵉrôš*, usually ‖ *'erez*, 'cedar') was a noble tree (xiv. 8, xxxvii. 24, lv. 13, lx. 13) whose timbers were used in building the temple (1 Kings v. 22) and the ship of Tyre (Ezek. xxvii. 5); probably the Phoenician juniper (20–40 feet), and to be distinguished from the 'juniper' *reṯem*, properly 'broom' (*Retama Rhoetam*) of 1 Kings xix. 4; Ps. cxx. 4; Job. xxx. 4. *The plane and cypress*] *tiḏhār ûṯᵉ'aššûr*. The etymology of both words is unknown. They occur elsewhere only in the list of trees described in lx. 13 as 'the glory of Lebanon' and (*tᵉ'aššûr*) in the consonantal text of Ezek. xxvii. 6. 'Box-tree' (V, T, RV) can hardly be right for *tᵉ'aššûr*, since the box has a maximum height of 25–30 feet and would hardly provide timbers for the deck of the ship of Tyre. The rabbis (so Volz) took it as the *sherbîn*, a species of evergreen conifer. It was perhaps *Cupressus sempervivens var. horizontalis L.* (*KB*, cf. RV mg.), the common Mediterranean cypress (80–100 feet). For *tiḏhār* conjectures are 'pine' (AV, RV), 'plane' (RV mg., RSV, Sa'adya, according to Volz), 'cypress' (LXX), 'elm' (V), 'ash' (Dalman, *TLZ* 51, 215). The identification must remain uncertain. Although the ash and elm are mainly trees of northern latitudes, there are species in Palestine and Iraq. But if we are looking for an exotic tree, the best guess is the Oriental Plane (*Platanus orientalis*), a native of the Levant and Persia.

19–20. *together . . . once for all*] These are the same word (*yaḥdāw*) in the Hebrew. Its literal meaning is '(in) its unitednesses' (*GK* 91 *k*). DI uses it 15 times (xl. 5, xli. 1, 19 f., 23, xliii. 9, 17, 26, xlv. 16, 20 f., xlvi. 2, xlviii. 13, lii. 8 f.) and the related *yaḥaḏ* 4 times. It binds together what are practically synonyms (in ver. 19 nouns, in 20 verbs) and is a good example of his voluminous style. But it is more than a rhetorical device. Unison and simultaneity are not far removed from 'all-of-a-suddenness'. There is more than a suggestion of suddenness in xlviii. 13 and it cannot be excluded from the present passage. Every line in 17*b*–19 begins with *I* (Yahweh) *will*. When Yahweh creates he does so, according to Hebrew ideas, *instanter*. Nor is it said that he will 'plant' (*nāṭa'*) saplings which are to grow slowly to maturity: 'plant' (AV, RV) in 19*a* is in the Heb. 'give' (i.e. 'put' ‖ *śîm*, 'set', 'put'). If the return was to be in the not-distant future, the trees would have to be full-grown if they were to serve the purpose for which they were intended. This raises the problem whether DI meant what he said, or whether it is only poetic licence which happened to anticipate modern irrigation and afforestation.

XLI. 21–29. YAHWEH IS THE ONLY GOD BECAUSE HE ALONE KNOWS AND DETERMINES THE FUTURE

21. עֲצֻמוֹתֵיכֶם] Either 'your strong' (Arab. *'azuma*) or 'your defensive' (Arab. *'aṣama*) *arguments*, it matters little which. There is no need to emend the text: עֲצְבוֹתֵיכֶם 'your idols' (*BH*), after Jerome's *idola vestra*, is not a good parallel. The summons is to the gods themselves to present their case, not to the worshippers to produce their idols, and the plural of עָצָב is always elsewhere עֲצַבִּים. P seems to have understood as מוֹעֲצוֹתֵיכֶם, 'your counsels', always, except in Prov. xxii. 20, in a bad sense.

22. יַגִּישׁוּ] Either (i) 'let (the gods) produce (their arguments)', which has already been said, or (ii) 'let (the worshippers) produce (their gods, i.e., idols)'. Read *Qal* יִגְּשׁוּ, *Let them* (the gods) *come forward*, with all major versions. וְנֵדְעָה אַחֲרִיתָן] It is usual to transfer these words to the end of the verse, giving a better || and more common metre (3:2 not 2:3). But the MT order is more logical. It is sufficient if the gods predict the future, without leaving 'us' the task of interpreting it.

23. וְנִשְׁתָּעָה וְנִרְא] Point וְנִשְׁתְּעָה וְנִרְא, lit. 'that we may be alarmed and fear'; see on ver. 10 (philological note).

24. מֵאָפַע] A patent scribal error for מֵאֶפֶס. וּמֵאֶפֶס . . . מֵאַיִן] Either (i) 'made of nothing', a not impossible hyperbole, or (ii) 'less than nothing', a minus quantity. *You are nothing at all!* covers both nuances.

25. וְיָבֹא] is occasionally transitive, as in Job xv. 21, xx. 22, cf. our 'go-for' (a person). But in view of the simile we should probably emend to ויבס: a *sāmech* could easily be omitted by haplography, especially in writing from dictation. Then point וַיָּבָס, *waw consec.*, *and he trampled*, following הֶעִירוֹתִי.

27. רִאשׁוֹן וגו׳] '*I* first *will say* unto Zion, Behold, behold them' (RV) is unintelligible (note the unrelated 'them'). When ראשון is used adverbially it is in fem. רִאשֹׁנָה. It is primarily an adjectival-noun, 'first', 'chief', and in Prov. xviii. 17 appears to mean 'first speaker', 'leading counsel' (G. R. Driver, 'Problems of the Hebrew Text and Language', in *Alttestamentliche Studien, Friedrich Nötscher Festschrift*, ed. H. Junker and J. Botterweck, 1950, pp. 46 f.). For the unintelligible הִנֵּה הִנָּם LXX has δώσω. This can hardly be for אֶתֵּן, which MT has in the ‖ stich. Driver suggests some such word as הֲכִינוֹתִי, 'I set up'. Q[a] reads הנה הנומה 'behold the speaker', הַנּוֹמֶה being presumably *Qal* participle of נום, which is related to נְאֻם ('utterance') and in post-biblical Hebrew means 'to speak', with participle נוֹמֶה as if from נָמָה. For OT examples of *Qal* participle of a verb ע״ו with *ḥōlem* see 2 Kings xvi. 7; Zech. x. 5 (cf. *GK* 72 *p*). The Scroll will then mean something like 'Here is one who will be spokesman for Zion'. But the Hebrew is clumsy and it is not clear who the spokesman is. It looks as if there was deep-seated corruption even before the Scroll was written.

28. וְאֵרֶא Point וָאֵרֶא, 'and I looked'. וּמֵאֵלֶּה] 'and from (= of) these'. Who are 'these'? LXX καὶ ἀπὸ τῶν εἰδώλων αὐτῶν may be for וּמֵאֱלֹהֵיהֶם, *and among their gods*. The Hebrew text could easily be altered on reverential grounds, since *ex hypothesi* heathen gods were not gods: cf. 2 Sam. v. 21, where 'for their images' LXX and 1 Chron. xiv. 12 have 'their gods', doubtless the original reading. Even if LXX is only interpreting, its interpretation seems right.

29. אָוֶן] 'vanity'. Read אַיִן (T, Q[a]), cf. אֶפֶס following. Perhaps אַיִן וָאֶפֶס (Q[a]).

Yahweh challenges the heathen gods to come forward and substantiate the claims made for them. Do they understand the significance of past events or can they predict the future? Let them do anything, either good or ill, to show that they are alive! Yahweh it is who has stirred up the conqueror. He will send a herald with good tidings for Jerusalem.

The passage is in two parts. Verses 21–24 imply that Yahweh is the only God because he alone can predict the future; vv. 25–29 assert, as an example, that it is he who has stirred up Cyrus. The inference is that he knows the future because he, in fact, determines it.

Verses 21–24 picture an assize at which the credentials of the gods are to be examined. This has been anticipated in xli. 1 f., where the peoples were summoned to the bar of judgement. Now it is the turn of their gods. As in xli. 1 f. (and v. 1–7) Yahweh is both Judge and a party to the dispute. The gods are ordered to present their *case* (*rîḇ*, see on xli. 11). For Yahweh as *King* of Jacob-Israel see also xliii. 15, xliv. 6. Even during the monarchy he had been the *de facto* King of his people (cf. vi. 5; 1 Kings xxii. 19; Judges viii. 23; 1 Sam. viii. 7); the human king was his vicegerent. Then (ver. 22) *Let them* (the gods) *come forward and tell us the course of events*, lit. 'the things which happen'; the expression embraces past and future, not the future only as in EVV. Of the insistent *tell . . . tell . . . tell*, the first refers to history in general, the second to the past, the third to the future. What the *events already happened* are has occasioned much discussion. The Hebrew is literally 'the former things' (*hārīʾšōnôṯ*). The word recurs in xlii. 9, xliii. 9, 18, xlvi. 9, xlviii. 3. The reference here is probably not to happenings in the remote past, as in xliii. 18, but to the early victories of Cyrus already described (xli. 2 f.), whose significance Yahweh had announced while as yet they were contemporary (cf. ver. 26). Did any 'god' discern their import? Does any even now understand *what they signify* (lit. 'what they [are]'), that we may *know* what will be *their outcome?* Or, if the gods are silent about the past, let them *tell us what the future holds*. Let them *do anything at all, be it good or ill*, to show some sign of life and animation. The conclusion is manifest: *you are nothing at all!*

24. *who chooses you is loathsome as you are*] Lit. 'loathsome (thing) he chooses you', which can be construed either as 'he who chooses you is loathsome' (cf. EVV), or 'he who chooses you (chooses what is) loathsome'. Heb. *tôʿēḇāh* ('abomination') is a common opprobrious epithet for an idol (e.g. xliv. 19). The thought is similar to that of Hos. ix. 10, 'and became detestable like the thing they loved'.

The most illuminating commentary is a story in Herodotus (i. 46–51), who relates that when Croesus of Lydia was faced with the prospect of having to measure his power with that of Cyrus, he took the initiative and prepared to attack Media, which had recently been absorbed by Persia. He sent lavish gifts to all the oracles of Greece and even beyond, praying them to let him know what would be the outcome of the campaign. 'We can understand that for all this Croesus got the best advice consistent with the ignorance and caution of the priests whom he consulted. The oracles told him that if he went against Cyrus he would destroy a great empire; but he forgot to ask, whether it was his own or his rival's' (G. A. Smith, *The Book of Isaiah*, ii, 2nd ed., 1927, p. 117). The oracles always took care to be on the right side, on the principle, 'Heads I win, tails you lose!' The Prophet had every reason to be satirical about idols. Even if he had never heard of Delphi, the oracles of the Babylonian gods did not inspire any greater confidence (cf. xlvii. 13).

In vv. 25–29 Yahweh states explicitly what he had already implied in the rhetorical question of ver. 2: *I stirred up one from the north and he came*, &c. Cyrus' empire, now incorporating Media and Lydia, stretched in an arc from east of Babylonia round to the Aegean. He could thus be said to come from both north and east; indeed, if Hebrew wanted to say 'north-east', it would have to name both points of the compass in parallelism. That Cyrus is to *invoke* Yahweh ('call upon my name') is a bold assertion and some would emend the text to 'one whom I call by his name'. It seems better to keep the more difficult reading, notwithstanding xlv. 3. Cyrus is Yahweh's 'shepherd' (xliv. 28) and 'anointed one' (xlv. 1). Moreover, for monotheistic faith all active enterprise is service of the one God, even though the human instrument is not aware of the import of what he is doing (cf. Mal. i. 11; Jer. xxv. 9).

25. *rulers*] *s^eg̱ānîm*, a loan-word from Akkadian, used of Babylonian (Jer. li. 23, 57) and Assyrian (Ezek. xxiii, 6, 12, 23) prefects.

26. A rhetorical question, addressed still to the (imaginary) gods; cf. 'your words'. *'Just so!'*] For this non-moral sense of Heb. *ṣaddîḵ*, 'right(eous)', cf. xliii. 9, 'It is true' (*'^emeṯ*). For vv. 27–29 see textual notes. The address is no longer to the gods but to the public assembled to support their case or to voice opinions on their competence.

28. *leading counsel . . . herald*] Probably the Prophet.

XLII. 1–4. THE SERVANT OF YAHWEH: HIS ENDOWMENT AND MISSION

2. יִשָּׂא] The acc. obj. ('his voice') comes at the end of the second stich after a second verb: cf. Num. xiv. 1. Or it may be abs. trans., 'cry aloud', as in iii. 7.

3. לֶאֱמֶת] Lit. 'according to faithfulness'. There is no need to point לְאֻמּוֹת, 'to the peoples' (*BH*). DI never uses the rare אֻמּוֹת but only לְאֻמִּים (xlix. 1, four times in all).

4. יָרוּץ] *Qal* imperfect רצץ, 'get broken'. For the spelling cf. Eccles. xii. 6 and see *GK* 67 *q*; unless we point יֵרוֹץ (*Niph.*).

Yahweh designates his Servant, whom he has chosen and endowed with his spirit to reveal his law to the nations. The Servant will work quietly, patiently, and without wearying, until the mission for which the nations are waiting is accomplished. For the translation cf. *NEB* at Matt. xii. 18–20 *passim*.

The speaker is Yahweh. The Servant is anonymous: LXX 'Jacob my servant . . . Israel my chosen' would give a 4:4 line in a 3:3 context and is interpretation based on xli. 8 f. It is not obvious who the audience are. They can hardly be the nations, who are referred to in the 3rd person. They are perhaps supernatural beings (cf. vi. 8; 1 Kings xxii. 19 f.), or the address may be to the Prophet himself (Lindblom, p. 15). The Servant is introduced as if already present but his mission (probably) and its fulfilment (certainly, cf. ver. 4) lie in the future.

1. Yahweh calls the Servant *my servant . . . my chosen*, words used of Israel in xli. 8, xliv. 1 f., xlv. 4. *I support*] Also of Israel in xli. 10. The sense of the verb is to grasp by or with the hand: Exod. xvii. 12; Prov. xxxi. 19. *on whom my favour rests*] Lit. '(whom) my soul (*nep̱eš*) accepts favourably'. 'My soul' is a common amplification of the pronoun 'I', with some emphasis. This may be expressed in English either through the predicate, as in Mark i. 11 ('I am well pleased', Gr. εὐδόκησα); or the meaning may be that Yahweh acts *ganz persönlich* (Volz). The words which Jesus heard at his baptism (Mark i. 11) are a conflation of Ps. ii. 7 and this passage. Jesus was conscious of combining in his own person the vocations of the Messiah-Son of man and the Isaianic Servant. The Servant is *endowed* with Yahweh's *spirit*: cf. xi. 2, where it is said that 'the spirit of Yahweh shall rest upon him (the messianic king), the spirit of wisdom and understanding, the spirit of counsel and might, the spirit of knowledge and the fear of Yahweh'. This is doubtless the original of Rev. i. 4, 'the seven spirits who are before God's throne'. Hebrew used several verbs for the spirit's coming 'upon' a man. In Judges and 1 Sam. it is usually 'rushed' (*ṣālaḥ*): Judges xiv. 6, 19; 1 Sam. x. 6, 10. In Ezek. xi. 5 it is 'fell' (*nāp̱al*), and in Num. xxiv. 2; Judges xi. 29; 1 Sam. xvi. 23, 'was' (= 'came'). Such possession by the spirit was temporary only. In xi. 2 the spirit 'rests' (*nûᵃḥ*) upon, as a permanent endowment. In the present passage *I have endowed him with* is lit. 'I have given (*nāṯan*) upon him'. This need not in itself indicate permanent endowment, since the same verb is used of the seventy elders (Num. xi. 25), whose inspiration was only temporary; but we can hardly doubt that the spirit is given to the Servant, no less than to the messianic prince, as an abiding possession. *he shall reveal my law*] Lit. 'he shall cause *mišpāṭ* to go out'. These words must be the key to the understanding of the passage, since they recur in ver. 3, and in ver. 4 the Servant is to 'establish' *mišpāṭ* in the world. Verse 2 excludes public proclamation, and vv. 3 f. imply that the Servant's task will demand unwearied patience with individuals rather than dealing with nations in the mass. The verb *yôṣî'* must therefore have the sense 'cause to go out' (from the mouth), i.e. 'speak', 'impart', 'reveal', a meaning it always has where the acc. obj. is not a material object: cf. xlviii. 20, Num. xiii. 32 f. Particularly relevant is Jer. xv. 19, where the meaning is 'if you speak what is precious, unmixed with what is worthless, you will be as my mouth'. The length of the Servant's task and his patience exclude an interpretation that he publishes *mišpāṭ* as a ruler issues edicts. What, then, is the *mišpāṭ* he is to reveal? The word was originally a forensic term (see on xli. 1) but no sense of English 'judgment' quite conveys its meaning here. Neither does RSV 'justice'. In Exod. xxi. 1 the plural *mišpāṭîm* is used of the moral and ritual 'judgments' (RSV 'ordinances') of the Book of the Covenant. Such collective judgments or legal pronouncements would shape the *mišpāṭ* ('custom', 'manner of life') of the people who acknowledged their validity: cf. 2 Kings xvii. 33, 'the manner of the nations', this with reference to their religious ceremonies. In the near context (vv. 26 f.) it is said that the Assyrian settlers in Samaria did not know the *mišpāṭ* of Yahweh, i.e. how to worship him; accordingly, an Israelite priest was delegated to teach them. The verb 'teach' is from the same √ as *tôrāh*, originally 'teaching', 'instruction', which is || *mišpāṭ* in ver. 4. Jeremiah complained that no one in Jerusalem knew 'the way (*dereḵ*) of Yahweh, the *mišpāṭ* of their God' (Jer. v. 4 f.). Skinner interpreted this in the sense of 'ethic' (*Prophecy and Religion*, p. 139) but that is too moralistic in the present context. Most commentators remark that *mišpāṭ* is here used absolutely, without the def. art., and that it has the comprehensive sense of the Islamic *dîn* ('judgement'), which embraces both faith and practice. Other suggestions are 'religion' (H. W. Robinson, *The Cross of the Servant*) and 'true religion' (Moffatt); but 'religion' (*religio*) has too general a connotation and (*pace NEB* at Acts xvii. 22, and Jas. i. 26 f. *θρησκεία*) is hardly a biblical word. Volz's *Wahrheit* ('truth') is too intellectual. 'Revelation' might do, since any *mišpāṭ* has something of the character of a revelatory pronouncement, but in its wide sense the noun is too abstract and we can transfer what is needed in it to the governing verb, which is good AV. In view of the primary meaning of *mišpāṭ* the emphasis is on the practice of religion rather than on its credal content (cf. Mic. vi. 8), not omitting (in the light of the 2 Kings xvii references) appropriate worship. All things considered we may opt for the *SOED* (i. 1115 *a*) definition of divine as distinct from human law: 'The body of commandments which express the will of God with regard to the conduct of His intelligent creatures'. *my law*] Heb. 'law' simply, but the word needs some definition in an English translation. Since the language is poetry *mišpāṭ* without the article could mean 'the law', but it cannot in this context mean the Mosaic law. Revealed law, as distinct from such *νόμος* as the heathen, although *ἀνόμως*, may be thought to have by nature (cf. Rom. ii. 11–16), is *mišpaṭ yahwêh* (Jer. viii. 7).

2. The seven negatives in this and the following verses must emphasize the contrast between the Servant and others who might compete for the title. The contrast may be with the early *n*ᵉ*ḇî'îm*, or it may be with denunciatory prophets like Amos. Some think the contrast is with Cyrus and that the Servant was intended as a foil to Cyrus.

3. A fine example of litotes. Isaac Watts interprets perfectly:

He'll never quench the smoking flax,
But raise it to a flame;
The bruised reed He never breaks,
Nor scorns the meanest name.

Both figures imply that the Servant will never despair of even the most abandoned outcast. *broken reed*] 'Reed' in its primary botanical sense, as in Akk. *ḳanû*, Gr. κάννα. EVV 'bruised' is now anachronistic: Heb. *rāṣûṣ* means 'broken': cf. Eccles. xii. 6; Ezek. xxix. 7; Dan. ii. 40. *snuff out the smouldering wick*] Lit. 'extinguish the dimly burning flax'. For the figure cf. xliii. 17; see also 2 Sam. xiv. 7; 2 Chron. xxix. 7. The adjective 'smouldering' (*kēhāh*) is used of the failing sight of Eli (1 Sam. iii. 2: cf. Gen. xxvii. 1; Deut. xxxiv. 7; Job xvii. 1). For the improbable suggestion that the Servant himself is the broken reed see *SS*, p. 91.

4. *With faith undimmed and spirit unbroken*] Lit. 'He will not burn dimly or (himself) be broken', referring back to the figure in ver. 3. Torrey took the words to mean 'he will not chide or deal harshly'. This is based on a second √*kāhāh*, which is found ἅπ. λεγ. in 1 Sam. iii. 13, and √*rāṣaṣ* in sense 'oppress', 'deal harshly', in lviii. 6; 1 Sam. xii. 3 f.; Amos iv. 1. The suggestion is attractive and would provide a good example of DI's habit of playing on homonyms. An objection to it is that ver. 4 would be only a repetition of what has already been said of the Servant's manner of working in ver. 3. *he will establish*] Heb. *'aḏ yāśîm*. RSV 'till he has established' could suggest that the Servant will break down as soon as his work is finished. But *'aḏ* can have the sense of 'while', 'all the time that' (cf. 1 Sam. xiv. 19; Ps. cxli. 10). The Hebrew only means that the Servant will carry through his task to its completion. The verb 'establish' is the same as that used of the 'planting' of trees in the desert (xli. 19*b*). *the world*] The inhabited earth as known to the Hebrews (Gen. x). It is ‖ *the shorelands* (*'iyyîm*), which correspond to 'the nations' of ver. 1. It is worth noting that the windows of the OT were more open to the west than to the impenetrable further east. There is something prophetic in this (cf. Acts xvi. 9 f.). *teaching*] *tôrāh*, originally 'teaching', has in the total context of the passage almost the sense of 'revelation'. *are waiting*] *yᵉyaḥēlû*; is ‖ *yᵉḳawwû* (see on xl. 31) in li. 5, and conveys the same suggestion of expectant hope. This is not to say that the nations are conscious of longing, still less that they are aware of what they long for. Nevertheless,

Far and wide, though all unknowing,
Pants for Thee each mortal breast.

There have been sharp conflicts of opinion on the question whether the Servant is depicted as king or as prophet. Those determined to see in him the Messiah or a royal figure (e.g. Sellin in his Zerubbabel-Jehoiachin periods) naturally try to prove the former, and those who see in him Israel, or a prophet, or DI himself (e.g. Sellin in his last phase) the latter. But while the king might be said to be custodian of *the* Torah (cf. Deut. xvii. 18 f.) and to administer it through his officers, *tôrāh* in the sense of this passage was not initiated by him (*contra* G. Östborn, *Tora in the OT*, Lund, 1945, pp. 56 f.), but either by priests (usually) or prophets (viii. 16, xxx. 9 f.; Zech. vii. 12). On the whole, the Servant looks more like prophet than king, but it is probable that he should not be placed in either category to the exclusion of the other. The dominant impression is that of a peripatetic missionary (so Volz). Except that Jesus said that he was sent only to the lost sheep of the house of Israel (Matt. xv. 24), the passage is a strikingly accurate forecast of his teaching ministry.

XLII. 5–9. THE CALLING OF THE SERVANT

6. וְאַחְזֵק] The juss. 1st pers. is rare and it is usual to point this and the two verbs following as *waw consec*. It matters little, since the final result of the call is still in the future. וְאֶצָּרְךָ] Can be either from יצר ('form', RV mg.) or נצר ('keep', EVV). DI uses יצר more frequently (8 times of 'forming' Israel) than נצר (indubitably only xlviii. 6, xlix. 6), but the logical order, after *take you by the hand*, seems to require *keep* (i.e. protect) here.

Yahweh, the true God and Creator, addresses one ('thee') whom he has called and appointed to be a light to the nations, to open the eyes that are blind and to deliver those in captivity. He will not surrender to idols the praise due to him alone. What he formerly announced has come to pass and he will announce new happenings before they unfold.

This is a difficult passage. The main problems are: (1) its relation to vv. 1–4 preceding and (2) the identity of 'thee' in ver. 6, in other words, whether the passage belongs to the cycle of 'Servant Songs', which the majority of scholars limit to xlii. 1–4, xlix. 1–6, l. 4–9, lii. 13–liii. 12.

(1) A number of scholars have argued for the unity of vv. 1–7 (or 1–9). The majority view is that 1–4 and 5–9 are separate units and this is the view taken here. It is most natural to take ver. 5, with its 'Thus says Yahweh' and its participial relative clauses (cf. xliii. 16 f.), as the beginning of a new section.

(2) If the prophecy were a closely knit composition, 'thee' would be the Servant of vv. 1–4. But on the 'small units' theory this cannot

be assumed. Some scholars (M. Haller, S. Mowinckel, Hans Schmidt, W. E. Barnes, Sidney Smith, see *SS*, pp. 76, 85, 133 for references) think that vv. 5–9 are addressed to Cyrus. This view is tenable only with difficulty. True, Cyrus is 'called' (xlv. 3 f., xlvi. 11, xlviii. 15), 'in righteousness' (xlv. 13). Yahweh has taken his right hand (xlv. 1) and he is to free the exiles (xlv. 13). But it is difficult to imagine him as *b*ᵉ*rîṯ ʿām* (ver. 6) on any interpretation of the expression, not to speak of as 'a light to the nations', an expression used of the Servant in xlix. 6.

We must conclude that 'thee' is the Servant. But this does not entirely resolve the difficulty. We are not yet in a position to say whether the Servant of vv. 1–4 is the Israel of xli. 8, or, as many hold, an individual Servant κατ' ἐξοχήν. Even those who think that the Servant of the 'Songs' is Israel generally admit that the 'Songs' are in some ways different from passages like xli. 8, and therefore treat them separately: e.g. Wheeler Robinson, *The Cross of the Servant*. The question to be decided here is whether xlii. 5–9 is to be related to vv. 1–4 or to 'Israel' passages like xli. 8. We must therefore examine the passage in detail.

5. The 'hymnic' introduction with its participial clauses is characteristic of DI. *the* L*ORD—he is God*] *hā'ēl yahwêh*, 'the (true) God, Yahweh'. *hā'ēl* occurs without Yahweh following in about twenty passages (e.g. 2 Sam. xxii. 31, see *BDB* 42 *b*, 6(*a*)), generally with adjectival or similar qualification; in the absolute sense, 'the Deity', followed by Yahweh, only here and Ps. lxxxv. 8 (*9*). LXX κύριος ὁ θεός is probably paraphrase; so is האל האלוהים of Qᵃ. *and stretched them out*] Cf. xl. 22. *spread out*] *rôḳaʿ*, lit. 'beat out', the same verb as for the overlaying of the idol in xl. 19. *with* (lit. 'and') *its teeming life*] *w*ᵉ*ṣe'*ᵉ*ṣā'êhā*, a reduplicated form from √ 'go out'. The word, apart from xxii. 24, is peculiar to Isa. xl–lxvi and Job. Its use here is a good example of zeugma. *the peoples*] *hāʿām*, strictly a singular collective, 'people'. But the context requires the plural collective sense of 'peoples'. Levy compares the occasional use of Arab. *ʿāmm* as the 'totality' (of creatures). This would give a strict parallel to *whatever moves about in it*, though the parallel would be equally sound if 'peoples' referred to human beings, as it surely must in ver. 6. *life*] lit. 'spirit'. For this use of 'spirit' = 'breath' (of life) cf. Ps. civ. 29 f., where animals are endowed with it; also 'the breath of the spirit of life' of all living creatures (Gen. vii. 22), though *rûᵃḥ* there may be a gloss (LXX, V, omit).

6. *called*] Israel (xli. 9, xliii. 1, liv. 6), the Servant (xlix. 1) and Cyrus (see above) are all said to be 'called'. *for a saving purpose*] Lit. 'in righteousness' (cf. xlv. 13, of Cyrus). 'Righteousness' and 'salvation' are parallel and almost synonymous in xlv. 8, xlvi. 13, li. 6, 8. *I take you by the hand*] Cf. xli. 9, 13 (of Israel), xlv. 1 (of Cyrus). *the mediator of my covenant with the peoples*] Heb. *b^e^rîṯ ʿām*. Assuming for the moment that *b^e^rîṯ* means 'covenant' (cf. Akk. *birîtu*, 'fetter'), there are three possible interpretations of the expression: (i) 'covenant people', meaning Israel; (ii) '(the mediator of my) covenant with the people', the people being Israel and the mediator a Servant *κατ' ἐξοχήν* (cf. xlix. 5); (iii) '(the mediator of my) covenant with the peoples', the mediator being either Israel or a Servant *κατ' ἐξοχήν*. Sense (i) is possible on the analogy of 'wonder of a counsellor' = 'wonderful counsellor' (ix. 5; cf. Gen. xvi. 12; Prov. xv. 20, xxi. 20), though the natural expression for 'covenant people' would be *ʿam b^e^rîṯ*, and 'covenant people' is not a good || with 'a light to the nations'. Sense (ii) gives a fair || with what follows, is consistent with a mission of the Servant to Israel prior to a mission to the nations (cf. xlix. 5 f.), but gives to 'people' a more restricted sense than it has in ver. 5. Sense (iii) gives to (human) 'peoples' a more restricted sense than it may have in ver. 5, but this need occasion no surprise in DI. A covenant with mankind, or even with all creation, has an analogy in the rainbow-covenant of Gen. ix. 8–17. Even if it had not, DI's attitude to the nations does not preclude but rather supports (xlv. 22, xlix. 5 f.) such an idea. It has been suggested, originally by Torczyner (see *SS*, p. 133), that *b^e^rîṯ* here means 'vision', i.e. 'a vision vouchsafed to the people(s)'. This would relate the word to Akk. *barû*, 'see', *birûtu*, 'vision', and would give a perfect || to 'a light to the nations', 'peoples' and 'nations' both being genitives of object. An objection is that *b^e^rîṯ*, 'covenant' occurs some 300 times and it would hardly be obvious even to a contemporary that in this one instance it meant 'vision'. But DI lived in Babylonia and used occasional homonyms (see on xli. 2). The word may convey a *double entendre* and it is possible that 'A light that will be a revelation (*ἀποκάλυψιν*) to the heathen and glory to thy people Israel' (Luke ii. 32) is reminiscent of *b^e^rîṯ* = 'vision'. *my covenant*] The covenant, like the 'law' in ver. 1, is Yahweh's.

7. It is grammatically possible to take the infinitives as gerundial (*GK* 114 *o*) with Yahweh as subject, i.e. 'by my opening,' &c. (similarly in xlv. i, xlix. 5, 8), but it is more natural to take the 'you' of ver. 6 as the subject. *to open the eyes that are blind, to bring the captives out of the dungeon,* &c.] Refers most naturally to the physical privations of the exiles (cf. xlvii. 6), but it may refer to the spiritual darkness (cf. ix. 2, (*1*)) of Israel (xlii. 18–20) or even of the nations and their rulers (lii. 15). It is difficult to restrict the universalism of DI or to limit his *dungeon* and *prison* to 'iron bars' and 'cages'. 'The release of the captives from prison is not to be taken as liberation from exile but rather in a spiritual sense, a liberation of all the peoples from bondage. All of ver. 7 is a development of *light to the nations*' (Muilenburg).

All things considered, xlii. 5–9 has more affinity to the Servant Song vv. 1–4 than it has to 'Israel' passages like xli. 8–10. It is as if Yahweh, having introduced the Servant, proceeds to give him his commission. But none of the other Servant Songs begins with such a 'self-predication' as ver. 5; none is so polemic as ver. 8; none refers to the 'former' and the 'new' things (ver. 9); and the 'you' at the end of ver. 9 is plural, not the singular 'thee' of ver. 6. The whole is similar to xlix. 7–12, which, as it proceeds, describes the deliverance of Israel from exile. It is probable that both xlii. 5–9 and xlix. 7–12 are connecting links between the Servant Songs they follow and the main body of the prophecy. Some hands of LXX omit 'for a light to the nations', which would leave a defective line like xlix. 8*bα*, and it may be that xlii. 5–9 and xlix. 7–12 were originally 'Israel' passages which have been adapted to 'Servant' contexts. For further discussion see *SS*, pp. 128–35.

9. *former prophecies*] Lit. 'former things'. See on xli. 22. The reference again is probably to the rise of Cyrus but it may be more general, to pronouncements made through earlier prophets. In either case, Yahweh is not only 'up to date' with news but will pronounce authoritatively upon it. That is a difference between him and the *idols* (see on xl. 19) to whom he will not surrender the honour due to him alone. *new things*] See on xlviii. 6.

XLII. 10–17. THE NEW SONG

10. יוֹרְדֵי הַיָּם] Although the expression occurs in Ps. cvii. 22 it is tempting to read יִרְעַם הַיָּם, as in Ps. xcvi. 11, xcviii. 7, where also the words are followed by וּמְלֹאוֹ. The zeugma אִיִּים וְיֹשְׁבֵיהֶם is no more violent than is Ps. xcviii. 7*b*.

11. יִשְׂאוּ] See on xlii. 2.

14. אַחֲרִישׁ אֶתְאַפָּק] Synchronistic asyndetous imperfects following perfect (*Tenses* §§ 34, 163 Observation 1; *GK* 120 *c*).

15. אִיִּים] Gives no sense here. The original may have been צִיָּה/צִיּוֹת, which occurs in a similar context in xli. 18.

16. לֹא יָדָעוּ] Suspicious in || stichs and makes heavy going. Omit in first stich. A copyist may have felt that *dereḵ*, 'way', needed some definition. But it means '(on their) journey', cf. Gen. xxiv. 21;

1 Kings xviii. 27, xix. 7. לְפָנֵיהֶם] Should perhaps be transferred to the second stich.

The whole earth is bidden to sing a new song of praise to Yahweh. He is going out as a warrior. Then, speaking in his own person, Yahweh declares that he has long imposed silence on himself. Now he will cast off restraint, make havoc of all obstacles, and order a way in which even the blind cannot get lost.

The passage invites comparison with a group of Psalms of which the *Venite* is one, especially xxxiii. 3–22, xcvi, xcviii, cxlix, which similarly begin with the summons to 'Sing to Yahweh a new song'. The Psalms have a common pattern, that of the 'community thanksgiving'. Following (i) the summons to praise, there is (ii) a glorification of Yahweh either as world-creator and/or victor over the nations and/or their gods, and finally (iii) an announcement of his coming to judge the world. Whether the pattern was created by DI and adopted by the psalmists, or vice versa, has been much discussed, but the general opinion now is that DI was making use of a well-established Psalm-type.

To judge from the Psalms, xlii. 10–17 is a single poem, notwithstanding its changes of metre (cf. Ps. xcviii) and subject in vv. 14–17. It consists of (i) the summons to praise (vv. 10–12), (ii) descriptions of Yahweh under the figures of a warrior and a woman in labour (13–15), leading up to (iii) the now familiar theme of the exodus from Babylon (16 f.). The metrical irregularities are due to the passionate utterance (e.g. the staccato ver. 14). For Yahweh's intervention in a summons to praise cf. Ps. xcv. 8–11.

Comparison with the Psalms makes it clear that the violent similes in vv. 13–15 are not so incongruous with their context as they at first seem, and that if vv. 16 f. correspond to the Psalmists' picture of Yahweh's coming to judge the world, the Prophet must have thought of the return of the exiles as the triumphant culmination of Yahweh's purpose. A new world will be born of the divine travail. Similarly, the 'new song' of Rev. v. 9 is in an eschatological context.

10f. The new song is to be sung by *the whole earth* (*miḳᵉṣêh hā'āreṣ*), lit. 'from the end of the earth'. This does not mean from a point at the farthest distance, but 'from one end of the earth to another'; cf. Gen. xix. 4, where *miḳḳāṣêh* means 'without exception' (RSV 'to the last man'); Gen. xlvii. 2, 'from the end of his brothers' = 'from all his brothers'; Isa. lvi. 11; Jer. li. 31; Ezek. xxxiii. 2. The geographical horizons are *the shorelands* (see on xl. 15) to the west, and, to the east, *the wilderness and its cities . . . the settlements where Kedar dwells*. For 'cities and their villages/settlements' see Joshua xv. 21–61.

Cities (*ʿārîm*, √ unknown) might be large (Gen. x. 12: Deut. i. 28) or small (Gen. xix. 20; Eccles. ix. 14). They were walled (Lev. xxv. 29; Num. xxxv. 4) and fortified (2 Sam. xx. 6). Tadmor (Palmyra) and Sela (Petra) were such 'wilderness' cities. They had their 'daughter' villages (*bānôṯ*, Num. xxi. 25, xxxii. 42) or 'settlements' (*ḥaṣērîm*, the word used here). These were unwalled (Lev. xxv. 31), their inhabitants taking refuge in the cities in times of danger. Kedar (xxi. 16, lx. 7 and mg. refs.) is typical of the Bedouin nomads and in Jer. ii. 20 is parallel with 'the isles', to denote east and west, as here. The name is from a √'be dark', probably with reference to their goat-hair tents (Song i. 5). *the denizens of the rocks*] The parallel *the tops of the mountains* is against taking *selaʿ* ('crag', 'rock', AV) as a proper name (RV, RSV). The verbs in 11*b* are onomatopoeic and suggest inarticulate animal cries: cf. *the sea and all that fills it* (ver. 10). All nature is to praise Yahweh (cf. xliii. 20; Ps. xcvi. 11 f., xcviii. 7 f.). The passage anticipates the doctrine of the redemption of all creation (Rom. viii. 19–21).

13. *a warrior*] *gibbôr*: the corresponding Arab. *ǧabbâr* is one of the 'beautiful names' of Allah (*Qur'ān* lix. 23). *he will rouse himself to fury*] Cf. RSV. For this reflexive sense of *yāʿîr* (*Hiph.* *ʿûr*) see Ps. xxxv. 23. Yahweh is a solitary figure, without allies (cf. lix. 16 f., lxiii. 1–6); it is his own fury that he rouses. *fury*] *ḳin'āh*, √ 'to become intensely red'. *show himself mighty*] Lit. 'act as a *gibbôr*'.

14. The figure changes to that of a woman in labour. Yahweh himself is the speaker. *I have long been inactive*] For this sense of 'keep silent' cf. Judges xviii. 9; 1 Kings xxii. 3. *with all my might*] For *yaḥaḏ*, 'together' = 'altogether', 'completely', cf. Ps. xix. 9 (*10*), xxxvii. 38, lxxiv. 8; Isa. xxvii. 4; Jer. v. 5. *gasp* and *pant* are onomatopoeic, synonyms, and simultaneous. The 'together' gives them a kind of superlative force.

15. Describes the effect of these seemingly incongruous rages: mountains and hills will be devastated, rivers turned to desert wastes, and standing pools dried up. This is the opposite of the desert transformed to oasis of xli. 18 f.

16. *blind*] Best understood figuratively rather than literally. The returning exiles were not physically but spiritually blind and deaf (cf. vv. 18 f., xliii. 8). Words like 'way' and 'path' often refer, especially in parallelism, to moral direction and course of life. This is naturally most frquent in the Wisdom literature but it occurs also in the prophets (e.g. lix. 8, Jer. vi. 16, xviii. 15). To draw fast distinctions between the literal and figurative uses of such words is often impossible. This is a major difficulty in the interpretation of

DI. That he looked for the physical rehabilitation of Israel seems certain, but he was equally concerned with moral regeneration. *I will not leave them undone*] Cf. RV mg. In the preceding stich the verb is perfect of divine resolve (see on xli. 10): 'these are the things I have determined to do'. The object 'them' of the second verb 'leave' or 'forsake' (*ʿăzaḇtî*) has 'these things' as its antecedent, not the returning exiles. The closest approximation to the meaning 'omit to do' for 'forsake' is Gen. xxiv. 27, where Abraham's servant blesses Yahweh 'who has not forsaken (i.e. left unexercised) his steadfast love' (cf. Ruth ii. 20; Ps. xxxvii. 8).

The 'berserker rage' of this passage is objectionable to the modern reader, even though it is relieved by the abrupt change of figure in ver. 14. The figure of the warrior-god goes back to the Exodus (Exod. xv. 3). An even more violent picture is that of the blood-stained warrior of lxiii. 1–6. Our instinct is to say that such passages are out of place in Holy Scripture, that they are not patient of a Christian interpretation. Before we say that, we should look at the sequel. It was natural for the Hebrews to assume that when God visited the world in judgement there would be carnage: blood would be shed. When he did come, in the Incarnation, blood was shed; but it was man, not God, who shed it, and the blood that was shed was not man's, but the blood of the incarnate Son of God. There are two possible sequels to the anthropomorphic-anthropopathic conception of the warrior-god: it will either be outgrown and give place to an abstract monotheism, or it will find its culmination in the doctrine of the Incarnation. That is what happened. The Hebrews firmly believed that God is personal; they could never think of him as indifferent to the fate of the world. He would *act*—that is the permanent significance of the violent similes in this paragraph. He *did* act, but in a very different way from what was expected of him (cf. John iii. 17). We might call this the 'inverse' fulfilment of prophecy. Isa. xlii. 13–16 is patripassianism *in nuce*.

> I think this is the authentic sign and seal
> Of Godship; that it ever waxes glad,
> And more glad, until gladness blossoms, bursts,
> Into a rage to suffer for mankind.

That is Browning's way of saying what the Hebrew prophet said long ago.

XLII. 18–25. THE BLIND AND DEAF SERVANT

19. וְעִוֵּר . . . עִוֵּר] This is poor parallelism. We expect וְחֵרֵשׁ, so 2 MSS. and Σ; but they may have been making an obvious correction.

20. רָאִית] Read רָאִיתָ (*Keth.*). יִשְׁמָע] About 60 MSS. are said to read תִשְׁמָע, but this again may be deliberate alteration of a clumsy line. The harder reading may be explained as 'a transition from an address to a statement' in vigorous poetic language (*GK* 144 *p*).

22. הָפֵחַ בַּחוּרִים כֻּלָּם] Lit. 'a trapping in holes all of them'. The verb is ἅπ. λεγ. *Hiph.* infin. abs. פחח, a denominative from פַּח, 'bird-trap'. The Masora probably intended בַּחוּרִים, 'young men' (so T.). The || requires 'in holes', best pointed בְּחוֹרִים. מְשִׁסָּה] Read לִמְשִׁסָּה, with Q[a].

25. חֵמָה אַפּוֹ] The versions are no more guarantee (*BH*) that they read חֲמַת than are EVV ('the fury of his anger'). Even Q[a] חמת is not decisive. The harder MT reading may be explained as 'permutation', a variety of apposition, with a certain additional force (*GK* 131 *k*).

Yahweh's blind and deaf servant is bidden to see and hear. It is not as if he were deprived of the organs of sight and hearing. His present plight is due to his stubborn disobedience in the past.

The passage contains a number of grammatical solecisms, quick changes of person (vv. 20, 24), infins. abs. (vv. 20, 22), and 'the servant of Yahweh' (ver. 19) occurs in a context in which Yahweh himself is the speaker. It reads more like a poet's notes than a finished poem. Some alterations of text can be made with support from MSS. and versions, but it is equally possible that copyists and translators were trying to smooth out a text which they felt was inconsistent with itself. The sentence 'and they were not willing in his ways to walk' has an Aramaic ring and seems inserted between two parallel stichs. This need not mean that the passage is not from DI, but, if it is his, it looks as if it has been expanded. (Jeremiah, especially, contains denunciatory passages which look as if they have been rationalized by scribes who were puzzled by them.)

The blind and deaf servant is obviously Israel and the verses may owe their place here to the catchword *blind*, which relates them to the preceding paragraph. The Prophet was perfectly frank about the moral and spiritual blindness of his people (cf. xliii. 22–28). The main emphasis is that it was Yahweh who brought upon his people the disaster of the exile, in order to discipline them to obedience, and not, as some of them might be only too ready to argue, the Babylonians. When we look back to the history of the Israelite kingdoms, we may easily assume that it was inevitable that they would be engulfed by Assyria and Babylonia. The prophets insisted that their fall was a divine judgement on their disobedience, not simply a political misfortune due to the fact that they were weak and their enemies strong. This lesson was burned into the consciousness of the post-exilic community: cf. Neh. i. 5–11, ix. 6–38; Dan. ix. 4–19; Ps. cvi.

19. *he who has been granted my covenant of peace*] Heb. *m^e^šullām*, *Pu'al* participle. LXX 'their rulers' probably read as *môš^e^lîm*; cf. P *šallîṭā'*, 'ruler'. But parallelism requires some equivalent of *the* LORD'*s servant.* J. L. Palache's theory that Meshullam was the name of the Servant of Yahweh (*The 'Ebed-Jahveh Enigma in Pseudo-Isaiah*, 1934) is wholly improbable (see *SS*, pp. 89 f.). The comparison with Arab. *muslim*, 'one who is submissive (to God)' has no OT analogy. The word is probably to be understood in the light of *b^e^rîṯ š^e^lômî*, 'my covenant of peace' (liv. 10; cf. Ezek. xxxiv. 25, xxxvii. 26; Num. xxv. 12; Mal. ii. 5 (cf. Š. Porúbčan, *Il Patto nuovo in Is.* 40–66, 1958, p. 53). 'Covenant' and 'peace' are also associated in Job v. 25: 'Your covenant will be with the stones of the field, and the wild creatures of the field will be at peace with you.' *the* LORD'*s servant*] May have been expanded from *'aḇdî*, 'my servant'.

21. *for his righteousness' sake*] 'Righteousness' is almost meaningless to the present-day reader but there is no substitute for it in this context, unless it be 'saving purpose'. We have seen (see on xlii. 6) that 'righteousness' (*ṣeḏeḵ*) in DI is almost synonymous with 'salvation' (*yeša'*, *y^e^šû'āh*, *t^e^šû'āh*); in other words, it tends to move away from the purely ethical sense of justice (*mišpāṭ*). 'We see therefore that in Second-Isaiah the word *tsedeq–ts^e^dāqāh* (righteousness) has come to mean "salvation". The Righteousness of God shows itself in his saving work . . . in the Prophets and in the Psalms the salvation *motif* steadily becomes supreme' (N. H. Snaith, *The Distinctive Ideas of the OT*, p. 92). Other words associated with 'righteousness' are 'fidelity' or 'faithfulness' (*'^e^meṯ*) and 'steadfast love' (*ḥeseḏ*), e.g. Ps. lxxxv (cf. A. R. Johnson, *Sacral Kingship in Ancient Israel*, pp. 125 f.). Another line of approach to the expression 'for his righteousness' sake' is to compare it with 'for my own sake' (xliii. 25, xlviii. 11) and 'for my name's sake' (xlviii. 9), which point to Yahweh's essential nature as the ground of his dealings with men. *his law*] Heb. *tôrāh*, 'law' simply. This can hardly be, for the original DI, 'The Law' (of Moses), i.e. the Pentateuch, but it is probably more specific than 'teaching' (xlii. 4). In ver. 24 it is 'his law' (*tôrāṯô*). The phrases *to walk in his ways* and *obey his law* are Deuteronomic in tone and support the view that the original passage has been subjected to editorial revision.

23. *from now on*] *l^e^'āḥôr*, meaning as in xli. 23.

25. *but he did not understand*] *w^e^lô' yāḏā'*. But the phrase may mean 'unawares', 'when he did not expect (it)': cf. xlvii. 11; Ps. xxxv. 8.

XLIII. 1–7. ISRAEL, YAHWEH'S FAMILY, RANSOMED AND REPATRIATED

4. אָדָם] 'mankind' seems too wide a || to 'peoples'. It is usual to read אֲדָמֹת ('lands'), *tau* omitted by haplography. To this it is objected (Volz) that the plural 'lands' is found only in the doubtful Ps. xlix. 12 and that its meaning would have to be 'pieces of (cultivated) soil'. But why should it not mean that? Verses 3*b* and 4*b* are closely || and מִצְרַיִם more often stands for the highly productive land of Egypt than it does for the Egyptians. Can it be the Egyptian nomes?

7. כֹּל הַנִּקְרָא] The suggestion to read כֻּלֹּה נִקְרָא, 'the whole of it (Israel) is called', is not to be followed. The Massoretic word-division gives a closer connexion with ver. 6 and brings out more forcibly Yahweh's relation to individual Israelites.

Yahweh, who created Israel, will protect his people in all perils that threaten them. He will give the rich lands of Africa as the price of their freedom, and gather them from all the countries to which they have been dispersed.

1. The passage is connected with the preceding by *Yet now*, an indication that at least the nucleus of xlii. 18–25 is from DI. And the assurance that flames will *not* now scorch is intended as a contrast with the flames that *did* scorch (xlii. 25). The hopeless plight in which the exiles now find themselves is to be followed by a future rich in promise. We expect Yahweh to say 'Rejoice!' Instead, as if remembering their despondency, he says *Fear not!* (repeated in ver. 5, cf. xl. 9, xli. 10, 13 f., xliv. 2, liv. 4—the words run like a thread through the prophecy). That Yahweh created the world and its peoples has already been elaborated (xl. 12–26, 28, xlii. 5). Now he is said to have *created* and *formed* Israel; cf. xliii. 21, xliv. 2, 21, 24. *Created* is used of the divine activity in the first creation story (Gen. i–ii 4*a*); *formed* (*yāṣar*) is characteristic of the second (Gen. ii. 7 f., 19). The word is used particularly of the work of a potter (xxix. 16, xli. 25; Jer. xviii; similarly in Phoenician and Ugaritic). At the end of ver. 7 a third word *I made* is used. This, the ordinary word for 'made', is common to both creation stories (Gen. i. 7, 16, 25 f., ii. 2 f., 4*b*, 9, 18). *I have redeemed you*] See on xli. 14. *I have called you by name*] Cf. xlv. 3 (Cyrus). The meaning is that Israel has been called for a specific purpose; cf. Bezalel (Exod. xxxi. 2). It is one of the paradoxes of OT religion that when the Hebrews came to believe in one only God, they continued to think of him as having a special relation to themselves. At first sight monotheism seems inconsistent with any

doctrine of election. But so long as the election was to service it is entirely credible (cf. H. H. Rowley, *The Biblical Doctrine of Election*, 1950). Jesus was a Jew, and he would have been unintelligible had he appeared anywhere else in the world than where he did and without the long training in the knowledge of God to which the Jews had to submit themselves.

2. Fire and water are mentioned together in Ps. lxvi. 12 as embracing extremes of danger. The reference here is general rather than to dangers attending the homeward journey to Palestine. The passing through the waters may be reminiscent of the Exodus, and the story of the burning fiery furnace (Dan. iii) is probably a development from the motif of passing unscathed through fire.

3. *the Holy One of Israel*] See on xli. 14. *your deliverer*] Cf. xlix. 26. The word (*môšîaʿ*) occurs without the pron. sf. in xliii. 11, xlv. 15, 21, where it is best rendered 'saviour' in the wildest sense. The √ meaning in *Qal* is 'to be wide, spacious', *Hiph.* 'give width to, liberate'. It has a correspondingly wide content. What it means in the present passage is explained in what follows. Yahweh will give the rich lands of Africa as the price of his people's ransom. *Seba* is to be distinguished from Sheba (Ps. lxxii. 10 (*11*)), on the Arabian side of the Red Sea; it was the country south of Nubia (Heb. Cush). Cush and Seba correspond roughly to Upper Egypt and the Lower Sudan. Together with Egypt proper they were all of Africa known to the Hebrews (Gen. x. 6 f.). The text is generally taken to mean that Yahweh will give the African territories to Cyrus in return for his liberation of the exiles: cf. on xlv. 15, where Egypt, Nubia, and the Sabeans are mentioned together. No part of Africa had been included in the Babylonian Empire, so Egypt, Nubia, and Seba may be thought of as 'extras' to what Persia would naturally gain by the conquest of Babylon. In fact, it was not until Cambyses, Cyrus' successor, that the Persians invaded Egypt. It is clear that it was not DI's expectation that Israel would exercise world-dominion.

5–7. After a repeated *Fear not*, Yahweh asserts that he will bring back his exiled family from the four points of the compass. The juxtaposition of masc. and fem., *sons* and *daughters* (cf. xlix. 22) expresses entirety (*GK* 122 *v*). Already in the sixth century the Jews were widely scattered. Some had fled to Egypt (Jer. xliii), taking Jeremiah with them; others had (earlier?) founded a colony at Elephantine, near the first Cataract (see on xlix. 12). A substantial number from the northern tribes had been deported to Assyria. Jeremiah (Jer. xxxi. 1–22) and Ezekiel (Ezek. xxxvii. 15–28) looked for a reunion of all Israelites under a ruler of the house of David.

They thought, not of two kingdoms, but of one people of God, and when DI speaks of Israel and Jacob in parallelism, as he frequently does, it is this one people ('all the descendants of Israel', xlv. 25) he has in mind; cf. G. A. Danell, *Studies in the Name Israel in the OT*, 1946, p. 262. He did not concern himself with the question whether Palestine could support them all (see on xlix. 14–21); what he was concerned with was the unity of the family of God. *who belongs to me*] Lit. 'who is called by my name'. The thought is the same as in ver. 1, though it is somewhat differently expressed. The full expression is 'my name is called over them', in token that they belong to me; cf. Deut. xxviii. 10; Jer. xiv. 9, xv. 16. Not only is Israel Yahweh's, but individual Israelites. *that my majesty might be clearly seen*] Lit. 'for my glory', as though Israel, ransomed and restored, is the final evidence of the majesty which all mankind is to see (cf. xl. 5) and acclaim.

XLIII. 8–13. THERE IS NO GOD EXCEPT YAHWEH AND HIS PEOPLE ARE HIS WITNESSES

8. הוֹצִיא] Q[a] הוציאו, probably rightly; or may be intended as infin. abs. (= imptv.) with *ī* in final syll. (*GK* 74 *l*).

9. נִקְבְּצוּ] *Niph.* perfect (cf. LXX συνήχθησαν), not jussive (EVV) or imperative (RV mg.). יַשְׁמִיעֻנוּ] The suffix is difficult to construe, since not all of 'us' were there. Read יַשְׁמִיעוּ (Q[a]).

10. עַבְדִּי] Can be either (i) a second subject; 'and my servant (is also my witness)', or (ii) a second predicate: 'and (you are also) my servant'. The second is more natural. The singular 'my servant' is supported by all versions except P, and notwithstanding the ‖ *my witnesses*, is to be preferred. DI uses the plural only in liv. 17 and possibly xliv. 26 (which see).

12. וְהוֹשַׁעְתִּי] Makes a four-beat stich, looks suspiciously like a dittograph of וְהִשְׁמַעְתִּי, and breaks the connexion between the key verbs in ver. 9. וַאֲנִי־אֵל] Metre and sense are improved if ver. 13 begins here. Q[a] omits the copula, a further improvement. Verses 12 and 13 consist each of a tristich.

13. מִיּוֹם] The only other identical use of this expression is in Ezek. xlviii. 35, where it must mean 'from now on'. LXX ἔτι ἀπ' ἀρχῆς (similarly T, V) may have read מֵעוֹלָם, but as likely as not was interpreting.

Yahweh gives the order for his people to be brought into a general assembly of the nations. Has any god ever foretold the future? If so, let him bring evidence that will convince the court. Presumably no witnesses are forthcoming. Yahweh then turns to Israel: 'You are my witnesses.' Their very giving of evidence is to strengthen their faith and open their blind eyes to what is obvious. Yahweh is LORD, the only God and Saviour, now and for ever.

The paragraph has no obvious connexion with what precedes. Its closest links are with xli. 21–29, xlii. 18, and xlviii. 14. The setting is forensic (see on xli. 1–4) but is less vividly portrayed than in similar passages. A new feature is that the Israelites are summoned as Yahweh's witnesses in his controversy with the gods and their devotees. They look unimpressive witnesses enough, without insight or perception; *blind, yet have eyes, and deaf, although they have ears.*

8. *Bring in*] Lit. 'bring out', the figure being of captives whose sight has been impaired by long confinement in darkness (xlii. 18–22). Brought *out* from imprisonment they are now to be brought *in* as witnesses.

9. The court sits. *Who among them foretold this?*] There are no grammatical antecedents to *them* and *this*: *them* can hardly be the nations, since it has never been suggested that they could predict. *Who* and *them* must refer obliquely to the gods, who are challenged to produce witnesses from among their own worshippers. *this*] must refer to something specific, most likely the conquests of Cyrus: cf. xlviii. 14 ('these things'), xli. 1–4, 25 f. *foretold*] For Heb. 'told' (*higgîḏ*) in sense *foretold* cf. 2 Sam. vii. 11. The verb is imperfect, not perfect as in xli. 26, xlviii. 14. Perhaps the meaning is 'Who . . . can explain this': for this sense of Heb. 'tell' cf. Judges xiv. 12–14 (Samson's riddle); 1 Kings x. 3; Dan. ii. 2. Then *announced* (impf.) must be frequentative, 'was in the habit of announcing'. *that the court may say*] Lit. 'that they (the audience) may hear and say'.

10. *that you may know*, &c.] It has been suggested that the original was 'that they may know . . .'. But the whole emphasis is that Israel's witnessing will strengthen her faith. Indeed, half the paragraph is addressed to the witnesses, who otherwise would be incidental to the picture. *I am He*] See on xli. 4.

11. *I, I alone, am the LORD*] 'I, I am Yahweh', here means more than 'I am the God whose name is Yahweh'. The meaning is 'I am God, the sole Deity'. A comparison with passages like xlv. 5 f., 18 ('I am Yahweh and there is no other') and xlv. 22, xlvi. 9 ('I am God and there is no other') makes this quite clear (cf. S. H. Blank, 'Studies in DI', *HUCA* 15, 1940, pp. 14 f.). When Yahweh says *Before me no god was formed*, he obviously does not mean that he himself was formed. The words are an ironical reference to the idol-gods. He, and he alone, always was God and always will be. *Saviour*] See on 'your deliverer', xliii. 3.

12. *foreign god*] Lit. 'foreigner', cf. Deut. xxxii. 16; Jer. ii. 25, iii. 13; and for the full expression Ps. xliv. 20 (*21*), lxxxi. 10.

13. *and shall be ever the same*] Lit. 'also from now on I am He'. For 'I am He' in sense 'I am the same', see on xli. 4.

XLIII. 14–15. BABYLON IN PANIC

14b. This passage has occasioned much discussion and many emendations have been suggested. But as Duhm said, the difficulty is not to find something possible, but something convincing, in place of what we have. MT as pointed makes reasonably good sense: lit. 'for your sakes I send (pf. of divine resolve) to Babylon and will bring down (as) fugitives all of them and (= *scilicet*) the Chaldeans in the ships of their shrill cry'. בָבֶלָה] Q[a] reads בבבל, 'against Babylon', which is more forcible. Otherwise the Scroll agrees with MT apart from the usual orthographic variations. וְהוֹרַדְתִּי] LXX ἐπεγείρω, OL *suscitabo*, P *wa'ytîṯ* ('make come'). But MT looks sound. בָרִיחִים] LXX φεύγοντες, V *vectes* ('bars' = בְּרִיחִים, AV mg.), both support MT. בָּאֳנִיּוֹת רִנָּתָם] LXX[A] ἐν κλοιοῖς δεθήσονται, from which an original בַּעֲנָקוֹת רֻתָּקוּ, 'shall be bound in neck-chains', or similar, has been conjectured. But Torrey points out that δεθήσονται may be an inner-LXX corruption of δεηθήσονται 'shall cry for mercy'. (LXX sometimes has δέησις, 'entreaty', for רִנָּה). Then κλοιοῖς, 'collars', 'pillories', or the like, may be a further corruption of πλοίοις ('ships') to agree with δεθήσονται. That leaves us with the MT intact, and the only question is how we should point and translate it. To point בַּאֲנִיּוֹת, *in lamentationibus*, 'their rejoicing (shall be turned) to lamentations' (cf. RSV), is reading too much into a sentence that has no verb. (Duhm supposed that a verb had fallen out, but metrically there is no room for one.)

A tentative alternative translation might be:

> For your sakes I send against Babylon,
> and will drive them all downstream in coracles,
> the Chaldeans in their proud ships.

Torrey refers to יוֹרְדֵי הַיָּם בָּאֳנִיּוֹת (Ps. cvii. 23), which he translates 'those who embark on the sea in ships'. Another example of Heb. 'go down into' = 'embark in' is Jonah i. 3*b*. There remains בָרִיחִים, of which the *bêth* may be the preposition 'in'. 'In ריחים' would give a construction exactly similar to Ps. cvii. 23 and a perfect ‖ to בָּאֳנִיּוֹת following, if ריחים (or ? רוחים—there is often no appreciable difference between *waw* and *yôdh* in Q[a]) were some kind of wide or low craft ('vessel') like the *ḳuffa*, the circular coracle still used on the Euphrates. Arab. *'inâ* (= Heb. אֳנִי) *raḥraḥ*, 'a wide and low vessel', is from √*rḥḥ*, and is a domestic utensil, though it is interesting that 'vessel' has the same range of meaning in Semitic as it has in English. But Jer. xxii. 14 speaks of 'spacious (מְרֻוָּחִים) rooms', √רָוַח. True, the *kuffa* is a poky craft, but it could be an ironical ‖ to 'proud ships'. Or, if we must have something spacious, why not hastily constructed 'rafts'? These suggestions are offered with hesitation, since in the wide range of terms for shipping in Akkadian there is no cognate to רוחים; but the word might be descriptive rather than a technical term.

This passage might be only a fragment, were it not that it has both a declarative prologue and an epilogue, if the words may be permitted for what are only distichs. That so short a passage is so 'framed' suggests that its content (14*b*) had special importance. For the first time in the prophecy Babylon and the Chaldeans are named, but it is not yet said whom or what Yahweh is to send or 'let loose' (*Pi'ēl*, cf. Job xii. 15) against them. This is probably intentional and it is unimaginative to read 'I will send him', i.e. Cyrus (cf. *BH*). The framework (vv. 14*a*, 15) is in what are by now familiar terms. For Yahweh as King of Israel cf. xli. 21, xliv. 6. *in their proud ships*] Lit. 'in the ships of their shrill cry/cries'. This has been taken to mean (i) the ships in which they take such pride (cf. RV), or (ii) to refer to the shouts with which the rowers timed their rowing (cf. AV). On either interpretation, *in their proud ships* is a fair paraphrase. The Chaldeans were a Semitic people who settled in the lower Euphrates valley and after a long struggle wrested Babylon from the Assyrians, by whom it had been conquered, and established the Chaldean or 'neo-Babylonian' empire after the fall of Nineveh in 612 B.C.

XLIII. 16–21. THE WONDERS OF THE NEW EXODUS

Yahweh had once made a path through the sea and, as if assuming command of a hostile army, had engulfed it in the resurging waters. He now announces his intention to do 'a new thing', in which the elements of water and dry land will be reversed. He will make pathways through the desert waste and supply his people with water. Even the creatures of the wild will honour him for this.

The homeward journey through the transformed desert has been described in xli. 17–20, but without explicitly comparing and contrasting it with the Exodus. Here that contrast is intentionally drawn. Verses 16 f. must refer to the passage of the Red Sea and the fate of the Egyptians. EVV translate all but one of the verbs by the present tense, as though they express general truths. They could all be rendered by the past tense (see on xl. 13): *made* and *led out* are participles, and the Hebrew participle takes its tense from its context; in *they sink down, nevermore to rise* (lit. 'they do/will not rise') the verbs are imperfect, probably to give a more vivid picture, as though the hearers are either transported into the past, or the past brought into their present, for them to *see* what is happening; in *they are extinguished*, *quenched* the verbs are statives perfect and EVV rightly translate them to describe accomplished facts.

17. *who led out*] For this as a military term see on xl. 26. It is as if Yahweh assumes command of the Egyptian host and leads it to destruction. *a whole army in mass formation*] Lit. 'army and strength together', putting the accent (*'athnaḥ*) on 'together' (*yaḥdāw*), *metri causa* and because in DI it gathers up what precedes (*contra* AV, RV). *quenched like a wick*] For the figure see xlii. 3. Our modern phrase would be 'snuffed out like a candle'. The chivalry of Egypt was utterly powerless against Yahweh: cf. Exod. xv. 21.

18. *the past*] Heb. *rī'šōnōṯ*, 'former things'; cf. xli. 22, xlii. 9, xliii. 9, xlvi. 9, xlviii. 3. Whatever the word may mean elsewhere in DI, here it must refer to the Exodus, notwithstanding that it is without the def. art., which anyhow is no matter in poetry.

19. *a new thing*] Cf. xlii. 9, xlviii. 6 (both plur.). Here the reference is clear, to the new Exodus. *spring up*] The verb, whether in its literal or figurative meaning, is used of the germination (or sprouting) of plants, generally with emphasis on its suddenness (cf. lviii. 8); hence *now*. *surely you must know it!*] Lit. 'do you not know it?' Q^a 'do you not know?' simply. LXX καὶ γνώσεσθε αὐτά avoids the parenthesis but sounds trivial. MT is understandable in the light of xl. 21, 28. For 'is it not?' (*h^{a}lō'*) in sense 'it certainly is', cf. 'Is not this David?' (1 Sam. xxi. 11 (*12*) and frequently). The meaning must be something like 'You might have known I would do something of the kind!' **paths**] So Q^a. MT 'rivers', which appear in ver. 20 (cf. xli. 18). The reading of the Scroll is preferred because it reproduces the 'way' || 'path' of ver. 16. That it has 'paths' (plur.) is no objection. There could only be one 'path' = 'way' through the Red Sea. The word (*n^{e}ṯīḇōṯ*) is mostly used in the plural, even when || *dereḵ*, 'way', in the singular (e.g. xlii. 16), and it conveys something of the suggestion of 'bypaths' (cf. Jer. xviii. 15).

20. For the thought cf. xlii. 11 and passages cited there. It is not said that *the creatures of the wild will honour* Yahweh because he has made the desert more tolerable for them—they would doubtless prefer it in *statu quo*!—but because he has made it more tolerable for his chosen people. There is in the OT no conception of 'nature' as 'the creative and regulative physical power which is conceived as operating in the physical world and as the immediate cause of all its phenomena' (*SOED.* s.v. iv. 1). No Hebrew poet could have written of

'. . . . . a sense sublime
Of something far more deeply interfused,
Whose dwelling is the light of setting suns,
And the round ocean and the living air,
And the blue sky, and in the mind of man:
A motion and a spirit, that impels
All thinking things, all objects of all thought,
And rolls through all things.'

Nature or, it would be better to say, the world of created things, stood over against God. The mountains and hills could 'break forth into singing, and all the trees of the field clap their hands' (lv. 12; cf. Ps. lxv. 13). Man and beast could rejoice and praise God together, as in the present passage, and 'the restitution of all things to their first state of perfection' is imagined in passages like xi. 6–9. The Hebrews knew nothing of the redemption of the 'soul' apart from the redemption of the body, and the honour which the creatures of the wild are to give to Yahweh contributes to the eschatological picture of paradise restored. *wolves . . . owls*] These desert 'howlers' are named together in xxxiv. 13; Mic. i. 8; Job xxx. 29. *wolves*] Heb. *tannîm*. RV, RSV 'jackals'. But since in xiii. 22, xxxiv. 13 f. they are associated with *'iyyîm*, which are undoubtedly jackals (Arab. *ibn 'âwâ*), the meaning is more probably 'wolves' (Arab. *tînân*); so Post, *HDB.*, i. 620*b*; G. R. Driver, *PEQ.*, 87, 1955, p. 135. *owls*] *b^enôṯ ya'^anāh*. An 'unclean' bird (Lev. xi. 16; Deut. xiv. 15); not the 'ostrich' of Job xxxix. 13, unless, which is doubtful, *r^enānîm* there is a corruption of *y^e'ēnîm* (cf. Lam. iv. 3, *Qere*). It has generally been taken to mean 'daughters of greed' (Syr. *ya'nâ*, 'greedy'), i.e. 'ostriches'; so LXX, V, P, RV, RSV. But *ya'^anāh* may be related to Arab. *wa'na*, 'stony land'. It was probably some kind of owl: AV always 'owl(s)'; Driver, 'eagle-owl' (*PEQ.*, 87, 1955, pp. 12 f.). The word 'daughters' has no reference to sex (*GK* 122 *b*, *i*).

21. *that they might rehearse my praises*] Lit. '(that) they may/might/should recount (over again) my praise': a final clause (so RV, RSV) without any formal link with what precedes (cf. *GK* 120 *c*). For Yahweh as Israel's 'praise' (*t^ehillāh*) cf. Deut. x. 21. The word is from the same √*hll* as *Halleluyah*, and the meaning is that Israel is to 'recount' Yahweh's 'praiseworthy acts' (*t^ehillôṯ*, cf. Ps. ix. 14, (*15*); lxxviii. 4+) in the manner of 'Halleluyah' Psalms like cv–cvii.

XLIII. 22–28. FRIVOLOUS SACRIFICES BETOKEN A SINFUL HISTORY

25. לֹא אֶזְכֹּר] Add עוֹד with Q[a]. This is metrically probable.

28. וַאֲחַלֵּל שָׂרֵי קֹדֶשׁ LXX *καὶ ἐμίαναν οἱ ἄρχοντες* (Q+*σου*) *τὰ ἅγιά μου* has been thought to depend on a text וַיְחַלְּלוּ שָׂרֶיךָ קָדְשִׁי, 'and your princes profaned my sanctuary'. In that case 28*a* should go with 27 to make up a tristich. It may be so; but 27 seems a comprehensive indictment enough as it stands, and if there must be a tristich in the paragraph, it is more likely to be in the final than in the penultimate verse. MT gives a perfectly good sense. In any case point וָאֲחַלֵּל and וָאֶתְּנָה. The Massoretic pointing probably intended the words as predictions (cf. RV).

Yahweh says emphatically that it was not to him that the Israelites offered their lavish sacrifices. Not that he had demanded such slavish toil from them. On the contrary: it was they who had made a slave of him with their sins. But it was entirely in keeping with his nature that he should wipe out their sins. Let him and them together review the past and see whether there was any justification for their conduct. They had been insubordinate ever since they began to be a people. That was why he had brought their state and its institutions to an end.

The verses do not appear to have any relation to what precedes, notwithstanding that they begin with 'And'/'But' (AV)/'Yet' (RV, RSV), on which see below.

The passage (cf. 23*b*) cannot be a complaint on Yahweh's part that the Israelites had not brought him sacrifices. It is ironical and too grave in tone to mean simply that Israel need not reproach herself because she had not sacrificed during the exile; that Yahweh had not required sacrifice, if only because sacrificial worship was impossible in the conditions of the exile, with the implication that obedience was equally, or more, acceptable to him. It is an indictment of Israel from the beginnings of her history—'your first father sinned'. There is evidence enough that Israel offered sacrifices on a lavish scale (e.g. i. 11–14; Amos iv. 4 f., v. 21 f.). No doubt the sacrifices were offered officially to Yahweh, no doubt also that those who offered them assumed that they were offering them to Yahweh. But Yahweh says plainly that they were not offered to *him*, and he seems to say that he did not want them. The passage is not so forthright in its condemnation of sacrifice as are those in Amos and Isaiah, though there is much in it that seems to disparage sacrifice.

22. This verse is capable of more than one translation, and it was probably as open to *double entendre* for those to whom it was addressed as it is for us. The ambiguities, if such they are, are due to the various nuances of the verb *ḳārā'* ('call'), of the particle *kî* ('that', EVV 'but'), and the preposition *b*^{e} ('with', EVV 'of'). The primary meaning of *ḳārā'* is 'call', sometimes with direct accusative of the person called, but more frequently predicate and object are connected by a preposition 'to', i.e. 'call (to) so-and-so'. Among extensions of its meaning are (i) 'invite' (especially to a feast, 1 Kings i. 9 f., 19), (ii) 'call upon' = 'invoke' (God in prayer), lv. 6; Judges xv. 18; 1 Sam. xii. 17 f.; so EVV here. *Do not imagine . . . that it was me you invited to your feastings*] Heb. 'But not me you invited.' The 'and' = 'but' has a certain rhetorical force ('by any means', 'at all'), which it is difficult to render without being clumsy. 'It sure wasn't me!' would express it exactly but is slang. An equally correct translation is 'Do not imagine that it was me you invoked', i.e. to judge from the following context, with accompanying sacrifices (cf. Ps. cxvi. 17), though when the verb is used in this sense it is generally of simple and direct appeal to God in prayer. The sacrifices, on either interpretation, are an essential element in the picture. *to your feastings*] At any sacrifice the Deity might be thought of as 'entertained' by his worshippers. Pre-exilic sacrifice was eucharistic rather than penitential, and the sin-offering (*ḥaṭṭā'ṯ*, Lev. iv) and guilt-offering (*'āšām*, Lev. v), so prominent in post-exilic sacrifice, are conspicuously absent here. The *me* is emphatic by position, and, by implication, in vv. 23*a*, 24*a*, though it would be clumsy in those verses to keep putting the pron. obj. before the verb. To whom, then, were the sacrifices offered, if not to Yahweh? The implication, probably, is that they were offered, wittingly or unwittingly, to 'some foreign god you fancied' (xliii. 12). *or that you went so far as*] Heb. '(to the point) that'. For this sense of *kî* cf. xxii. 1; Gen. xx. 9+ (*BDB.*, 472*b*. f.). EVV 'but' can be equally correct, *kî* being used in an adversative sense after a negative (cf. Gen. xvii. 15+). *to weary yourself on my account*] For *b*^{e} ('with') in sense 'on account of' cf. lvii. 10; Ps. vi. 6 (7), lxix. 3, (4). But admittedly 22*b* can be rendered 'for you were (had become) weary of me'.

23. *your holocausts of sheep*] In the 'burnt-offering' or 'holocaust' (*'ôlāh*, 'that which ascends', either to the altar, or from the altar in sacrificial smoke) the whole carcase of the animal was burnt (Lev. i) and the worshipper had no share in its flesh. The word for 'sheep' (*śêh*) means 'one of a flock', whether sheep or goat (Lev. i. 10). Here it is collective. A bull was an equally legitimate offering (Lev. i. 3–9) and, *a priori*, more meritorious because more expensive. But if the worshippers were inclined to be niggardly, they would make it convenient to offer a sheep or goat. Is there a hint of that here? (cf.

AV, RV, 'small cattle'). 'Your starveling sheep/goats' would perhaps be overdoing it. *or do me honour with your sacrifices*] Perhaps with the suggestion 'You did very well out of them yourselves!' The *sacrifice* (*zeḇaḥ*, lit. 'slaughter') or 'peace-offering' (so EVV for *šelem*, Lev. iii) was the staple offering in pre-exilic times. Prior to the Deuteronomic legislation (Deut. xii) any slaughter of domestic animals was a 'sacrifice'. The flesh, whether of cattle or sheep/goats, was eaten by the worshippers and the officiating priest, and if a man preferred beef to mutton, it would cost him more but there was more of it. *I did not make you slave*] The noun *'eḇeḏ*, 'slave', 'servant', and the corresponding verb have a wide range of meanings. The *Hiph.* of the verb is found about a dozen times, and always (e.g. Exod. i. 13, vi. 5; Jer. xvii. 4) in sense 'reduce to slavery', except in the late 2 Chron. xxxiv. 33, where its severity has been relaxed to a routine cultic meaning. *at preparing grain-offerings*] Heb. 'with *minḥāh*', a word meaning 'gift' or 'present', sometimes euphemistically for tribute (e.g. Judges iii. 15), hence any offering to God, whether of grain or animals (Gen. iv. 3–5). In P it has come to have the specialized meaning 'grain-offering' (so Lev. ii). This does not mean that P was the first to use it so: 2 Kings xvi. 13, 15, says that Ahaz 'burned his whole-offering and his *minḥāh* (both with acc. part. *'eṯ*) and it is arbitrary to delete 'and the *minḥāh*' in Judges xiii. 19, 23 (so G. F. Moore, *Judges*, p. 322). No civilized god could be expected to eat his meat without bread of some kind! The meaning *grain-offering* in the present passage (*contra* EVV, exc. RV mg.) is supported by the || *frankincense*, the more so since frankincense was an essential ingredient in the grain-offering (Lev. ii. 1; see also Jer. xvii. 26, 'burnt-offerings and sacrifices, grain-offerings and frankincense'). The preparation of grain-offerings demanded patience and skill (Lev. ii, *passim*) like 'slaving' in the kitchen, and *minḥāh*, especially with the verb *slave at*, would have some overtone of 'tribute'. *weary you*] 'make you toil'; almost 'wear you out' (cf. Mal. ii. 17). *by demanding frankincense*] Lit. 'with (*bêth* of price, *GK* 119 *p*, "at the price of") frankincense'. *frankincense*] A luxury product, associated with gold and myrrh, imported from Sheba (lx. 6; Jer. vi. 20; Song iii. 6, iv. 6, 14; Matt. ii. 11).

24. *fragrant cane*] *Calamus aromaticus*, another luxury import. The sense is ironical and the meaning throughout the passage is much the same as in Jer. vi. 20: here Yahweh says that Israel did not buy cane for *him*, there that they did but that he did not want it. The sentence is alliterative (*lō' ḳānîṯā llî ḇakkesep̱ ḳānêh*), 'you did not gain cane for me for cash', but not so cacophanous. Engl. 'cane' probably derives, via Gk κάννα, from Heb. *ḳānêh*, Akk. *ḳanû*. *or soak me with* *the fat of your sacrifices*] For 'soak' (*Hiph. rāwāh*) cf. lv. 10, of rain soaking the earth. The Deity's share of the *zeḇaḥ* was 'all fat and no lean' (cf. Lev. iii. 3 f.). It is as if Yahweh says, 'I am heartily glad you didn't!'

25. *I, in very truth I, do wipe out your transgressions*] This is a little ponderous even in the Hebrew: 'Í, Í am he (that) wípes out your transgréssions for my ówn sake (? five stresses). Although some MSS. of LXX, notably א and A, omit 'for my own sake', reasons for deleting it are not compelling. Part of the difficulty is the use of the pronouns 'I' and 'he' in close proximity. The 'he' may be simply a connecting link between the subject 'I' and the predicate (*GK* 141 *g*, *h*) in what is a noun sentence ('wipes out', *môḥêh*, is a ptc.), giving additional emphasis to the already duplicated 'I' (see on xl. 1). The longer form of the 1st pers. pron. ('*ānôḵî*) may also be deliberate. (It is relatively infrequent in the Hebrew of the period, but cf. xlv. 12.) But there is probably an overtone of the 'monotheistic formula' ('I, I am he who wipes out'), notwithstanding that elsewhere in DI this is '*anî hû*' (see on xli. 4). In that case it is worth noting that here, as in xlvi. 4, the 'monotheistic formula' is not simply a definition of Yahweh as he is 'in himself', but is brought into relation with his saving work. *transgressions*] Or 'acts of flagrant disobedience' (cf. ver. 27), properly 'rebellions' (cf. Job xxxiv. 37). *because I am what I am*] Heb. *leᵉmaʿanî*, 'for my own sake', occurs in xxxvii. 35 = 2 Kings xix. 34; Isa. xlviii. 11. It has much the same meaning as 'for the sake of my name' (*lᵉmaʿan šᵉmî*), which occurs in xlviii. 9; Ezek. xx. 9, 14, 22, 44. But in 'for the sake of my/thy/his name' there is usually emphasis on Yahweh's good name, fame, or reputation: so especially in Ezek. (though see xx. 44). The same is true of 'for my own sake' in Isa. xlviii. 11 (though cf. ver. 9). But here Yahweh's wiping out of Israel's transgressions springs from pure grace; he forgives because it is his nature to do so: cf. Ps. xxiii. 3, xxv. 11, xxxi. 3 (*4*); also the expression 'for the sake of thy steadfast love' (*ḥasdᵉḵā*), Ps. vi. 4, (*5*), xliv. 26 (*27*).

26. The language is forensic but the scene is not described in such detail as in similar passages (see on xli. 1–7). It is almost as if Yahweh says: 'Sue me if you will; there may be something I have forgotten! Let us argue the matter in court; you shall state your case and endeavour to get a favourable verdict'.

27. *Your first father*] Must be Jacob (cf. Hos. xii. 3), not Abraham. Abraham was the ancestor of Arabs and Edomites, as well as of Israel, Jacob of Israelites only. *those who should have been my spokesmen to you*] Heb. *mᵉlîṣêḵā*, 'your interpreters'. The suffix may be either subjective or objective. Here it has something of the force of both: the 'interpreters' were Israelites sent by God *to* Israel. The word (*Hiph.* ptc. *lîṣ*) means 'interpreter' in Phoenician and is found three times in OT outside this passage: in Gen. xlii. 23 the meaning is clear; in Job xxxiii. 23 (RSV 'mediator') it is || 'messenger'/'angel' (*mal'āḵ*); in 2 Chron. xxxii. 31 it is used of 'the envoys (RSV) of the princes of Babylon'. Nils Johansson (*Parakletoi*, 1940, p. 47) renders *Fürsprecher*, 'intercessors', and the meaning may be somewhat wider than (false) prophets, and include the kings (and priests?), who were intermediaries between Yahweh and Israel (see the beginning of ver. 28). Except in the *Hiph.* participle the verb has the bad sense of 'scorn', 'deride' (cf. Job xvi. 20; Ps. cxix. 51). An interpreter may have been so called because he had every opportunity to deceive both the parties he was engaged to serve. *flagrantly disobeyed me*] Heb. 'rebelled against me': see on 'transgressions' (ver. 25).

28. Lit. 'and I profaned (*wā'aḥallēl*, cf. xlvii. 6) the holy princes'. If we keep the rendering 'profane(d)' (EVV), 'profane' must be in the sense opposite to 'sacred'—so 'de-sacrated', somewhat as the fruit of the vine, after being 'holy' (i.e. given to the sanctuary, Lev. xix. 23–25) in the fourth year, was thereafter 'profaned', i.e. put to everyday or secular use (cf. Deut. xx. 6, xxviii. 30; Jer. xxxi. 5; where 'use/enjoy the fruit' [EVV] is in Heb. 'profane it': see Jer. xxxi. 5, RV mg.). The term *consecrated princes* (*śārê ḳōḏeš*) is used of priests (RV 'princes', RSV 'officers of the sanctuary') in 1 Chron. xxiv. 5. But this usage is late, after the functions of the kings had passed to the priesthood. In DI the reference, assuming that the text is sound (see above), is almost certainly to the 'sacral' kings. *and abandoned Jacob to destruction*] Lit. 'and gave Jacob to the ban' (*ḥērem*). In early times this would have meant annihilation (cf. 1 Sam. xv. 3), but here the word is used rather more loosely. *those who reviled him*] Heb. *giddûpîm*, an intensive plural (*GK* 124 *e*), 'reviling(s)' i.e. reviling words; cf. li. 7.

XLIV. 1–5. THE INCREASE OF 'THE LORD'S' PEOPLE

2. יְשֻׁרוּן] LXX, P, and some MSS. T, read יִשְׂרָאֵל. They are supported by four Hebrew MSS. but that they were interpreting is evident from the expansive ὁ ἠγαπημένος 'Ισραὴλ of LXX (see below). V *rectissime* and minor Gr. versions also support MT.

4. בְּבֵין] Read כְּבֵין with 10 MSS., Q[a], LXX, T.

5. יְכַנֶּה . . . יִקְרָא Point יִקָּרֵא (so *Σ*, cf. xlviii. 1) and יְכֻנֶּה (P).

Yahweh will take measures to ensure the increase of his people in numbers and influence. This increase is likened to the rapid growth of trees that flourish where there is abundance of water. Not only so, but non-Israelites will signify, both by word and by written declaration, their allegiance to Yahweh.

Like xliii. 1, which also follows a reproach, the passage begins with an anacrustic *But now*, and is a message of consolation. Once more, Jacob-Israel is Yahweh's *servant*, his *chosen* (both words repeated for emphasis in ver. 2), *made* and *formed* by him: see on xli. 8–10, xliii. 7. Again, too, there is the encouragement to banish fear and to expect the divine help: same references. There had been some danger that the Israelite community would dwindle in exile. (The North Israelites who were deported to Assyria are lost to history.) Some no doubt were attracted by the splendours of Babylon, and Jer. xxix. 6 is evidence that there had been unwillingness to marry, in the expectation of a speedy return. The pouring out of *water* and *copious rains* (ver. 3) does not refer to the transformation of the desert in preparation for the new Exodus (as in xli. 17 f., xliii. 19), but to the increase of the Israelite population, which will be effected by the out-pouring of Yahweh's spirit. The only problem presented by the passage is whether ver. 5 refers to the reclamation of defaulting Jews, or to proselytes from the heathen. If it is to the latter, the thought is introduced abruptly, and yet the language seems to require this interpretation: no Israelite born would need to call himself Jacob, or to add the name Israel to his own.

2. *in the womb*] Cf. xliv. 24, xlix. 1, 5. Heb. 'from the womb' must mean 'from (the time you were conceived in) the womb', not 'from (the time you came out of) the womb'. The words go with the preceding *who formed you* (so the Massoretic punctuation), not with *and will help you* following. The initial 'forming' of a people, as of a person, is *in the womb* (Job xxxi. 15; Ps. cxxxix. 13–16; cf. Job x. 8–11). Israel's 'forming', like Jeremiah's (Jer. i. 5), was antenatal. There may be reminiscence of the antenatal struggle between Jacob and Esau (Gen. xxv. 22 f.). Indeed, according to Genesis, all previous history had been a preparation for the calling of Israel (see on xli. 8–10), though that, strictly, is outside the thought of the present passage. *Jeshurun*] The name is attested from Deut. xxxii. 15, xxxiii. 5, 26; Ecclus. xxxvii. 25. It is presumably an honorific name for Israel, and related to *yāšār*, 'upright', in contrast to Jacob ('deceiver', 'overreacher', cf. Gen. xxvii. 36, xxxii. 28). The form is similar to Zebulun, Jeduthun, and some have thought that the ending *-ûn* is a diminutive. (Diminutives are often used to express affection.) This view is now for the most part abandoned (*GK* 86 *g*) but *BL* (p. 501) still inclines to it.

3. *the thirsty*] Heb. *ṣāmē'* is masculine and strictly should not be translated 'thirsty land' (as RV mg., RSV), since all words denoting land are feminine, unless of course the masculine could be used in the first stich without serious violation of grammar. But in any case the following context indicates that *thirsty* (land) and *dry ground* are metaphors for 'those who are thirsty'. *copious rains*] 'streams' (RV, RSV), if rivers are intended, is going beyond the meaning of Heb. *nôzᵉlîm* (√ 'descend'). Note the following 'upon' and cf. xlv. 8, 'let the skies rain victory'; Job xxxvi. 28, 'which the skies pour down'. *I will pour my spirit*] For a similar metaphor (but with *šāpak̠*, not *yāṣaḳ*) see Ezek. xxxix. 29; Joel ii. 28 f. (*iii. 1 f.*); Zech. xii. 10. Whether this implies that the OT conceived of 'spirit' (*rûᵃḥ*) as fluid substance (so Volz, *Der Geist Gottes*, 1910) need not concern us here. But Volz is right when he says that there is no thought in the present text of spiritual energies, that 'the *rûᵃḥ* here is the divine energy which creates physical life, as in xxxii. 15; Ps. civ. 30; or as in Ezek. xxxvii, where it wakens the dead bones': see also on xlii. 5. *my blessing*] Cf. Mal. iii. 10, where 'blessing' is 'emptied out' from the opened 'windows of heaven'. *your children . . . your children's children*] Heb. 'your seed . . . your offspring' (*ṣe'ᵉṣā'ĕk̠ā*, see on xlii. 5). T 'sons and sons' sons'. 'Seed', 'offspring', 'progeny' are now somewhat archaic and besides convey the suggestion of remote posterity. That is unlikely to be the meaning here: Lev. xxii. 13 (cf. 1 Sam. i. 11) speaks of a widow who has no child (*zera'*, 'seed'), and Job xxi. 8 says of the wicked, 'their children ("seed") are established in their presence, and their offspring before their eyes'.

4. *grow apace*] Heb. *ṣāmaḥ*, like Engl. 'sprout', is not confined to the initial germination of plants: cf. Exod. x. 5; Ezek. xvii. 6; Eccles. ii. 6. **like* the verdant poplar*] Heb. *kᵉb̠în ḥāṣîr*. It is now certain that the difficult Heb. *bên* in this passage is not the preposition 'between' but the 'ben-tree' (*SOED*, i. 168*a*, s.v. *sb.*³), a species of *moringa* (*SOED*, *s.v.*), remarkable for the intense greenness of its leaves. The word is found in Arabic, Aramaic–Syriac, and Akkadian (Muss-Arnolt, *Assyrian Dictionary*, 178*b*). It was probably the *Populus euphratica*, pointing *bên pᵉrāt̠* in the hitherto enigmatical Gen. xlix. 22. See J. M. Allegro in *ZAW* 63, 1951, pp. 154–6 and 64, 1952, pp. 249–51. *watercourses*] Heb. *yib̠ᵉlê māyim*, 'conduits of water'. Except in Ecclus. l. 8, the word occurs only in xxx. 25, where it is associated with *pᵉlāg̠îm*, artificial irrigation canals fed by a river (cf. Ps. xlvi. 4 (*5*); Prov. xxi. 1). RSV 'flowing streams' is restrictive for an expression which could include both rivers and Babylonian canals.

5. *will sign himself as 'The LORD's*] Heb. 'will write his hand "To Yahweh" '. Most commentators take this to mean that the convert will brand or tattoo his hand with the word 'The LORD's', this with reference to 1 Kings xx. 41; Ezek. ix. 4; Rev. vii. 3 (on the forehead), and Rev. xiii. 16 (on the right hand or the forehead). But Israelite religion discouraged self-mutilation (Lev. xix. 28). The 'binding' of passages like the *Shema* on the hand and forehead is enjoined in Deut. vi. 8, xi. 18; Prov. vii. 3; cf. Exod. xiii. 16; but it is doubtful whether 'will write his hand "To Yahweh" ' can mean even this, though the thought may not be far removed from it. The √*ktb may* originally have meant 'to engrave' (cf. Gr. *γράφειν*) and early writing was epigraphic, but that is not to say that the verb *kāṯaḇ* retained the sense of 'incise'. Still less is there any example of *kāṯaḇ* = 'incise' with two accusatives. 'His hand' could be instrumental accusative, 'write with his hand'. But with what else should a man write? It is just possible that it may be accusative of place, and so 'upon his hand', but this would be needlessly obscure. When Yahweh says 'I have graven you on the palms', he says so unambiguously (*'al-kappayim ḥaḳḳōṯîḵ*, xlix. 16). Some would read *beyāḏô* for *yāḏô*, supposing that a *bêth* has been omitted by haplography. But if this means 'on' (Kissane) or *in* (Volz) his hand, Hebrew would surely have said *'al*: so all the passages cited in the foregoing, to which add Exod. xxxix. 30. It is best to take 'his hand' as acc. obj., as we might write 'Witness my hand . . .'. The meaning of ver. 5 is that converts to Yahwism will testify their allegiance both by word of mouth and/or in writing. *and add to his name the surname Israel*] Lit. 'and be titled (*yeḵunnêh*) with the name Israel': cf. xlv. 4, where Yahweh says to Cyrus, 'I give you a title of honour'; Job xxxii. 21 f. (AV, RV, 'give flattering titles'); Ecclus. xliv. 23, xlvii. 6. The verb is related to Arab. *kunyā*, a kind of surname whereby a man, after the birth of a son, comes to be styled '*Abū* (Father of) So-and-So'. In the same way a proselyte will style himself a 'son (*ben*) of Israel'.

Nothing is said of any mass-conversion of the heathen: the proselytes are to come in by ones and twos, as indeed they subsequently did (cf. lvi. 3–8). The passage is remarkable as being perhaps the earliest in which what we may call the Church is conceived of as a community transcending the boundaries of race. In the ancient world there was no thought of a supra-national or supra-racial faith (cf. 1 Sam. xxvi. 19). A man's religion was determined by his birth, or it might be that a people who were incorporated into an empire would adopt the religion of the conquering power. Only in the NT does the Church become truly international. This was necessitated by the very nature of the Gospel and was made possible by the Roman Empire, which admitted to its citizenship men of diverse races. It was anticipated and foreshadowed by the Prophet of the Exile.

XLIV. 6–8. YAHWEH IS THE ONLY GOD

6. LXX omits the first יהוה, probably rightly: xli. 21 has מֶלֶךְ יַעֲקֹב with יהוה earlier in the verse. Here מֶלֶךְ־יִשְׂרָאֵל is defined by יהוה צְבָאוֹת following.

7. וּמִי־כָמוֹנִי] Add יַעֲמֹד וְ with LXX (στήτω καὶ). מִשּׂוּמִי עַם־עוֹלָם וְאֹתִיּוֹת] Lit. 'from my placing an/the ancient people' makes no sense, especially in relation to what follows. It is usual to emend to מִי הִשְׁמִיעַ מֵעוֹלָם אֹתִיּוֹת, 'who announced (sing.) coming events long ago?' but this is not a suitable || to the next stich, in which the verb is plural. If we must conjecture, why not מַשְׁמִיעֵי (constr. before מִן, cf. xxviii. 9) מֵעוֹלָם אֹתִיּוֹת? (Torrey reads מַשְׁמִיעַ.) This would make a passable protasis (the ptc. being *casus pendens*) to a conditional sentence with the force of 'those who ages ago announced coming events should be able to tell us (*or* can doubtless tell us, *waw apodosis*, cf. Exod. xii. 15; 1 Sam. ii. 13; Prov. xxiii. 24: *GK* 116 *w*, 159 *i*) what the future still holds'. If they could do the one they should be able to do the other (cf. xlii. 9). לָמוֹ] Read לָנוּ (T).

8. תִּרְהוּ] No √רהה is attested. It is simplest to read תִּירְאוּ (Q[a] תיראו). Torrey says this would be an anticlimax after תִּפְחֲדוּ, but see Mic. vii. 17; Deut. ii. 25, xi. 25. Others emend to תִּרְהֲבוּ, in Arabic, Syriac, and Akkadian sense 'be alarmed'. The verb is found in iii. 5; Ps. cxxxviii. 3; Prov. vi. 3; Song vi. 5; Ecclus. xiii. 8, though not in the required sense except perhaps in the Song passage. It is much the same whichever of the two emendations we adopt. הִשְׁמַעְתִּיךָ] Either delete the suffix or, better in this context, read the plural הִשְׁמַעְתִּיכֶם. וְאַתֶּם עֵדָי וגו׳] These words are, metrically and grammatically, difficult to construe: lit. 'and yóu are my wítnesses / is there a Gód except mé ? / and there is no Róck. I know nóne' (? 2:2:2). It is usual to read אֱלֹהִים for אֱלוֹהַּ (*mêm* omitted by haplography), but אלוה and צור are || in Deut. xxxii. 15; Ps. xviii. 31 (*32*), of which the present passage may be reminiscent. בַּל־יָדָעְתִּי] looks at first sight like a dittograph of מִבַּלְעָדַי, but DI's fondness for paronomasia is against deleting it, or (with Köhler) substituting מִבַּלְעָדַי for it at the end of the verse. That מבלעדי could have something of the force of 'without my knowledge and approval' is clear from Num. v. 20; 2 Kings xviii. 25 = Isa. xxxvi. 10; Jer. xliv. 19. This is exactly what we want: 'Is there a God without my knowledge?' (Answer: 'Certainly not!') Put affirmatively this means, *There is no other God to my knowledge*, and finally, catching up the paronomasia, *nor any Rock. I know none.*

The content of this passage is similar to that of xliii. 8–13. The text appears to have suffered in transmission but it can be restored by reference to LXX and, for once in a way, by conjectural emendation. Yahweh is again introduced as *Israel's King* (see on xli. 21, xliii. 15) and *Redeemer* (see on xli. 14). To this is added, for the first time in the prophecy, the title *the LORD of hosts* (*Yahwêh ṣᵉḇā'ôṯ*). From now on it appears with some frequency: xlv. 13, xlvii. 4, xlviii. 2, li. 15, liv. 5. In two of these passages (xlvii. 4, liv. 5) it is associated with Yahweh as Israel's Redeemer (as here) and with the title 'the Holy One of Israel'. The expression occurs in all 279 times, of which 245 are in the prophets. (There is none in Gen.–Judges.) The earliest forms were 'Yahweh the God of hosts' (14 times) and 'Yahweh the God of the hosts' (*haṣṣᵉḇā'ôṯ*, Amos iii. 13, vi. 14; Hos. xii. 6). The shortened *Yahwêh ṣᵉḇā'ôṯ* is found 255 times. It has been thought that the 'hosts' were originally the armies of Israel, this because of the association of the expression with the Ark (1 Sam. iv. 4 f.; 2 Sam. vi. 2; cf. 1 Sam. xvii. 45, 'Yahweh of hosts, the God of the battle-ranks of Israel'). However this may be—1 Sam. xvii. 45 is probably a late passage—in the prophets, where Yahweh so frequently threatens Israel, the hosts can hardly be the armies of Israel. The view that the hosts are the stars (cf. Judges v. 20) is open to the objection that the stars are 'the host (sing.) of heaven' (Deut. iv. 19, xvii. 3; 2 Kings xvii. 16, xxi. 3, 5+; cf. Gen. ii. 1; Isa. xl. 26). The same applies to the angels (Joshua v. 14 f.?; 1 Kings xxii. 19; Ps. cxlviii. 2 *Keth.*; and so, probably, read the singular in Ps. ciii. 21). All in all, and in view of the fact that *ṣᵉḇā'ôṯ* is without the def. art., it is best to think of the 'hosts' as 'the content of all that exists in heaven and earth' (so W. Eichrodt, *The Theology of the OT*, i, pp. 192–4; similarly O. S. Rankin, 'Names of God', in *A Theological Word Book of the Bible*, ed. A. Richardson, p. 95). This must surely be the sense in the present text. The titles *Israel's King and Redeemer*, *the LORD of hosts*, are gathered up in the comprehensive *I am the first and I am the last*; *there is no God but me*: cf. xli. 4, xliii. 10 f., xlv. 5 f., xlviii. 12. These words are the original of 'I am the Alpha and the Omega' (Rev. i. 8, 17, xxi. 6, xxii. 13).

7. The gods (presumably) are again challenged to a legal process. *If anyone thinks he is like me, let him . . .*] Lit. 'and who is like me, let him . . .'. The construction is similar to Jer. xlix. 19, lit. 'and who(ever) is chosen, I will appoint him'. (There is hardly any limit to the constructions of quasi-conditional sentences in Heb.; cf. *GK* 159 *a*, *b*) *and state his case*] Lit. 'and arrange it to/for me'. The verb (*'āraḵ*) is used of setting forth a legal case: Job xiii. 18, xxiii. 4. In xli. 22 the gods had been challenged to explain the significance of

events in the past, and to announce future happenings. They might with some show of confidence claim that they had done the former. Very well! Let them *tell *us* what the future still holds!* *ages ago . . . long ago* (ver. 8)] Heb. *mēʿôlām . . . mē'āz*. It is not possible to define precisely the *termini a quo* of these expressions. The first is used in xlii. 14 and xlvi. 9, and in Gen. vi. 4; Joshua xxiv. 2, and the Mesha Inscription line 10 can only mean 'long ago'. The second (lit. 'from then') occurs in xlv. 21, xlviii. 3, 5, 7, 8, where it means rather indefinitely 'in time past', and in Gen. xxxix. 5; Exod. v. 23; Joshua xiv. 10; 2 Sam. xv. 34; Isa. xiv. 8; Jer. xliv. 18, with the implication 'quite recently'. Obviously, both expressions in the present context must refer to times within history. Even *mērô'š* ('from the beginning'), xl. 21, xli. 4, 26, xlviii. 16, must not be pressed too hard. These terms have a way of fading into one another. At the same time, in DI, with his conceptions of God's 'eternity' and a beginning of time, we are on the verge of the illimitable: both expressions occur in Ps. xciii. 2, cf. Ecclus. xlii. 21 (E. Jenni, *Das Wort ʿōlām im AT*, 1953, p. 29). History is under the control of the Prime Mover of all things.

8. *There is no other God to my knowledge*] As though conceding that he might conceivably be ignorant, though of course the words also mean *there is no God but me*, as in ver. 6 (see grammatical note, *supra*). The final *I know none* is decisive enough. Torrey would take it as a subordinate adjectival clause, '(whom) I do not know'. But the negative *bal* is against this. Although it is the common negative in Phoenician, and in Hebrew is a poetical synonym of the ordinary *lô'*, it has a certain sharp emphasis, e.g. in xliii. 17, xliv. 9 (*ter*). *Rock*] This epithet for God would sound bizarre if it occurred only here. But it occurs 33 times in OT, chiefly in Deut. xxxii. and Ps.: see the Concordance. It is often || God and Yahweh. That it did not originate with DI is obvious from the fact that it is found in conjunction with *selaʿ* ('crag'), *miśgāḇ* ('inaccessible height'), *mᵉṣûḏāh* ('fastness'), features which are familiar in Palestine but absent in Babylonia: cf. Ps. xviii. 2 (*3*). Other peoples than Israel might be said to have their 'rock' (Deut. xxxii. 31, 37; 1 Sam. ii. 2; 2 Sam. xxii. 32), though this was only make-believe on their part: so here. When Yahweh says of other gods, *there is no rock*, he implies that he is *the* Rock (cf. Deut. xxxii. 4). The OT never says that Yahweh is *like* a rock but that he *is* the Rock. The word 'designates Jehovah, by a forcible and expressive figure, as the unchangeable support or refuge of His servants; and is used with evident appropriateness, where the thought is of God's unvarying attitude towards His people' (S. R. Driver, *Deuteronomy*, *I.C.C.*, p. 350; see also J. Begrich in *ZAW* 46, 1928, pp. 254 f.).

XLIV. 9–20. THE STUPIDITY OF IDOLATRY

9. הֵ֫מָּה] The *puncta extraordinaria* (*GK* 5 *n*, *BL* § 6 *r*, *s*) probably indicate that the letters are a dittograph from the preceding word. They are otiose and in Q[a] are inserted above the line.

10. וּפֶסֶל נָסָךְ] *Waw apodosis*, construction similar to ver. 7 preceding.

12. מַעֲצָד] Only here and Jer. x. 3. (Nothing can be based on the conjectural emendation מַעֲצָד for מַעֲרָצָה in Isa. x. 33.) But MT 'The ironsmith the axe' hardly makes sense. And what should an ironsmith be doing with a woodworker's (Jer. x. 3) tool which appears to have been something like a bill-hook (cf. Gezer Calendar, line 3, 'the month of the cutting [עצד] of flax', Arab. *miʿḍad*, 'reaping-hook')? Torrey emends to מְעַצֵּב, 'The ironsmith cuts the metal', but this destroys the ‖ with חָרַשׁ עֵצִים, 'the woodworker' in ver. 13. LXX *ὤξυνεν τέκτων σίδηρον* omits מַעֲצָד and repeats יחד (pointing יָחַד) from the preceding verse (similarly P). It seems best to omit מַעֲצָד. וּפָעַל] Read יִפְעַל.

14. לִכְרָת] Read כָּרַת or יִכְרֹת, unless we take the infinitive to indicate purpose: 'He goes out to cut'. Or a preceding הָלַךְ, 'he goes', may have been omitted by haplography. ארן] (*sic*) The *ἅπ. λεγ.* אֹרֶן (Akk. *erinu*, ? *Laurus nobilis*) is attested from Q[a] and T, but the minuscule *nûn* (*GK* 5 *n*) suggests that the reading was uncertain. To read אֶרֶז, 'cedar'—so some MSS.—is open to the objection that cedars have already been listed. The Hebrew is clumsy and catalogical. LXX is shorter, probably based on כָּרַת־לוֹ בַּעֲצֵי יַעַר נָטַע אֹרֶן וְגֶשֶׁם יְגַדֵּל. This shorter text may be original. (The same applies to other parts of the passage, to judge from comparison of the text with the versions.) It is curious that LXX read ארן as אָדֹן, 'the Lord' (*dāleth* and *rêsh* could be indistinguishable in the old script—ᐊ), though it mistook it as the subject, not the object, of נָטַע—*ὃ ἐφύτευσεν ὁ κύριος*. It is tempting to translate 'he plants an Adonis(-tree)'. Although Adonis-Tammuz was mostly associated with the revival and decay of annual vegetation (cf. the Adonis-plantations of xvii. 10, RSV 'pleasant plants'), there are indications of his earlier (?) association with trees: cf. W. W. Graf Baudissin, *Adonis und Esmun*, p. 103; I. Engnell, *Studies in Divine Kingship*, pp. 25 ff. *et passim* and literature cited. On the other hand, nowhere, so far as is known, is the equation Adonis = Adonis-tree found. Nor does Isa. xliv. 9–20 point to a specifically Adonis cult.

15. יַשִּׂיק] *Hiph.* שלק, 'cause to ascend', i.e. 'burn'. לָמוֹ] If this cannot mean 'to it', it would seem necessary to emend to לוֹ, though the writer is not too particular about his concords: e.g. מֵהֶם in this verse.

16. There are differences of reading in this verse as between MT, Q[a] and LXX. It is usual to emend the second חֶצְיוֹ to גֶּחָלָיו, 'its embers', this—it is said—with reference to LXX, to the reading in ver. 19, and because two halves make a whole and so there could be nothing left over (as in ver. 17). LXX[B] and Q[a] repeat חציו, followed by גחליו. The argument from LXX is therefore overstated, the more so since MSS which do not repeat חציו say nothing about 'coals'. We should not expect arithmetical exactitude in satire of this kind. It would be just like the writer to say that after the two halves had been burned, the foolish man, now warmed and fed, proceeded to make a god out of the bits and pieces. יֹאכֵל יִצְלֶה] The order of these words should probably be inverted: cf. LXX. רָאִיתִי] Q[a] נגד, 'I am warm in front of the fire', lacks the assonance and vividness of the last three words of MT.

18. טַח] Either *Qal* pf. 3rd pers. sing. masc. טחח with impersonal subject: 'it is smeared (*as to*, acc. of specification) their eyes'; or, with the same parsing, since the verb precedes the subject, it may disagree in gender and number (*GK* 145 *o*).

There is now more reluctance to say that this passage is not from DI than there was in the generation following Duhm. If it were missing it would not be missed, but the same could be said of a score of other passages in the prophecy. Verses 21–23 would follow ver. 8 more naturally than they do ver. 20, though this is not a conclusive argument that they should. By some, but not by Duhm, the passage is read as prose: e.g. *BH* and Volz, though the latter thinks that its Deutero-Isaianic origin is 'quite credible'. Parallelism is discernible throughout but it is not great poetry. It was not intended to be; it is a kind of 'Skeltonical' doggerel which suits its theme admirably. It is not addressed to makers of idols but is a satirical description of their antic stupidity. If it was intended for an audience contemporary with the Prophet, they must have been exiles who were in danger of being seduced by the idolatry around them. Let them see it for what it really is! Though again, what is castigated is not idolatry in the grandiose manner of xl. 19 f. but a paltry home-made variety, almost a casual sequel to the drudgery of house-warming and cooking. The two Aramaisms, *yaśśîḳ* (ver. 15, elsewhere only in the late Ps. lxxviii. 21 and Ezek. xxxix. 9) and *yisgoḏ/'esgōḏ* (vv. 15, 17, 19, elsewhere only xlvi. 6, *which see*) are suspicious, even though by the time of the exile Aramaic may have begun to oust Akkadian. Aramaisms in Hebrew OT are mostly early, when the two languages were not yet fully differentiated, or late, when Hebrew was in decline.

On the whole, it is probable that xliv. 9–20 is not from DI, any more than Jer. x. 1–10 (16) is from Jeremiah. Did the Prophet essay such an anatomical description of idolatry? Not that it matters very much, or that the passage is irrelevant in its context. The commandment 'You shall not make yourself a graven image' is, on the prophetic level of discourse, the logical sequel to 'You shall have no other God in my presence' (Exod. xx. 3 f.). Someone, if not DI himself, was almost bound to point that out in a context which insists so strongly on the transcendence and sole deity of Yahweh.

It has been said that 'the prophet seems nowhere to reveal any true understanding of the pagan mind on this subject. He does not sense the numinous quality in the idol, the thing that evoked wonder and awe and reverence and fear before it' (Muilenburg, *in loc.*). This is broadly true, though it needs some little qualification. In point of fact, classical writers could be just as caustic about idolatry as this passage is: e.g. Horace (*Satires* i. 8 ff.), who is quoted by commentators, among them Muilenburg:

> Olim truncus eram ficulnus, inutile lignum,
> Cum faber, incertus, scamnum faceretne Priapum,
> Maluit esse deum.

Notwithstanding its grim but boisterous satire, xliv. 9–20 does at least seem aware of the almost crazy fear evoked by the idol. And in so far as Muilenburg's comment is true, it might support the conclusion that the passage is from a lesser man than DI. Though not necessarily: not even a prophet would have appreciated the Hindu philosophy of idolatry, supposing that it could have been expounded to him. A Hindu yogi would justify the practice of idolatry, not for himself, but for the masses who know no better, the 'lesser breeds' who are to all intents and purposes polytheists. The OT knows nothing of the distinction between an idol in which the god is supposed to reside, and which may therefore be said to be identical with the god, and a symbol intended to remind the worshipper of God's presence. We may regret that, if only because the ancient Hebrews contributed nothing to the plastic arts. But such a distinction is hard to maintain, with the result that the Jew, to be on the safe side, almost without exception eschewed animal symbols, even in two dimensions, altogether. When all is said, crude idolatry is no better than the Bible depicts it. If we look for a reasoned anti-philosophy of idolatry, we can find it in Wisd. xiii. f. And the conclusion there is no less devastating than it is here. The truth is that monotheism with its aniconic, and pantheism-cum-polytheism with its iconic—to use an inoffensive adjective—worship, are based on different, and perhaps irreconcilable, conceptions of Reality.

9. *empty-heads*] *tôhû*, see on xl. 17. *their darlings*] *ḥamûḏêhem*. Cf. Dan. xi. 37, 'the darling (*ḥemdaṯ*) of women', i.e. Tammuz. *their* *devotees*] Lit. 'their witnesses'. Some would emend to *ʿaḇᵉḏêhem*, 'their servants' or 'worshippers', of which also *devotees* could be a valid paraphrase. But 'their witnesses' should be retained. Just as the Israelites are Yahweh's 'witnesses' (cf. ver. 8 immediately preceding; xliii. 10, 12), the idol-gods may be said to have their witnesses (xliii. 9). Indeed, 'their witnesses' may well be a catchword prompting the placing of this passage after ver. 8.

10. *to no purpose or use*] Lit. 'in order not to profit'. The negative *biltî* with infinitive conveys the suggestion of purpose, as though the result had been the intention.

11. *his accomplices*] *ḥᵃḇērâw*. To read this as 'workers of spells' (*ḥôḇᵉrâw*) with reference to T (so *BH*), is to go beyond what T ('their worshippers') says.

13. *crayon*] *śereḏ*, ἅπ. λεγ., probably 'red chalk' (cf. 'red ochre', RV mg.). *chisels*] *maḳṣûʿôṯ*, ἅπ. λεγ. 'scraping tools', Arab. √*ḳḍʿ*. 'Set-squares' (Arab. √*ḳṭʿ*, cf. the 'corners' of Exod. xxvi. 23 f.; Ezek. xli. 22) would give an equally suitable meaning in the context: cf. Torrey *in loc.*

14. *selects*] Lit. 'takes'. For this sense cf. Deut. i. 15, 23; Joshua iii. 12; 1 Kings xi. 37. *makes his choice*] Lit. 'strengthens for himself'. For this sense of 'strengthen' = 'secure' (for one's advantage) cf. Ps. lxxx. 17 (*16*).

15. *prostrates himself*] √*sgd* is that from which *masǧid*, 'mosque', lit. 'place of prostration', is derived.

17. *his idol*] Comes in lamely and some (e.g. Levy, Kissane) would delete. But the bathos was probably intentional.

19. *a loathsome thing*] *tôʿēḇāh*, one of a number of stock opprobrious epithets for 'idol' (cf. C. R. North, 'The Essence of Idolatry', in *Von Ugarit nach Qumran, Festschrift für Otto Eissfeldt*, hrsg. J. Hempel und L. Rost, 1958, pp. 151–60). The word itself is old enough but Torrey is probably right when he says, 'It is hardly likely that תועבה was already a current synonym for "god" (i.e. idol) in the time of the Second Isaiah'. But, as he observes, it may have been substituted for an original *ʾᵉlôhîm* ('god') or the like, as in 2 Kings xxiii. 13.

Little remains to be said on a passage which is on the whole straightforward. Notwithstanding its apparent doggerel simplicity, it shows acute observation and psychological penetration. The meticulous fuss of the whole business! The material from which the idol is made! Wood, remnants after a man has lighted his fire and cooked his food (this last detail thrice repeated, vv. 15 f., 19)! The climax of irony comes when the accuser puts the indictment into the mouth of the idol-worshipper, as if he would perforce acknowledge the truth of it, if only he had any sense (ver. 19)!

XLIV. 21–23. YAHWEH'S JOY AND PRIDE IN ISRAEL

21. תִנָּשֵׁנִי] The only other example of a *Niph.* with pron. sf. is in Ps. cix. 3, where the verb has acquired the transitive sense 'attack'. Some would point תִנְשֵׁנִי (*Qal*), 'you must not forget me', so some versions and RV mg. This accords well with *Remember* at the beginning of the verse, but a less pleading and more forceful negative seems called for. Fischer (*in loc.*) conjectured תַשִּׁאֵנִי (*Hiph.* נשא, 'beguile', 'deceive', cf. Gen. iii. 13). This is now supported by Q[a] תשאני.

These verses are one § in RV, two in RSV. Much of their content is paralleled elsewhere (cf. xli. 8, 14, xlii. 11, xliii. 1). Some regard them as two short independent units, or perhaps fragments, vv. 21 f. and 23. Some think that ver. 21 originally followed ver. 8, and although feeling in a matter of this kind is no certain guide, it does seem a more natural sequel to vv. 6–8 than to vv. 9–20. Others take ver. 23 as an introduction to the divine pronouncement in 24–28, on the ground that in OT liturgies a pronouncement is sometimes prefaced by a hymn of praise (as in xlii. 10–17; Ps. lxxxi, xcv). Since the relation of their parts to their contexts, and to one another, is uncertain, they are here for convenience treated together.

21. **play false with**] Lit. 'deceive' (see textual note). Lest the textual emendation should seem to rob the text of the assurance 'you will not be forgotten by me' (EVV), see xlix. 15.

22. *I have wiped out*] Cf. xliii. 25. As rapidly and completely as clouds disperse before the rising sun (Hos. vi. 4, xiii. 3; Job vii. 9, xxx. 15), so Yahweh has wiped out his people's *rebellious past* (lit. 'rebellions'). So far in the prophecy the redemption of Israel has referred to the coming release from Babylon. Here the word has taken on a deeper meaning, that of redemption from sin and guilt: cf. Jer. xxxi. 18, 34; Ps. cxxx. 8). With such an assurance Israel may *come back* to Yahweh with entire confidence.

23. *deep abysses*] 'The nether world' (RSV) or 'Pit' (Ezek. xxvi 20, xxxi. 14, 16, 18, xxxii. 18, 24; Ps. lxxxviii. 6 (7); Lam. iii. 55), i.e. Sheol (Deut. xxxii. 22; Ps. lxxxvi. 13). In Ps. vi. 5 (*6*) (cf. Ps. lxxxviii.

5 f.) Sheol is assumed to be outside Yahweh's jurisdiction, a place where no one praises him. But already in Amos ix. 2 those who 'dig into Sheol' are mistaken if they imagine they have escaped from Yahweh. The present passage is in line with Ps. cxxxix. 7–9, where heaven, earth and sea, and Sheol, are all within his domain. See further lv. 12 for the acclamation of mountains and forest. *and points to Israel as his crowning achievement*] *yiṯpā'ār*; cf. xlix. 3, lx. 21, lxi. 3; lit. 'will get himself glory (or beauty) by means of Israel'. The verb is not the usual one for 'glory' (√*kbd*), though it is || with it in lx. 13. With a human subject it conveys the suggestion of boasting: cf. x. 15; Judges vii. 2, or, ironically, 'assuming the honour', so Moses to Pharaoh, Exod. viii. 5. It is used only thirteen times, of which eight are in Isa. xl–lxvi. The cognate languages give no clue to the meaning of the √, but the nouns *pᵉ'ēr* and *tip̄'ereṯ* suggest that the action of the verb was accompanied by the wearing of finery, particularly on the head. A *pᵉ'ēr* was some kind of festive garland or head-dress (of a bridegroom, lxi. 10; of feminine fashion, iii. 20; of priests' 'turbans', Exod. xxxix. 28; Ezek. xliv. 18; or as a sign of gladness instead of mourning, lxi. 3; Ezek. xxiv. 17, 23). The more frequent *tip̄'ereṯ* is used of women's finery (iii. 18), of festive garments (lii. 1), of jewels (Ezek. xvi. 17, 39, xxiii. 26), of the adornment of the temple (lx. 7), and in the alliterative expression *'ᵃṭereṯ tip̄'ereṯ* (lxii. 3; Jer. xiii. 18; Ezek. xvi. 12, xxiii. 42; Prov. iv. 9, xvi. 31), which RSV translates, fairly enough, 'beautiful crown', except at lxii. 3, 'crown of beauty', and Prov. xvi. 31, 'crown of glory', both very appropriately. To translate that Yahweh 'will show himself off by means of Israel' would not be quite reverent but it would bring out the picturesque in the text. We need not imagine anything bombastic, any more than in Prov. xvi. 31: 'A hoary head is a crown of glory' (or 'a beautiful crown'). In lxii. 3 the promise is that Israel is to be 'a crown of beauty in the hand of Yahweh' and there is much in Isa. xl–lxvi to suggest that the redeemed Israel is his proudest achievement.

XLIV. 24–28. THE CURTAIN RISES FOR CYRUS

24. מֵאִתִּי] Some of the best MSS, and *Qere*, read 'from with me', i.e. very nearly 'by myself' (AV). The compound preposition מֵאֵת is quite normal Hebrew, though the sense 'originating from' (Yahweh) is comparatively infrequent: but see Joshua xi. 20; 1 Kings xii. 24; and, of the word of prophecy, Jer. vii. 1+. *Qere* gives a good || to לְבַדִּי preceding and is still favoured by Volz and Fischer. But *Keth.* מִי אִתִּי, 'who was with me?' is to be preferred: it is supported by Q[a] מיא אתי, by LXX (*τίς ἕτερος*) and V, and is the kind of rhetorical question which DI loves. The meaning is much the same either way: 'who was with me?' implies 'by myself (alone)', and vice versa.

25. בַּדִּים] Elsewhere only xvi. 6; Jer. xlviii. 30, l. 36; Job xi. 3. In the first two and last of these passages the meaning must be 'idle talk' (RSV 'boasts', 'babble'), similarly Phoenician and Syriac, and (conjecturally) lviii. 13 (RSV 'talking idly'). Here and in Jer. l. 36, if the readings are correct, the word must have the concrete sense of 'idle-talkers', but in view of the || קֹסְמִים (see below) it is tempting to read בָּרִים (see on אדן/ארן, xliv. 14 above), the *bārū*-priests, whose functions were similar to those of the Roman *haruspices*. The word is Akkadian and DI would be familiar with it. But the memory of it would be lost to later scribes. Once more, perhaps, a conflate translation, *wordy prognosticators*, may be permitted. יְשַׂכֵּל] A variant of יסכל, so Codex prophetarum Cairensis and Q[a]. For lexicons see under ס.

26. עַבְדּוֹ] Can be read either as 'his servant' (so, as pointed, EVV) or 'his servants' (pointed עֲבָדָו). There are frequent examples of defective writing of 3rd pers. sing. masc. sf. with plural nouns (see *GK* 91 *k*). The || *his envoys* is in favour of 'his servants': so LXX[A] and T. It is impossible to dogmatize, but on the whole the Massoretic pointing is to be preferred: see below. וּלְעָרֵי יְהוּדָה תִּבָּנֶינָה] There is much to be said for regarding this stich as an expansion (so Köhler). The only other tristich in 24–28 is in 24*b*, where it heightens the poetry. Here it weakens it and the sing. sf. in *her ruins* refers back to Jerusalem. The addition, if such it is, is quite in the spirit of the original (cf. xl. 9).

28b. Lit. 'and saying of Jerusalem, "She shall be (re)built" and the temple, "You shall be (re)founded".' (cf. RV). This is difficult to construe and it is usual to read הָאֹמֵר (so LXX, V) for וְלֵאמֹר and וְלַהֵיכָל (so V) for וְהֵיכָל. Duhm transferred 28*b* (with some verbal corrections) to 26*b*, and Mowinckel (*Det Gamle Testamente*, iii, *in loc.*) would omit it altogether. Volz finds 28*b* 'suspicious' because of its badly preserved text, its repetition of what is said in 26*b*, and because DI nowhere else mentions the temple. But he ends by keeping it, with the verbal corrections already mentioned. His final word is that in the text as it stands it is Cyrus who orders the rebuilding of city and temple, cf. Ezra i. 2, vi. 3. This was already remarked by Dillmann–Kittel (*Der Prophet Jesaja erklärt*, 1898, p. 401) with reference to xlv. 13. This may well have been the sense of the original (is it the intention of RSV?): 28*a* would make an abrupt termination and some explication of Yahweh's *purpose* through Cyrus seems called for. The meaning will then be: 'by (explicative *waw*) saying of Jerusalem, "It is to be rebuilt", and to the temple (וְלַהֵיכָל), "You shall be refounded" ', i.e. substantially *by ordering* (Arab. sense of אמר, mostly late in Heb. but cf. 1 Sam. xvi. 16; 1 Kings xi. 18; Job ix. 7—any word of a king is a command) *Jerusalem to be rebuilt and the temple foundations relaid.* Or we could keep וְהֵיכָל as an accusative of specification: 'and (in regard to) the temple'; though why Jerusalem should be spoken *of* and the temple *to* does not appear, and further corrections of the text would be dubious (see further below).

This paragraph must be one of the longest sentences in the OT. Verse 24*a* introduces Yahweh as speaking; 24*b*–28 contain what he says. What he says consists of a single majestic tristich (two if we keep the second stich of 26*b*; but see above) followed by seven distichs or couplets. The tristich contains three participles and all the couplets except the last (28*b*) begin with a participle and are followed by a finite verb in the second stich. In vv. 25, 26*a*, and 28*a*, the verbs are in the 3rd pers.; in 26*b*, 27 they are in the 1st. The sentence is skilfully wrought but must have been difficult to control, especially if the prophet got 'excited' about it, and it need occasion no surprise if in the last couplet (28*b*) the concord is not such as a modern grammarian would approve. Since in 24*b* Yahweh begins with 'I who' we almost expect the finite verbs and pron. sfs. to be in the 1st pers. throughout; 'who nullify . . . and make crazed . . . my servants . . . my messengers . . . I bring to completion', &c. It is an interesting example of a prophet speaking *of* at the same time as he is speaking *for* God. By all the rules, this is temerity on his part. But it may be simply that the participle with the article is usually 3rd pers. and the Prophet forgot himself in defiance of orthodox grammar.

The passage is in the nature of a dénouement. Cyrus has already been more or less openly referred to (xli. 2 f., 25). Here he is to be named. And it is as if when it comes to the annunciation the Prophet keeps the name back as long as he can, so heightening the effect of the revelation when it comes. But the relative clauses are not so much padding, repetitions calculated to excite his audience to the impatience of boredom. Most of the detail in vv. 25–27 is new, and if it excites impatience it is the impatience of expectancy. The general trend of the argument is that Yahweh is the sole Creator, that he is Lord of history, that what he announces through the prophets is verified by subsequent events, and that events now converge upon Cyrus, *my shepherd.*

24. your Redeemer] See on xli. 14. *who formed you in the womb*] See on xliv. 2. *all that is*] Heb. *kōl*, 'all'. This is the nearest the OT comes to the conception of 'the universe' as we understand it and DI was the first, indeed the only, writer to use the word so in this its simplest form: *hakkōl* ('the all', Jer. x. 16, li. 19; Eccles. i. 2; cf. Ps. ciii. 19, cxlv. 9) is almost certainly later. The usual expression for the created world is 'the heavens and the earth' (Gen. i. 1, or, more inclusively, Exod. xx. 11; Neh. ix. 6) and this survived into NT times (cf. Matt. xi. 25; Acts xvii. 24). Volz thinks that *all* here includes history as well as revelation. To be sure, it can; creation and history are closely related in DI. But to judge from the immediately subsequent context, it is creation the Prophet has in mind at this point; history is the theme of the verses that follow. *who stretched out the heavens . . . and spread out the earth*] See on xl. 22, xlii. 5. *I alone*] Heb. lit. 'according to my separateness'. Another new feature. Some idea of the isolation and solitariness implied in the word may be gained from xlix. 21, lxiii. 3; 1 Kings xix. 10, and the ‖ 'who was with me?' There is no hint that Yahweh was 'lonely', but only the Christian revelation could have obviated abysses of speculation. Even as it is, we peer into unfathomable mystery.

25. *nullifies the omens*] Lit. 'breaks the signs'. The signs or *omens* (*'ôṯôṯ*) announced by prophets (cf. 1 Sam. x. 7, 9) were assumed to be irrevocable. To outward appearance at least, Babylonian prophets were as sure of themselves as were the prophets of Israel. Nevertheless, Yahweh 'breaks their signs'. *wordy prognosticators*] See textual note. For the Babylonian *bārū*-priests or 'seers' see A. Haldar (*Associations of Cult Prophets among the Ancient Semites*, 1945, pp. 1–12), who says that their chief function was 'to acquire and communicate knowledge of the will of the gods concerning future events' (p. 2). This they did by various means, notably by inspecting the entrails, especially the livers, of sacrificial animals (Haruspicy). *diviners*] Heb. *ḳôsᵉmîm*. Their speciality was divination by means of arrows (Belomancy), see the vivid description in Ezek. xxi. 18–23 .

23–28. *makes . . . crazed*] Cf. AV, RV. RSV 'makes fools of', similarly *BDB*, *KB*. Heb. *yᵉhôlēl* (*Pôʿēl*, *hālal*). The semantic relations of the various senses of the √ are difficult to make out: *Piʿēl* = 'praise', *Hithpaʿēl* = 'boast'; *Hithpôʿēl* = 'act like a madman' (1 Sam. xxi. 14; Jer. xxv. 16, l. 38, li. 7; and, of madly raging chariots, Jer. xlvi. 9; Nah. ii. 5). Köhler derives the *Pôʿēl* conjugations from a different but homonymous √, though there is little evidence for this in the cognates. *Pôʿēl* is found only twice outside this passage and in both of them (Job xii. 17; Eccles. vii. 7) 'crazed' will pass as well as 'foolish': cf. Ps. cii. 9 (*8*); Eccles. ii. 2 (*Pôʿal*). Folly and madness are near allied: cf. Eccles. i. 17, ii. 12, vii. 25, x. 13. If a note on Engl. 'fool' may be permitted: it comes from Lat. *follis*, 'bellows', in late popular Lat. 'wind-bag' (*SOED*., s.v.). This would suit the present context admirably. *refutes*] Lit. 'causes to return backward'. Cf. 1 Cor. i. 20.

26. *carries out*] For this sense of Heb. 'cause (word) to stand' (*mēḳîm*) cf. 1 Sam. xv. 11, 12; 1 Kings vi. 12. The ‖ *executes*, lit. 'brings to completion', means much the same. *his servant*] See textual note. If we read as 'his servants', these are the prophets (cf. Amos iii. 7). If we keep the traditional pointing, *his servant* may be Israel (cf. ver. 21 preceding; xliii. 10, which see), or, more likely, for once in a way, DI himself. We have noted his temerity in this passage. In the following context Yahweh's *word* and *purpose* are concerned with the rehabilitation of Jerusalem and the part Cyrus is to play in it, and this is a major feature in DI's message. *the purpose announced through his envoys*] Lit. 'the counsel of his messengers' (so EVV). But this 'counsel' is not advice that 'his messengers' give to Yahweh, as Hushai and Ahithophel might counsel Absalom (2 Sam. xvii. 14). It is Yahweh's *purpose* (or 'plan', 'intention'; cf. v. 19, xlvi. 10 f.; Mic. iv. 12; Ps. xxxiii. 10 f., cvii. 11), a purpose none can 'break' or 'refute' (xiv. 26 f.), and which *his envoys* (the prophets generally) are commissioned to announce. *rebuild*] *'ᵃḳômēm* (*Pô'ēl*, *ḳûm*; cf. lviii. 12, lxi. 4), probably intended to link up with *who carries out* (*mēḳîm*) *the word of his servant* at the beginning of the verse.

27. *the ocean-deep*] *ṣûlāh*, ἅπ. λεγ. But the related *mᵉṣûlāh* is used of the deep sea (Ps. lxiii. 22 (*23*), cvii. 24; Jonah ii. 3 (*4*)) and in Exod. xv. 5; Neh. ix. 11 (cf. Zech. x. 11) of the Red Sea. Note also the two words for 'dry ground' in Exod. xv. 21 f., corresponding to the two verbs for the drying up of the deep in this verse. Yahweh's control of nature is the theme of ver. 24. Here, where the scene has shifted to history, there is some allusion to the Exodus: see also on li. 9. There is also, in the Hebrew, word-play between the *ruins* of ver. 26 and the *run dry* of 27.

28. *my shepherd*] *rô'î*. For *shepherd* as the designation of a ruler see on xl. 9, and cf. 2 Sam. v. 2; Jer. iii. 15, xxiii. 1–4; Ezek. xxxiv (esp. vv. 23 f.). The word so used was common in the ancient world: cf. Hammurabi *Code* 51, Homer ποιμένα λαῶν. There are those who would point *rē'î*, 'my friend'. Even if it were so, the word is not that used of Abraham in xli. 8. Solomon had an official called 'the king's friend' (*rē'êh hammeleḵ*, 1 Kings iv. 5, Nathan) and Hushai was 'David's friend' (2 Sam. xv. 37, xvi. 16 f.). But we cannot base on this the idea of Cyrus as Yahweh's 'friend' in the sense of vizier. Moreover, *rēᵃ'* has the general sense of boon-companion, and that would never do here. *will*] *ḥēp̱eṣ*: originally 'pleasure', but already in Judges xiii. 23 the verb is acquiring the sense of 'intend'. In lviii. 3, 13 the meaning is 'business' (cf. RSV mg.). Here and in xlviii. 14; liii. 10 it is almost synonymous with the *purpose* of ver. 26; indeed, in xlvi. 10 the words are parallel.

XLV. 1–7. CYRUS YAHWEH'S ANOINTED PRINCE

1. לְרַד] *Qal* infin. constr. רדד. For the *pathaḥ* see *GK* 67 *p*. A pointing לֹרד = לְהוֹרִיד is unnecessary. The sense 'beat down' is the same as in xli. 2. The *lāmedh* indicates the purpose or intention of *whose right hand I grasp* following.

2. הֲדוּרִים] RV 'rugged places' (RSV mg. 'swellings') assumes a sense of √*hdr* otherwise unattested unless we cf. Arab. IV. 'swollen', 'inflated' (of the belly), and post-biblical Heb. 'rounded', 'zigzag'. Skinner quotes Ovid's *tumidi montes* and Milton's 'tumid hills'. But it seems best to read הֲרָרִים, 'mountains': so Q^a, LXX ὄρη. For the reduplicated *rêsh* see *GK* 93 *aa*. The meaning is much the same anyhow, especially with the verb that follows. MT may have been influenced by current Talmudic Hebrew. אֲוַשֵּׁר] Read *Qere* אֲיַשֵּׁר, as in ver. 13. For the sense cf. xl. 3.

6. מַעֲרָבָה] Lit. 'its place of setting', though there is no need to insert *mappîq* in the *hē*: cf. *GK* 91 *e*.

Cyrus is addressed as Yahweh's anointed prince, whom he has summoned by name. Yahweh declares that he will go before him in person, break down all opposition of armies and fortifications, and give him access to vast hidden wealth. He will do this because of Israel, and that the world may know that he is the sole God and the determiner of weal and woe.

The passage is to all appearance a direct address to Cyrus. It is generally assumed that the address proper begins at ver. 2. This would be very abrupt and it is arguable that the inverted commas should come before *To his anointed prince*. True, in ver. 1 there are quick transitions between the 3rd and 1st pers. (cf. xliv. 26) and we expect either 'to his anointed prince . . . whose right hand he grasps', &c. or 'to my anointed prince . . . whose right hand I grasp', &c. In what we have, majesty is combined with a certain intimacy. The passage as a whole is in epistolary form. The substance of it begins at ver. 2, but we expect an exordium or salutation such as we find in Ezra iv. 11, vii. 12 (2 Kings v. 6, x. 2 would be no exceptions) and in the Near East generally (see *ANET*, pp. 321 f., 475–92). This is not to say that we are to think of a formal letter or even address. Ezekiel addressed 'the word of the LORD' in highly polished verse to

Tyre (Ezek. xxvii. f.), to Pharaoh (xxix, xxxi. f.), and indeed to all and sundry; but this is not to say that he expected what he said to reach their ears. As between DI and Cyrus the case may be different. Cyrus was not so far away and the Prophet must have known that his 'word of the LORD' might be reported to him. That was probably his intention. Max Haller ('Die Kyros-Lieder Deuterojesajas', in *Eucharisterion* Hermann Gunkel, pp. 276 f.) even conjectured that DI was for a time in the entourage of Cyrus, but this is hardly to be taken seriously. Duhm (on xliv. 26–28) was more cautious. We may picture DI much as Ezekiel describes himself (Ezek. viii. 1, xiv. 1 f., xx. 1–3, xxxiii. 30). The elders would visit him and he would deliver Yahweh's pronouncements to them as occasion arose. But what he said in the name of Yahweh to Cyrus was intended as much for them as it was for Cyrus. From all we know of Cyrus, even if this word of the LORD was fully reported to him, he did not take it very seriously. But that is not to discredit DI: he was, as it were, working out an interpretation of events which was broadly true even though it was beyond the comprehension of the leading human actor in it.

Much has been written about the verbal similarities of this passage to the Babylonian-Persian court-style, as though the Prophet imitated the style the better to impress Cyrus. There can, of course, be no question of DI's borrowing from the Cyrus-cylinder (see *ANET*, pp. 315 f.), which was written after the fall of Babylon. The correspondences between the cylinder and DI are soon enumerated. In line 12 Cyrus has it that 'he (Marduk) pronounced the name of Cyrus . . . pronounced his name to be ruler of all the world': cf. *who summon you by name . . . I address you by name*, vv. 3*b*, 4*b*. In line 22 Cyrus boasts that Bel and Nabu love his *rule*; in xlviii. 14 he *himself* is described as 'whom Yahweh loves', but this is outside the present passage. The most striking correspondence is that between *whose right hand I grasp* and, as it is usually translated, 'He (Marduk) sought out a righteous prince, after his own heart, whom he might take by the hand' (line 12). In *ANET* this is rendered—whether finally or not remains to be seen—'He scanned and looked (through) all the countries, searching for a righteous ruler willing to lead him (i.e. Marduk) (in the annual procession)'. In DI Yahweh says to Cyrus *I myself will go before you* (ver. 2, note the thrice repeated 'before'); in the cylinder Cyrus speaks of Marduk 'going at his side like a friend and helper' (line 15). On the whole, then, the similarities between DI and the court-style are general, and may be explained as deriving from general Semitic idiom. In fact, as will appear, what is said about Cyrus has been assimilated to the Prophet's thinking rather than the Prophet's thinking to any court-style.

1. *anointed prince*] Heb. *māšîaḥ*, 'messiah'. That Yahweh should call a non-Israelite king so must have been shocking to the Prophet's contemporaries (cf. vv. 9–13) but we may easily read into it more than was intended. Cyrus has already been given the royal title of *shepherd* (xliv. 28). In a sense all DI's thinking is eschatological but the word 'messiah' had not yet acquired all the eschatological content which it came to have in later messianic dogma. Oddly enough, it is never used in the OT of the future messianic king—Dan. ix. 25 f. refers to the high priest. It was a title of reigning Hebrew kings: 1 Sam. xxiv. 6 (7) (Saul); 2 Sam. xix. 21 (*22*) (David); Ps. ii. 2, xviii. 50 +; but it always denotes the king's relation to Yahweh, not to Israel. In the late Ps. cxv. 15 the word 'anointed ones' is used metaphorically of the patriarchs. Similarly here, though Cyrus was of course a king. But he was certainly never ceremonially anointed in the name of Yahweh. What the word implies is that he is Yahweh's vicegerent. The nearest approach to such a title of a non-Israelite king is in Jer. xxv. 9, xxvii. 6, xliii. 10, where Nebuchadrezzar is called 'my servant', a word used of David (2 Sam. vii. 5 and some 30 times) in his capacity as king. *whose right hand I grasp*] Cf. xli. 13, xlii. 6 (of Israel); Jer. xxxi. 32; Ps. lxxiii. 23. *beat down nations . . . kings*] Cf. xli. 2. *strip kings of their weapons*] Lit. 'unloose the loins of kings', in sense of disarm and so render helpless: cf. 1 Kings xx. 11, 'Let not him that girds on (his armour) boast himself as he that puts (it) off' (lit. 'unlooses'). Weapons were fastened to a loin-belt: 2 Sam. xx. 8; Neh. iv. 18 (*12*). *doors . . . gates*] For the distinction between doors and gates see Neh. iii. 3, 13–15. A 'gate' (*šaʿar*) was a solid structure comprising doors (*deläṯayim*, dual, for swinging doors, cf. AV 'the two leaved gates'), bolts, and bars. In a small city 'the gate' would correspond to our 'square'. It was the market (2 Kings vii. 1, 18) and the place where the elders 'sat' and administered justice (Deut. xxi. 19 f., xxii. 15 +). Herodotus (i. 179) says of Babylon 'There are a hundred gates in the circuit of the wall, all of bronze with bronze uprights and lintels' (cf. ver. 2*b* and for the wording there, Ps. cvii. 16).

3. *buried*] Heb. *ṭāman*, 'hide', generally conveys the sense hide in the earth: cf. Gen. xxxv. 4; Exod. ii. 12; Joshua vii. 21 f.; Jer. xiii. 4–7. For the fabulous wealth of Babylon cf. Jer. l. 37; li. 13. *that you may know*] Duhm omits and takes what follows in the sense 'for I am Yahweh'. His reason is that access to the wealth of Babylon is no ground for knowledge on Cyrus' part that 'I am Yahweh'. Köhler also omits, presumably on metrical grounds. They may be right. It would ease the problem of Cyrus and the fulfilment—or non-fulfilment—of the Prophet's expectations concerning him, if we could

omit the words here, and read 'one whom I call by name' instead of 'one who will invoke me' in xli. 25 (which see). But we are not free to seek a solution of a theological problem by uncertain textual emendations. Even so, the fulfilment of the expectations concerning Cyrus, indeed the whole problem of the Prophet's interpretation of history, would still have to be faced.

3–4. *summon . . . address you by name*] Cf. xliii. 1, of Israel.

4. *I give you a title of honour*] Cf. xliv. 5 (which see).

5–6. In these verses Yahweh's dealings with Cyrus merge into assertions of Yahweh's sole Deity, with which cf. xli. 4, xliii. 10 f.

7. This verse definitely excludes any dualistic interpretation of reality such as characterizes Zoroastrianism. But it is unlikely that it was directed against Zoroastrianism as such or against the faith of Cyrus in particular. We have no reason to assume that Cyrus was a Zoroastrian and, if he was, it would have been extremely maladroit of the Prophet to engage in polemic against him. It is even doubtful whether the Prophet was thinking of dualism as we understand it. Dualism of a kind is implicit in any polytheism, in which health may be bestowed by one god and pestilence sent by another. *weal . . . woe*] Heb. *šālôm . . . rāʿ*, lit. 'peace . . . evil'; 'evil' in sense of 'calamity', as in Amos iii. 6. For *šālôm* Q[a] has *ṭôḇ*, 'good'; the meaning is the same. The verse is a variation of the theme, 'There is no God but Yahweh'. Monotheism is not a faith that encounters no moral difficulties. To say, as the OT does, that all happenings in nature are due to the personal agency of God creates a problem for the modern mind, but this is not the place for a discussion of it.

XLV. 8. VICTORY AND SALVATION

מִמַּעַל] Lit. 'from above'; but for the sense 'above' cf. Amos ii. 9; Deut. iv. 39; v. 8 +. Of course, the moisture would be distilled 'from above'. תִּפְתַּח] There is no need to add רַחְמָהּ, 'her womb' (Duhm) or to point תִּפָּתַח (*Niph.*), since 'the Qal can stand alone with the ellipse of the natural object' (G. R. Driver, 'Hebrew Notes', *JBL* 68, 1949, p. 59). וְיִפְרוּ] The masc. plur. verb is difficult. If the text is right, the subject must be 'heaven and earth' (so AV, RV?). There is a sense in which this is right (see below), but the grammar is difficult, because it proposes an understood pron. subj. drawn from two different distichs. We should probably read either וְיִפְרַח (so conjecturally Torrey and Kissane, now supported by Q[a], cf. xxxv. 1 f.), or the sing. וְיֵפֶר, either way with יֶשַׁע as subj. The former is preferable, since *blossom* . . . *burst into flower* gives a better sequential parallel than 'bear fruit . . . blossom'. תַּצְמִיחַ] The *Hiph.* will bear the sense *burst into flower* (*GK* 53 *d*) without emending to *Qal.* אֲנִי י״ בְּרָאתִיו] Although the accusative 'it' can be expressed by the masc. sf., we expect the feminine בְּרָאתִיהָ (*GK* 135 *p*), unless the masculine refers to Cyrus, which is improbable. The words are wanting in Q[a], perhaps rightly, though the text of the Scroll in this verse does not inspire full confidence: e.g. it omits יַחַד, which surely is original.

This verse may be an independent piece or it may be a hymnic conclusion to vv. 1–7. Whichever it is, it is a perfect miniature in verse. The skies are bidden to *rain victory*. The fecund earth is to *open her womb*. The issue of this 'marriage' of heaven and earth is to be *prosperity* and *salvation*. The idea had erotic associations in Baal religion, but here it has been sublimated into what is now pure metaphor: cf. lv. 10. *distil . . . rain*] *har'îpû . . . yizzᵉlû*. For a similar picture, with these verbs in the reverse order, cf. Job xxxvi. 27 f. The first has the sense of 'trickle', 'drip' (Prov. iii. 20; Ps. lxv. 11 (*12*), where the figure is that of a laden cart dropping its contents in its tracks: cf. RSV). *burst into flower*] To bring out the force of *yaḥaḏ*, 'together', explained at xli. 19 f. *victory . . . prosperity . . . salvation*] *ṣeḏeḳ . . . yešaʻ . . . ṣᵉḏāḳāh*. These words in DI are near synonyms: see on xli. 2, xlii. 6, 21. (There is no definable difference between the masculine and feminine forms *ṣeḏeḳ/ṣᵉḏāḳāh*.) Their meaning ranges between *victory* and *salvation*. It would obviously be wrong to limit 'righteousness/salvation' in this passage to military victory or material prosperity, and the translation offered is an attempt to convey the full breadth of the Prophet's conception. To the Hebrew way of thinking 'salvation' and 'prosperity' are like the obverse and reverse sides of a coin.

An alternative translation of *ṣeḏeḳ/ṣᵉḏāḳāh* is, of course, the old-fashioned 'righteousness':

. . . let the heavens rain righteousness;
let the earth open her womb,
  that salvation may blossom
  and righteousness burst into flower.

This would bring out the essential 'harmony' between the natural and moral orders, between Kant's 'starry heavens above' and 'the moral law within'. Wordsworth brings out the interrelation between the moral and physical orders in his *Ode to Duty*:

Thou dost preserve the stars from wrong;
And the most ancient heavens, through
  Thee, are fresh and strong.

Here in DI the direction is from the natural to the moral order. Leaving aside the concept of 'God', it is doubtful whether man has as much freedom to derange the physical order as he sometimes assumes he has.

XLV. 9–13. THE DISPOSER SUPREME OF NATURE AND HISTORY

9. חֶרֶשׂ אֶת־חַרְשֵׂי אֲדָמָה] Lit. 'an earthen vessel with (i.e. by the side of = like cf. Jer. xxiii. 28*b*) the earthen vessels of the ground.' This is passable Hebrew but it gives to את a somewhat different sense from what it has in the preceding stich, in other words the || seems defective. RSV 'an earthen vessel with the potter' keeps the ||, apparently taking its cue from Torrey's 'a potsherd with *him who formed* (חָרַשׁ, "maker", "fashioner", constr. of חָרָשׁ) the earth'. Another suggested reading is הֲיָרִיב ⟨יֵצֶר⟩ אֶת־יֹצְרוֹ חֶרֶשׂ אֶת־חֹרְשֵׁי אֲדָמָה 'Shall (the pottery) strive with the potter (or) the ploughland with them that plough?' This is based partly on LXX, which Torrey rightly says 'makes such terrible work of this verse'. It necessitates emending the exclamatory הוֹי רָב into an interrogative, besides introducing a second figure which confuses the picture. (Play on √s חרשׂ/חרשׁ would be over subtle). It seems best to keep MT. The sense of the exclamatory הוֹי can be conveyed in English in both stichs by interrogatives: see the translation. The second stich is explanatory of רָב in the first and the || is not unduly forced. וּפָעָלְךָ אֵין יָדַיִם לוֹ] It is usual to emend to וּפָעֳלוֹ אֵין־יָדַיִם לָךְ 'and his work, "You have no hands" '(cf. LXX οὐδε ἔχεις χεῖρας). But it suffices to read וּפֹעַל כִּ[י] וגו״, 'and the (finished) work, (that) "He has no hands" '. RSV 'Your work has no handles' is surely wrong: 'handles' would be יָדוֹת (*GK* 87 *o*).

11. וְיֹצְרוֹ הָאֹתִיּוֹת שְׁאָלוּנִי] These words have occasioned much discussion and it is fairly certain that 'my sons' and 'the work of my hands' following should be in || stichs (*contra* RV). It is usual to read הַאַתֶּם תִּשְׁאָלוּנִי, 'Are *you* to ask me?', or similar. But הָאֹתִיּוֹת, 'the coming things', is not so out of place in the context as may at first appear: cf. xli. 23, where the word is followed up in ver. 25 by הַעִירוֹתִי, similarly ver. 13 here. It is probable that הָאֹתִיּוֹת should go with וְיֹצְרוֹ preceding: cf. Q[a] יוצר האתות, 'who shapes the future (or "the signs"?)'. For that matter יֹצְרוֹ can mean the same (cf. *GK* 90 *o*). This would give a 2:2:2 line similar to those in the divine declarations in xliii. 16, xlv. 18. The imperative שְׁאָלוּנִי is ironical (see *GK* 110 *a* with exx.) and the sense will be 'Is it for you to question me about my children?'

13. וְגָלוּתִי] There is no need to read וְגָלוּת עַמִּי, either on the authority of LXX (cf. *BH*) or *metri causa*. MT means 'my exiled people' anyhow. The metre in the passage is a mixture of 3:3 and 3:2.

It is as unthinkable that any man should argue with Yahweh as that potter's clay should argue with the potter! Yahweh, who shapes the course of history, repeats that he created heaven and earth and mankind, and that he has roused 'him'—obviously Cyrus—to action for a saving purpose, that of rebuilding Jerusalem 'my city' and setting his exiled people free.

The passage is the only piece of invective in chs. xl–lv. It is generally agreed that it is directed against those of DI's compatriots who were scandalized by his making Yahweh assert that he would carry out his purposes through the agency of a 'shepherd' and 'anointed prince' who was not one of his own 'children'. Evidently he has other 'children' (lit. 'sons') than Israelites. Kissane appears to argue that the meaning in ver. 9 is that Cyrus cannot refuse the role he is called upon to play. This necessitates his placing ver. 11 before ver. 9 and altering the Heb. *hôy rāḇ* (lit. 'Ah! He who would strive') to *h^{a}yārîḇ* (lit. 'Can the thing fashioned strive?'). (That the exclamatory Hebrew can be expressed in English by an interrogative is another matter: see above.) Besides, it makes the problem of Cyrus more difficult than it is already. Cyrus is not a clay figure or puppet, and Jeremiah (xviii. 1–10) had already implied that not even the divine 'Potter' is always successful at the first attempt.

The figure of the potter, his 'hands', and his material is skilfully and consistently maintained, but it is impossible to convey this in English without sounding clumsy and irreverent: e.g. 'Who is he that would cavil at his Potter? But see the notes following.

9. *cavil at*] The Heb. verb is *rîḇ*, for which see on xli. 11. A translation 'bring an action against' would be permissible, but nothing quite so formal is intended here. *Maker*] Lit. 'Potter' (*yôṣēr*). *a piece of common earthenware*] For the literal rendering of the Hebrew see grammatical note above. The √ meaning of *ḥereś* ('earthen vessel') is something that scratches or is rough. Such vessels might be glazed (Prov. xxvi. 23) but ordinarily they were cheap enough to be broken without much concern (xxx. 14; Jer. xix. 11; Lam. iv. 2; cf. Ps. ii. 9) or after being used for ceremonial purposes (Lev. vi. 28 (*21*), xi. 33, xv. 12). That places like the Valley of Hinnom (Jer. xix) were strewn with broken sherds is confirmed wherever sites have been excavated. The same word is used both for an undamaged vessel and for a broken fragment (Job ii. 8). The words 'earthen vessels of the ground' can therefore mean either (i) vessels made of earth, as Yahweh is said to have 'formed (*wayyîṣer*) man of dust (*'āp̄ār*) from the ground' (*hā'^{a}ḏāmāh*), as a potter moulds clay (Gen. ii. 7), or (ii) broken sherds like the many that strew the ground, in which case the sense would be 'What is he better than a common (or discarded) sherd?' *the potter*] Lit. 'its potter', the same word as *his Maker* preceding. *skill*] Or 'dexterity', Heb. 'hands'.

10. *As well might a son say to his father*] Lit. 'Ah! he who says to (his) father!' The very idea is preposterous, not to say impious! The context requires the sense 'his own father'. For omission of the pron. sf. where it would refer back to the subject, cf. Mal. i. 6, 'A son honours (his) father'. *his mother*] Lit. 'woman', again without pron. sf., but the || requires 'mother'. For 'woman' = 'mother' cf. *NEB* at John ii. 4, xix. 26 (Gr. γύναι).

11. *take me to task*] Or 'put me to the question'. *what I do*] Lit. 'the work of my hands', continuing the figure of the potter: cf. *the (finished) work*, ver. 9.

12. Cf. xl. 22, xlii. 5, xliv. 24. *and set all their host in motion*] Lit. 'and all their host I commanded'. The similarity in sound of *ṣiwwêṯî*. 'I commanded', and *hammôṣî'* ('who leads out') in xl. 26 is striking but probably accidental.

13. *I, too*] To bring out the force of the separate pers. pron. *have stirred him up*] See on xli. 2, 25. *for a saving purpose*] Cf. xlii. 6 (of Israel). *I will direct all his ways aright*] Cf. xl. 3, xlv. 2. *he shall build my city*] Cf. xliv. 28. *payment . . . bribe*] These words are used together, but in the reverse order, in Mic. iii. 11. 'payment' (*m*ᵉ*ḥîr*) is for value received (2 Sam. xxiv. 24; 1 Kings x. 28, xxi. 2). The best illustrations of *šōḥaḏ* ('bribe') here are 1 Kings xv. 19; 2 Kings xvi. 8, where one king offers money to another king to induce him to take sides in a war. It is difficult to reconcile what Yahweh says here with what he says in xliii. 3 f. and (perhaps) xlv. 14. We must either suppose that the Prophet was not concerned to be consistent, or that he was capable of 'nodding' occasionally. All attempts to resolve the inconsistency are forced and we must conclude that the fundamental truths of prophecy are not dependent on precision in matters of detail.

XLV. 14–25. FROM HEATHENISM TO ISRAEL AND TO GOD

14. יְגִיעַ . . . וּסְחַר] As pointed means 'the wealth (as product of toil) . . . and the wares of'. This is said to be an unsuitable || to Sabeans and many would emend to יְגִעֵי . . . וְסֹחֲרֵי, 'the toilers . . . the merchants'. In any case, the wealth and wares would be brought by the Egyptians and Nubians. Point יְגִיעַ . . . וְסֹחֵר, taking both words as collectives, *the toilers and the merchants*. סֹחֵר is collective in xxiii. 2, and in Job iii. 17 יְגִיעֵי (sing. יָגִיעַ, 'weary') is a *kaṭîl* form similar to אָסִיר, 'prisoner', פָּקִיד, 'overseer'. אֵלַיִךְ] Read וְאֵלַיִךְ (cf. Q^{a}).

16. כֻּלָּם יַחְדָּו] If the text is right, the *'athnaḥ* should be with יחדו. Volz, *metri causa*, deletes as a gloss and regards כלם as a dittograph from the preceding word. But it is tempting to read כָּל־נֶחֱרָיו, *all who rage at him* (for this sense see on xli. 11). LXX has *οἱ ἀντικείμενοι αὐτῷ*, similarly in xli. 11; cf. also ver. 24 below.

19. תֹּהוּ] Accusative of place, *in the void*, though a prefix *bêth* may have been omitted by haplography.

23. צְדָקָה] If the meaning is (*the*) *truth* (cf. צֶדֶק, ver. 19), the word may be the subject of יָצָא, notwithstanding the discord in gender: cf. *GK* 145 *o*. Some would read בִּצְדָקָה, 'in truth/righteousness', with דָּבָר as the subject of the verb.

24. לִי אָמַר] Lit. 'to me he (or "one") said'. The unrelated pronouns are difficult and various emendations have been suggested. The commonest is to read לֵאמֹר and transfer it to the beginning of the verse, after LXX. But LXX in the context hardly inspires confidence. Q^{a} ליא יאמר evidently took the verb as *Niph.* יֵאָמֵר, since it always writes the *Qal plene*, יואמר. The לִי may correspond to the Arab. *li* (short *i*), the so-called '*li* of command' (Wright, *Arabic Grammar*, i, p. 291 B), which gives an imperative sense when affixed to the jussive; cf. *GK* 143 *e*). The meaning is then, 'it shall be said'. יָבוֹא וְיֵבֹשׁוּ] Read יָבוֹאוּ with 21 MSS. Q^{a} has יבואו יבושו. For a similar asyndetous construction cf. xli. 3.

In these verses the introductory 'Thus says Yahweh' occurs at ver. 14 and again at ver. 18. In vv. 14–17 Yahweh announces that the peoples of the Nile Valley are to come bearing tribute to 'thee'. They are to come with a deference approaching worship, and confess that God is with 'thee' only and that there is no other God. Although God is *Saviour* he is nevertheless *a God who conceals himself*. In vv. 18 f. Yahweh, the purposive and sole Creator of heaven and earth, asserts that he has never been inaccessible, or ambiguous in his declarations to Israel. There follows (vv. 20 f.) a reiterated summons to the *survivors of the nations* to *assemble and come* to a judicial inquiry. Who was it that announced 'this' long ago? Yahweh asserts that it was he. The climax is reached in vv. 22–25, in which Yahweh bids all the ends of the earth turn to him and be saved. He declares on oath, upon his own assurances—*by myself*—that every knee shall bend and every tongue swear fealty to him.

On the small units theory these verses consist of two (vv. 14–17, 18–25; Mowinckel, Köhler), or three (vv. 14–17, 18 f., 20–25; Volz) separate pieces. There is no case for subdividing 18–25, except into stanzas or 'strophes', and the *kî* ('for') appears to join the verses to what precedes. In ver. 14 'thee', if the 2nd pers. sing. fem. of the massoretic pointing is correct, must be either Israel (cf. xli. 14) or Zion-Jerusalem (cf. xl. 1 f.), and this fact is evidence for regarding 14–25 as a unit. The case may be different if 'thee' is to be identified with Cyrus. The suffixes can be pointed as masculine *'ālêḵā*, &c., without altering the consonantal text, though in Q[a], the earliest evidence of interpretation, the suffixes in 14*b* are feminine (*kî*), with final *yôdh*. The Cyrus interpretation is as old as Jerome, Ibn Ezra, and Grotius (so Skinner), and has been revived by Skinner, Mowinckel, and others; though not by Volz, who nevertheless regards 14–17 as a separate piece. Chapter xliii. 3 would seem to point to Cyrus, but only to be contradicted by xlv. 13 here. Cyrus would fit 14*a* well enough, but hardly 14*b*. 'They shall make supplication (lit. "pray") to you' presents some difficulty on either interpretation, since everywhere else the *Hithpa'ēl* of the verb is used of prayer to a god (xliv. 17), or, usually, to Yahweh. Accordingly it has been conjectured that for 'to you' we should read 'to your God' (*'el 'elôhêḵā*). This is not necessary. What is implied is clear from the content of the prayer, *God is with you, and there is no other*, which is not strictly a prayer but a confession that the person addressed is the intermediary between the speakers and God. This role is better filled by Zion-Israel than by Cyrus, especially in view of the close connexion between 14–17 and 18–25.

Another difficulty is to decide whether the speaker in 15–17 is the Prophet (RSV), or whether the verses are a continuation of the confession of the Sabeans (so Muilenburg, commenting on RSV, though he admits that 'there is much to be said for either view'). If we could emend 'thou' (*'attāh*) to 'with thee' (*'ittāḵ*), with Duhm and others, we should have to decide for the latter, but the textual evidence for this is slender. On the whole, vv. 15–17 are best understood as an utterance of the Prophet, who marvels at the wondrous ways of Yahweh. A similar problem is presented by vv. 24 f., see below.

14. *the Sabeans*] See on xliii. 3. *tall*] Lit. 'men of stature' (*middāh*), as in Num. xiii. 32; 1 Chron. xi. 23. A word with the same spelling is once found in Neh. v. 4 of 'tribute' (Akk. *mandattu*). This would give a suitable meaning ('bearers of tribute') here, and for gifts from the kings of Seba see Ps. lxxii. 10. Nevertheless, *tall* is to be preferred. Herodotus twice (iii. 20, 114) reports that 'the Ethiopians are said to be the tallest and best-looking people in the world'. In Isa. xviii. 2, 7, they are 'a nation tall (*memuššāḵ*, lit. "long drawn out") and smooth'. *shall make pilgrimage*] *ya'aḇōrû*, lit. 'shall pass over'.

For this sense of the verb see Amos v. 5; Ps. xlii. 4 (*5*); and cf. Isa. lxii. 10. For the expectation that all peoples would one day come as pilgrims to Zion cf. ii. 2–4, lxvi. 18–23; Zech. xiv. 16; and for their bringing of lavish gifts Isa. lx. Since the destination of a pilgrimage is a place rather than a people, *you* (2nd pers. sing. fem., 'thee') is Zion-Jerusalem rather than Israel, though in DI 'Jerusalem' and 'Israel' are more or less synonymous (see on xl. 2). *they will pay court to you*] Lit. 'they will go after (or "follow") you'. A cultic expression, especially frequent in Deut., for 'going after' Yahweh (Deut. xiii. 4 (*5*); 1 Kings xiv. 8; Jer. ii. 2) or other gods (Deut. vi. 14; 1 Kings xviii. 18; Jer. ii. 23). *coming with manacled hands*] Lit. 'in chains shall they pass over'. Many scholars omit, whether on metrical grounds, or because the clause is felt to introduce an incongruous feature into the picture. (The Africans are presumed to come of their own free will.) But there is no case for omission *metri causa*, even though 'they shall pass over' is repeated from the preceding line: the case is similar to 'lift it up, have no fear' in xl. 9. As to incongruity, the chains are manacles (cf. Jer. xl. 4), not fetters, which would make the journey impossible. They could be fastened on by the Africans themselves, probably as an assurance that they were coming with no hostile intent. Herodotus (iii. 23) tells of an 'Ethiopian' prison in which all the prisoners were bound with gold chains—'for in Ethiopia the rarest metal is bronze'. It makes no difference even if this was only hearsay. *they will bow low*] *yištaḥ*ᵃ*wû*. For the same word used of deference to a Hebrew king, by kings, see Ps. lxxii. 11.

15. *conceals himself*] *mistattēr*. This *Hithpa'ēl* form could have the sense 'shows himself protective', on the analogy of *Hithpa'ēl nḳm*, 'show one's self vengeful' (Ps. viii. 2 (*3*); cf. *siṯrāh*, 'protection' [Deut. xxxii. 38]; *mistôr*, 'place of protection' [iv. 6]). It is arguable that *who conceals himself* is incongruous with *Saviour*; but ver. 19, 'I have never spoken in secrecy' (*bassēṯer*) seems to refer back to *mistattēr* here and to confirm the traditional interpretation of the word. The paradox *a God who conceals himself . . . Saviour* is forceful and in the last resort true.

> There is in God, some say
> A deep but dazzling darkness . . .
>
> (Boethius, quoted by Helen Waddell in *The Wandering Scholars*, Pelican Books, p. 27)

which explains the fascination of the mystics' quest. Nowhere in the OT is the thought of the 'hidden' God, the *deus absconditus* of theology, so plainly stated as here. At first sight it is so un-Hebrew that some scholars, on very slight textual evidence (see *BH* note), would emend to 'with thee (Israel) God hides himself' (see above), and put the words into the mouths of the Sabeans. But the thought of God as 'hidden', notwithstanding that he is Revealer and Saviour, is not unfamiliar in the OT: cf. Ps. xcvii. 2 and the story of Yahweh's placing Moses in the cleft of the rock and covering him with his hand to shield him from the untempered rays of the divine glory, Exod. xxxiii, 17–23. It is implicit in the name Yahweh/Ehyeh, 'I am who I am', which by all the rules is a bad definition, since it puts into the definition the thing to be defined. Yet what would we have? That God is *deus absconditus* is a corollary of any doctrine of divine transcendence (cf. Rom. xi. 33; 1 Tim. vi. 15 f.). There is a sense in which nature, with its mingled revelation and mystery, is a necessary barrier between God and ourselves, lest we should be blinded by excess of light: cf. Browning, *Bishop Blougram's Apology*, the lines beginning 'Pure faith indeed—you know not what you ask'. *Saviour*] Here used absolutely, almost as a proper name: cf. xliii. 11 and 'Most Holy', xl. 25.

18. The hymnic introduction is even more than usually elaborate. Yahweh *created the heavens* and *formed the earth* and firmly established it. It is an orderly creation, not a *chaos* (*tôhû*, see on xl. 17 and cf. Gen. i. 2) but a habitable world.

19. Not only is Yahweh's creation orderly but his word is clear. He has *never spoken in secrecy* (cf. xlviii. 16), *in some place in the land of darkness* (*ḥōšeḵ*). Here also reference may be made to Gen. i. 2, where darkness is said to have been upon the original 'deep'. That Yahweh has never spoken in secrecy is no contradiction of ver. 15, that he is *a God who conceals himself*. Any doctrine of revelation assumes that God is unknown and unknowable except in so far as he chooses to reveal himself, that man cannot by searching find out God (Job xi. 7). What is meant is that God does not make himself deliberately obscure, so that men are driven to *seek* (*biḳḳēš*, here a cultic term, as in lxv. 1; 2 Sam. xxi. 1 and often) him by superstitious, or occult, or orgiastic means. He speaks *the truth* (*ṣeḏeḳ*). For the word 'righteousness' in this sense as opposed to a lie (*šeḳer*) cf. Ps. lii. 3 (5); Prov. xii. 17. Volz (*in loc.*) has it that 'O.T. religion is at once grand and simple: it is the religion of the layman', the religion of Abraham, Moses, and the prophets, and, we may add, of the great rabbis. *right*] *mêšārîm*, a plural of amplification (*GK* 124 *e*). The word conveys the sense of what is straightforward, combined with moral excellence. For *ṣeḏeḳ* and *mêšārîm* similarly used together, see Prov. i. 3, ii. 9. Of course, something of the senses of 'victory' and 'salvation' still attach to *ṣeḏeḳ*.

20–21. The divine self-predication widens out into a summons to the nations to *assemble yourselves and come* (*wāḇō'û*), *with one* *accord draw near*. For 'with one accord' (*yaḥdāw*) Q[a] has 'and come' (*w*[e]*'ēṯāyû*, cf. xli. 5, 25). This gives a closer || with 'and come' preceding, but is not to be preferred. The summons is to something like the now familiar assize-inquest (cf. on xli. 21–24, xliii. 9–13, xliv. 6–8), though the tone is less menacing. *The survivors of the nations* are presumably those who have survived the world-shattering events which are the theme of the preceding chapters. But the expression could mean 'fugitive nations' (appositional genitive, cf. *GK* 128 *f*). The two themes of the stupidity of idolatry and the total inability of the gods to foretell the future are repeated, but there is a recognition that what the idolaters have done, they have done in ignorance rather than out of wilful wickedness. *who carry about their wooden idols*] The reference is to the custom of carrying the statues of the gods in procession on festal occasions (cf. xlvi. 1 f.).

21. *advance your arguments*] Cf. xli. 21. *by all means let them* (*sc.* the gods) *confer together*] For a similar abrupt transition from 2nd to 3rd per. (*GK* 144 *p*) cf. xlv. 8. T 'by all means confer together' (2nd pers.) is a permissible interpretation. *Who announced this long ago, in time past declared it?*] The unrelated demonstrative *this* is more likely to refer to a specific event or events, than to the fulfilment of prophecy in general. Chapter xlvi. 10 f. gives the clue to its meaning here: the reference is to the exploits of Cyrus. *long ago*] *miḳḳeḏem*, generally refers to the distant past (Mic. v. 2 (*1*); Hab. i. 12; Ps. lxxiv. 12, lxxvii. 11 (*12*), lxxviii. 2, cxliii. 5), but the root meaning ('be in front', 'precede') does not demand anything more than 'beforehand'. Job (xxix. 2) wishes he were 'as in the months of *ḳeḏem*, as in the days when God watched over me' (cf. also Isa. xlvi. 10 f.). *in time past*] *mē'āz*, lit. 'from then'. This could be quite recently (Exod. iv. 10; 2 Sam. xv. 34; cf. Gen. xxxix. 5; Exod. v. 23; Isa. xiv. 8). It is not improbable that the reference is to the 'prophecies' now extant in xiii. 2–4, (5–16), 17–22, xxi. 1–10 (cf. Jer. li. 11, 28), in which Babylon is to be overthrown by the Medes. That these Median prophecies exercised the minds of later generations is clear from Dan. v. 31, according to which 'Darius the Mede received the kingdom' immediately after the death of the Babylonian Belshazzar. They are presumably earlier than the time (550–49) when Cyrus captured Astyages. Isaiah xiii is said to be 'the pronouncement concerning Babylon which Isaiah the son of Amoz saw'. It is, of course, practically certain that the pronouncement was not Isaiah's, but if chs. xiii–xxiii were included, much in their present form, in the original proto-Isaiah (i–xxxix), the 'Median' prophecies in them may have had something to do with the final collocation of xl–lxvi with i–xxxix: see C. R. North, 'The "Former Things" and the "New Things" in Deutero-Isaiah', in *Studies in O.T. Prophecy*, T. H. Robinson *Festschrift*, ed. H. H. Rowley, 1950, 124 f. Whether xiii. 2–4, 17–22, as Deutero-Isaiah (it may fairly be conjectured) knew it, was prefixed by xiii. 1 is uncertain, even doubtful, but if the Median prophecies were in circulation in the 'Isaiah School', he might well regard them as of sufficient antiquity for *miḳḳeḏem* to have the sense of 'long ago'.

22–25. The summons becomes a universal appeal, though the verbs are still in the imperative mood, as indeed they are in the 'Come unto me, all who . . .' of Jesus (Matt. xi. 28), which, like the present passage, follows a self-predication. It is fair to regard *be saved* as a *Niph. tolerativum* (*GK* 51 *c*), 'let yourselves be saved'. Or the second imperative can contain the assurance 'you shall be saved' (cf. *divide et impera*, *GK* 110 *f*). *the farthest ends of the earth*] The far, of course, includes the near; for the ancients the farthest horizon was circular, even though the earth was flat. Yahweh's gaze to 'the ends of the earth' is often menacing (e.g. 1 Sam. ii. 10; Ps. ii. 8 f.). Not so here (see also lii. 10; Ps. xxii. 27, (*28*)), in what is one of the high peaks of OT religion. The stress is on the individual (cf. xliv. 5)—*every knee . . . every tongue*. It is not a mass conversion that is envisaged but a confession which men will utter as individuals. For the sense *swear fealty* of *Niph. šāḇa'*, cf. Ezek. xvi. 8, where Yahweh says he 'plighted troth' (so RSV) to Jerusalem. The New Covenant in Jer. xxxi. 31–34 is announced as with 'the house of Israel', though the terms in which it is expanded (vv. 33 f.) show that it was to be made effective by the regeneration of individual Israelites. The present passage marks an advance even upon that, since it embraces individual Gentiles. *be recalled*] Lit. 'return': see on lv. 11.

24–25. RSV takes these verses as an utterance of Yahweh. But would Yahweh refer to himself as 'Yahweh' and 'him'? RSV has not understood *lî 'āmar* (for which see above), which it renders 'it shall be said of me (Yahweh)'. The verses, like 15–17, are best understood as words of the Prophet. Even so, some ambiguities remain.

24. *victory*] *ṣᵉḏāḳôṯ*, may be taken as an intensive plural, as in xxxiii. 15 (cf. *GK* 124 *e*), or the reference may be to Yahweh's 'saving/victorious/righteous deeds' of redemption: cf. Judges v. 11 (*bis*, RSV 'triumphs'); 1 Sam. xii. 7; Ps. ciii. 6. Either way, the range of meanings is wide: cf. 'the truth', ver. 19 above; and on xli. 2, xlii. 6, 21. *unto him . . . at him*] By both pronouns probably, by the second almost certainly (see on ver. 16 above, and cf. xli. 11), we are to understand

Israel rather than Yahweh. It is usual for the Prophet's thought to begin and end with Israel, Yahweh's witnesses to the world. There may be some significance in the choice of preposition in *unto him* (*'āḏâw*, not the more usual *'ēlâw*, 'to him', as in *'ēlayiḵ*, ver. 14). *'aḏ* is stronger, more 'adhesive', than *'el*, as though Gentile and Jew will be united into one community: cf. xliv. 5.

25. *sing their victory hallelujahs*] *yiṣdᵉḵû wᵉyiṯhalᵉlû* lit. 'shall be victorious (RSV "shall triumph") and glory' (see on xli. 16); 'paeans of victory' might serve, but the 'paean' was essentially Greek. The natural way for Hebrews to 'triumph and glory (*hiṯhallēl*) in Yahweh' would be to sing 'Hallelujah' psalms such as Ps. civ–cvi, cxi–cxiii, cxv–cxvii, cxxxv, cxlvi–cl. These Psalms are full of the 'praiseworthy' deeds of Yahweh.

XLVI. GODS IMPOTENT AND THE LORD GOD OMNIPOTENT

1. נְשֻׂאֹתֵיכֶם עֲמוּסוֹת] 'your things carried are borne', can hardly be right in what is a description of Bel and Nebo and 'their effigies'. Read either נְשֻׂאֹת כְּמוֹ עֲמוּסוֹת (Volz) or נְשֻׂאֹת כְּמַעֲמָסוֹת, 'carried like burdens': cf. LXX ὡς φορτίον. The gender of נְשֻׂאֹת is determined by מַעֲמָסוֹת/עֲמוּסוֹת (Zech. xii. 3), not by עֲצַבֵּיהֶם.

8. וְהִתְאֹשָׁשׁוּ] *Hithpô'ēl 'āšaš*. None of the many explanations is entirely convincing. The versions differ widely, not because they had different readings but because they did not understand the word. AV, RV ('shew yourselves men') take as a denominative from אִישׁ. RSV ('consider') follows P. Assuming that the text is sound, two alternatives seem open: (i) To relate to Arab. *'assasa*, Akk. *ašašu*, Rabbinical Heb. אשש, 'found', 'establish'; hence, as the second of two imperatives (see on xlv. 22), 'you shall be firmly established' (cf. RV mg.); (ii) In a Sumerian–Akkadian glossary *aššišu* is equated with *šēmû* (Heb. שמע), 'listening', from which G. R. Driver (*JTS* 32, 1931, p. 365) infers the meaning 'show yourselves attentive or obedient'. This has a narrower philological basis than has (i) but it suits both the immediate and the general (cf. שִׁמְעוּ, vv. 3, 12) context better.

11. עֲצָתוֹ] Read עֲצָתִי with *Qere* and LXX.

12. אַבִּירֵי] LXX reads as אֹבְדֵי, 'you who have lost (heart)', but MT is supported by 'rebels' (ver. 8).

This chapter is best treated as a unity, notwithstanding that vv. 5–7 (8) are somewhat loosely related to their context (see below). The first theme (vv. 1–4) is the contrast between Yahweh who carries his people, and the Babylonian gods which are lifeless blocks needing to be carried about by their distraught worshippers. The classic exposition of it is in Sir George Adam Smith (p. 198): 'The truth is this: it makes all the difference to a man how he conceives his religion—whether as something he has to carry, or as something that will carry him.' Verses 9–12 revert to the theme of the fulfilment of prophecy and the role of Cyrus, and end with the assurance that Yahweh's victory and the deliverance of his people will not be long delayed.

1. *Bel . . . Nebo*] The two most prominent gods in the Babylonian pantheon. Bel, the equivalent of the Canaanite Baal ('Lord'), was originally a title of the Sumerian god Enlil, but from the time of the Babylonian Hammurabi it became an epithet of Marduk (cf. Jer. l. 2), and the Babylonian form of the creation epic tells how Marduk became the champion of the gods by destroying Tiamat. Nebo (Bab. Nabu, 'speaker', probably related to Heb. *nāḇî'*, 'prophet'), the son of Bel-Marduk, was the patron of wisdom and the art of writing, and his function was to write on the tables of destiny the fates decreed by the gods for the coming year. This was at the New Year Festival, when he was brought from his own temple at Borsippa, some miles south-west of Babylon, and accompanied his father Marduk in the festival procession. It is probable that Nabu was the patron-god of the Babylonian-Chaldean dynasty, since its three most important kings, Nabopolassar, Nebuchadrezzar, and Nabonidus, had names compounded with his. *crouches . . . cowers*] The translation happens to catch something of the alliteration of the Heb. *kāra'* . . . *ḳōrēs*. The first of these verbs usually describes a going down on one's knees: so xlv. 23; Judges vii. 5 f.; 1 Kings viii. 54; 2 Kings i. 13; Job iv. 4; and cf. *keră'ayim*, 'shin-bones', Amos iii. 12. The second is found only here, but is obviously related to *ḳeres*, 'hook' (as bent), Exod. xxvi. 6, and *ḳarsōl*, 'ankle', 2 Sam. xxii. 37/Ps. xviii. 36 (*37*). *have been made over to*] Lit. 'have become to (for)'. A common meaning of Heb. 'X becomes to Y' is that X becomes the property of Y: e.g. Deut. x. 9; Judges xi. 31; 1 Kings xi. 3. The pack-animals are the custodians of the effigies; indeed, it is as if the effigies, and, *ipso facto*, the gods themselves, have become their property!

2. *They crumple up completely*] Still conveying something of the alliteration of the Heb.; lit. 'they crouch, they cower together'. The Heb. 'together' (*yaḥdāw*, see on xli. 19 f.) does not refer to the two gods but to their total collapse. 'Their knees and ankles give way' would be a fair alternative translation; see above on the associations of the verbs. This is no description of a festival procession but of panic

flight; cf. xliii. 14. *they cannot carry their burden to safety*] The grammatical subject is Bel and Nebo, since the verb is masculine. The
logical subject is the pack-animals, which are feminine collective
(*ʿᵃyēp̱āh*, vs. 1). What the text describes is a confusion of idols, gods,
and exhausted animals. The scene is entirely different from that in
the account of the return of the ark from Philistia to Bethshemesh
(1 Sam. vi. 11 f.). *trudge*] *hālāk̠āh*, 'go' or (commonly) 'walk'. The
three consecutive long vowels convey the suggestion of utter
weariness. That the passage (like xliii. 14) is predictive, not a description after the event, is clear from the fact that there was no stampede
to evacuate Babylon of its gods before it fell to Cyrus. Nor did Cyrus
banish the gods from their temples; instead, he 'restored the gods of
Sumer and Akkad, which Nabonidus had brought into Babylon,
unharmed to their own shrines' (*Cyrus Cylinder*, lines 33 f.), and be-
sought them all to ask Bel and Nabu to grant long life to him and
to Cambyses his son (ibid., lines 34 f.): see *ANET*, p. 316*b*. Nevertheless, the description is true enough in its own way. There is an amus-
ing account of a scene in India in W. T. Grenfell, *Forty Years for
Labrador*, p. 302: 'The townspeople seemed to see nothing out of the
way in the following item in the local newspaper: "Last evening,
during the course of the procession, the Diety (*sic*) most unfortunately
fell off into the drain. By the concerted efforts of the worshippers,
however, he was restored to his position at eight o 'clock".'

3. *family* (lit 'house') *of Jacob*] This would include those who traced
their descent from the former Northern Israel: see on xliii. 5–7.
remnant] *š̠ᵉʾērît̠*, √ 'be left over'. The word generally conveys a suggestion of pitiful smallness: e.g. xliv. 16 f.; Amos i. 8, v. 15; Jer.
xlii. 2; and see on xliv. 1–5.

4. *even to*] *wᵉʿad̠* = 'up to and including': see on xlv. 24. *I remain
the same*] Lit. 'I am he': see on xli. 4, and cf. Ps. cii. 27 (*28*) (EVV
'thou art the same'); similarly Mal. iii. 6, 'I, the LORD, do not
change'. The separate pers. pron. 'I' occurs five times in this verse,
with cumulative emphasis. Even the acc. obj. 'you' (Israel) is not
expressed, though it is implied from ver. 3. It is as if Yahweh is all.
support] *ʾesbōl*. The verb is always used of carrying a heavy load: cf.
liii. 4, 11; Gen. xlix. 15 ('he bowed his shoulder to bear'); Lam. v. 7.
Of the related nouns, *siḇlōt̠* is used of the slave labours imposed
on Israel in Egypt: Exod. i. 11, ii. 11, &c.; and *sēḇel* of the corvée
in 1 Kings xi. 28. *I have made a beginning*] *ʿāśît̠î*. The word looks
simple enough but its meaning here is not easy to determine. EVV
'I have made' appear to take it as referring to the 'making' of Israel
as a people. The absence of the acc. obj. is no objection (see above),
but in the other two passages (xliii. 7, xliv. 2) where Yahweh is said

to have 'made' Israel, the word is supplemented by 'created' and/or 'formed'. Volz (*ich walte*) evidently had some hesitation about 'made', though he does not discuss the matter beyond saying that ver. 4 has 'all sorts of peculiar expressions' but that the text need not be altered. (It has been suggested that we should read *nāśā'ṯî*, 'I carried': see *BH.*) The two main senses of '*āśāh* are 'do' and 'make', roughly in the proportions 5:2. The probability is that it is here used absolutely in the sense 'act (decisively)': see on xli. 4. The difficulty is to find a suitable translation: 'acted' is abrupt and vague; 'performed' in the Jacobean sense (e.g. at Ezek. xxxvii. 14, lit. 'spoken and performed'—no acc. obj. in Hebrew) might do, but 'the performing God' of Isaac Watts now sounds rather ridiculous. There remains the question of the *terminus a quo* of the divine action here. It could be the Exodus: 'I made a beginning'. This would relate the word to the birth of Israel (ver. 3 and cf. Hos. xi. 1, xii. 9 (*10*), xiii. 4). Or it could be more recently: 'I have made a beginning', with reference to the career of Cyrus (ver. 11 and cf. xli. 4, xliv. 23). *I myself will support and carry you*] The Hebrew order is 'carry' ('*eśśā'*) and 'support' ('*esbōl*). In an Aramaic papyrus from Elephantine (E. G. Kraeling, *The Brooklyn Museum Aramaic Papyri*, 1953, No. 5) a man frees his woman slave and her daughter on the condition that they serve and provide (*sbl*) for him and his son. From this, and the fact that in old Babylonian legal documents the verb *našû* (= Heb. *nāśā'*) is similarly used in the sense 'support', 'provide for', J. Rabinowitz ('A note on Isa 46[4]', *JBL* 73, 1954, p. 237) suggests that legal terminology is the source of the phrase in vv. 3 f. here. This is a dubious inference. In another Brooklyn papyrus (op. cit., No. 9, line 17) a man makes over part of his property to his daughter 'because she maintained (*sbl*) me when I was old (*sb*, cf. *śêḇāh*, ver. 4 here) in days'. All that can be inferred is that the semantic development of Heb.–Aram. *sbl* is similar to that of the Latin–English 'support'/'maintain'. It is just possible that the repeated '*esbōl*—the verb is not used of carrying the Babylonian gods in vv. 1 f.—has already acquired something of the sense 'provide for' in old age: cf. Ps. lxxi. 18; Ruth iv. 15. At least it is sound homiletics. Yahweh is not just a beast of burden.

5–8. Some, e.g. Volz (vv. 5–7), Köhler (vv. 5–8), Mowinckel (vv. 6–8) regard these verses as secondary. It is arguable that 'Remember this' (ver. 8) refers back more naturally to ver. 4 than it does to vv. 5–7. On the other hand, the carrying of the idol in 7*a* is a close link with vv. 1 f. and adds a new feature to the preceding descriptions of idolatry. On the whole, the passage is more relevant where it stands than are the other 'idol interludes' in DI.

5. Cf. xl. 18, 25, in a similar 'idolatry' context.

6. Cf. xl. 19, xli. 7, xliv. 15, 17. *balance*] *ḳānêh* ('reed'). Properly the 'beam' of a balance, but used, as in English, for the scales themselves.

7. *They carry it laboriously*] Lit. 'They carry it they support (*yisbᵉlû*) it'.

8. *you rebels*] The address is to the Prophet's own people, not to Gentiles: cf. xliii. 27, xlviii. 8.

9a. *what happened ages ago*] Lit. 'the former things (*rî'šônôṯ*, cf. xli. 22, xlii. 9, xliii. 9, 18, xlviii. 3) from ancient time' (*'ôlām*, see on xliv. 7). The most likely reference is to the Exodus, as in xliii. 18. For 9*b* see on xliii. 11. *God . . . very God*] *'ēl . . . 'ᵉlôhîm*. The second of these words for God is not particularly emphatic: it is simply that Hebrew avoids using the same word in ‖ clauses.

10. *my purpose . . . my will*] *'ᵃṣāṯî . . . ḥep̄ṣî*. The meanings of the words here are exactly the same as in the Cyrus context xliv. 26–28, which see.

11. *a falcon*] *'ayiṭ*: onomatopoeic, 'screamer'. No particular species of bird is indicated. Scavengers are implied in xviii. 6; Gen. xv. 11; Ezek. xxxix. 4; and 'vulture' might serve here. (Some vultures are solitary.) But in Job xxviii. 7 the word is ‖ *'ayyāh* (Lev. xi. 14; Deut. xiv. 13, some kind of falcon). 'Falcon', with its 'stooping' flight would suit Cyrus well. Falconry was practised in the East as far back as 1200 B.C. *the man who shall carry out my purpose*] Lit. 'the man of my counsel' (= purpose, see on xliv. 26). Obviously, no man 'counsels' Yahweh (cf. xl. 13): he decides his own counsel. The genitive is therefore subjective, 'my counsel-man', not objective as in xl. 13, 'the man who counsels him'. *In short*] An attempt to bring out the staccato threefold *'ap̄* ('also') of the Hebrew: see on xli. 10. *I have resolved*] *yāṣartî*, lit. 'formed', 'shaped' (see on xliii. 1) sc. 'in my mind'.

12–13. The difficulty here is to translate, without alternative renderings, the words *ṣᵉḏāḳāh* (AV, RV, 'righteousness') and *tᵉšû'āh* (AV, RV, 'salvation'). See on xli. 2, xlii. 6, 21. The two words are almost synonyms in DI and their scope is wide. 'Victory' is here, and 'deliverance', but the ethico-religious concepts of 'righteousness' and 'salvation' can hardly be lacking in the climax of an utterance by Yahweh himself. It is a fair inference that we are far from victory and deliverance because we are far from righteousness: cf. xlii. 18–25. *I will give in Zion my gift of salvation*] Lit. 'I will give in Zion salvation'. The Heb. 'give' is here used in its not infrequent sense of 'put', 'set', 'place', and the metaphor is similar to that in xli. 19, 'I will place (Heb. 'give') in the wilderness the cedar', &c. The thought is that of salvation as a permanent endowment or 'planting', but it is not easy to find the right English word for it. Any one of the words 'grant', 'bestow', 'appoint', even 'establish', might serve. Another facet of the Heb. 'give' is 'show', 'display': cf. Ezek. xxvii. 10, lit. 'they gave your splendour'; Exod. vii. 9, lit. 'give for yourselves a miracle'. *to Israel my pride*] For 'pride' (*tip̄'ereṯ*), see on xliv. 23. It is here used much in the sense of Goldsmith's 'A bold peasantry, their country's pride'. The phrase could be translated 'my glory (*or* beauty) to Israel', taking *tip̄'artî* as a second object of 'give' in the preceding stich, not as an appositional qualification of 'Israel'. But a second object so far removed from the verb could hardly be other than ambiguous, especially in view of the different prepositions —'*in* Zion', '*to* (or *for*) Israel'.

XLVII. BABYLON'S PRIDE AND FALL

3–4. וְלֹא אֶפְגַּע אָדָם גֹּאֲלֵנוּ וגו׳] Lit. 'and I will not meet man our Redeemer', &c. אדם in the not infrequent sense 'any one', as in Lev. i. 2. The primary sense of פגע is 'meet by chance', 'fall in with'. The meeting may be unexpected by the subject (Exod. v. 20, xxiii. 4; 1 Sam. x. 5), by the object (Gen. xxxii. 1 (*2*); Amos v. 19), or by both parties (Ruth ii. 22). The verb takes either the direct object (so here), or, more often, governs its object by ב. Derivative meanings are to meet with hostile intent (usual), with a request (Gen. xxiii. 8; Ruth i. 16), or with kindness (only lxiv. 4 outside the present passage). All MSS. of LXX read אדם but some also begin ver. 4 with *εἶπεν* (or *λέγει*), either reading אָמַר, or assuming it to make sense of what follows. Some moderns read אָדָם אָמַר, supposing אָמַר to have been omitted by haplography. Others substitute אָמַר for אָדָם. In that case we must either (i) point אַפְגִּעַ (*Hiph.*, so P, and cf. liii. 12, lix. 16), 'I will not interpose (to save you)', though, since Yahweh is the avenger, the question of his intervening to save from someone else hardly arises; or (ii) point אֶפָּגַע (*Niph.*), 'I will not be entreated'. Another expedient is to read יִפְגַּע for אֶפְגַּע (so V, Σ), 'and no one shall intervene (to save you)'. The general sense is the same whatever we read. On the whole it seems best to keep MT in the sense 'I will parley with no man', and to bracket ver. 4, which is prose and introduces 'us' (= Israel) in a context in which Yahweh is the speaker. Yahweh is the speaker throughout the poem but his first mention of himself is in 'I will take vengeance'. A glossator may have felt that the 'I' needed definition and his choice of גֹּאֲלֵנוּ may be due to the fact that it was the function of the 'avenger of blood' (גֹּאֵל הַדָּם) to avenge, though the verbs גאל and נקם are never actually brought together except in lxiii. 4. The gloss, if such it be, is a conflation from xli. 14 and xliv. 6. גאל and פגע are associated in Num. xxxv. 19, 21.

7. גְּבֶרֶת עַד] The Massorah takes עַד with what follows, 'to the point that you did not', &c. (cf. Job xiv. 6). Many moderns take it with גְּבֶרֶת, lit. 'queen in perpetuity'. This may seem superfluous after לְעוֹלָם and the major versions omit the word. Q[a] reads עוד, 'still', for which at the end of a sentence cf. Gen. xlvi. 29; Jer. xiii. 27. *I shall go on being a queen for ever* well expresses Babylon's unconscionable pride. Volz omits from עַד to לִבֵּךְ as repetitive from ver. 6 and because of the unrelated אֵלֶּה, 'these'. But DI is fond of repetitions, into which he always introduces a new emphasis. 'These things' presumably refers back to ver. 6, and, anyhow, English can refer loosely to 'all this' and 'the end of it' (אַחֲרִיתָהּ), for which Q[a] has אחרונה, with no appreciable difference of meaning.

8. וְאַפְסִי] The suffix is an obsolete case-ending (*GK* 90 *l*). This is more terse than the pron. sf., which anyhow would mean 'I am not'.

10. רָעָתֵךְ] 'your wickedness' is more arresting than Q[a] דעתך 'your knowledge', which is entirely appropriate in the next line.

12. MT looks overloaded and it is tempting to omit בַּאֲשֶׁר יָגַעַתְּ מִנְּעוּרָיִךְ (so Duhm, Köhler), which has no proper ‖ and may have been repeated from ver. 15. Volz supposed that it was the first half of a line of which the second half has been lost. Q[a] has a shorter text, simply ועד היום, 'and until to-day' for נִלְאֵית (13) . . . אוּלַי. Muilenburg seems inclined to follow the Scroll in ver. 12: 'It is possible that the lines omitted by the Dead Sea Scroll are a satirical gloss'. But much else in the poem is satirical. He appears to keep נִלְאֵית, which anyhow must be genuine. On the whole it is best to keep the text as it stands, with some reservation about 'in which you have toiled from your youth'.

13. עֲצָתָיִךְ] The mixed pointing, the noun being singular and the suffix as for plural (*GK* 91 *l*; *BL* § 29*b*[1]), may conceal textual corruption. Many would read יוֹעֲצָיִךְ, 'your counsellors' since 'counsels' cannot 'stand up'. But the subject of יַעַמְדוּ is probably the nouns following. It is little matter, since 'counsels' imply 'counsellors'. מֵאֲשֶׁר] It is usual to omit the *mêm* as a dittograph (cf. LXX, P), otherwise the subject of יָבֹאוּ is vague and indefinite. But that may be intentional, the undefined subject—for the Prophet, though not for the 'prognosticators'—referring back to the 'disaster', 'ruin', and 'crash' which are to 'come upon' Babylon in ver. 11. In any case, what the fates decreed depended on observations in this or that 'quarter' of the sky. The construction would be eased if for the plural יָבֹאוּ we could read the singular יָבוֹא. This was conjectured by Duhm and is now supported by Q^{a}.

15. סֹחֲרַיִךְ] The proposal to read שֹׁחֲרַיִךְ in the sense 'your magicians' (see on שַׁחְרָהּ, ver. 11 below) is unconvincing. The spelling with *sāmech* is attested by Q^{a}. The √s סחר/שחר have such a wide range of meanings that סֹחֲרַיִךְ could mean 'your magicians', but it is practically certain that the usual sense 'your traffickers' is intended: see exeg. note below.

This magnificent taunt-song is a single poem. The fact that its sub-divisions are not obviously clear—some say that there are five, others that there are six—is sufficient indication of this. We have not to do with separate pieces which have been put together to form a unity, as in xl. 1–11. Nor must we expect, in a longish Hebrew poem, to find stanzas so regular as in *The Faerie Queene*. The first two paragraphs are obvious enough: in vv. 1–4 Babylon is a luxury-loving lady who is to be degraded to the status of the meanest slave; in vv. 5–7 she is a heartless tyrant; in vv. 8–9 bereavement, sudden and irreparable, is to come to her; in vv. 10–11 she is to be engulfed in utter ruin. In vv. 12–13 she is bidden to call her sorcerers and astrologers to save her, if they can! In vain, their only concern, and that of her 'traffickers', is to save themselves, regardless of her fate (vv. 14–15).

The 'tenses' of the verbs indicate that the poem is predictive, not descriptive after the event. Babylon did, of course, fall to Cyrus, and Herodotus speaks of 'the poverty which followed upon the conquest with its attendant hardship and general ruin'. But it was still one of the wonder-cities of the world, rather like Venice in her decline.

The tone of the poem, notwithstanding the 'I will take vengeance' of ver. 4, is less vengeful than Nahum's taunt-song against Nineveh. Babylon's ill-treatment of the Jews is briefly described but does not stand in the foreground. The indictment is directed more against her overweening pride and utter heartlessness (cf. xiv. 4–21). This, perhaps, is the main reason why Babylon, not Assyria, came to be the type of Antichrist (cf. Rev. xvii–xviii). The Assyrians were ruthlessly cruel. Nineveh was sacked and passed into oblivion. Babylon lived on and even enjoyed a brief revival of her earlier splendour under Alexander the Great. Nebuchadrezzar was a great king, with qualities different from those of an Assyrian Tiglath-Pileser. But he survived in legend, not unjustly, as swell-headed and rather ridiculous (Dan. iii–iv). And so Babylon went into a slow decline, to become the standing example of what happens to a civilization made rotten by wealth and self-indulgence. It is one of the main themes of prophecy, beginning with Amos (Amos vi. 1–7). Dives did not intend to be cruel, but he was cruel nevertheless (Luke xvi. 19–31).

1. *Get down*] May sound colloquial but is what the peremptory imperative means here. EVV 'Come down' is from the standpoint of someone at ground level, but the speaker is Yahweh. *among the rubble*] Lit. 'in the dust'. The grand lady's 'throne' is to be the dust. For dust in the (here anticipatory) sense of rubble cf. 1 Kings xx. 10; Ezek. xxvi. 4, 12; Neh. iv. 10 (*4*). *virgin city of Babylon*] Lit. 'the virgin (of) the daughter (of) Babylon'; appositional genitives (*GK* 130 *e*), cf. our 'the city of London'. Babylon is personified as a woman (cf. Britannia), virgin, and as yet unconquered and unravished. For similar personifications cf. xxxvii. 22 (Zion); Amos v. 2 (Israel); Jer. xlvi. 11 (Egypt). *sit*] Repeated for emphasis. *dainty and voluptuous*] Cf. Deut. xxviii. 54, 56, 'tender and delicately brought up'.

2. To grind with millstones was the task of the lowest menial slaves: Exod. xi. 5 and see plates 185–6 in *AOTB*. Note the onomatopoeia: *ḳᵉḥî rēḥayim wᵉṭaḥᵃnî ḳāmaḥ*. *uncover your tresses*] Cf. AV and to be preferred to 'remove thy veil' (RV, cf. RSV). The noun *ṣammāh* (√ 'draw together') can mean either 'plaited hair' or 'veil' (so LXX, P). It occurs elsewhere only in Song iv. 1, 3, vi. 7, where AV 'within thy locks' means 'behind your tresses', which hang over the face, partially hiding it. The verb *uncover* (*Piʿēl gālāh*) seems decisive, since everywhere else its acc. obj. is something uncovered, not something removed: so in the present context, 'bare your thighs'. We might point the verb *gōllî* (*Qal gālal*), lit 'roll away', though the object of this is usually a stone (e.g. Gen. xxix. 3) and it would be making heavy work of a veil. Yet AV and RV mean much the same. It was immodest and humiliating for a 'dainty' lady to uncover her hair: cf. 1 Cor. xi. 2–13. She therefore wore a veil to conceal it and could only uncover her hair by removing her veil. *train*] *šōḇel*, ἅπ. λεγ. but evidently a trailing garment: cf. *šibbōleṯ*, 'flowing stream' (Ps. lxix. 15 (*16*)), 'ear of grain' (Gen. xli. 5). Qᵃ has *šûlayiḵ*, 'your skirts': cf. vi. 1; Jer. xiii. 22, 26; Nahum iii. 5. The two words are from related √s (*šbl*/*šwl*) and the Scroll has substituted a more familiar word. *thighs*] Heb. *šôḳ* has much the same ambiguity as Engl. 'leg', usually the lower leg of a man, the upper of an animal. The former is illustrated from the bronze doors of Balawat, in which women captives are holding up their skirts to their knees (A. Jeremias, *Das AT im Lichte des Alten Orients*, 4. Aufl., p. 689). But to wade through rivers a woman would need to bare her thighs, and in Ps. cxlvii. 10; Song v. 15 the word can hardly be restricted to 'shanks'.

3. *You will suffer rape*] Lit. 'Your nakedness will be uncovered'; but to 'uncover the nakedness of' = 'to have intercourse with': Lev. vi. 6–19. The 'virgin' Babylon is to be deflowered. Or, if we prefer the literal translation, the meaning may be that Babylon is to suffer the public humiliation of the adulteress: cf. Ezek. xvi. 37; Hos: ii. 10 (*12*). *shame*] For *ḥerpāh* as 'disgrace' consequent on sexual humiliation see 2 Sam. xiii. 13. If we prefer the literal translation of the first stich, 'shame' will be 'pudenda', though the word is not elsewhere found in exactly that sense.

5. *the dark*] Here = imprisonment: cf. xlii. 7, xlix. 9. *queen*] For this sense of *g^e^ḇîrāh* ('lady', 'mistress') see 1 Kings xi. 19, xv. 13, and cf. 'Venice, the Queen of the Adriatic'.

6. *I ceased to regard them as any longer mine*] Lit. 'I profaned (*ḥillaltî*, i.e. "de-sacrated", see on xliii. 28) my inheritance'. Yahweh's 'inheritance' or 'property' (*naḥ^a^lāh*) is hardly ever the land of Israel (though see Jer. ii. 7 and perhaps four times). It is his *people* Israel (1 Sam. x. 1 and some two dozen times, sometimes with 'people' ‖ 'inheritance', as here). As Yahweh's property Israel is sacred or 'holy' (*ḳōḏeš*) to him (Jer. ii. 3) and under his inviolable protection. The opposite of *ḳōḏeš* is *ḥōl*, 'profane' in the sense 'common', or, as we should say, 'secular' (Lev. x. 10; 1 Sam. xxi. 5). In Ezek. xxii. 26 'they profaned my holy things' means that they treated them as if they had no sacred meaning. So here, Yahweh's people have forfeited their sacrosanctity, and he no longer treats them as 'holy'.

7. *you gave not a thought*] Lit. 'you did not remember', in sense of Job xxi. 6, xli. 8 (*xl. 32*); Lam. i. 9; Eccles. xi. 8. One cannot 'remember' the future except in the original sense 'bear in mind'.

8. *you pampered jade*] *'^a^ḏînāh*. 'Pampered' in the original sense of 'crammed with food'; cf. Jer. li. 34, 'he has filled his belly with my delicacies' (*'^a^ḏānāy*); Neh. ix. 25, 'so they ate, and were surfeited and became fat, and luxuriated (*yiṯ'add^e^nû*, almost "wallowed") in thy great goodness'. *I am, and there is none else beside*] So verbatim Zeph. ii. 15 (Nineveh). The words by themselves could mean no more than that 'nobody else matters'. But in the light of xlv. 5 f. and the elaborations of the theme in xiv. 13 f. and Ezek. xxviii. 1–10 (Tyre) we are to think of self-deification. Babylon had no standard except herself by which to judge herself.

9. *at one fell stroke*] *k^e^ṯummām*, lit. 'according to their completeness'. But a possible meaning is 'all unawares' (to themselves): cf. 1 Kings xxii. 34, where a man draws his bow *l^e^ṯummô*, 'according to his innocency', i.e. without deliberate aim (EVV 'at a venture'). In that case loss of children and widowhood are forces which strike Babylon

without, as we should say, premeditation on their part. This is probably how LXX (ἐξαίφνης) understood the expression. *in spite of . . . for all*] Heb. 'with . . . with'. For this sense of the preposition cf. Num. xiv. 11 and Engl. 'with all his faults I love him still'. Babylonian magical rituals were almost incredibly elaborate. The *incantations* (*kᵉšāp̱îm*) here were protective, intended to ward off disaster. The word *kešep̱* is Babylonian (*kišpu*) and a typical incantation formula runs: *kaššāpu ikšipanni kišpi ikšipanni kišipšu* = 'The enchanter has enchanted me; (with the) enchantment (with which) he has enchanted me, do you enchant him!' The Hebrew word for 'spells' (*ḥᵃḇārîm*) is from a √ 'bind', 'tie' (Akk. *abāru*), and the repetition of the spells was accompanied by the symbolical tying of knots in a rope. The fullest catalogue of magic practitioners in the OT is in Deut. xviii. 10 f., where EVV 'sorcerer' and 'charmer' are for *mᵉḵaššēp̱* and *ḥôḇēr ḥāḇer* (lit. 'knotter of knots') respectively.

10. *misled you*] *šôḇᵉḇāṯēḵ* (*Pôʿlēl šûḇ*), 'turned you back', almost 'led you by the nose': cf. Ezek. xxxviii. 4, 'I will turn you back (from your intended course) and put hooks into your jaws' (Yahweh to Gog).

11. The sudden destruction which is to overwhelm Babylon is expressed by three alliterative nouns: *rāʿāh* ('evil', 'disaster'), *hōwāh* (√ 'to fall', elsewhere only Ezek. vi. 26, 'ruin upon ruin'), *šôʾāh* (onomatopoetic, cf. Zeph. i. 15). Some such words as 'rack', 'ruin', 'crash' may serve to represent them. They are pictured as demons such as the Babylonians might hope to scare away with din. *to charm away*] *šaḥrāh*. Could mean 'its dawn' (*šaḥar*, cf. AV, RV). But 'charm away' (Arab. *saḥara*) is more likely: cf. RV mg. Another possible meaning is 'to control' (Arab. *saḫara* II = 'to tame', 'control'). Some would emend to *šaḥᵃḏāh*, 'to bribe it off' (cf. *šōḥaḏ*, 'bribe'). This would give a good ‖ to 'appease' in the next line, but is unnecessary. *appease*] *kappᵉrāh*, i.e. buy off by payment of a ransom (*kōp̱er*, cf. xliii. 3), so Gen. xxxii. 21; Prov. xvi. 14. 'Expiate' (RSV), the more usual sense of the verb, is surely wrong here.

13. The meaning is the same, whether we read 'counsels' or 'counsellors', or render 'counsels' or *consultations*. All three are involved: cf. 2 Sam. xvi. 20–xvii. 14. Babylon is *worn out* (cf. Job xvi. 7, RSV) to the point of impatience (cf. vii. 13) by conflicting counsels. Let the astrologers (*those who divide up the heavens*, &c.) *stand to and save* her! *the quarters which indicate what is to be befall you*] Lit. 'from where (what is coming—unexpressed part. subj., cf. *GK* 144 *d*, *e*) will come upon you'. Many omens were based on terrestrial phenomena, but the emphasis here is on celestial phenomena such as eclipses, planetary conjunctions and the like: cf. M. Jastrow, *The Religion of*

Babylonia and Assyria, chs. xix–xx. For the Babylonians, what happened on earth was determined by the motions of the heavenly bodies. For the Prophet, the courses of the stars and the course of history were alike under the control of Yahweh: cf. xl. 26, xlv. 7.

14. So far from the astrologers being able to save Babylon, they will be powerless to save themselves. They will be like stubble consumed by fire. It will not be a comfortable fire at which to warm themselves or to sit by, but a raging furnace. It will be a case of save himself who can!

15. Babylon will be left alone to her fate. *Such is all they care about you*] Lit. 'Such they have become for you'. The way in which, here, as in ver. 13, the compound substantive subjects are placed after the very simple verbs, is rhetorically effective. *with whom you have trafficked*] Lit. 'your merchants' (*sôḥ^{a}rayiḵ*, √ 'go around'). The word introduces a new feature into the poem, but one that is characteristic in denunciations of rich but decadent world powers: so Nahum iii. 16, of Assyria, where the word is *rôk^{e}lîm* and has the sense of 'footing it around'; Isa. xxiii. 1–8; Ezek. xxvii. 12–36 (Tyre). In Isa. xxiii. 17 f., which is perhaps secondary to the song of the prostitute that precedes it, this 'trafficking' is something wanton. Nowhere is the association of trafficking, luxury, and wantonness so vividly described as in Rev. xviii (Babylon = Rome), which is obviously based on Isa. xlvii. Babylon's 'traffickers' have only dealt with her for what they themselves could get out of it, and when disaster comes they leave her to her fate without scruple. *each goes his own random way*] Lit. 'each in his own direction they wander (confusedly)'.

XLVIII. PROPHECY AND HISTORY

The question whether DI consists of short pieces or longer poems is nowhere more difficult to decide than in this chapter. According to Köhler, Volz, and Mowinckel, the chapter contains four pieces, vv. 1–11, 12–16, 17–19, 20–21 (22). For Muilenburg it is a single poem, with two major divisions (vv. 1–11, 12–21) of four strophes each (vv. 1–2, 3–5, 6–8, 9–11; 12–13, 14–15, 16–17, 18–19) and a closing lyrical finale (vv. 20–21). He argues that 'a stylistic analysis provides a clue . . . to the essential unity of the poem', and instances the use (in the Heb.) of the verbs 'hear' (vv. 1, 3, 5, 6, 12, 14, 16), 'call' (vv. 1, 2, 8, 12, 13, 15), 'speak' (vv. 15, 16), 'declare' (vv. 3, 5, 6, 14, 20), and the nouns 'Jacob' (vv. 1, 12, 20) and 'name' (vv. 1, 2, 9, (11), 19). That there is an 'essential unity' in the chapter is not in dispute. That Israel's past has been sinful is a theme common to vv. 1–5 and 18–19. But the links between the several parts are by no means so close as they are in chs. xlvi and xlvii. On the whole, this half-way stage in the prophecy leaves the impression that it is a gathering together of related themes rather than an artistic unity. In the circumstances it may make for clarity if we divide the chapter into the paragraphs of the RV.

XLVIII. 1–11. PROPHECY, PAST AND CONTEMPORARY

1. מִמֵּי יְהוּדָה יָצָאוּ] 'went out from the waters of Judah' conveys little meaning. In Deut. xxxiii. 28 and Ps. lxviii. 26 (27), the ancestor Jacob-Israel is a 'fountain' (Deut. עַיִן, Ps. מְקוֹר), but the comparison is somewhat remote. Elsewhere in DI Judah is only mentioned twice (xl. 9, xliv. 26, 'the cities of Judah'). To read וּמִיהוּדָה 'and from Judah' (LXX) is objectionable on metrical grounds. (Some 40 MSS. have the longer but meaningless וּמִימֵי.) It is usual to read וּמִמְּעֵי, 'and from the bowels of': cf. Gen. xv. 4, 'one who shall go forth (יֵצֵא) from your bowels'; similarly 2 Sam. vii. 12; Isa. xlviii. 19; 2 Chron. xxxii. 21. Some of the rabbis (cf. T. 'seed') took 'waters' here as a euphemism in this sense.

6. There seems nothing we can do about the abrupt change in the pron. subj. from singular to plural, unless we make the homiletical point that it is for *individual* Israelites to testify. But the change from singular to plural pronouns is common enough, especially in Deut.

7. וְלִפְנֵי־יוֹם וְלֹא] Assuming that מִיּוֹם (xliii. 13; Ezek. xlviii. 35) means 'from now on', לפני־יום should mean 'until now'. MT may have been amplified from לְפָנִים, 'formerly', with little difference of meaning. The text runs more smoothly if we may read לֹא for וְלֹא, with Q[a].

8. פִּתְּחָה] The pointing as *Piʿēl* probably has *Niph.* נִפְתְּחָה in mind: similarly in lx. 11 and cf. xxxv. 5.

9. וּתְהִלָּתִי] If the text is right, the force of לְמַעַן in the first stich must extend over this second. This is infrequent, but examples can be quoted (e.g. xv. 8, lviii. 10, lxi. 7: cf. *GK* 119 *hh*) where it would be pedantic to amplify the text.

11. כִּי אֵיךְ יֵחָל] 'for how should it be profaned?' The verb has no subject and the stich is a beat short (2:2). LXX *ὅτι τὸ ἐμὸν ὄνομα βεβηλοῦται* may have read שְׁמִי, or it may only have been interpreting. It is tempting to take the phrase as a gloss (so Duhm) based on Ezek. xx. 9, 14, 22, which has much in common with this passage: see on xliii. 25. Among other expedients is one to take תְּהִלָּתִי from ver. 9 and insert it here; but that would necessitate a further change of יֵחָל to תֵּחָל.

The main argument of this section is that Yahweh long ago predicted the course of his people's history, in order that as events happened they should have no excuse for attributing them to any idol-god. Similarly now, on the eve of their liberation, he predicts *new things*, this for the sake of his *name* and because he knows how prone they are to misinterpret the courses of events.

The passage has occasioned much perplexity. It is even harsher in tone than xlii. 18–25, xliii. 22–28, and xlvi. 8, and may seem inconsistent with the message of 'the prophet of consolation'. Nor are the strictures in it addressed to a section only of the exiles, like those in xlv. 9–11, but to the whole nation throughout its history, which is even accused of idolatry. Indeed, the general tone, and even some details, are reminiscent of Ezekiel. Accordingly, Duhm supposed that an original consolatory poem of DI has been interpolated by a kind of interlinear commentary in which Israel's past is strongly condemned. This type of interpretation was widely accepted by Duhm's successors. Details vary but a fair example of it is to be seen in Moffatt's translation, in which vv. 1*b*, 2, 4, 5*b*, 7*b*, 8*b*–10 are bracketed. The change from the 2nd pers. of ver. 1 to the 3rd of ver. 2 could indicate that the verses are composite. On the other hand, DI is quite capable of an abrupt transition from 2nd to 3rd person; see on xlv. 8, 21, though those are single sentences in which the changes of person are explicable on rhetorical and stylistic grounds. The interpolation theory was still supported by Mowinckel in *Det Gamle Testamente*, iii. 1944, but most recent commentators incline to the view that the passage, much as we have it, is from DI. It is pointed out that he was no mild enthusiast, that he certainly encountered opposition (see on xlv. 9–11), and that he was concerned to penetrate to the underlying causes of things. Also it is difficult to see what motive an editor could have in turning his mildness into harshness, especially when the general tendency was to tone down the asperities of the prophets. The suggestion has been made (by Volz) that the passage is an address given by the Prophet on one of the days of penitence and fasting which the exiles observed in Babylon (cf. Zech. vii. 3–5). Whether this is so or not, the suggestion is a valuable one. It would be surprising if DI did not exercise some kind of public ministry, as his predecessors had done.

The question whether the passage has been expanded is of course one for higher, not lower, criticism, since there is no textual evidence for the deletion of the disputed sentences. There is not, and never can be, any certainty that the original text was shorter than what we have. But if, on higher critical grounds, we could be reasonably certain that a passage has been expanded in the MT, should we be justified in deleting the 'insertions'? The answer must be, in general,

No! We cannot recover the original autographs, or exact copies of them. If, on textual evidence, we have to say that this or that was not in the original text, we may be justified in deleting it, as the RV sometimes does. Individual scholars may, on higher critical grounds, decide against the genuineness of a passage, and bracket it in their commentaries, though the probability is that they will find the contents of the waste-paper basket as interesting as what they keep. But it is improbable that any oecumenical committee will ever delete a passage from the Bible solely on higher critical grounds. That is Holy Scripture which has the sanction of Christian tradition. No one would dream of deleting xliv. 9–20 from the Bible, even if he were convinced that it is not from DI. And the insertions, if such they be, in xlviii. 1–11 say no more than is said again and again by the prophets. So let them stay, even though some may have reservations about them.

1. *who swear by . . . and invoke*] To 'swear by' (Deut. vi. 13, x. 20) and 'invoke' (Heb. *yazkîrû*, lit. 'call to remembrance', cf. xxvi. 13; Gen. xl. 14, xli. 9; Ps. xx. 7 (*8*)) were cultic acts, and support the suggestion that this passage was spoken by the Prophet at some assembly for worship. *good faith . . . sincerity*] *'ᵉmeṯ . . . ṣᵉḏāḳāh*, lit. 'truth . . . righteousness'. For the association of these in the taking of oaths cf. Jer. iv. 2; Zech. viii. 8.

2. *the holy city*] *'îr haḳḳōḏeš*, came to be the common designation of Jerusalem (lii. 1; Neh. xi. 1; Dan. ix. 24; Matt. iv. 5, xxvii. 53), and the name (*el-ḳuds*) by which it is still called by Muslims.

3. *Long ago I foretold the events of times now past*] Lit. 'The former things (*hārî'šônôṯ*) long ago (*mē'āz*) I declared'. For 'the former things' see on xli. 22, xlii. 9, xliii. 9, 18, xlvi. 9. Sometimes the reference is to the early victories of Cyrus; in xliii. 18 it must be to the Exodus; in xlvi. 9 it may be to the Exodus, or, more generally, to events in the past. The reference here is not entirely clear. A case can be made out for yet another reference to the victories of Cyrus (cf. C. R. North, 'The "Former Things" and the "New Things" in Deutero-Isaiah', in *Studies in OT Prophecy*, ed. H. H. Rowley, pp. 123 f.), in which case *mē'āz* should be translated 'in time past', a rendering which is perfectly admissible: so 2 Sam. xv. 34, and cf. Exod. iv. 10, v. 23; Isa. xiv. 8; Jer. xliv. 18, EVV 'since' (comparatively recently). But on the whole it is more likely that 'the former things' here are, in a general way, the significant events in Israel's history. Prominent among them would be the Exodus. According to Gen. xv. 12–16, which must be comparatively early (? JE), Yahweh foretold the Egyptian bondage and Exodus to Abraham. Whether DI was

acquainted with this tradition in a literary form we cannot say, but it must have been current in his time. Or 'the former things' may be the disasters predicted by the prophets from Amos to Jeremiah. An objection to this is that if they were calamities, Israel could hardly point to them proudly as the work of their 'idols' (ver. 5*b*). But is 5*b* original? Assuming the possibility that it is not, we are free to take 'the former things' as including the exile and to interpret ver. 3 accordingly. Thus, it was supposed in the ancient world that the fortunes of nations depended on the power of their gods, and even that they reflected the struggles of the gods in the supernatural world: Dan. x. 13, 20 f.; cf. Deut. xxxii. 8. Hence, if a people suffered disaster, it was because its god was powerless to save it. Therefore, if Yahweh had not announced the exile beforehand, and insisted that it was he who was bringing it about, Israel would have assumed that Bel-Marduk was stronger than he. Indeed, it is not impossible that 'my carved idol and my molten image' in ver. 5*b* is aimed at apostasy on the part of some of the exiles to Bel-Marduk. *I declared and made known what they would be*] Lit. 'from my mouth they went out and I caused them to be heard'. For 'my mouth' cf. xl. 5, xlv. 23, lv. 11. The anthropomorphism should not be taken literally. For words to 'go out from the mouth' is a way of saying that they are solemnly and irrevocably spoken: cf. Judges xi. 36; Jer. xliv. 17. *acted*] See on xli. 4.

4. That Israel had always been self-willed is a recurring reproach in the later Elohistic and Deuteronomic tradition, but the language here is not just copy-book stuff. *stubborn*] *ḳāšeh*, lit. 'hard'. The usual expression is 'hard of neck', cf. the next stich: so Exod. xxxii. 9, xxxiii. 3, 5; Deut. ix. 6, 13. It passed over into the NT σκληροτράχηλος (Acts vii. 51) and so, with some biblical flavour, into Engl. 'stiff-necked'. *rigid as iron*] Lit. 'a sinew (*gîḏ*) of iron'. *and your brazen effrontery*] Lit. 'and your forehead bronze': cf. Jer. iii. 3, 'the forehead of a prostitute'.

5. *my idol*] *ʿoṣbî*. The singular form, *ʿōṣeḇ*, is only found here. It was probably vocalized to conform to *bōšeṯ*, 'shame(ful thing)'. *metal image*] *pesel wᵉnesek*. EVV take as two images, but the expression was almost certainly a hendiadys. The double subject precedes the verb in the singular. In the story of Micah the Ephraimite, Micah's mother gives him silver with which to make a *pesel ûmassēḵāh*: Judges xvii. 3 f., and in xviii. 31 the image is called Micah's *pesel*; cf. Deut. xxvii. 15. *set them in motion*] Lit. 'commanded them': cf. xlv. 12.

6. *All that you have seen you are now to behold*] Lit. 'Thou hast heard behold it all'. The imperative expresses a distinct assurance (*GK*

110 *c*) and *behold* something of the suggestion 'perceive the meaning', as in Job (xv. 17, xxiv. 1, xxxiv. 32). *and it must be your part to make it known*] Lit. 'and you, will you not declare?' (*taggîḏû*), almost in the sense of 'bear witness'; cf. xliii. 10. Indeed, Volz would read *tāʿîḏ*, 'testify', though he translates it *zugeben*, 'will you not have to admit it?' This may be the meaning of MT, 'you will have to admit it': cf. iii. 9; Ps. xxxviii. 18 (*19*). The question is rhetorical and expects the answer 'Yes'. *new things*] *ḥᵃḏāšôṯ*, as distinct from 'the former things' of ver. 3. The sing. *ḥᵃḏāšāh* in xliii. 19 refers to the transformation of the wilderness. The plural in xlii. 9 is undefined, though it is said that they will be announced in due course. It is now clear that they refer to Cyrus' conquest of Babylon.

7. For the bearing of this and the previous verse on the date of DI see Introduction (*supra*, p. 3). *created*] The verb *bārāʾ* (see on xl. 26) is used not only of the initial creation but of God's creative activity in history: see also xli. 20, xliii. 1, 7, xlv. 7 f., liv. 16, lvii. 19, lxv. 18; Jer. xxxi. 22; Ps. li. 10 (*12*).

8. *firmly closed*] Lit. 'not opened'. Litotes, cf. on xlii. 3. *a rebel*] Cf. xliii. 27, xlvi. 8.

9. *For my name's sake*] Here *name* with some emphasis on 'reputation': see on xliii. 25, and cf. ver. 11, 'the honour due to me'. *I am slow to anger*] Lit. 'I lengthen (*ʾaʾᵃrîḵ*) my anger'. That Yahweh is *ʾereḵ ʾappayim*, 'long-tempered', is one of the attributes in his self-predication to Moses (Exod. xxxiv. 6; cf. Num. xiv. 18; Neh. ix. 17; Ps. lxxxvi. 15, ciii. 8, cxlv. 8; Jonah iv. 2; Nahum i. 3). If the Jews had had a mind to list 'beautiful names' of Yahweh, this would have been one of them; and although in Ezek., and perhaps in this passage, Yahweh is sensitive about his good name, it is his nature to be 'long-tempered'. *renown*] For this sense of *tᵉhillāh*, 'praise', in conjunction with 'name', cf. Zeph. iii. 19 f. *restrain*] *ʾeḥᵉṭom*. The √ is ἅπ. λεγ. in OT but the cognate languages show that its literal sense is 'muzzle'. *otherwise*] *lᵉḇiltî*, lit. 'in order not to', with infinitive of purpose.

10. This verse would present no difficulty if we could translate the first verb *ṣᵉraptîḵā* by 'I bought you' (Akk. *ṣarāpu*, 'to buy'). The preposition following (*bᵉ*) would then be a normal example of the '*bêth* of price' (*GK* 119 *p*): 'I bought you, but not for money'. To buy for nothing seems a contradiction, but the purchaser is Yahweh, who, when he redeems (xliii. 1, xlviii. 20; Ps. lxxiv. 2, lxxvii. 15 (*16*)) Israel, does not pay anything. Indeed, in lv. 1 men are invited to buy grain (*šiḇᵉrû*, cf. Gen. xli. 57, xlii. 2) 'without money'. But nowhere else in the OT can the √*ṣārap̱* (about two dozen times) possibly have the meaning 'buy'. If we translate *I have assayed you*, we are in some difficulty with the b^e following. Its frequent sense 'with' (AV) is meaningless here. RV 'as' probably took it as *bêth essentiae* (*GK* 119 *i*), but 'I have assayed you, but not as silver (is assayed)' is, to say the least, obscure. RSV 'like' is based on a conjectural emendation (k^e for b^e), and, even so, makes little sense. In passages like 'Every man shall be put to death for (b^e) his own sin' (Deut. xxiv. 16), the 'for' has a causal force, but such cases can equally well be examples of an extended use of the '*bêth* of price', similar to those in Gen. xviii. 28; 1 Sam. iii. 13. The meaning will then be that Yahweh has 'assayed' Israel, but not for any silver that has accrued to him from the process! The exile has brought him neither pleasure nor profit; Israel has been mostly 'dross' (i. 22, 25; Ezek. xxii. 18–22). *I chose you*] The meaning, on the normal sense of the verb (*b^eḥartîḵā*), must be that Yahweh, without expecting to find any good metal in Israel, nevertheless chose her. In Aramaic the word commonly has the meaning 'to test'; similarly in the Heb. *Niph.* (Prov. viii. 10, 19, x. 20), gold and silver are 'choice', i.e. chosen, because they have been tested. Volz cites two MSS. which read *b^eḥantîḵā*, 'I tested you' (*bāḥan* is sometimes ‖ *ṣārap̱*). This reading is now supported by Q^a and may be original. *in the furnace of affliction*] In Deut. iv. 20; 1 Kings viii. 51; Jer. xi. 4 'the iron furnace' (*kûr*) is Egypt, and the emphasis is on torment rather than on testing. In Ezek. xxii. 18, 20, 22; Prov. xvii. 3, xxvii. 21 the *kûr* is a smelting-pot or crucible. It is probable that in this verse both the Egyptian bondage and the exile are in mind. It is an historical fact that out of the 'dross' that was Israel, some precious metal was extracted.

11. See on xlii. 8, xliii. 25.

XLVIII. 12–19. THE CONTEMPORANEITY OF HISTORY

14. כֻּלְּכֶם . . . בָּהֶם] 'all of you (? Israelites, ? the nations) . . . among them' (? the nations and/or their gods). Some 40 MSS. read בָּכֶם, 'among you'. But there has never been any suggestion that the Israelites have predicted, or should be able to predict, the future. Q^a has יקבצו כולם וישמעו, 'let them all assemble and hear', the 'them' being presumably the gods (cf. xli. 22); but the summons to them to 'hear' seems irrelevant. Since, in any case, we must do the best we can with pronouns that have no antecedents, it is best to keep the MT. יהוה אֲהֵבוֹ וגו׳] Lit. 'Yahweh loves him he will carry out his purpose against Babylon'. The difficulty here is that Yahweh is in the 3rd person, whereas in the preceding and following contexts he is the speaker. LXX omits יהוה. Duhm and others get tolerable sense and metre by reading אֹהֲבִי יַעֲשֶׂה חֶפְצִי, 'he whom I love will carry out my purpose'. Q[a] has אוהבי but otherwise makes 'pie' of the text (יהוה אוהבי וישה *sic*). Volz thinks that the original has been modified on reverential grounds. Yet he hesitates to adopt Duhm's emendation because it would imply a closer intimacy between Yahweh and Cyrus than does the (by some) conjectured רֵעִי ('my friend') in xliv. 28, and would put Cyrus on the same footing as Abraham (cf. xli. 8). His way out of the difficulty is to take יהוה אֲהֵבוֹ as a titular or symbolic name (cf. vii. 3, viii. 1) by which even Yahweh can call Cyrus, and read חֶפְצִי for חֶפְצוֹ: so ' "He-whom-Yahweh-loves" will carry out my purpose'. But apart from its clumsiness, this reading does not get rid of the statement that Yahweh 'loves' Cyrus. If we keep MT we must bracket 14*b* as a later expansion. But it looks basically original, not the kind of marginal comment that a scribe would dare to invent. וּזְרֹעוֹ כַּשְׂדִּים] 'and his arm the Chaldeans'. We must either read בַּכַּשְׂדִּים or suppose that the ב in בְּבָבֶל governs also כַּשְׂדִּים; see on ver. 9 above. LXX *τοῦ ἄραι σπέρμα χαλδαίων* must be for וּ[בְ]זֶרַע כַּשְׂדִּים. This may be right but there is no compelling reason for adopting it.

15. וְהִצְלִיחַ] LXX, P, read as for וָאַצְלִיחַ, 'and I have prospered'. There is no essential difference between this and MT. Yahweh is the prime mover throughout.

Although this passage seems mostly repetitive, it contains a suggestion that is profoundly significant, viz. that of the 'contemporaneity' of history. The first hint of this is in ver. 4, where the only translation that brings out the full implication of the context is neither 'I knew how stubborn you were', nor 'I know how stubborn you are', but 'I *knew* how stubborn you *are*'. The address is to all Israel throughout her history: 'therefore I told you long ago', before the birth of any living Israelite. Underlying it is the concept of the corporate personality of the nation in the past and in the present. so now, in vv. 18 f., what is said is not 'If only *your fathers* had paid heed to my commandments, then your peace would have been like a river . . .', but 'If only *you* had paid heed'. Yahweh is contemporary with all history: 'ever since anything came to pass, there am I' (ver. 16; cf. xli. 4). Not only so, but the present generation of Israelites is, in a sense, contemporary with Israel's history throughout its course. Whether we should press this so far as to make it imply that contemporary Israel shared the guilt of their forefathers is, perhaps, an academic question. But in the classic confessions of Nehemiah (Neh. i. 5–11), Ezra (Neh. ix. 6–37), and Daniel (Dan. ix. 4–19), no attempt is made to lay the blame entirely on former generations.

The Greeks may have been far better historians than the Hebrews, but they had no conception of any 'theology of history'. They saw 'the rhythm of the Universe as a cyclic movement governed by an impersonal Law. . . . Hence, in the Graeco-Roman World and in the Indian World . . . History was rated at a low value' (A. Toynbee, *An Historian's Approach to Religion*, pp. 8 f.). For the Hebrews, history had a beginning, in the creation (which the Greeks never really believed in), a purpose determined by God, and it would have a consummation.

12. *whom I called*] See on xlii. 6, xliii. 1. *I am he, I am the first, I, too, am the last*] See on xli. 4, xliv. 6.

13. *My hand laid the foundation of the earth*] The most detailed description of Hebrew cosmogony, apart from Gen. i, is in Ps. civ. 1–9, in which the earth is founded on pillars driven down into the abyss of subterranean waters: cf. also Ps. xxiv. 2, cii. 25 (*26*); Prov. iii. 19; Job xxxviii. 4–6. Q[a] has the dual 'My hands laid'. This seems more logical; but Yahweh could quite easily lay the earth's foundations with one hand. MT 'my hand . . . my right hand' is normal parallelism and a way of saying that both Yahweh's 'hands' were employed. *they sprang into being*] Lit. 'they stood up together' (*yaḥdāw*, see on xli. 19 f.).

14. The best that can be done with the unrelated pronouns is to take *you* as the nations (cf. xliii. 9, xlv. 20) and *them* as their gods (Cf. xli. 22, 26). **He whom I call 'Friend'**] Lit. 'My friend' (see textual note above). The reference is to Cyrus (cf. xliv. 28) and no matter what we do with the text, it must remain that Yahweh is said to 'love' Cyrus or that Cyrus is his 'friend'.

15. The repeated *I, I* and the four emphatic and swiftly moving verbs (cf. xli. 20) are characteristic of DI and in keeping with the momentousness of what is taking place. *undertaking*] Heb. 'way'. For 'way' = journey = undertaking cf. Gen. xxiv. 21, 40, 56; Joshua i. 8.

16. *Never . . . have I spoken in secrecy*] Cf. xlv. 19. *ever since anything came to pass*] Heb. *mē'ēṯ heyôṯāh*, lit. 'from the time of its becoming', the *min* ('from') marking the *terminus a quo*. Precisely what the 3rd pers. sing. fem. sf. 'its' refers to is not indicated, but the ‖ *from the beginning* points to events long past: cf. vv. 3–5, xl. 21, xli. 4, though see also xli. 26 *in re* Cyrus. Duhm is probably right to insist that 'its becoming' cannot refer to the creation, but he is probably wrong in saying that 'from the beginning' and 'from the time of its becoming' (*seit es geschieht*) look no farther back than to the career of Cyrus. *there am I*] 'Before Abraham was, I am' (John viii. 58) comes almost inevitably to mind. *and now the Lord God has sent me and his spirit*]

'And his spirit' is a second object, not a second subject, of 'sent'. In the OT the spirit never sends but is always sent. The sentence is prose and the 'me' can hardly be anyone but the Prophet. But why should the Prophet interject a reference to himself into a context in which Yahweh is the speaker? It is the only such reference in the prophecy, except the doubtful 'and I said' of xl. 6 (see *supra*, p. 70) and, possibly, l. 4–9 (see *infra*, pp. 203–4). Volz emends to read *w*^{e}-*'attāh 'ešlāḥennû l*^{e}*'orḥô*, 'and now I send him (*sc.* Cyrus) on his way'; but no reliance can be placed on this. Most critics, although there is no textual evidence for it, regard the words as a later addition to the text. A stronger case could be made for their retention if the whole verse were an utterance of the Prophet, but to say 'Never from the beginning have I spoken in secrecy . . . there am I' is Yahweh's prerogative (cf. xlv. 19). It is just possible that a member of (perhaps) the Trito-Isaianic circle could, without meaning to be presumptuous, make the Prophet utter the whole verse, and indeed the verse does hang loosely between ver. 15, which has a certain finality about it, and ver. 17, which (*pace* Muilenburg) looks as if it begins a new strophe. But perhaps it is best to retain 16*a* and to bracket 16*b* as a later insertion based on lxi. 1, in which the speaker is less reticent than DI appears to have been. A similar case of 'interjection' is Mic. iii. 8, which also looks secondary.

17. *for your profit*] Lit. 'in order to profit' (*Hiph.* infin. *yā'al*). This verb (some 20 times) is nearly always accompanied by a negative or used in a question requiring a negative answer: e.g. Job xxxv. 3, 'What am I better off than if I had sinned?' The only exceptions are xlvii. 12 (ironical); Job xxx. 13 ('they promote my ruin', *si vera lectio*), and here, where, as the next verse shows, Yahweh's teaching had been wasted on his people. It was a case of 'How often would I . . .!' (Luke xiii. 34). Israel's history had been a tragedy of wasted opportunities.

18–19. *Would that you had paid heed to my commands!*] 'Oh that thou wouldest hearken' (RV mg.) is a perfectly possible translation of this first stich: cf. lxiv. 1 (*lxiii. 19*), but the following stich can hardly be translated 'then should thy peace be' (*way*^{e}*hî*). The reference, then, is to the past rather than to the future. The past is irrevocable, but there is nothing in the passage to suggest that there is no longer any hope for Israel. That would be a negation of DI's message. Indeed, 19*b* implies, almost as a certainty, that Yahweh's promises to Abraham (cf. Gen. xiii. 16, xxii. 17) will be fulfilled, and, if it stood alone, would contain not a condition but a promise and assurance. Divine grace is ever renewed. The sense of the whole is 'Would that you had (but you did not), and yet you still may. . . '. *a river*] *nāhār*, perennial and smooth flowing, not a wadi (*naḥal*). *the waves* (lit. 'rollers') *of the sea*] Everywhere else a description or symbol of turbulence, but here ‖ 'river' must be a simile of abundance and fullness.

19. *your descendants*] *ṣe'eṣā'ê mē'êḵā*, lit. 'the offspring (cf. xlii. 5, xliv. 3) of your bowels': cf. textual note on verse 1 above. *its grains*] *me'ôṯâw*, plural of *mā'āh*, with 3rd pers. sing. masc. sf. The word is ἅπ. λεγ. in OT but in post-biblical Hebrew means 'seed' and in Aramaic 'small coin'. The minor Greek versions have κέγχρος. *obliterated*] *yikkārēṯ*, lit. 'cut off'. For the appropriate figure of a *name* not being 'cut off' or 'erased' cf. lv. 13, lvi. 5; Ruth iv. 10. *destroyed*] For *šāmaḏ* ‖ *kāraṯ* cf. 1 Sam. xxiv. 21 (*22*); Ps. xxxvii. 38. For *name* ‖ *children* (*zera'*, properly 'seed'), almost = 'family', 'descendants', cf. lxvi. 22.

XLVIII. 20–22. HOME FROM BABYLON!

Deliverance is so certain and so near that the prophet cries, '*Go out from Babylon, haste away from Chaldea!*' The verse is swift moving, with only two beats to the stich. 'Tell it out' (*hôṣî'ûhā*, ver. 20) is only one word, and though it carries two beats, it is as if the verse marks time, very much as in the 'It stood still' (*ya'amōḏ*) of Job iv. 16 and (possibly) 'is dumb' (*ne'elāmāh*) of Isa. liii. 7. *Say* (*'imerû*) is anacrusis. Verse 21 may be scanned as 2:2/3:3, in which case the poem slows down as it reaches its climax, as a river slows down at the end of its course (so *BH* and cf. xl. 3–5). But it can equally well be scanned as 2:2/2:2/2:2 (so Köhler). Either way, vv. 20–21 are an exquisitely wrought poem. Verse 22 is prose and is word for word the same as lvii. 21, except that it has 'Yahweh' instead of 'my God'. It may be a Trito-Isaianic (?) expansion, intended to mark the close of the first half of the prophecy. But in view of ver. 18 it is not inappropriate here.

20. *haste away*] *bireḥû*, generally has the sense 'flee' (so EVV here), though in Song viii. 14 'make haste' (so EVV) is obviously right. At the same time, something of the urgency of 'flee' is intended by the word here. The summons is to be interpreted in the light of Jer. li. 6: 'Flee (*nûsû*) from the midst of Babylon . . . do not be destroyed in her punishment' (cf. Rev. xviii. 4). The exiles, if they do not make haste, will be in similar peril to Lot (Gen. xix. 15–17); the destruction that is coming upon the city (xlvii. 11) may overtake them. *Chaldea*] *kaśdîm*. The word usually stands for the Chaldean people (so AV, RV here), but it can also stand for the country where the Chaldeans dwelt (so RSV and cf. Jer. l. 10, li. 24, 35, and 4 times Ezek.). *The* LORD *has redeemed his servant Jacob*] See on xli. 8, 14.

Even more important than that the exiles are free is the fact that it is Yahweh who has *redeemed* them, and they are to proclaim the glad tidings to all the world. And indeed, even if this second Exodus was less marvellous than the Prophet anticipated, it did excite wonder —or so the Jews persuaded themselves—among the nations (Ps. cxxvi. 2).

21. This verse is a recollection of the first Exodus, which in itself is a sure promise for the second: cf. xli. 18, xliii. 19 f. *and that they thirsted not*] Lit. 'and they thirsted not' (so AV, RV). RSV omits 'and', but the conjunction is intended as a link with the preceding verse. Events future and past are parts of the one redemptive process: see on vv. 12–19 above. It would perhaps be going too far to include verse 21 as part of the *oratio recta* beginning 'The LORD has redeemed . . .'. Nor is the translation offered to be pressed to the point of saying that the verb 'Say' is followed by two acc. obj. clauses, one *oratio recta* and the other *oratio obliqua*. Perhaps the conjunctive 'and' may be understood as suggesting the sense 'and (do not forget that)'. This is certainly what is implied. *he made water flow . . . by splitting the rock so that water gushed out*] Lit. 'he made water flow . . . and he split the rock and water gushed out'. The Exodus tradition records two occasions on which Moses struck a rock and water gushed out (Exod. xvii. 6; Num. xx. 11), but this passage is not a conflation of the two incidents. EVV 'he clave/struck' picture only one occasion. The *waw consec.* 'and he split' is explicative of, not subsequent to, 'he made water flow'. The sentence is similar to Gen. xl. 23: 'the chief butler did not remember Joseph and (*waw consec.* = but) he forgot him' (cf. *GK* 111 *l*). *so that water gushed out*] Again the *waw consec.* may be construed as expressing the logical consequence of what precedes (*GK*, same ref.).

22. *peace*] *šālôm* here must not be restricted to weal or prosperity (cf. xlv. 7). Indeed, the *šālôm* of the wicked was a continual puzzle to the righteous: cf. Ps. lxxiii. 3.

CHAPTERS XLIX–LV

Some of the major themes of chs. xl–xlviii are absent from these chapters. There are no references to Babylon or to Cyrus, no polemics against idolatry, no summonses to assize-inquests, and no appeals to the fulfilment of former prophecies. The address is to Zion-Jerusalem rather than to Jacob-Israel. Apart from the Servant Songs, three of which are in xlix–lv and only one (xlii. 1–4) in xl–xlviii, the main concern is with the rehabilitation of Jerusalem rather than with the release from Babylon.

There is, nevertheless, general agreement that xlix–lv are from DI. (For dissident opinions—none of them by any scholar now living—see R. H. Pfeiffer, *Introduction to the OT*, pp. 453 f.). A contrary view has been revived by J. Morgenstern, in a series of articles (still proceeding) in *HUCA*, vols. xxvii. *sqq.*, 1956 *sqq.* Morgenstern argues that a major catastrophe befell Jerusalem in 485 B.C. 'Accordingly all of Isa. 34–35 and 49–66, including . . . the Suffering Servant sections . . . we have had to ascribe to Trito-Isaiah, with the specific understanding that by Trito-Isaiah is meant, not a single prophet, perhaps a disciple of Deutero-Isaiah, as has not infrequently been suggested, but rather a long succession of prophetic personalities over a protracted period, extending from 520 B.C. to well into the fourth century B.C.' (op. cit., xxix, 1958, pp. 2 f.).

That the Jerusalem Jews were in trouble with their neighbours over an attempt to rebuild the walls of the city, has long been recognized. This may have been in the reign of Xerxes I (485–465 B.C.), and Ezra iv. 7–23 purports to give the text of a letter to Artaxerxes I (464–424 B.C.) together with the king's reply ordering that the work of rebuilding should cease. There is no reason to doubt the substantial genuineness of the letter or of Artaxerxes' reply. But Morgenstern is surely exaggerating when he says that 'early in 485 B.C. . . . a severe catastrophe befell the Jewish community in Judah . . . perhaps the most tragic in all Jewish history until the advent of Hitler' (op. cit., pp. 1 f.). In any case, it is no matter, so far as the interpretation of Isa. xlix–lv is concerned, whether the plight of Jerusalem was what it was at any time between 586 and 538 B.C., or what it was in a conjectured situation between 485 and Nehemiah's coming to the city in 444.

A very few scholars, while agreeing that chs. xlix–lv are from DI, have supposed that they were 'delivered' in Palestine after the liberation edict of Cyrus. The most recent is R. Levy, *Deutero-Isaiah: A Commentary*, 1925, pp. 12, 220. Again, it is no matter, so far as their interpretation is concerned. The reason for the general view that chs. xl–lv are a unity, to be dated before any return to Palestine, is that the closing vv. (lv. 12 f.) recur to the main theme of the approaching exodus from Babylon, an exodus which presumably had not yet taken place.

XLIX. 1–6. THE SERVANT OF YAHWEH: HIS ADDRESS TO THE NATIONS

5. לֹא] So *Keth.* This makes perfectly good sense: 'and that Israel be not swept away', lit. 'gathered up': cf. lvii. 1 (*bis*), where נֶאֱסָפִים = 'taken away' (EVV), xvi. 10; Jer. xlviii. 33. For a similar negative following a positive cf. xlv. 1*b*. But *Qere* לוֹ, 'to him', is supported by

9 MSS., A, T, and Q^a, and is to be preferred. There is no substantial difference of meanings as between the two readings. וָאֶכָּבֵד] Point וְאֶכָּבֵד and transfer 5*b* to follow ver. 3. The poem moves by stages of two distichs each. Verse 5*b*, as it stands, is in parenthesis and RV brackets it. עֻזִּי] T interprets, and Q^a reads, עֶזְרִי, 'my help'. This may be right (cf. ver. 8; l. 7, 9) but there is no compelling reason for adopting it.

6. וַיֹּאמֶר] Repetitive after the אָמַר of ver. 5. The word is anacrusis and may have been inserted, to avoid ambiguity, after 5*b* had been misplaced. נְצִירֵי] So *Keth.* and Q^a. *Qere* and some MSS. have נְצוּרֵי. In both readings 'kept safe' or 'preserved' (EVV) seems intended (√נצר I, Arab. *nẓr*, 'guard', 'keep'). But this is a very imprecise ‖ to 'tribes'. In view of the different *scriptio plena* spellings it may be that the original was נִצְרֵי and that the word should be related to √נצר II, Arab. *nḍr*, 'grow green'. It will then have some such meaning as 'offshoots': cf. xi. 1, xiv. 19 (?), lx. 21; Dan. xi. 7; Ecclus. xl. 15 (‖ שֹׁרֶשׁ, 'root'). This gives a passable ‖ to 'tribes' in the preceding stich and the reference will be to the scattered remnants of Israel: cf. xliii. 5 f.

In this, the second Servant Song, the speaker is the Servant himself. He addresses himself to the distant peoples, to whom he had first been commissioned (xlii. 1–4). He tells them that Yahweh had designated him to his service even before he was born, then equipped and kept him—it is not said for how long—in readiness for his task. His major endowment is incisiveness of speech, speech that goes straight to its mark. Yahweh has given him the honourable title 'Israel'. Between vv. 3 and 4 time must have elapsed during which the Servant says emphatically that he has laboured in vain, though he has not lost faith in God or in the ultimate success of his mission. His task so far (ver. 5*a*) has been to try to 'bring back' Jacob-Israel to Yahweh. Yahweh tells him that it is little matter that he should rehabilitate the tribes of Jacob. Instead, the Servant assures his audience, Yahweh has widened the scope of his mission: 'so I make you a light to the nations, that my salvation may reach to the end of the earth'. This had been Yahweh's original intention, cf. xlii. 1–4.

1. *far shores . . . distant peoples*] The Servant's audience is as wide as Yahweh's in xli. 1. *before I was born*] Lit. 'from the womb'; see on xliv. 2 (of Israel) and cf. Jer. i. 5, 'Before I formed you in the belly I knew you, and before you came out from the womb I set you apart'. *he named my name*] Heb. *hizkîr š^emî*, lit. 'he caused my name to be mentioned', cf. 2 Sam. xviii. 18. The corresponding Akk. *šuma zakāru*, 'to name a name', is common. The expression is ‖ *he* *called me* and so is more specific than 'he gave me my name' simply. It is rather 'he designated me by name'.

2. *He made my mouth like a sharp sword*] Cf. the frequent expressions 'with the mouth (EVV "edge") of the sword' (e.g. Deut. xiii. 15 (*16*)), i.e. without quarter, and the sword that 'devours' (lit. 'eats'), Deut. xxxii. 42. A more expansive ‖ is xi. 4, where it is said of the messianic king: 'he will strike the earth with the rod of his mouth and with the breath of his lips he will slay the wicked', and which is the literary original of Rev. i. 16, ii. 16; cf. 2 Thess. ii. 8. This, however, is not to say that the Servant must be a king or a military figure. Jer. xxiii. 29, 'Is not my word like a fire and like a forge-hammer that shatters rock?', is in a context that has to do with prophets: cf. Hos. vi. 5; Eph. vi. 17; Heb. iv. 12. The 'sharp' word of the Servant is the word of a prophet rather than the edict of a king. *a polished arrow*] *ḥēṣ bārûr*. Cf. Jer. li. 11, where RSV has 'sharpen the arrows'. But for 'sharp' we should expect *ḥēṣ šānûn*, cf. Isa. v. 28; Ps. xlv. 6, cxx. 4; Prov. xxv. 18. An arrow would consist of shaft and point (cf. Ps. lvii. 4 (*5*), 'spears and arrows') and anyone polishing the shaft would naturally see that its tip was sharp. *quiver*] Cf. Lam. iii. 13, 'He made the arrows (Heb. "sons") of his quiver penetrate my kidneys'. The figures in this verse give us no warrant for picturing the Servant as a 'meek and mild' person. On the contrary, the word of the LORD is a formidable weapon, and it is because the Servant's task is arduous and dangerous that Yahweh does not send him to it until he has been properly equipped to face it.

3. *you Israel*] Heb. 'Israel'. There has been much discussion about the genuineness of 'Israel' here. Nearly all the protagonists for an individual interpretation of the Servant have deleted the word. F. Praetorius (*Nachträge und Verbesserungen zu DJ*, 1927, pp. 31 f.) is one of the very few who retain it. On the other hand, some who argue for the collective interpretation (e.g. H. W. Robinson, Köhler) are content to delete it, this because the Servant appears to be distinguished from Israel in vv. 5 f. Metrical grounds have been urged both for and against deletion. The metre of the poem is 3:3 and if we delete 'Israel' we must give three stresses to 'in whom I pride myself'. This is possible (cf. 2*aβ*, 4*bβ*) but not probable. The versions all have 'Israel' and the only MS. which omits it is Kennicott 96, which is said by Volz to be a good, but by J. A. Bewer ('Two Notes on Isaiah 49. 1–6', in *Jewish Studies in Memory of George A. Kohut*, ed. S. W. Baron & A. Marx, 1935, pp. 86–90) a careless MS. Even if K96 were a good MS., we should hardly be justified in following it in defiance of the otherwise unanimous textual evidence. No one would ever have deleted the name were it not that it is

suspect on dogmatic grounds. It must therefore be retained. Yet it needs some qualification, if 'Israel' has a mission to Israel (vv. 5 f.). Even if (see below) it is Yahweh, and not the Servant, who is to 'bring back Jacob-Israel', it is strange that Yahweh should speak *of* Israel when speaking *to* 'Israel'. The AV 'O Israel' takes 'Israel' as a vocative and construes it with what precedes. RV and RSV take it as in apposition to 'my Servant'. It should, of course, be construed with the qualifying relative clause that follows (cf. *GK* 155 *d*) and some force should be given to *b*^{e}*ḵā* in the Hebrew: lit. 'Israel which in you I take pride' = 'you Israel in whom I take pride', with no comma after 'Israel'. Those nineteenth-century commentators who argued for an individual Servant while still retaining 'Israel' were accustomed to understand it in the sense of 'the true (embodiment of) Israel'. Praetorius (loc. cit.) says the idea is similar to *l'état c'est moi* ('ähnlich "in deinem Lager ist Österreich" '), and this solution is not to be dismissed out of hand. A similar interpretation is that of E. Burrows: 'It is to be observed that "Israel" is not a term of address (vocative), and not merely an apposition to "my Servant", but a name which is predicated. It need not therefore be an indication of the Servant's proper name. It can be understood as a name of honour applied to him for the reason indicated in the last clause . . . it is here honorific' (*The Gospel of the Infancy and other Biblical Essays*, p. 63). *I take pride*] See on xliv. 23.

4. *But I said*] The pronoun is emphatic. *I said* = 'I thought', as often with this verb. *to no purpose*] *l*^{e}*rîḳ*, 'for emptiness', cf. Job xxxix. 16. *entirely in vain*] *l*^{e}*ṯôhû w*^{e}*heḇel*, 'for chaos (see on xl. 17) and vapour' (lvii. 13, the 'vanity' of Eccles.). *assuredly*] Is good AV (7 times). Current Engl. 'surely' can express little more than hope, not the complete confidence of the Servant. For the emphatic force of Heb. *'āḵēn*, cf. xl. 7; Gen. xxviii. 16; Exod. ii. 14. It expresses a strong contrast, especially after 'I said', as of something wrongly imagined: cf. liii. 4; Jer. iii. 19 f. (RSV). *the Lord will declare his confidence in me*] Lit. 'my *mišpāṭ* is with Yahweh'. The precise sense of *mišpāṭ* is difficult to determine here. The ‖ to it is *p*^{e}*'ullāh*, 'recompense', for which see xl. 10. The best commentary on the passage is 1 Cor. iv. 1–5, in which Paul says it is the Lord who judges (*ἀνα-κρίνων*) him and that every man will receive his commendation (*ἔπαινος*) from God, *ἔπαινος* corresponding to 'recompense' here. The Servant, like the Psalmist (Ps. lxxiii. 13–15) has been inclined to take a despairing view of his situation, but on further reflection he thinks better of it. He is not exactly involved in a legal dispute with Yahweh, but if we must give to *mišpāṭ* something of its usual judicial connotation, he is expressing his conviction that Yahweh's

verdict on his service will be a favourable one (cf. l. 8 f.), and accompanied by some token of approval. The suffix in 'my judgement' is objective, 'the judgement passed on me'.

5. *to bring Jacob back to him,* &c.] There is obvious difficulty in these words, if the Servant is the nation Israel. How can Israel 'bring back' Israel? Accordingly, protagonists for the collective theory have argued that the infinitives in this and the next verse are gerundial (cf. *GK* 114 *o*), with Yahweh as their subject. Two translations have been offered on the basis of this interpretation: (i) 'But now, says Yahweh . . . in that he brings back Jacob to himself, and that Israel will not be swept away (*Qere* reading) . . .' (so Hitzig, *Der Prophet Jesaja, übersetzt und ausgelegt*, 1833, p. 540); (ii) 'And now, says Yahweh . . . in that he brought back Jacob (out of Egypt) to himself and gathered Israel to himself (in the wilderness) . . . it is too little . . . that I should raise up Jacob's tribes . . .' (so K. Budde, *Die sogenannten Ebed-Jahwe Lieder*, 1900, p. 23). These translations are grammatically possible, but they are awkward and involved, and most exponents of the collective theory have now abandoned them. Instead, it is quite properly argued, Israel could have a mission to Israel, very much as we say that the first mission of the Church is to the Church.

6. *that you should be my servant*] Lit. 'from your becoming a servant to me'. Duhm called this 'a barbarous sentence' and omitted it as a gloss. But there is an exact parallel in Ezek. viii. 17. Duhm is left with a 4-beat stich in a 3:3 context. His real reason for the omission was that his 'leprous rabbi' (Peake) Servant was not the kind of leader to carry through a political restoration of Israel, and so he makes Yahweh the subject of the infinitives in vv. 5 f. *to re-establish*] This is a fair translation of *lᵉhāḳîm*, 'to cause to rise up', since Israel in the exile was 'down'. *the tribes of Jacob*] Since 'tribes' are political entities, the task envisaged in 6*a* would seem to be a political task. *to restore*] *lᵉhāšîḇ* (*Hiph.*). In ver. 5 'to bring back' is *lᵉšôḇēḇ*, (*Pôʿlēl*). Is there any difference of meaning between the two forms, as that the *Pôʿlēl* implies moral and spiritual, the *Hiph.* political, restoration? In 'He restores my soul' (*nepeš*, Ps. xxiii. 3) the verb *yᵉšôḇēḇ* is *Pôʿlēl*, but in Lam. i. 16 *nepeš* is acc. obj. of *mēšîḇ* (*Hiph*). The *Pôʿlēl* is found only 11 times, but it must have a political reference in lviii. 12; Jer. l. 19; Ezek. xxxix. 27. The choice of the one form in ver. 5 and of the other in ver. 6 may therefore be purely stylistic. Or the poet may have intended moral and spiritual restoration in ver. 5, political in ver. 6. He would be less conscious of any difference between the two than we are. DI was certainly concerned about both. In any case, ver. 6 seems to say that the

Servant is to abandon any concern he may so far have had about the political rehabilitation of Israel, and, instead, address himself to the nations. There is no mention of any mission to Israel in xlii. 1–4. Perhaps the Servant had misconstrued his orders and only by trial and error come to see where his real duty lay. For a similar situation in the NT see Acts xiii. 46 f. In any case God takes no refusal from his servants (Exod. iii–iv; Jer. i). If they complain about the difficulties of their task, instead of releasing them from it, he will appoint them to one wider, and, as they come to learn, more exacting. *a light to the nations*] See on xlii. 6. There can be no question of the genuineness of the expression here. *that my salvation may reach*] So, correctly, RV mg., RSV, as against AV, RV.

XLIX. 7–13. THE REVERSAL OF ISRAEL'S FORTUNES

7. לִבְזֹה נֶפֶשׁ] This expression has occasioned much discussion. בְּזֹה is presumably intended as *Qal* infin. constr. בזה, 'to despise': for similar spellings cf. Gen. xlviii. 11, l. 20; Ps. ci. 3. So, literally, 'a despising of *nep̄eš*' = 'one despised in *nep̄eš*' (abstract for concrete, *GK* 83 *c*, similar to *mastēr pānîm*, 'a hiding of face', liii. 3. There is no difference of meaning between בְּזֹה and בְּזוּי ('despised', *Qal* ptc. pass.), which has sometimes been conjectured and is now supported by Q[a]. The meaning is 'deeply despised' (see below). Others take the expression to mean 'self-despised' (cf. LXX), but this would seem to require בֹּזֶה (*Qal* ptc. act., so Kissane) followed by נַפְשׁוֹ (G. R. Driver, *JTS* 36, 1935, p. 401; Praetorius, *Nachträge u. Verbesserungen zu Deutero-Jesaias*, 1927, p. 33). מְתָעֵב] Point מְתֹעַב (*Pu'al*).

8. לְהָקִים אֶרֶץ] Only two beats. Some would add צִיָּה, 'a desert land', after xli. 18, liii. 2; but there can be no certainty about it.

9. דְּרָכִים] It is usual to read כָּל־דְּרָכִים, with LXX. Q[a] has כול הרים, 'all mountains'. But 'mountains' is not required by the ‖ שְׁפָיִים (see on xli. 18), even though sand-belts may be as much as 700 ft. high.

11. הָרַי] 'my mountains', sounds oddly. P and T read as הָרִים, cf. LXX πᾶν ὄρος. If MT is an abbreviation for הרים (so Volz), the copyist, in view of the ‖ מְסִלֹּתַי, was only asking to be misunderstood.

12. סִינִים] The conjectural reading סְוֵנִים is as old as Michaelis (1775) and is now attested by Q[a] סוניים.

This passage has much the same relation to the Servant Song that precedes it as xlii. 5–9 has to xlii. 1–4. But whereas xlii. 5–9 reads more like a 'Servant' than an 'Israel' passage, xlix. 7–13, as it proceeds, has all the marks of an 'Israel' passage descriptive of the homeward journey to Palestine: cf. xli. 17–20. Accordingly, xlix. 7–13 has been claimed as a Servant Song less often than has xlii. 5–9: e.g. Volz takes xlix. 7–13 as an Israel but xlii. 5–9 as a Servant passage.

Two verses (7 and 8) begin with 'Thus says the LORD', and on the widely current theory that the prophecy is made up of some fifty separate pieces, each of them should begin a new piece. Verse 7 is brief, perhaps a fragment, yet in conformity with his theory (see *supra*, p. 4 f.) Gressmann divided 7–13 into two Servant Songs, vv. 7 and 8–13 (*Der Messias*, pp. 299 ff.). There are similarities between ver. 7 and the last Servant Song (cf. lii. 15, liii. 3), as there are also between it and typically 'Israel' passages like xlviii. 17. The 'one who is deeply despised' must either be Israel, or—on any theory that the Servant is to be distinguished from Israel—the Servant *κατ' ἐξοχήν*. In vv. 8–13 Yahweh addresses one whom he has 'answered', 'helped', and 'protected', and whose task is to resettle the land (of Palestine) and release the prisoners (now in exile). This looks very like the political task which Yahweh has said he no longer requires of the Servant. A glance at 8*bα* shows it to be a defective line (metre 2:2) and a verbal repetition of xlii. 6*b*, except that there MT adds 'a light to the nations'. To add to the complexity, the words 'a light to the nations' are wanting in the first hand of LXX^B at xlii. 6, but are found in P at xlix. 8. It is tempting to suppose that they have been borrowed from xlix. 6, where there is no doubt of their genuineness. The problem of xlix. 7–13 would be much simplified if we could omit from ver. 7 all except the introductory formula, together with 'Thus says Yahweh' and *bα* from ver. 8. We should then be left with what was originally an assurance of restoration to Israel:

7. This is the word of the LORD,
Israel's Redeemer and Holy One:
8. 'In the hour of my favour I respond to your need,
in a day of deliverance I come to your aid;
that you may resettle the land,
and recover possessions now deserted.'

This, we may conjecture, was later expanded to serve as a suitable link between the Servant passage and what follows. The case is similar to that of xlii. 5–9 (see *supra*, p. 113). Such a 'solution' of what is a stubborn difficulty is offered with due reserve. Anyone who has tried to cope with the literature on the Servant problem knows that it is full of what are now discarded reconstructions of the text, made to fit in with some *a priori* theory of who the Servant was (see *SS*, ch. 5). For this reason the suspected expansions are neither omitted, nor even bracketed, in the translation, and the commentary below is based on MT as we have it.

7. *deeply despised*] So RSV for *ḇᵉzōh nep̱eš*; similarly Duhm, Volz. Reference is commonly made to Ps. xvii. 9, 'my deadly enemies' lit. 'my enemies against the soul' (*nep̱eš*), and Ps. xxii. 6 (7), *bᵉzûy ʿām*, 'despised by the people'. But the closest analogy is to be found in the expression *mar nep̱eš*, 'bitter in soul': so 1 Sam. i. 10 ('deeply distressed'), xxii. 2 ('bitterly discontented'); Job iii. 20; Prov. xxxi. 6 ('embittered'). Similarly lvii. 15. 'humble in spirit' (*šᵉp̱al rûaḥ*). There is no reason why we should not read something of 'self-despised' into the words. Few people are uninfluenced by what others think and say of them. *loathed by the nations*] *mᵉṯōʿaḇ gôy*. There is no precise ‖ to the use of the sing. *gôy*, 'nation', here, unless it be at lv. 5, where a collective sense (German *Leute*, so Duhm) is surely intended; similarly *ʿām*, 'people(s)', in xlii. 5. The words *gôy* and *ʿam* are more or less synonyms and are sometimes in parallelism (e.g. ver. 22). The chief difference between them is that although *gôy* is used of Israel, it comes increasingly to denote non-Hebrews, until in rabbinical Hebrew a *gôy* is a Gentile. *tyrant rulers*] *môšᵉlîm*, in sense of xiv. 5. *will see*] The understood object is the reversal of Israel's fortunes. *and stand to attention*] Lit. 'and rise'. For examples of such deference see Judges iii. 20; Job xxix. 8. *princes . . . will prostrate themselves*] Cf. Ps. lxxii. 11.

8. *In the hour of my favour*, &c.] Quoted in 2 Cor. vi. 2. For OT‖s see lviii. 5, lxi. 2; Ps. lxix. 13 (*14*). The Hebrew perfects express certainty. *and I will protect you*, &c.] See on xlii. 6. *that you may resettle*, &c.] For a literal translation see RSV. The meaning is that the returning exiles are to repeople and recover the land which Yahweh gave as a possession to Israel (Deut. iv. 21). But however desirable this may have been, it seems something of an anticlimax to *I will . . . make you the mediator of my covenant with the peoples* (see on xlii. 6), and confirms the suspicion that those words were not in the original text. Whether the subject of the infinitives in 8*bβ* is Israel (or the Servant?)—*that you may resettle the land*—or whether it is Yahweh—'by (my) resettling the land' (cf. li. 16, where the subject of the infinitives must be Yahweh)—it is impossible to decide on grammatical grounds. We may have it both ways if we say that the exiles were to resettle their homeland but that it was only Yahweh who could enable them to do it.

9a. Has the same place in the structure of this passage as ver. 7 has in xlii. 5–9. *darkness*] i.e. imprisonment, as in xlii. 7, xlvii. 5.

9b–10. For the figure of the returning exiles as sheep cf. xl. 11, also xxxv. 7 for the same general picture. *scorching sand*] *šārāḇ*, elsewhere only xxxv. 7, of parched ground.

11. *put in order*] Lit. ‘raised’.

12. Cf. xliii. 5 f.; Ps. cvii. 3. The verse may originally have stood after ver. 18: cf. lx. 4. *Syene*] Reading *s*^{e}*wēnîm* (see textual note). Heb. *sînîm* was once supposed to be China, and this explanation, according to Levy, ‘still has a measure of probability’. LXX has Persia, V *terra australis*. There is little doubt that it was Ezekiel’s *s*^{e}*wēnēh* (Ezek. xxix. 10, xxx. 6, to be distinguished from the *sîn*, RSV Pelusium, of xxx. 15 f.), the *swn* of the Elephantine papyri, the modern Aswan. Exactly when the Jewish garrison was first stationed there is not known, but Jer. xliv. 1 already speaks of Jews who lived ‘in the land of Pathros’ (the Egyptian name means ‘Land of the south’).

13. For the thought of all nature rejoicing in God’s redemptive work cf. xlii. 10–12, xliv. 23, lii. 9, lv. 12 f.

XLIX. 14–21. THE REPOPULATION OF ZION

14. יהוה וַאדֹנָי] Q^{a} has ואלוהי, ‘and my God’, written over ואדני. This is not the original reading, but it is evidence that the Qumran community read the tetragrammaton as ’^{a}*ḏônāy*, and, following the general rule, avoided the same word in ‖ stichs. We may do the same and translate אדני as ‘my God’.

15. מֵרַחֵם] Intended as *Piʿēl* infinitive plus prefixed מִן with negative force ‘away from’; lit. ‘so as not to have compassion on’. This is quite possible (cf. *GK* 119 *y*). But Kittel’s suggestion (*BH*) to read מְרַחֵם (*Piʿēl* ptc.) is a sound one. The meaning will then be ‘a compassionate (mother)’. Since the gender is implicit in the sense, the word does not need the feminine ending (*GK* 122 *c*, similarly Arabic). This seems required by אֵלֶּה, ‘these’, in the next line.

17. בָּנָיִךְ] Point בֹּנַיִךְ, ‘your builders’, with V, T, and now Q^{a}; similarly in liv. 13. But there is surely a *double entendre* here: see below.

18. כֻּלָּם] Transfer *athnaḥ* to the preceding word.

21. אֵלֶּה] Read וְאֵלֶּה with many MSS., LXX, V. The *waw* corresponds to enclitic ‘then’ in English.

This passage is closely related to the preceding: *But* (*waw consec.*) *Zion says*. There may also be intentional word-play between ‘will have compassion’ of ver. 13 and the ‘compassionate mother’ of 15. Volz treats vv. 7–26 as a single poem prophesying ‘the several phases of the national salvation’. Muilenburg takes ch. xlix as a single poem, ‘The Servant of the Lord: Called, Commissioned, and Comforted’, in twelve strophes. Volz’s position is reasonable enough: the themes in vv. 7–26 are closely related and progress to a climax at the end of the chapter. But for the purpose of exposition it is convenient to deal with them separately.

Verses 14–21 begin with Zion's lament that Yahweh has forsaken her. This anticipates the figure of Zion as the wife of Yahweh (l. 1; liv. 1–8), though the marriage relationship is not yet explicit. But Yahweh's love for the city is even greater than that of a mother for 'the son of her womb'. (The double relationship of Yahweh to Israel, as Husband and as Father, appears already in Hos. ii, xi. 1 f.). His eagerness to see the city rebuilt is as great as that of any architect to see his design take shape. The builders (Zion's children) appear as if from nowhere—though ver. 12 should perhaps follow ver. 18. There are so many of them that the city is too small to contain them. The astonishment of the bewildered 'mother' is complete: 'Where can all these have come from?' They must be those who have been born in all the places to which Israelites, from the former northern and southern kingdoms, have been scattered. While the city has lain forsaken, 'children', unbeknown to her, have been born to her.

The picture will strike us as grotesque unless we are careful to distinguish between reality and simile, especially in ver. 18*b*. The city Zion is personified as a woman: cf. xlvii. But a woman can hardly 'put on' her children as a bride puts on her jewellery. Either the children are *like* so many jewels which the mother puts on, or, if our picture is of the city Zion, her children man her walls and/or have their names entered on something like a roll of honour. And the sanguine expectation is that all will be worthy: cf. liv. 13, lx. 21.

15. All the commentators remark that nowhere in the OT, except in Jer. xxxi. 20, is the love of Yahweh for his people so poignantly expressed as here. 'This love is greater than mother-love, stronger than the strongest human feeling, more intimate than the closest bond of nature' (Volz). Yet when Volz says it is not yet love for the individual soul but for the chosen people and city, he is stating a contrast which is very near to breaking down. A city apart from its inhabitants is an abstraction, and although Yahweh is concerned about walls, those who build and live inside them ('all of them', vv. 18 f.) come clearly into the picture. Similarly, Jeremiah's New Covenant (Jer. xxxi. 31–34) is with the nation, but as it becomes defined it includes, almost of necessity, individual Israelites: 'they shall all know me'. *these . . . I*] Note the contrast: the *I* is emphatic. We should say 'they', but Heb. 'these' is in sharper focus.

16. *I have engraved you*] The verb 'engrave' (*ḥāḳaḳ*) is used of Ezekiel's 'portraying' (EVV) Jerusalem 'upon' a brick (Ezek. iv. 1), also (probably) of inscribing on copper (Isa. xxx. 8, where Heb. *sēper* = Akk. *siparru*, 'copper', and cf. the copper scroll from Qumran). Some kind of tattooing seems intended. The meaning is sometimes taken to be that Yahweh has tattooed the name Zion on his palms as a lover tattooes the name of his beloved. But there is no analogy for this in OT (not even in xliv. 5, which see). The object of 'engraved' is 'you', i.e. the city, and the ‖ is 'your walls'. Yahweh's 'stigmata' are sketches of the city he loves and of which he is reminded whenever he looks at his hands.

17. *your builders*] There is an obvious play on 'your builders' (*bônayiḵ*) and MT 'your sons' (*bānayiḵ*): see textual note above. In this verse Zion's builders are her 'sons': contrast lx. 10, which is probably based on xlv. 13.

18b. Cf. lxi. 10 and contrast Jer. iv. 30; Ezek. xxiii. 40. *fasten them on*] *tᵉḳaššᵉrîm*, cf. the *ḳiššûrîm*, finery of some sort (iii. 20; Jer. ii. 32, necklaces?, sashes? √ 'bind on').

19. *those who swallow you up*] For the vivid metaphor expressing swiftness and entirety cf. Job vii. 19, 'let me alone while I swallow my spittle'; Jer. li. 34.

20. *make room for me*] *gᵉšoh-llî*, almost an impatient 'get out of my way', cf. Gen. xix. 9. *for us*] Heb. 'for me', but the subject is 'the children', who speak 'with one voice'.

21. *who has borne?*] The verb is masculine (*yālaḏ*) and the meaning could be 'who has begotten?' The *Qal* is used of a father's begetting in the J source of the Pentateuch; cf. Gen. iv. 18. But 'borne' is probably right here, the masculine being used for feminine, as in *mᵉraḥēm*, ver. 15. *exiled and turned away*] Wanting in the leading MSS. of LXX and may be a later addition. The words are metrically superfluous, 2:2 inserted in a 3:3 distich. *where, then, have these come from?*] *wᵉ'ēllêh 'êpôh hēm*. Could conceivably mean 'what sort (of children) are these?' i.e. 'are they really mine?' with reference to Judges viii. 18 (*'êpôh* = *qualis?*). But Moore (*Judges*, I.C.C., *in loc.*) denies that the word could have this sense. Nevertheless, 'are these really mine?' does convey what is almost incredulity on Zion's part.

XLIX. 22–26. THE TURNING OF THE TABLES

22. אֲדֹנָי] Wanting in LXX and Qª. The shorter formula is usual: cf. ver. 25; l. 1.

24. צַדִּיק] We expect עָרִיץ, as in ver. 25. This is supported by LXX (ἀδίκως), P, V, and is now confirmed by Qª.

25. כִּי־כֹה אָמַר יהוה] Some would transpose these words to the beginning of ver. 24. As they stand, they break the connexion between strophe and antistrophe. This could be for additional emphasis, though that is hardly needed. It may be that the words are not original. The case would then be similar to Jer. ix. 21 f., (*20 f.*), where a perfect elegy has been weakened by the well-meant insertion of 'Speak, thus says the LORD' (cf. LXX *in loc.*). וְאֶת־יְרִיבֵךְ] Lit., 'and with those who contend with you'. LXX, P, T, appear to have read as וְאֶת־רִיבֵךְ. The את will then be the acc. part. and the literal translation, 'and I myself will conduct your רִיב '.Q[a] has it both ways, ריבך with an additional *yôdh* written over the word. The meaning is much the same either way.

Yahweh has only to signal to the nations and they will release Zion's children and conduct them home with all ceremony. Kings and queens will be their attendants. The passage lacks the universal charity of xlv. 20–35. But its purpose is different and its tone can sound harsher than it really is. The detail 'lick ("up" is rightly omitted by RV, RSV) the dust' is less objectionable than in Ps. lxxii. 9; Mic. vii. 17. What saves the royal attendants from degradation is the additional word 'on your feet'. The ‖ is 'with their faces to the ground they shall bow low to you' (cf. xlv. 14). The gestures are spontaneous on their part. Orientals are more demonstrative than we when showing homage or affection. What is implied is that they will kiss the feet of their one-time slaves, with something of the abandon described in 2 Kings iv. 27; Matt. xxviii. 9, without noticing the dust that covers them. Verse 26 is not a picture of crude cannibalism. True, it could help to inflame Jewish chauvinism in later eschatological pictures. What it means in its context is that the panic-stricken Babylonians will consume one another in internecine strife. (Herodotus relates [iv. 63]—though it may not be strictly relevant in this context—that it was a Scythian custom for every soldier to drink the blood of the first man he killed.) But although these verses have a strongly nationalistic colouring, nationalism is not the last word. The section ends, as is usual with DI, on a theocentric and universalist note: 'all mankind shall know that I am the LORD . . .'.

22. *signal*] *nēs*. In Ezek. xxvii. 7 ‖ *miprāś*, 'canvas', 'sail'. An ensign or rallying-flag of some kind, generally set conspicuously on a hill: cf. xiii. 2, xviii. 3, xxx. 17. For close verbal ‖s to 22*a* see v. 26, xi. 12, lxii. 10. *in their arms*] Lit. 'in (their) bosom', properly the fold of a garment: cf. Neh. v. 13, 'I shook out my bosom'; Ps. cxxix. 7. We need not take the passage so literally as that the boys are to be carried in bosom-folds and girls on shoulders. We can 'scramble' the ‖ stichs and still retain a vivid picture. For a similar picture see lx. 4, where toddlers are to be carried astride the hips.

23. *foster-fathers*] Cf. Num. xi. 12 (Moses). *those who wait for me*] See on xl. 31.

24–25. These verses are a fine example of poetic inversion: *what he has seized . . . captives . . . captives . . . what he has seized.* For other examples cf. li. 6, 8, liii. 3 f. *tyrant . . . bully*] These words are not too strong for Heb. *gibbôr . . . ʿārîṣ*. The general sense of the former is 'strong (man)', 'warrior', and Yahweh is so called in xlii. 13. The corresponding Arab. *ǧabbâr* has usually a pejorative sense, 'tyrant', and in Hebrew the *Hithpaʿēl* of the √ (only xlii. 13; Job xv. 25, xxxvi. 9) is probably a denominative, 'act the *gibbôr*', with every suggestion of violence. The general sense of √*ʿrṣ* is 'inspire awe' or 'terror' (cf. xlvii. 12), and Jeremiah describes Yahweh in a saviour-sense as *gibbôr ʿārîṣ* (xx. 11). The adj.-noun is usually ‖ words like 'wicked', 'insolent', 'overbearing', 'ruthless', and describes the man who has no scruples about using force to get what he wants. If 'bully' seems too strong, 'ruthless' or 'despot' will serve.

26. *devour their own kin*] Lit. 'eat their (own) flesh'. For 'flesh' (*bāśār*) in sense of near kin cf. lviii. 7; Gen. ii. 23 f., xxix. 14, xxxvii. 27. *blood . . . wine*] For the inevitable association cf. lxiii. 1–3; Mark xiv. 23 f.; John vi. 55 f.; 1 Cor. xi. 25. *heady wine*] *ʿāsîs*, the freshly pressed out juice of the grape: cf. Mal. iv. 3 (*iii. 21*), 'and you shall crush the wicked and they will be ashes under the soles of your feet'. It could be potent stuff (Joel i. 5; LXX at Amos ix. 13; Joel iii. 18 (*iv. 18*) renders γλυκασμός, cf. the γλεῦκος of Acts ii. 13). The first juice, squeezed from the grapes by their own weight, was reckoned better than the second yield extracted by the press. But the choice of what was an unusual word was probably determined by the fact that the 'new wine' (AV in the Joel passages, AV mg. at Isa. xlix. 26, Amos ix. 6) was the blood of men newly slain.

26. *Deliverer*] See on xliii. 3. *Redeemer*] See on xli. 14. *the Mighty One of Jacob*] *ʾaḇîr yaʿaḳōḇ*. An ancient poetical name for God (Gen. xlix. 24, the Blessing of Jacob), which survives also in lx. 16; Ps. cxxxii. 2, 4; cf. 'the Mighty One of Israel' (i. 24). The √ ('to be strong') is the same as that of *ʾēḇer*, 'pinions' (xl. 31). It is probable that *ʾaḇîr* was originally pronounced *ʾabbîr*, which is used of angels (Ps. lxxviii. 25), men, and animals, and that the pointing *ʾaḇîr* was a justifiable theological conceit of the rabbis. If the expression ever meant 'the bull of Jacob' (cf. Ps. xxii. 12 (*13*), l. 13; RSV at Isa. x. 13), such a meaning could hardly survive the issue of the controversy over the 'calves' of Bethel and Dan. Indeed, a change from *'abbîr* to *'ᵃḇîr* was intended to avoid any association with idolatry (see Skinner, *Genesis*, I.C.C., on xlix. 24).

L. 1–3. SEPARATION, NOT DIVORCE

2. מִפְּדוּת] Lit. 'away from rescue' (מִן privative). A pointing פְּדוּת (infin. constr.) would give no appreciable difference of meaning. תִּבְאַשׁ] Q[a] תיבש, 'dry up'; similarly LXX. But if the passage is reminiscent of the Exodus (see below), MT is to be preferred: cf. Exod. vii. 18, 21, 'The fish in the Nile died and the Nile stank'. Also, a change from תבאש to תיבש is easier to account for than the other way round.

In this passage the theme of the relationship between Yahweh and his people as that of husband and wife (see on xlix. 14–21) comes into clear focus. The 'mother' is Zion and Yahweh's address is to her children (see the preceding section and note 'your mother'). They might suppose that their plight was due to one or the other of two causes: (i) Either Yahweh had formally divorced their mother, or (ii) he had sold them to some creditor. Neither of these suppositions had the slightest reason. (i) According to the Deuteronomic law, a husband might divorce his wife at will. But so that he might not divorce her in a fit of temper or without due deliberation—once she had been married to another man he could never remarry her —he had to write her a certificate of divorce (Deut. xxiv. 1–4; cf. Jer. iii. 1; Mark x. 2–4). The question, *Where, pray, is your mother's writ of divorce?* is rhetorical and expects the answer, 'There never was one!' Yahweh had not divorced Zion, though he had broken off relations with her (cf. Hos. iii. 3). (ii) If a man was distrained by his creditors, he might compound with them by selling his children as slaves (cf. Exod. xxi. 7; Neh. v. 1–5; Matt. xviii. 25), or, if he died, a creditor might take his children as slaves (2 Kings iv. 1). There is a note of reproof in the question *which of my creditors is it to whom I sold you?* Any suggestion that Yahweh had 'creditors' is preposterous. The reason for the exile was his people's *iniquities* and *flagrant disobedience* (lit. 'rebellions'), not any cooling of affection or straitened circumstances on his part. They were in no position to arraign their mother, as Hosea's young children are bidden to do (Hos. ii. 2–5 (*4–7*)). They were of responsible age. We should see in mother and children the concept of corporate personality. The suggestion that the mother is the people as a whole (*die Gesamtbevölkerung*, Volz), and the children the individual Israelites, should not be pressed. There was collective responsibility, in the past and extending into the present. The only thing that now stands in the way of Zion's restoration is her own want of faith. When Yahweh sends his prophet with the message of pardon, he meets with no response. Verse 2 doubtless reflects the experience of the Prophet and is a good example of the 'word of the LORD' which is also a word of the prophet.

Yahweh, whose power over nature is absolute, is fully capable of delivering his people: vv. 2*b*, 3. The logical connexion of these verses with what precedes is not immediately obvious. What has power over nature to do with Israel's release from Babylon, let alone with her moral and spiritual recovery? (similarly in xliv. 26–28). (Much the same question might be asked concerning the relation of the nature miracles of Jesus [e.g. Mark iv. 35–40] and his saving grace.) There are two interpretations of vv. 2*b*, 3. Some think that the rebuking of the sea refers to the stilling of the 'deep' (*tᵉhôm*) at the creation (Gen. i. 2), or to Yahweh's universal control of nature; others that the reference is to the crossing of the Red Sea at the Exodus (cf. Exod. xiv. 21, xv. 8). The obvious interpretation is that the passage—like li. 9 f. (which see) and Ps. lxxiv. 12–17—has in mind creation, command of nature, *and* redemption (the Exodus). Similarly, ver. 3 well describes sandstorms such as the exiles in Babylonia must have seen, storms which may darken the sky more completely than an eclipse of the sun, and be reminiscent also of the plague of darkness (Exod. x. 21–23). The assurance conveyed by the passage is that present deliverance of his people is no more difficult for Yahweh to accomplish than his deliverance of them in the past, or, for that matter, his disposition of universal nature in the present. For this reason the verbs, which are in the 'imperfect', are best translated by present tenses, though they could, being in poetry, be legitimately treated as aorists.

1. *with which I sent her away*] The simplest translation of the Hebrew is 'whom I sent away' (cf. AV), and it would make no difference to the meaning of the passage if we so translated it. Clearly, the mother has been 'sent away' (ver. 2). But she has not been formally divorced. The antecedent to the relative *'ᵃšer* is 'the writ of divorce', and the relative does not usually take a preposition when the antecedent is expressed (xlvii. 12 and lvi. 4 are exceptional, xlvii. 15 normal). Although *šillaḥ* ('send away') is used almost as a technical term for 'divorce' (to the passages quoted above add Mal. ii. 16), it has a wider content of meanings. The regulative term is 'the writ of divorce' (*sēp̄er kᵉrîṯûṯ*) and the plain sense of the rhetorical question is that no such writ was ever executed. The disputation style of the verse is similar to that later employed by Malachi (Duhm). *Nay!*] *hēn*, as distinct from the more usual *hinnēh* (see supra, p. 80), generally calls attention to some fact on which action is taken, or a conclusion

based. It may therefore sometimes have almost the contrary sense of 'Yes!' (cf. Gen. iii. 22, xi. 6).

2. *so shortened*] *ḳāṣôr ḳāṣ^erāh*, infin. abs. Not 'so short', but 'become so short'. Hebrew stative verbs have a 'dynamic character' and 'designate first of all the "becoming" of the conditions and qualities in question' (T. Boman, *Hebrew Thought compared with Greek*, p. 31). No prophet would ever have committed himself to the sentiment of the psalmist, 'this is my grief, that the Most High no longer has the strength he had' (Moffatt at Ps. lxxvii. 10, without committing ourselves to the validity of his translation; though cf. RSV). *rescue*] *p^eḏûṯ*, lit. 'ransom'. The √*pāḏāh* has much the same meaning as *gā'al* (see on xli. 14), with which it is ‖ in Jer. xxxi. 11; Hos. xiii. 14. But although in commercial transactions 'ransom' was accompanied by the payment of an assessed price (e.g. Exod. xiii. 13), when God ransoms Israel, any such thought is entirely absent. Yahweh paid nothing to the Egyptians when he 'ransomed' his people from them (Deut. vii. 8). *to set (you) at liberty*] A mild translation of a vb. (*haṣṣîl, Hiph.*) which commonly expresses forcible capture, snatching away (Gen. xxxi. 9; 1 Sam. xvii. 35; Amos iii. 12). For *hiṣṣîl* ‖ *pāḏāh* see not only here, but Jer. xv. 21: 'I will snatch you from the hand of the wicked and rescue you from the grasp of the ruthless'. *Surely not!*] Heb. *hēn*, see above. *If I were to rebuke the sea*, &c.] Cf. Ps. cvi. 9 (reference to Exodus); Nahum i. 4 (reference general). *its ocean tides*] *n^ehārôṯ*, lit. 'rivers' (so EVV). But the ‖ is 'the sea' and the meaning must be something like 'the ocean depths': cf. xliv. 27 (‖ *ṣûlāh*); xlviii. 18 (‖ 'the waves of the sea'); Ps. xciii. 3 (EVV 'the floods'); Hab. iii. 8 f.; Jonah ii. 4 ('the *nāhār* surrounded me'). Note also the similarity of language to Ps. cvi. 9, where the corresponding word is *t^ehômôṯ* ('deeps'). *desert*] Heb. *miḏbār*, normally 'wilderness' (see on xl. 3), and this will do if the passage has the Exodus in mind (cf. Ps. cvi. 9). But in passages like Deut. xxxii. 10; Job xxxviii. 26; Ps. cii. 6 (7), the meaning must approximate to 'desert' and this will be its meaning here if the emphasis is on Yahweh's devastating power over nature. It is worth noting that 'I should dry it up' (√*ḥārēḇ* I) in the preceding stich can be read as 'I should lay it desolate' (√*ḥārēḇ* II, Arab. *ḫariba*), and so increase the 'desolation' content of *miḏbār* following.

3. *blackness*] *ḳaḏrûṯ*: cf. 1 Kings xviii. 45, 'the skies grew black (*hiṯkadd^erû*) with clouds'. The reference could be to a solar eclipse, though the √ is not found in a context that demands such a meaning. For *ḳaḏrûṯ* as a sign of mourning see Jer. iv. 28, and for *sackcloth* frequently.

L. 4–9 (11). THE GETHSEMANE OF THE SERVANT

4. לָעוּת] The reading is attested by both Qumran Scrolls, and is apparently *Qal* infin. constr. of עות. But the meaning is uncertain. V *sustenare* (RV, RSV, 'sustain') appears to take this as an Aramaized form of עוש (Arab. *ġāṯa* IV, 'aid'), found only in Joel iv. 11, where the reading is dubious, though the name יְעוּשׁ, 'helper', is found in Gen. xxxvi. 5 and a few other passages. AV, RV mg. 'to speak a word in season', relates the word to עֵת, 'time'. LXX εἰπεῖν is thought by some to be for לַעֲנוֹת, 'to answer', but is probably an attempted interpretation of a word not understood. Similarly T לְאַלָּפָא, 'to teach', from which an original לִרְעוֹת, 'to shepherd', 'feed', has been supposed. But this is pure guesswork. G. R. Driver (in a private communication) equates with Arab. *'awā(y)*, 'to incline', and compares with נוּד לְ, 'to nod towards' = 'to console' (Job ii. 11). Since no emendation is reliable we must give to לעות the most fitting sense we can in its context. What we require is some word that will serve to express communication between an experienced teacher and someone who is 'weary'; 'sustain' or 'console' cannot be far wrong. אֶת־יָעֵף] For the acc. part. in poetry with a word without the article cf. xli. 7. דָּבָר] Instr. acc. If we keep the *athnaḥ* on דבר, the line will be 2:2. יָעִיר . . . יָעִיר] Overloaded and repetitious. Some would delete one בַּבֹּקֶר as a dittograph; but see below. It is more likely that the first יעיר should be deleted. It is marked by *pasek* (*GK* p. 59, n. 2), an indication that the early scribes were dubious about it.

5. אֹזֶן . . . אֲדֹנָי] This stich is partly repetitious and its ‖ or complement, if there was one, has been lost. It adds nothing to the description and its פָּתַח is weaker than the יָעִיר of the preceding line. Some would delete it.

6. הִסְתַּרְתִּי] 'I did not hide' makes perfectly good sense. But Q[a] הֲסִירוֹתִי 'I did (not) turn (my face) away', is attractive and the meaning much the same.

10. שֹׁמֵעַ] Many (e.g. Duhm, Köhler, Volz) read יִשְׁמַע (jussive, 'let him hear'). This is not necessary.

11. מְאַזְּרֵי] Lit. 'who gird (sparks)'. Many read מְאִירֵי, 'who light', after P (so RSV), and quote xxvii. 11; Mal. i. 10 for the *Hiph.* of אוֹר in the sense 'kindle (fire)'—the normal sense is 'give light to'. This would anticipate אוּר, 'flame', in the next line. But on the principle that the harder reading is to be preferred, we should keep MT, which gives a more vivid picture. The reflexive *Hithpa'ēl*,

מִתְאַזֵּרִי, might seem more exact, and Volz reads this, quoting Ps. xciii. 1 in support. But the *Pi'ēl* for once in a way may have something of a reflexive force: אזר is a verb of 'putting on' and such verbs (e.g. לָבֵשׁ, Gen. xxxviii. 19 and frequently) imply clothing one's self (cf. *GK* 117*y*).

Verses 4–9 of this passage sound like a soliloquy; or if, like xlix. 1–6 they are addressed to an audience, there is no clear indication who the audience are. They could conceivably be the 'you' of vv. 10 f., but this might have been made more explicit. It seems clear that vv. 10 f. are intended as a follow-up to 4–9, but they have little or no literary affinity either with the generally recognized 'Servant Songs' or with the prophecy as a whole. Moreover, if they are a unity, they are a very loosely knit unity: in ver. 10 Yahweh is in the 3rd person, in 11 he is the speaker—'from my hand'.

The speaker in vv. 4–9 begins by saying that Yahweh has given him a disciplined tongue and ear, and he asserts that he has not been disobedient to his divine commission. He has been subjected to physical violence and insult. He expects that renewed and even more severe trials await him, but he is confident that his Vindicator (Yahweh) will justify him and that his adversaries will come to naught.

Many of the older (pre-Duhm) commentators thought that vv. 4–9 were autobiographical, that the speaker in them was the Prophet (Isaiah or Deutero-Isaiah: see *SS* p. 41 f. *et passim*). This view has naturally been revived by those who think that the Servant of Yahweh was the Prophet himself. But whether or not the Prophet was the Servant, the passage almost certainly embodies something of the Prophet's experience, and there is reason to believe that DI encountered opposition (cf. xlv. 9–13).

Since Duhm it has been usual to regard vv. 4–9 as the third in a cycle of four Servant Songs. It differs from the other three in that the word 'servant' does not occur in it, and its metre is variously 3:2, 2:2, 2:2:2 (see Köhler, p. 42), not 3:3. But these are not serious objections. We need some middle term between xlix. 1–6 and lii. 13–liii. 12 if we are to understand how the situation in the latter has come about. It is probable that vv. 10 f. were composed, either by DI or by an editor, to be a suitable transition between the Song proper and what follows (cf. the relation of the first two Songs to their following contexts). They are earlier than the Qumran Scrolls and the LXX, and are the first evidence we have that vv. 4–9 were interpreted as referring to the Servant ('his servant', ver. 10, is retrospective).

Torrey and Muilenburg (but not Kissane) regard ch. l as a unity, but no analysis of 'stylistic features' (Muilenburg, p. 579) can establish any convincing substantive relation between vv. 4–9 (11) and 1–3. DI's style is so distinctive that we might almost expect to find common stylistic features between any two widely separate pieces.

4. *The Lord God*] This longer form, instead of the more usual 'The Lord', is characteristic of this poem: vv. 5 (?), 7, 9. It may be for greater impressiveness, or it may be *metri causa*: 'The Lord has given' (*yahwêh nāṯan lî*) would be an unimpressive beginning. *an expert tongue*] The translation is Levy's (*in loc.*), with reference to Jer. ii. 24, 'a wild ass used to (*limmûḏ*) the wilderness'; cf. also Jer. xiii. 23, 'accustomed to do evil'. G. R. Driver (in a private communication) takes *limmûḏîm* here as an intensive plural 'teaching(s)', similar to *giddûp̄îm*, 'reviling(s)' in xliii. 28, with much the same meaning as Levy's. At the end of the verse it has the sense of 'those taught', 'disciples', as in viii. 16, liv. 13. DI not infrequently uses the same word in slightly different senses in adjoining contexts. *so that I am skilled*] Lit. 'to know', cf. Jer. i. 6, 'I do not know (i.e. I am not skilled) to speak'. *he wakens*] *yāʿîr*, the same forcible verb as in xli. 2; cf. also Zech. iv. 1. *morning by morning*] This duplication of *babbōḳer* occurs frequently enough (xxviii. 19; Exod. xvi. 21, xxx. 7; a dozen times in all) for it to be unimaginative to delete one of the two words. The metre is 2:2:2, as in 7*b*, 8*a*. The meaning of 'in the morning' is 'as soon as it begins to be light': cf. Gen. xxix. 25, xliv. 3; 1 Kings iii. 21. The Servant is no laggard. We are reminded of Thomas Ken's

> Awake, my soul, and with the sun
> Thy daily stage of duty run;
> Shake off dull sloth . . .

5. *nor have I turned back*] i.e. been apostate (Ps. xliv. 18 (*19*)) or treacherously unfaithful (Jer. xxxviii. 22).

6. This verse, however we may account for it, is a startling anticipation of the maltreatment of Christ on the morning of the crucifixion. Ps. cxxix. 1–3 is often quoted by those who see in the Servant the nation Israel, as an illustration of the way in which a community can be personified as an individual: cf. also Isa. i. 5 f. *those who flogged me*] *makkîm*, 'strikers'. The word can be used of striking in a private quarrel (Exod. xxi. 12–20), but in the present context (cf. ver. 8) we are probably to think of public chastisement. For 'strike' = 'beat' or 'scourge' by authority, cf. Deut. xxv. 2 f.; Jer. xx. 2, xxxvii. 15. *who tore (at my beard)*] *môr^eṭîm*: cf. Ezra ix. 3; Neh. xiii. 25. *spitting*] For spitting as a gesture of contempt cf. Deut. xxv. 9; Job xxx. 10.

8. The language in this and the next verse is unmistakably that of the law-court: see on xli. 1. *my Vindicator*] *maṣdîḳ*, lit. 'he who

declares me to be *ṣaddîḳ*', i.e. in the right. For this as a legal term, in the declarative sense of NT δικαιόω, cf. Deut. xxv. 1; 1 Kings viii. 32. He who justifies the wicked (*maṣdîḳ rāšā'*), or condemns the righteous (*maršîaʿ ṣaddîḳ*), is guilty of enormity abhorrent to Yahweh (Prov. xvii. 15). The Servant anticipates that he may be the victim of an unjust accusation. But Yahweh will be at hand, not only to conduct his case but to secure, and pronounce, his acquittal. *impeach*] For the forensic sense of Heb. *rîḇ* see on xli. 11 and cf. Job xiii. 19, xxxi. 35. *Let us take our stand together*] i.e. before the judgement seat, as the daughters of Zelophehad did before Moses, Eleazar, and the rulers (Num. xxvii. 2, 5). *my opponent*] *baʿal mišpāṭî*. This is the only example of the idiomatic use of *baʿal* ('owner') with *mišpāṭ* ('suit in law', 'case'; cf. Job xiii. 18). It could presumably mean 'my legal adviser', had there been any such in OT times. But quite obviously it means 'my antagonist' or 'accuser'. The Servant bids him *come near to me!* (cf. xli. 1).

9. *will come to my aid*] Cf. xli. 10, 13 f. *win a verdict against me*] *yaršîʿēnî*, 'condemn me (*or* have me condemned) as guilty' (cf. liv. 17). But we are not necessarily to think of the Servant as charged with a breach of the moral law. The verb can be used of civil relations (Exod. xxii. 9 (*8*) or even of a trumped-up charge (Job xxxiv. 17; Ps. xciv. 21; Prov. xvii. 15) of the kind brought against Jesus. That such perversions of justice could be common enough is clear from Amos v. 12. Again, the Servant is not describing a situation in which he actually finds himself. He is using forensic language to describe a situation he anticipates, or imagines, for himself. He expresses confidence that Yahweh will deliver him. It is just possible that he divines that it will only be at a post-mortem inquest that he is finally justified: cf. lii. 13–liii. 12. The text does not rule out such an interpretation. But it is more probable that the Servant does not yet know the sequel as it is unfolded in the final Song, in which Yahweh only justifies his 'righteous' (liii. 11) Servant after he has suffered the extreme penalty. Even Jesus prayed, 'Remove this cup from me' (Mark xiv. 36), and we should not expect the Servant, in his Gethsemane, to be more far-seeing than Jesus was. *wear out like a garment*] Cf. li. 6; Ps. cii. 27. *and become moth-eaten*] Cf. li. 8; Job xiii. 28.

10. *Who?*] This can be either the interrogative 'Who?' (EVV, Torrey, Köhler, Kissane) or the indefinite 'Whoever' (Duhm, Volz). If it is the former, where does the question end? At 'the LORD'? (Köhler, Kissane), at 'his servant'? (RV), or at the end of the verse (Torrey, RSV)? These uncertainties are eased if we take the pronoun as the indefinite 'Anyone who', followed by the relative 'that' (*'ᵃšer*) in the next line, as in Deut. xx. 5 ff.; Judges x. 18. We have then a description of 'Anyone who fears the LORD, obeying the word of his servant, who (nevertheless) gropes in darkness and has no glimmer of light'. This is an experience the saints know well. There is still much to be said for the AV, which puts the question mark after 'no light'. In that case it is much the same whether we take 'Who' as interrogative ('Who . . . has no light?') or indefinite ('Whoever . . . has no light'). To this there follows the admonition, '*Let him trust in the name of the* LORD . . .'. This is exactly what the Servant has done in a similar distressful situation, and the verse is an admirable summary, and application, of vv. 4–9. *fears the* LORD] Or 'reverences', or even 'worships' (cf. 2 Kings xvii. 25). There is no emphasis on cringing fear. The sense is something like that of English 'a god-fearing man'. *obeying the word of*] For *šāmaʿ bᵉḳôl*, lit. 'listen to the voice of', in this sense, cf. Deut. iv. 30 and frequently in Deuteronomic writing. *glimmer of light*] *nōgah*, as distinct from the more usual *'ôr*, 'light': cf. Amos v. 20. *the name of the* LORD] See on xlviii. 9. But here 'the name (*šēm*) of Yahweh' is almost a synonym for Yahweh himself, the sum-total of his attributes: cf. Exod. xxxiii. 19 and its sequel in xxxiv. 6. In post-biblical times 'the Name' came to be a substitute for the tetragrammaton (YHWH), which from motives of reverence was no longer pronounced. It is even found in the late OT passage Lev. xxiv. 11. Even if it is there a scribal substitute for the ineffable name, that only shows that 'the name of Yahweh' was coming to be used hypostatically for Yahweh himself. A study of the concordance, beginning with the key-passage Exod. iii. 15, will show how natural and even inevitable, on OT premisses, this development was.

11. The picture in this verse is a vivid one, of those who start a fire by means of friction or flint (cf. the Arabic and Syriac senses of √*ḳdḥ*). The fire gets out of control and rings them round so that they cannot escape from it. *By all means*] An attempt to represent the *hēn* ('Behold') at the beginning of the verse. *flames*] Cf. RV: 'light' (AV, RSV) is not strong enough. The pointing is not *'ôr*, but *'ûr*, for which cf. xxxi. 9 (‖ 'furnace'), xliv. 16, xlvii. 14; Ezek. v. 2. *This is what you may expect from me*] Lit. 'From my hand this has happened (perf. of certainty) to you'. *you shall die and go to a place of torment*] The Hebrew is so condensed as to be obscure: lit. 'you shall lie down to (*lᵉ*) a place of torment' (*maʿᵃṣēḇāh*). RSV has 'you shall lie down in torment' (similarly AV, RV). Muilenburg says with reference to 'torment'—the word is ἅπ. λεγ.—'There is no reference to a place here'. It is true that the preformative *mêm* need not indicate a 'place where'; but it very commonly does (*GK* 85 *e–i*) and we should expect that with 'lie down to' (*šāḵaḇ lᵉ*), notwithstanding Job xi. 18; Hos. ii. 18 (*20*), 'lie down in safety' (lit. 'according to security'). The general sense of the preposition *lᵉ* is that of direction towards, not 'in' (*bᵉ*) in a locative sense. The construction of the sentence is pregnant and its closest analogies are li. 14, 'he shall not die (and go) to the pit', and Job vii. 21, lit. 'For now I shall lie to the dust; and thou shalt seek me, but I shall not be', where 'lie down to' must have the meaning 'die (and be laid in)'. For other examples of 'lie' = 'lie in death', cf. xiv. 18; Ps. lxxxviii. 5 (*6*); Job xx. 11, xxi. 26; Ezek. xxxii. 21; also the expression 'lie down (i.e. die and be buried) with one's fathers' (1 Kings ii. 10). In the present context *maʿᵃṣēḇāh* means 'a place of (fiery) torment', very nearly 'Gehenna'. The conception is late (cf. lxvi. 24; Mark ix. 47 f.) and the (perhaps unconscious) reason why Muilenburg says that 'there is no reference to a place here' is that he has committed himself to the view that l. 10 f. is an integral part of a carefully constructed poem of DI, who is relatively early. Verse 10, then, is a commentary on the security of those who fear Yahweh and obey his Servant; ver. 11 is a commentary on the fate of those who are recalcitrant.

LI. 1–8. VICTORY, DELIVERANCE, AND RIGHTEOUSNESS

1. בּוֹר] Properly 'cistern'. May be an explanatory gloss to the *ἅπ. λεγ.* מַקֶּבֶת. But it makes no difference to the sense.

2. וַאֲבָרְכֵהוּ וְאַרְבֵּהוּ] The versions read as *waw consec.*, doubtless rightly. *GK* (107 *b*, n. 2) quotes this as a case where וְ is 'no doubt a dogmatic emendation for וַ in order to represent historical statements as promises'. That Israel's population was to increase in the present and future is promised elsewhere in DI (xliv. 3 f.).

4. עַמִּי וּלְאוּמִּי] A few MSS. have the plur. עַמִּים וּלְאוּמִּים, similarly P, no doubt rightly. לְאֹם is nowhere else used of Israel (Gen. xxv. 23 is not really an exception) and the form לאומי is *ἅπ. λεγ.* G. R. Driver ("Abbreviations in the Massoretic Text", *Textus I. Annual of the Hebrew University Bible Project*, 1960, p. 115) suggests that the words are examples of the abbreviation of the plural termination *îm* to *î*. It may be so, but why should the abbreviation be so sporadic? (Driver quotes only two exactly similar examples in Isa.). Another explanation is that the archetypal MS of MT Isaiah was written—in parts—from dictation and that the scribe did not hear the final *mêm*. The *mêm* of the plural termination was not an articulated labial but a nasal sound similar to Engl. *ng* (*nûn* in Arab., Aram.). The singulars 'my people . . . my nation' would not excite subsequent query, because in vv. 1 and 7 the address is obviously to Israelites. Or it may be that the singular forms are dogmatic emendations in the context. אַרְגִּיעַ] The Masora evidently took as *Hiph.* Impf. 1st pers. sing. of רגע II, 'cause to rest', and included it in ver. 4 (so AV, RV). Most moderns take as from רגע I, 'I will cause to flash', or the like (cf. רֶגַע, 'moment') and construe it with ver. 5 (cf. LXX and RSV 'speedily'). G. R. Driver (in a private communication) thinks the verbal form has become a stereotyped adverb, 'in a flash', cf. Prov. xii. 19. Another possibility is that the form is a fossilized and partly mutilated (*î* for *a*) elative (Arab. *'ap'al*), of which one or two examples like אַכְזָב, 'false', אֵיתָן, 'perennial', survive in Hebrew. These suggestions do not involve emendation of קָרוֹב following. Some such sense as 'my victory is immediately near' cannot be far wrong.

5. יָצָא יִשְׁעִי] Two stresses only. We expect three, unless, as some suggest, וּזְרֹעַי עַמִּים יִשְׁפֹּטוּ should be deleted as a partial dittograph. LXX καὶ ἐξελεύσεται ὡς φῶς τὸ σωτήριόν μου may be for יָצָא כַנֹּגַהּ יִשְׁעִי (cf. lxii. 1), or יצא alone could carry the meaning 'go out (i.e. rise) like the dawn': cf. xiii. 10; Gen. xix. 23; Judges v. 31; Hos. vi. 5.

6. נִמְלָחוּ] ἅπ. λεγ., ? 'be torn to shreds' (Arab. *malaḥa*, and cf. מֶלַח 'rags', Jer. xxxviii. 11 f.). A and Σ 'shall be salty' must have related the word to מֶלַח, 'salt'. They were probably guessing at the meaning of an unfamiliar word, but since Arab. *maliḥa* = 'become greyish', the sense of the Hebrew may be 'become murky like smoke'. Salt in OT times was not the refined white of to-day, but muddy grey (cf. Ezek. xlvii. 11). כְּמוֹ־כֵן] AV, RV, 'in like manner'. RSV 'like gnats' (cf. כִּנָּם/כִּנִּים, Exod. viii. 12–14). G. R. Driver (in a private communication) reads כַּמּוֹכֵן, 'like (spawn of) locusts' (Arab. *makin*). The figure is much the same. תֵּחָת] Usually taken as *Qal* impf. of חתת, 'be shattered' (AV, RV, 'be abolished'; RSV 'be ended'). In ver. 7 תֵּחָתּוּ is clearly from this verb, in a derivative sense 'be dismayed', 'scared' (cf. Job vii. 14; Jer. i. 17). An equally legitimate parsing is *Qal* impf. of נחת, 'go down'. But this verb is more common in Aramaic and nowhere in OT is it used of the setting of the sun (or victory), as יָצָא is in ver. 5 (see above). Even if it were, the general sense 'be destroyed' or 'annulled' would suit either vb.

This passage contains three short strophes (vv. 1–3, 4–6, 7 f.) beginning *Listen to me* (vv. 1, 7) and *Attend to me* (ver. 4). The vocabulary in vv. 4–6 has similarities to that of the first Servant Song, and van Hoonacker and W. B. Stevenson have suggested that they should be included in the Song cycle (see *SS*, p. 136 f.). This is improbable, since *mišpāṭ* and *tôrāh* are here mediated directly by

Yahweh, not by the Servant. Others have held that the verses are an intrusive variant of xlii. 1–4, or a patchwork of glosses. Begrich omits the verses from his study as 'very probably not genuine' (*SS*, loc. cit.).

The main difficulty in the interpretation of the passage is presented by the words *ṣeḏeḳ/ṣᵉḏāḳāh* (AV 'righteousness', vv. 1, 5, 6, 7, 8), *aʿ/yᵉšûʿāh* (AV 'salvation', vv. 5, 6, 8), *mišpāṭ* (AV 'judgement', ver. 4), and *tôrāh* (AV 'law', vv. 4, 7). The first two have come to be near-synonyms in DI (see on xlii. 21) and move within a radius of 'righteousness', 'victory', 'deliverance', and 'salvation'. In contemporary English 'righteousness' and even 'salvation' have an archaic flavour, even in religious parlance. Accordingly, in the *NEB* 'righteousness' (Gr. δικαιοσύνη) is 'to see right prevail' at Matt. v. 6, 'standard of conduct' at Matt. v. 20, 'justice' at Rom. iii. 5, but the translators have kept 'righteousness' at Rom. v. 21.

In the present passage it is well-nigh impossible to give precise English equivalents to a word like *ṣeḏeḳ*, which may have different shades of meaning in near contexts. (For discussion of the basic meaning of the word see A. R. Johnson, *Sacral Kingship in Ancient Israel*, 1955, *passim*). In ver. 1 *rôḏᵉpê ṣeḏeḳ* (AV 'ye that follow after righteousness') is similar to 'do righteousness' (RV) in lvi. 1, though li. 1–8 has not the legalistic flavour of lvi. 1–8. At the same time, li. 1–8 would be as much as home in Trito- as it is in Deutero-Isaiah. We cannot assume that *ṣeḏeḳ/yᵉšûʿāh*, even if we translate 'victory' or 'deliverance', have any immediate reference to victory over or deliverance from Babylon. Nor must we forget that DI was as concerned for the moral and spiritual reformation of his people as he was for their deliverance from Babylon.

1. *endeavour after right*] Heb. '*pursue ṣeḏeḳ*'. The question here is whether the emphasis in *ṣeḏeḳ* is ethical or soteriological-eschatological ('victory', 'deliverance'). Volz, 'notwithstanding some hesitation', opts for the latter (*Heil*), similarly Muilenburg. But RSV 'pursue deliverance' is almost a contradiction. One must 'wait' for deliverance, or one may 'yearn' for it; but Heb. *rāḏap̄* always implies strenuous activity on the part of the subject. The closest literary ‖ is in Deut. xvi. 20, where the sense must be, 'Justice, justice, is what you must strive to maintain', similarly Prov. xxi. 21, and cf. Ps. xxxiv. 14 (*15*), 'Seek peace, and pursue it'. The immediate ‖ *who seek the* LORD on the whole confirms the ethical emphasis in *ṣeḏeḳ*: cf. Zeph. ii. 3. The 'righteousness' which men pursue is Yahweh's righteousness. He is 'righteous' (? or 'victorious', *ṣaddîḳ*) and withal 'Saviour' (xlv. 21). When all has been said, the ethical and soteriological threads in DI's concept of Yahweh's *ṣeḏeḳ* cannot be neatly disentangled. Men may endeavour to do what is right but in the end

they are saved by faith. This may well be the implication in the rest of the strophe (see below, on ver. 2). *Think of*] Heb. 'Look to' (*habbîṭû*). *the rock*] P. A. H. de Boer, taking a cue from LXX, has argued that 'the rock' here is not Abraham but God (*Second Isaiah's Message*, 1956, pp. 58–67). To do this he points the vbs. 'hew' and 'dig' as actives. There are some thirty passages in which Yahweh is called 'the rock', the most notable in relation to the present passage being Deut. xxxii. 18, 'You were unmindful of the Rock that begot you, and you forgot the God who gave you birth' (*meḥôlelêḵā*). But this is not the metaphor de Boer sees in the text. He seems to say that God as 'the rock' and 'cistern' is the source from which Israel draws water, or finds shelter, by quarrying and digging. This is bizarre. And his plea that the passive verbs 'you were hewn' and 'digged' would need to be completed (in the Heb.) by 'from it' (*mimmennû* or *mē'ašer*) is not compelling. The language is elliptic, but not more so than 'a land (in which there is) no man' (Job xxxviii. 26), and there is no ambiguity. Duhm explained the ellipsis as *metri causa*. Moreover, *maḳḳeḇeṯ* ('quarry') in the ‖ stich, seems to be a reference to Sarah in ver. 2: cf. *neḳēḇāh*, lit. *perforata*, 'female'. Nor do de Boer's references to the rock, the boring (*hnḳbh*), and the stone-hewers (*hḥṣbm*) in the Siloam inscription strengthen his case: the boring was of the rock, not the *source* of the water.

2. *and I blessed him*] I.e. with children: cf. Gen. xxiv. 60; Ps. cxxviii. 3 f. Q[a] has 'and I made him fruitful', the right interpretation even if it is not the original reading. Abraham is presented as the ideal righteous (*ṣaddîḳ*) man (Gen. xviii. 19) and it is not improbable that DI has in mind the story told in Gen. xv. 1–6, in which Abram is distressed because he is childless. Yahweh bade him 'Look (*habbēṭ*, cf. the repeated *habbîṭû* in the present passage) at the heavens', and promised him that his descendants would be as numerous as the stars. 'And he believed Yahweh and he reckoned it to him as righteousness (*ṣeḏāḳāh*)'. Similarly, here, those who 'pursue righteousness'—and they were probably a minority in a small enough community (cf. xliv. 1–5)—are in effect exhorted to have faith.

3. The tenses (perf. and *waw consec.* impf.) are rightly taken by AV and RSV as indicating certainty. For *Eden . . . the garden of the* LORD cf. Gen. xiii. 10; Ezek. xxviii. 13, xxxi. 9; Joel ii. 3. Q[a] fills out the verse with 'sorrow and sighing shall flee', evidently taken from ver. 11: cf. xxxv. 10.

4. Lit. 'for *tôrāh* from with me goes out and my *mišpāṭ* for light to the peoples'. It is possible, though not on the whole probable, that the key words should be given the senses they have in xlii. 1–4. *for* *from me there issues the voice of authority*] Cf. ii. 3. *my ordinances*] The Hebrew noun is singular: 'RV 'my judgement', RSV 'my justice'. The latter is right if it means the sum-total of the moral and religious ordinances which Yahweh enjoins. What is not meant is any single judgement or legal decision. See on xli. 1, xlii. 1.

5. *my sovereign power*] Heb. 'my arms'. For 'arm' as a metaphor for 'power' or 'rule' cf. Ezek. xxx. 21. *shall rule*] Cf. RSV. Heb. *yišpōṭû*, 'shall judge'. *the far shores look to me with longing, expectant of my rule*] Lit. 'to me the coastlands wait (see on xl. 31) and to my arm they expect'. The construction is pregnant and the verbs are near synonyms.

6. The picture, if taken *au pied de la lettre*, is a melancholy one: heaven and the earth and its inhabitants have vanished, and Yahweh is left alone with his 'victory'/'righteousness'. It is possible to take the Heb. *kî* as 'if', 'though', and to translate as a concessive-conditional sentence: 'though the heavens should vanish . . . yet my victory would be for ever': cf. liv. 10, where RSV has 'For the mountains may depart . . .'. But this expedient is not necessary. What DI says is his way of asserting Bishop Blougram's terse 'God's all, man's nought'. The passage must be related to his message, and to that of the Bible, as a whole. Pure monism is entirely foreign to the thought of the Bible, and—Yahweh being what he is—the annihilation of heaven and earth was bound, sooner rather than later, to be followed by the creation of new heavens and a new earth (lxv. 17, lxvi. 22; 2 Pet. iii. 13). In this new creation Israel's 'descendants' and 'name' are to remain, and long life is to be the rule. But in the Apocalypse the new heaven and earth are—so it is implied—to be peopled by those who have passed through death to resurrection (Rev. xxi).

7. *you who know and do what is right*] Lit. 'knowers of *ṣeḏeḳ*', with emphasis on the ethical content of *ṣeḏeḳ*, as the ‖ indicates. But 'who know what is right' would be inadequate. Knowledge, for the Hebrews, especially 'the knowledge of God' (*daʿaṯ ʾᵉlôhîm*, Hos. iv. 1), is not intellectual understanding but *experientia*: cf. 'you know with all your heart and soul', Joshua xxiii. 14. When the participle 'knowing' is used in the construct state before a noun it has the sense 'expert in': e.g. hunting (Gen. xxv. 27), the sea (1 Kings ix. 27), reading (Isa. xxix. 11 f.), lamentation (Amos v. 16). 'To know righteousness' is a concise way of saying 'to know (how) to do right' (cf. Amos iii. 10), and the order is, 'If anyone wills to do . . . he shall know' (John vii. 17). *the people*] The noun is probably definite, though in poetry the article is wanting. The address is to the Israelite

community, though not all its members would qualify as 'knowers of right'. *in whose heart*] Heb. 'in their heart', 3rd person following 2nd person: cf. xlv. 21. The language recalls that of the New Covenant in Jer. xxxi. 33 f.: cf. Ps. xl. 8 (*9*); Ezek. xxxvi. 27.

8. *moth will eat them*] Cf. l. 9. *clothes-moth*] *sās*, ἅπ. λεγ., but common to the Semitic languages. Gr. σής (Matt. vi. 19) is probably a loan-word from Semitic. *triumph . . . victory*] Cf. ver. 6 and note the inversion (see on xlix. 24 f.).

LI. 9–11. HISTORY AND MYTH

9. עוּרִי עוּרִי . . . . עוּרִי] The normal accentuation is עוּרִי. Here it is varied for rhythmical effect, the rhythmical stresses being more lively than the grammatical: similarly Judges v. 12 (*GK* 72 *s*). הַמַּחְצֶבֶת] 'that hewed'. Qª has הַמֹּחֶצֶת, 'that smashed', cf. Job xxvi. 12. But there is no reason to alter MT.

10. הַשָּׂמָה] The Masora takes as the article (= אֲשֶׁר relative) with *Qal* perf. 3rd pers. sing. fem. Similarly הַשָּׁבָה (Ruth i. 22). But the original was probably the article with the *Qal* ptc. 3rd pers. sing. fem., and accent on the last syllable (הַשָּׂמָה).

11. שָׂשׂוֹן וְשִׂמְחָה יַשִּׂיגוּן] EVV take the nouns as accusatives: 'they shall obtain (lit. overtake) gladness and rejoicing'. It is better to take them as subjects: 'gladness and rejoicing shall overtake (them)'. The pron. obj. is understood (*Syn.*, § 73, Rem. 5) and it is unnecessary to emend to יַשִּׂיגוּם. נָסוּ] Read וְנָסוּ with xxxv. 10, and cf. Qª ונס.

This is the first of three impassioned summonses beginning 'Awake, awake' (AV, RV at li. 17, lii. 1). It is addressed to the 'arm of Yahweh' (cf. xl. 10, lii. 10, liii. 1; Luke i. 51). The figure of Yahweh's 'arm' as the instrument of deliverance and judgement is frequent in Deuteronomy, usually when recalling the Exodus, which Yahweh effected 'with a mighty hand and an out-stretched arm' (Deut. iv. 34). The original associations of 'Rahab, the sea-monster, the sea' (in Ugaritic the god *Yam*) and 'the great deep', were with the creation-myth. Job ix. 13 speaks of 'the helpers of Rahab', lit. 'storm(iness)', the creatures which Tiamat spawned to help her in her fight against the gods (*Enuma eliš*, i. 130–45, in *ANET*, p. 62*b*). In Job xxvi. 12 Yahweh is said to have 'smashed' Rahab, which is ‖ the sea (*hayyām*): cf. Ps. lxxxix. 10 (*11*). The 'sea-monster' (*tannîn*) is a mythological personification of chaos in Ps. lxxiv. 13, and probably in Job vii. 12; Isa. xxvii. 1 (in all three passages associated with 'the sea'). For 'the great deep' (*tᵉhôm rabbāh*) in Hebrew cosmogony see Gen. i. 2; Ps. civ. 6; Prov. viii. 27. The word is cognate with Tiamat, the chaos-monster of Babylonian cosmogony, and only occurs with the article (and in the plur.) at lxiii. 13; Ps. cvi. 9, where it refers to the Red Sea. 'Rahab', 'the sea-monster', 'the sea', and 'the deep' are all synonyms for the original chaos. The fullest form of the creation-myth is the Babylonian, in which Marduk slew Tiamat, 'split her like a shellfish into two parts' (*ANET*, p. 67, line 137), and with one half made a covering (the Heb. 'firmament') over the earth, to keep the waters of the original chaos from deluging the inhabited world. Heb. cosmology presented much the same picture: cf. Gen. i. 6–10; Job xxxviii. 8–11; Ps. civ. 6–9. The Hebrews had no liking for the sea, partly, no doubt, because they had no harbours to tempt them to maritime adventures, but mainly because 'the sea' stood for all that is turbulent and chaotic, threatening to reduce the ordered world to the chaos from which it had been screened at the creation. This motif runs through the Bible: 'there was no longer any sea' (Rev. xxi. 1) is more than the *cri du cœur* of a prisoner on a rocky islet; it is the triumphal assertion that any danger that 'the sea' would overwhelm the cosmos is finally removed.

If 9*b* refers to the creation, 10 refers to the Exodus and the deliverance at the Red Sea: 'that made the ocean-depths a pathway, for the redeemed to pass over'. Rahab is Egypt in Ps. lxxxvii. 4 ('Rahab and Babylon') and Isa. xxx. 7 ('Rahab sit-still'). The Hebrews took fragments from the creation-myth, like broken pieces of stained glass, and used them to embellish the story of the Exodus. They 'historicized' the myth, and it is broadly true to say that God's revelation in history was his answer to the human need that had found expression in what, to us, is crude mythology. Passages like the present and Ps. lxxiv. 12–17 refer equally to creation and redemption. It was as Redeemer that the Hebrews first came to know Yahweh. That they should come also to think of him as Creator was inevitable. They extolled him as Redeemer-Creator, with the main emphasis on his redeeming acts in history (cf. xliii. 14–17).

9. *Awake, awake*] Or 'rouse thyself'. For Heb. *'ûr* cf. xli. 2, and for the reiteration xl. 1. *exert thy might*] Lit. 'put on might'. Heb. *lāḇēš*, 'put on', is used of putting on armour (1 Sam. xvii. 5; Isa. lix. 17; Jer. xlvi. 4). The picture is probably of a heavily gauntleted forearm brandishing a sword: cf. Ps. lxxxix. 10 (*11*).

10. *dried up the sea*] Cf. l. 2. *redeemed*] The metaphors here and in 'ransomed' (ver. 11) should not be pressed: they are expressive ways of saying 'released . . . set free': cf. l. 2.

11. This verse is almost letter for letter the same as xxxv. 10, and some think it is a later borrowing from there. The connexion with ver. 9 f. is loose and, with its future reference, it might seem inconsequent. But something of the kind is called for and ver. 10 would be an abrupt ending. We have noted that Q[a] adds 'sorrow and sighing shall flee away' after li. 2. It is possible that such fragments of verse were current clichés in Deutero- and Trito-Isaianic circles, much as there are said to be stock phrases in the Homeric poems. It is obvious that DI was an individual, and the creative genius among those who produced what Caspari called *Lieder und Gottessprüche der Rückwanderer* (*BZAW* 65, 1934). But he was not above occasional borrowing (cf. xlii. 10) and this may have a bearing on the question whether he meticulously 'wrote' his poetry, or whether it was at first freely composed and transmitted orally. *crowned with never-fading gladness*] Lit. 'and never-ending (*'ôlām*) gladness upon their head(s)'. This may be only a poetical way of saying that they will be filled with intense and constant gladness. Or it may mean that they will garland themselves with festal wreaths of unfading flowers. That such wreaths were worn by merry-makers is clear from xxviii. 1, 3 f.; cf. Wisd. ii. 8, 'Let us crown ourselves with rosebuds, before they are withered'. The garlands, contrary to the normal course of nature, will be unfading: cf. 1 Pet. v. 4, 'You will obtain the unfading crown (*τὸν ἀμαράντινον στέφανον*) of glory', though we are not, before Hellenistic times, to think of wreaths worn by athletes: cf. 1 Macc. iv. 57; 2 Macc. iv. 9, 12.

LI. 12–16. 'FEAR NOT, YOU ARE MY PEOPLE'

12. מְנַחֶמְכֶם] It is usual to regard the final *mêm* as a dittograph and to read מְנַחֶמֵךְ (cf. LXX *σε*); but little reliance can be placed on minor emendations in what is (see below) a somewhat scrappy passage. In any case it is doubtful whether the plural suffix is intended to emphasize individuals and the following sing. vbs. collective Israel.

13. וַתִּשְׁכַּח] Q[a] ותשכחי, though its ותפחד agrees with MT.

16. לִנְטֹעַ] Lit. 'to plant', an anomalous word in this context, the nearest analogy being of 'establishing' a people (Jer. xxiv. 6). We expect לִנְטוֹת, 'to stretch out': (cf. vs. 13, xl. 22, xlii. 5, xliv. 24), and P either read this or understood the Hebrew so. Skinner defends MT and would even read נוֹטֵעַ, 'plants', in ver. 13, this on the theory (see below) that what is envisaged is new heavens and a new earth.

These verses form a bridge between two 'Awake, awake' passages. As they stand they must be taken as Yahweh's response to the appeal to his 'arm'. Yet they present a number of difficulties. Compared with the rest of DI they are 'jumpy' and inconsequent. The 'you' in 12*a* is masc. plur., in 12*b* it is fem. sing., and in 13 masc. sing. (in Q[a] fem. sing. and masc. sing.). The address is presumably to the exiles, thought of either as a community of individuals (12*a*), or personified as a woman (cf. xli. 14) or as a man (cf. xli. 8). Hebrew can pass abruptly from female to male personification (cf. xli. 8–13, 14–16). Ver. 16*a* has some similarity to the prose passage lix. 21 and also recalls passages in the Servant Songs (xlix. 2, l. 4), though this occasions no difficulty if the Servant is Israel and the Songs were in the first draft of the prophecy. The connexion between 16*a* and *b* is not very plain: 'I have put my words in your mouth . . . (lit.) to stretch out the heavens . . .'. Verses 15 f. seem loosely related to what precedes and consist of a quotation from Jer. xxxi. 35 and what sound like reminiscences of the Servant Songs. Duhm thought them a later addition and much the same view is taken by Volz, Fischer, and even Feldmann.

Torrey and Muilenburg, on the other hand, insist on the unity of li. 1–16. Indeed, it is almost as if the alleged fragmentariness of vv. 12–16 betrays them into over-statement of their contrary opinion. According to Torrey (pp. 394 f.) li. 1–16 is 'A composition lofty in tone and splendidly eloquent . . . one of the poems in which (the Second Isaiah's) pride in the literary dress of his productions is evident . . . The manner in which certain principal themes of 49 and 50 are plainly alluded to in ver. 16 is further evidence that these poems were written down by their author in the order in which we now have them'. There is nothing fortuitous in the relation between the two halves of ver. 16: 'It is none other than Yahwè, the creator and ruler of the world, who has chosen Israel. Cf. 42:5, 6; 44:24, and the other passages where the "founding of the world" and the call of Israel are put side by side' (p. 402). That may be so, but in xlii. 5 f. and xliv. 24 the order is not that Yahweh calls Israel as a preliminary to stretching out the heavens and laying the foundations of the earth. Muilenburg meets this difficulty by saying that in ver. 16 'the only probable meaning is that God is about to create a new world of righteousness, a new heaven and a new earth in the place of the old which will vanish and wear out (ver. 6: cf. 65:17; 66:22)': similarly Kissane. Again it may be so, though we should have expected it to be made more explicit. All things considered, li. 12–16 is the Achilles heel of the theory that DI 'wrote' and edited a book to which no subsequent additions were made.

12. *how is it that you live in fear?*] Lit. 'who are you and you fear?' For *mî* ('who?') in sense 'how' cf. Ruth iii. 16, 'How did you fare?' (lit. 'who are you?'); Amos vii. 2, 5, 'How (*mî*) can Jacob stand?'

man whose life is short-lived as grass] Lit. 'the son of man grass he is given (made)'. For the thought cf. xl. 6; Ps. ciii. 15. Or the picture may be of grass used as fuel in a stove (Matt. vi. 30; cf. Ezek. xv. 4, 6, vine prunings 'given' to the fire as fuel). For 'man' (*'ᵉnôš*) ‖ 'son of man' (*ben-'āḏām*) with the suggestion of mortal frailty, cf. Ps. viii. 4 (*5*); xc. 3.

13. *he sets about*] *kônēn.* The word is used of taking aim with bow and arrow: Ps. vii. 12 (*13*), xi. 2. *and what is?*] Lit. 'and where is?' The expected answer, as usual with Heb. *'ayyēh,* is 'Nowhere!' We should say, 'It matters nothing at all!' cf. 'Where would be the good of quarrelling . . . over it?' (Dickens).

14. *the burdened slave*] *ṣô'ēh,* 'stooping', an unusual word best illustrated from Jer. xlviii. 12, which pictures cellarers bending over jars of wine to empty them. *he shall not die and go down to the pit*] Lit. 'he shall not die to the pit', a pregnant construction, cf. l. 11. The *pit* (*šaḥaṯ*) is a synonym of Sheol, with which it is ‖ in Ps. xvi. 10, and to which men descend at death (Gen. xxxvii. 35). AV 'that he should not die in the pit nor that his bread should fail' is attractive in the light of Jer. xxxvii. 16–21 (note the detail about Jeremiah's ration of bread), but Heb. *lᵉ* ('to') cannot be forced into meaning 'in'. *even*] Not in Hebrew, but the connexion seems to justify a climactic force, 'much less shall he want for bread'.

15. *For*] Lit. 'and'. The Semitic languages use the conjunction 'and' lavishly, often in places where it seems superfluous to us: so frequently in the *Qur'ān* at the end of a passage, 'And God is the compassionate, the merciful'. This is not so much padding. Whether or not the verse is original in its context, the 'and' must be given some such force as 'This is as sure as that . . .'.

16. '*You are my people*'] See on xl. 1.

LI. 17–23. THE CUP OF WRATH

17. קֻבַּעַת כּוֹס] קבעת only occurs here and in ver. 22, though it is found in Akkadian, Ugaritic (*ḳb't*), and perhaps Egyptian (*ḳbḥw*), cf. Arab. *ḳub'a*, 'calyx'. כוס, which occurs in the preceding line, is here probably an explanatory gloss.

18. מְנַהֵל] Cf. xl. 11, xlix. 10; Ps. xxiii. 2. LXX παρακαλῶν (for מְנַחֵם?) may be due to careless reading: similarly P. But MT gives a better ‖ to 'take her by the hand'. Qᵃ has מנחל לך, 'to possess you', which can hardly be right, followed as it is by the 3rd person.

19. מִי אֲנַחֲמֵךְ] If the right reading, must mean 'How am I to console you?' (cf. RV and see on ver. 12). The versions read יְנַחֲמֵךְ and this is supported by Q[a] (so RSV).

23. The first stich is without any ‖. LXX adds *καὶ τῶν ταπενωσάντων σε* and Q[a] וּמְעַנַּיִךְ, 'and of those who humiliated you', almost certainly rightly.

An appeal to Jerusalem to rouse herself from the despair into which she has sunk. The speaker is presumably the Prophet, since Yahweh is referred to in the 3rd person (ver. 17) and himself speaks in vv. 22 f. Jerusalem's condition is due to Yahweh's having, with his own hand, given her 'the cup of his wrath' to drink. The ruinous state of the city during the years of the exile had only deepened the despair which found expression in the book of Lamentations. None of Jerusalem's 'sons', who must include the citizens born in her as well as her scattered children (xlix. 20–22), extends a helping hand to her (ver. 18), nor is sympathy forthcoming from those who have laid her waste or those who have been passive spectators of her misery (ver. 19). Indeed, 'her sons', like herself, are 'filled with (the cup of) Yahweh's wrath' (ver. 20). The passage closes with Yahweh's assurance that he has taken the cup from Jerusalem's hand and will give it to the tormentors who have arrogantly trampled on her.

Yahweh's 'cup' is described in a relatively late Asaph Psalm (lxxv. 8 (*9*)) as 'a cup in Yahweh's hand, with foaming wine, well mixed (with toxic ingredients). He pours out its contents and all the wicked of the world drink from it and drain it to the dregs', and become demented. Most OT references to the cup date from the time immediately preceding the exile: Jer. xxv. 15–28; Lam. iv. 21; Ezek. xxiii. 31–33; Hab. ii. 16. Very relevant to the present passage is Jer. li. 7: 'Babylon is a gold cup in Yahweh's hand, making the whole earth drunk; the nations drank of her wine and so became mad'. For NT continuations of the theme cf. Mark x. 38 f. and ‖s, xiv. 36 and ‖s; John xviii. 11; Rev. xiv. 10, xvi. 19. The thought is always present that those to whom God gives the cup are powerless to refuse it.

17. *Rouse yourself, rouse yourself*] *Hithpô'ēl*, reflexive intensive, rather stronger than the *Qal 'ûrî* of li. 9; lii. 1. *the cup of his wrath*] For the synecdoche cf. 1 Cor. xi. 26, 'as often as . . . you drink the cup'. *the goblet of reeling*] Not a normal English expression, though we can speak of a 'cup of kindness/consolation' (Jer. xvi. 7). The Heb. (*ḳubba'aṯ hattar'ēlāh*) is not intended as an elegant expression. 'Goblet of reeling' approximates in sound to it and is less infelicitous than 'bowl/goblet which made you reel/stagger' would be. Engl. 'goblet' is from Old French *gobel*, *gobeau*, of unknown origin, and it is tempting to surmise that it may have some relation to the Semitic-Egyptian word (see phil. note above).

18. *guide her . . . take her by the hand*] Jerusalem is pictured as groping about under the toxic effects of 'the cup'.

19. *condole with you*] *yānûḏ lāḵ*, lit. 'nod (the head) to and fro for you', the same gesture of sympathetic grief as shown by Job's friends and relatives (Job ii. 11, xlii. 11; cf. Ps. lxix. 20 (*21*): and note in these passages the same contiguity of condolence and consolation as in this verse). **who is there to* console you?*] Or 'comfort' (see on xl. 1). There had been no one since the stricken city had cried, 'No one consoles me' (Lam. i. 2, 9, 16 f., 21).

20. *at the top of every street*] Metrically superfluous and may be a gloss from Lam. ii. 19, iv. 1. The meaning is 'conspicuously', 'in full view'. *antelopes*] *tᵉʼô*. Only here and in a list of 'clean' wild deer in Deut. xiv. 5. The point of the comparison is that such animals are shy and defenceless, with no means of safety except in flight. *in a net*] The historical situation is that of the Babylonian siege of Jerusalem (2 Kings xxv. 1–4) but the exact meaning of the ἅπ. λεγ. *miḵmār* (EVV 'net') is not certain. The related words *miḵmereṯ*/*miḵmōreṯ* (Hab. i. 15; Isa. xix. 8) must mean 'net'. But perhaps we are to think of an enclosure or even a pit (cf. Ps. cxli. 10) into which driven animals fell, breaking their limbs in their terror. Ezek. xix. 8 describes such a pit, which could be netted over when a lion was caught in it.

21. *Therefore*] Köhler omits, presumably on metrical grounds. But if it is outside the metre, it is anacrusis and all the more forcible. Every word from this initial 'Therefore' to 'Behold' (*hinnēh*, ver. 22) is calculated to emphasize the coming reversal of Jerusalem's fortunes. To us the connexion with the preceding strophe may seem illogical and the requital of Babylon, which after all had been Yahweh's chosen instrument, almost savage. But we must not look for strict logic or exact arithmetic. Jerusalem had suffered 'double' (xl. 2) and Babylon had exceeded her commission (xlvii. 6). It was a case of the wicked swallowing up the man more righteous than himself (Hab. i. 13; cf. Isa. x. 5–19). So much can power coarsen those who possess it. *afflicted*] *ʿᵃniyyāh*. There may be an intentional contrast with the 'pampered' (*ʿᵃḏînāh*) Babylon in xlvii. 8.

22. *champions*] *yārîḇ*, 'pleads'. The verb is used of going to law with someone (xlv. 9, xlix. 25, l. 8), here of initiating or conducting an action on behalf of another (cf. i. 17; 1 Sam. xxiv. 15 (*16*); Mic. vii. 9). *I am taking*] Lit. 'I have taken', perfect of certainty. *cup of reeling . . . goblet of my wrath*] Note the inversion, cf. ver. 17.

23. '*Lie down for us to trample over you*'] Lit. 'Bow down that we may pass over'. For such barbarity cf. Joshua x. 24; Zech. x. 5. *and you* *lay full length on the ground . . .*] Lit. 'and you placed your back like the ground and like the street to the passers-by'. Although the address is to Jerusalem we are to picture 'the street' as crammed with her prostrate citizens. They lie, not on their bellies with their backs as 'pavement', but on their backs: see the rock-carving of Anu-banini in *AOTB*, Tafel CVIII, No. 254. The ordure of the streets (*ṭîṭ ḥûṣôṯ*, 2 Sam. xxii. 43; Zech. x. 5) would add to their shame and discomfort.

LII. 1–6. ZION, AWAKE!

1. עֻזֵּךְ] Qª has עוז, as in li. 9, but the suffix is supported by the ‖ תִּפְאַרְתֵּךְ. A reading עֶדְיֵךְ, 'your ornaments', has been suggested and might seem a better ‖; but it is purely conjectural. For עֹז in conjunction with תִּפְאֶרֶת see Ps. lxxxix. 17 (*18*).

2. שְׁבִי] 'sit down', reads oddly after 'stand up'. Read שְׁבִיָּה, notwithstanding that it occurs in the next line: note the repeated לִבְשִׁי (ver. 1) and מְבַשֵּׂר and מַשְׁמִיעַ (ver. 7). התפתחו] Read *Qere* הִתְפַּתְּחִי, notwithstanding that Qª agrees with MT. מוֹסְרֵי] 'fetters', √אסר, 'bind'. There is no need to read מִמּוֹסְרֵי (*BH*), as *Hithpaʿēl* readily takes an accusative (*GK* 54 *f*).

5. מִי־לִי] *Qere* מַה־לִּי, and so Qª. כִּי] *recitativum*, introducing what follows. יְהֵילִילוּ] *Hiph.* ילל, 'howl', 'wail', with unsyncopated ה (*GK* 70 *d*). If the spelling is right, the subject מֹשְׁלָו must be Israel's own rulers; similarly if we read (conjecturally) יְחֻלָּלוּ, 'are profaned' (see *BH* and cf. xliii. 28). A pointing יְהַלֲלוּ (*Piʿēl*), 'brag', in sense of Ps. x. 3, xliv. 9 (usual for the *Hithpaʿēl*) involves only a vowel change. מֹשְׁלָו will then be Israel's foreign rulers. Qª והוללו (*Pôʿēl* הלל) ought to mean 'and make fools of' (cf. xliv. 25), but is meaningless here, since it has no acc. obj.; but it does indicate how uncertain the original spelling is, and justifies our making the best sense we can in the context. נְאֻם־יהוה] Qª omits יהוה in the repeat of the phrase. This may be due to careless copying, or it may be one more indication of the scrappy build-up of vv. 4–6. מִנֹּאָץ] *Hithpôʿēl* נאץ, for מִתְנֹאָץ, with assimilated ת (*GK* 54 *c*). But the form may just as well be מְנֹאָץ (*Puʿal*).

6. לָכֵן . . . . לָכֵן] LXX, V, and Qª omit the second לכן.

The first two verses of this passage are an urgent summons to Zion-Jerusalem to put on her festal garments in anticipation of her near-approaching deliverance. Her sacred ground is no longer to be defiled by the presence of 'uncircumcised and unclean' foreigners. She is to shake herself from the dust in which she has lain prostrate (li. 23), and free herself from her neck-fetters.

Verses 7–10 would be a fitting sequel to 1 f., but the intermediate vv. 3–6 are more ragged than anything in the prophecy. There is parallelism in ver. 3, though the metre, outside the introductory 'For thus says Yahweh', is 2:3. What it says has no real connexion with 1 f. and all the indications are that it should be construed with what follows. Torrey, Volz, and Kissane contrive to put the verses into some semblance of poetry, but most commentators since Duhm regard them as prose (so *BH*, RSV). Notwithstanding that they contain traces of parallelism, they are cut up by parentheses—e.g. 'it is the word of Yahweh'—into prose fragments. Neither in thought nor in language are they convincingly Deutero-Isaianic, and even Muilenburg's verdict is that 'it is best . . . to delete the verses as a later insertion'.

1. *Wake up, wake up*] *ʿûrî*, the same peremptory summons as to 'the arm of Yahweh' (li. 9) and Deborah (Judges v. 12). The form is shorter than the 'rouse yourself' (*Hithpôʿēl*) of li. 17, which suggests a laboured 'coming-to' (cf. lxiv. 7 (*6*)), an effort to shake off the effects of the drugged 'cup'. Now Zion is sufficiently in control of her faculties to respond to the instant command. *sumptuous garments*] *bigᵉḏê tip̱ʾereṯ*. See iii. 18–22 for a catalogue of such 'finery'; also on xliv. 23. *the holy city*] See on xlviii. 2. *uncircumcised and* (therefore) *unclean*] To be uncircumcised was to be ritually impure, debarred from participation in the worship of Yahweh. According to the priestly legislation (P) foreigners were not admitted to the covenant which Yahweh made with Abraham and his descendants (Gen. xvii. 1–14) unless they submitted to be circumcised (Exod. xii. 48). Israelite antipathy to peoples uncircumcised, amounting to abhorrence and even contempt, was of long standing (Judges xiv. 3; 1 Sam. xiv. 6, xvii. 26, 36; 2 Sam. i. 20, with reference to the Philistines), and becomes increasingly pronounced in Ezekiel (Ezek. xxxii, ten times; xliv. 9). Even DI shared it, and the first major crisis in the Christian Church was over the question whether Gentiles should be admitted uncircumcised into its fellowship (Acts x. f.; Gal. ii).

2. *neck-fetters*] It was usual for captives to be tied neck to neck by a single long rope: see *AOTB*, Tafel LVII, No. 128.

3. *for nothing*] Heb. *ḥinnām*, 'gratis', can mean 'for no reason' (1 Sam. xix. 5), but the meaning here, as the ‖ shows, must be 'for no money payment' (cf. Gen. xxix. 15). Jerusalem had indeed been 'sold', but for her iniquities, not for money (l. 1). *without money*] Cf. xlv. 13; 1 Pet. i. 18. The redeem = buy back metaphor is not to be strictly applied (see on xli. 14).

4. *First, my people went down to Egypt as guests*] Lit. '(To) Egypt my people went down at the first to stay (*gûr*) there'. The order is peculiar but is probably not intended to convey anything recondite. Heb. *gûr*, 'sojourn' (as a resident alien) can carry more or less suggestion of receiving hospitality (1 Kings xvii. 20, *Hithpa'ēl*); and occasionally in the Psalms, of Yahweh's 'guests'; e.g. Ps. xxxix. 12 (*13*), 'I am thy passing guest': (cf. ξένος = 'foreigner', 'guest'). Jacob and his family at first received generous hospitality in Egypt (Gen. xlvii. 4–12), but the sequel was grim enough. That may be the allusion here: cf. Ps. cv. 23–25.

5. '*What do I find here?*']Lit. 'What to me here?' = 'What have I here?' in much the same sense as our exclamatory 'What have we here?' Whatever the precise content of the words, the general sense must be, 'Here is an impossible situation; something must be done about it!' *here*] Presumably Babylon, not Egypt or Assyria.

6. *on that day*] Frequent in eschatological prophecy (e.g. vii. 18, 20 f., 23), but nowhere else in DI, who always speaks as if the fulfilment of his expectations is to be in the near future. *that it is I, in very truth I, that speak*] Lit. 'that I am he (see on xli. 4) who speaks, behold me', and not very perspicuous.

LII. 7–10. 'HOW BEAUTEOUS ARE THEIR FEET...!'

7. נָאווּ] Variously parsed: (i) *Pi'lēl* נאו/נאה, 'be comely' (*BDB*, Bergsträsser, *Hebräische Grammatik* ii, § 20*a*); (ii) *pa* (*sic* = *Pa'ēl*) נאה (*KB*); (iii) *Niph.* אוה, 'desire' (*GK* 75 *x*; *BL*, p. 422). Most favour the last, in which case the corresponding adjective נָאוֶה must be related to the *Niph.* particle (*GK* 85 *n*). The cognate langg. do not attest a √נאה. In any case, contexts support some such meaning as 'beautiful' in Song (i. 5, 10, ii. 14, iv. 3, vi. 4, EVV 'comely', under constraint of the ‖ *yāp̄āh*, 'beautiful', of vi. 4; also Jer. vi. 2), and 'seemly/befitting' elsewhere (Ps. xxxiii. 1, xciii. 5, cxlvii. 1; Prov. xvii. 7, xix. 10, xxvi. 1). The word has much the same range of meanings as Gr. ὡραῖος, originally 'seasonable' (*NEB*. 'Beautiful' at Acts iii. 2, 10; 'welcome' at Rom. x. 15, in quotation from this passage).

8. קוֹל . . . קוֹל] The first קוֹל is interjectional: 'Hark!' See on xl. 3. For the second, Q^a has קולם, 'their voice' (cf. Ps. xciii. 3), but MT may stand.

This is a lyric poem of extraordinary vividness, much of it in a tripping 2:2 metre, with dimeter tristichs (2:2:2) in vv. 7*aβ*, 10*a*. Yahweh has achieved his victory over Babylon, and the Prophet sees in imagination a runner coming over the hills and approaching

Jerusalem with the news that the King himself is on his way, soon to make his triumphal entrance. For a detailed background picture cf. 2 Sam. xviii. 19–28, in which David waits in suspense for news of the battle between his forces and those of Absalom. The watchmen on the towers of the city are the first to catch sight of the oncoming messenger, and as they do so they raise a simultaneous shout of joy. Even the ruins of the city are to come alive and join in the acclamation. This goes beyond even the jubilation of sub-human nature, mountains, and forest trees (xliv. 23, xlix. 13, lv. 12) and 'the denizens of the rocks' (see on xlii. 11). What has been dead is to live again. Yahweh's victory is to be 'seen' by 'all the ends of the earth'. Nowhere does the combination of nationalism and universalism so characteristic of DI come to clearer expression than here. For a paraphrase of the passage, referring it to the proclamation of the Christian evangel, see Isaac Watts's hymn, 'How beauteous are their feet . . .!'

7. *How welcome is the runner*] Lit. 'How *nā'wû* (see phil. note; EVV 'beautiful') are the feet'. But feet are hardly beautiful, or, even of a runner, 'comely': cf. Gay's 'Rather comely than beautiful' (*SOED*, *sub. voc*). Nahum i. 15 (*ii. 1*) is probably a quotation from this passage. *over the hill-tops*] EVV 'upon the mountains'. But Heb. *'al* could have the force of 'over' (e.g. Song ii. 8, very pertinent here). The watchers in Jerusalem would have their first sight of the runner as he appeared on the Mount of Olives. But his journey would begin in Babylonia and the Prophet's imagination pictures him as he makes his way direct across the Syrian Desert, over hills and across ravines (xl. 3 f.), a distance of more than 500 miles. A Marathon-race indeed! *coming . . . with news*] *mᵉḇaśśēr*. The Hebrew verb generally conveys the sense 'carry good news' (1 Sam. xxxi. 9; 2 Sam. i. 20; Jer. xx. 15). But the news could be bad (1 Sam. iv. 17). In 2 Sam. xviii. 19 f., 26, the sense is neutral until the runner is within earshot (ver. 28). Here the expectation is of good news, as in the *Agamemnon*, but this is not said (*contra* EVV) until later in the verse, *who brings good* (*ṭôḇ*) *news* (cf. 2 Sam. xviii. 27). *'All is well!'*] Heb. *šālôm*, 'peace': so EVV at 2 Sam. xviii. 28. *deliverance*] *Or* 'victory', Heb. *yᵉšû'āh*, so also in ver. 10. The 2:2:2 line suggests a picture of the runner first on a distant hill, then descending into the valley separating it from one nearer the city, reappearing and once more disappearing, until he comes within earshot and cries, 'Your God reigns!' *'Your God reigns!'*] *Or* 'has become King'; cf. 'Yahweh reigns/has become King' of Ps. xcvi. 10, xcvii. 1, xcix. 1. It is on such correspondences as this between DI and psalms which are widely supposed to have been prominent in the ritual of an annual

autumn festival of Yahweh's enthronement as King, that Engnell and others base a theory that 'The 'Ebed Yahweh texts must . . . be characterized as *a prophetic remodelling* of a liturgical composition belonging to the Annual Festival' (see *BJRL* 31, 1948, pp. 1–42; *SS*², p. 230). For Yahweh as 'King' (of Israel) see xli. 21, xliii. 15, xliv. 6. This is the only text in DI where Yahweh is said to 'reign' and his kingship is universal, as in the Enthronement Psalms. In the context there is some suggestion that Yahweh has reasserted his kingly rule, which might, even to his own people, have seemed in abeyance during the Babylonian domination. For some sort of analogy see 1 Sam. xi. 14, if 'renew' the kingdom is a true reading (see *BH in loc.*).

8. The call of the runner is taken up by the city's *watchmen*, who would normally be posted on 'the roof of the gate by the wall' (2 Sam. xviii. 24). But the walls had been broken down (2 Kings xxv. 10). The Prophet is either idealizing or he imagines the watch-towers rebuilt for the occasion. *theirs will be an immediate view*] Lit. 'they will see eye to eye'. Engl. 'see eye to eye' is a Hebraism based on this passage but has acquired a different sense from that of the original, which means 'to see close up' (cf. Num. xiv. 14, EVV 'face to face'; Jer. xxxii. 4). *of the* LORD*'s return*] Taking the clause as acc. obj. of the verb 'see' preceding: Heb. *rā'āh bᵉ*, 'look/gaze at', stronger than 'see' simply (cf. 2 Kings x. 16; Mic. vii. 9 f.). So RSV and cf. RV mg. 'how'. AV 'when the LORD shall bring again Zion' is just possible, taking the *Qal šûḇ* as transitive (cf. Ps. lxxxv. 4 (5), and the idiom *šûḇ šᵉḇûṯ*, 'restore the fortunes of'), but it obliterates the picture of Yahweh's return to Zion in person (xl. 3–9). Qᵃ adds *bᵉraḥᵃmîm*, 'when Yahweh returns to Zion with compassion', which is similarly motivated by a desire to avoid what must have seemed too stark anthropomorphism. Already in Trito-Isaiah (lxii. 10), 'Prepare the way of the LORD' (xl. 3) has been toned down to 'Prepare the way of the people'.

9. Cf. xliv. 23, xlix. 13, li. 3, lv. 12. *one resounding shout of joy*] Heb. *rannᵉnû yaḥdāw*, 'shout together'. The verb is onomatopoeic and describes a ringing cry (*rinnāh*), usually of joy, sometimes of sorrow. Such a shout would echo through the *ruins of Jerusalem* (xliv. 26, xlix. 19, li. 3). *freed*] *gā'al*, lit. 'redeemed'.

10. *bared*] To 'bare' the arm was to draw it out of the breastfold in preparation for action (xlvii. 2; Ezek. iv. 7; and cf. xl. 10, li. 9; Ps. lxxiv. 11). *the ends of the earth*] Cf. xlv. 22. *victory*] *Or* 'deliverance (our God has wrought)', as in ver. 7, *or*, interpreting the word in the light of the whole biblical revelation, 'salvation' (so EVV).

LII. 11–12. FROM BABYLON AWAY!

11. טָמֵא אַל־תִּגָּעוּ] Q[a] reads בטמא: so otherwise invariably with נגע except when it is used absolutely, without acc. obj. (Job vi. 7; Lam. iv. 15). But in poetry so terse it would be pedantic to insist on 'restoring' the preposition.

12. כִּי ... כִּי. EVV 'For ... for'. If this is right, the 'for' = 'because' must be intended to stress that the preparations for the journey will be unhurried: those who carry the sacred vessels will have time to do everything without risk of breaking any taboo. But if that was the intention, it is rather like putting the cart before the horse. Another possibility is that the כִּי ... כִּי may convey an emphatic assurance, such as may be guaranteed by an oath (expressed or implied), as in xlix. 18. In such a case כִּי may be repeated with the second clause (cf. Gen. xxii. 16 f.) and neither particle needs to be translated. Its force will be brought out by the order in the English: e.g. 'Yahweh' is emphatic in the Hebrew because it stands at the end of the clause; in English it should stand at the beginning, 'the LORD himself'.

This spirited lyric recalls xlviii. 20 f., though the emphasis is different. There it is on the external circumstances of the exodus from Babylon, here it is on the deportment of the liberated exiles. The verses are a natural sequel to vv. 7–10, though their theme is exodus from Babylon, not the announcement of release to Jerusalem. The Prophet himself may well have intended them as a corollary from what precedes, and whether we deal with them separately, or join them to 7–10, is only a matter of exegetical convenience. Even Köhler (though not Mowinckel) takes 7–12 as a unit. Volz takes li. 9–11, 17–23; lii. 1–2, 7–12 as a single poem (*Dieses grosse Gedicht*), and on any showing they are a complex of related pieces, a kind of Pleiad.

The passage is a summons to the exiles to go out from 'there'. The verb 'go out' (*yāṣā'*) occurs three times. It can be used of marching in military formation (see on xl. 26), so far as there were such exercises in OT times. There are obvious reminiscences of the Exodus from Egypt, but this second exodus is to be without its anxieties and perils. The verses only picture the first stage of the journey home; for the subsequent stages we must fill it out from xli. 17–20, xl. 3–5, 10 f.

The passage is of some importance as showing that the Prophet was not indifferent to the externals of religion (cf. also lii. 1). He was concerned about the proper handling of the temple vessels. Notwithstanding his critical attitude toward animal sacrifices (see on xliii. 22–28), religion was not for him pure disembodied spirit, without external observances. He was enthusiastic for the rebuilding of the temple (xliv. 28). Of all the prophets, Jeremiah comes nearest to saying that the externals of religion are of no concern (cf. Jer. vii. 21 ff., xxxi. 31–34). Yet even he spoke of a return to the homeland, with all that that implied for the re-institution of the temple cultus. 'The religious life needs more for its full culture than repentance and prayer. There is a place in it for common prayer, for disciplined observance, for a sacred place with hallowed associations. There is need for festival and ritual where soul quickens soul in mutual self-dedication, where the past helps the present to realize the life which has helped and guided all the generations . . . If it was an exaggeration to make sacrifice an essential, it may be an equal exaggeration to demand its total abolition in the interests of purity of worship.' (A. C. Welch, *Jeremiah: his Time and his Work*, 1951, pp. 239 f.; cf. J. Skinner, *Prophecy and Religion*, 1951, *passim*). In Christianity the sacrificial system has been consummated and, in its cruder forms, abolished (Heb. viii–x). But Christianity, no less than Judaism, must have its cultic expressions (Heb. x. 25), its body as well as its soul.

11. The strophe begins with a repeated *sûrû, sûrû*, '*Away! Away!*' cf. li. 9, 17, lii. 1. *there . . . her*] Obviously Babylon (cf. xlviii. 20). By some the 'there' has been taken to imply that the prophecy was composed outside Babylon: in Palestine (Mowinckel), in Egypt (Marti), or in the Lebanon (Duhm). Torrey takes 'there' to imply 'from this *modern* Egyptian bondage'. The simplest explanation is that the summons to leave Babylon is issued (ideally) from Jerusalem (so Volz), which is the *locus standi* of the preceding sections. *unclean*] I.e. ritually and ceremonially. For the briefest summary of 'unclean' objects see Lev. v. 2 f.; Num. xix. 11–16 and mg. refs. Uncleanness (like holiness) was a quasi-physical property. To have contact with it was to contract it, and it was more contagious than holiness (Hag. ii. 11 f.). Idolatry was an especially potent source of it (Ezek. xx. 30 f.). Babylon was an 'unclean' land (cf. Hos. ix. 3; Amos vii. 17); uncircumcised foreigners were unclean (lii. 1) and it must have been difficult to avoid all contact with them. *march right away from her*] Lit. 'go out from her midst'. *rid yourselves of all impurity*] *hibbārû*, *Niph.* reflexive, stronger than 'be ye clean' (AV, RV). The implied impurity, like uncleanness, was ceremonial. The normal method of removing it was by ceremonial washings, followed by a longer or shorter period of quarantine (Lev. *passim*). This is not to say that DI was only, or even primarily, concerned with ritual cleansings. For him, as for his great predecessor (vi. 5), holiness and uncleanness had acquired a strongly ethical content. *you who carry*] Sc. the priests, probably 'the priests the Levites' (i.e. the Levitical priests) of Deut., not the priests *and* Levites of the post-exilic economy. *the sacred vessels*] Lit. 'the vessels of Yahweh'. An impressive, and probably exaggerated, inventory of these is given in Ezra i. 7–11. Judah had been a poor country since the time of Solomon and the temple treasury had more than once been depleted (1 Kings xiv. 26, 2. xii. 18, xiv. 14; and as recently as the reigns of Ahaz and Hezekiah, 2 Kings xvi. 8, xviii. 15). According to 2 Kings xxiv. 13 Nebuchadrezzar had 'cut in pieces (*wayᵉḳaṣṣēṣ*) all the vessels of gold in the temple of Yahweh, which Solomon . . . had made' (were there any of them left ?), counting them as so much bullion. This is said to have been 'as Yahweh had foretold', presumably referring to Jer. xx. 5. It is just possible that the editor of Kings read more into Jeremiah's *ûḇᵉzāzûm* (lit. 'and will plunder them'; AV 'spoil them' (*sic*), now archaic) than was intended. (Note also the contradiction in 2 Chron. xxxvi. 18 f.) Or it may be that 'cut in pieces' was intended to apply to all the metal fittings of the temple (2 Kings xxv. 13–17), some of which were too cumbrous to be transported intact. However that may be, the tradition that the most valuable temple vessels were kept in Babylon is too strong to be without foundation (cf. 2 Chron. xxxvi. 7, 10, 18 f.; Dan. i. 2, v. 2 f.).

12. *hurried escape*] *bᵉḥippāzôn*, lit. 'in trepidation/anxious fear', a clear reference to the literary tradition of the Exodus. In Exod. xii. 11; Deut. xvi. 3, the only other passages in which the word is used, the Israelites are said to have eaten the first Passover *bᵉḥippāzôn*. *still less*] Not in Hebrew. But the second member of a ∥ seldom just repeats, without adding anything to, the first; and flight is more demoralizing than haste. *in flight*] *bimᵉnûsāh*. In Exod. xvi. 5 Pharaoh was told that the Israelites 'had fled', but the Heb. there is *bāraḥ*, as in Isa. xlviii. 20 (see *in loc.*). In OT battles one side would usually turn tail at the onset of the other. There was little hand-to-hand fighting and most casualties were suffered during the headlong flight. *the Lord himself is going before you*] According to the pre-exilic Exodus tradition (JE, D) the ark, conceived of as the embodiment of Yahweh's presence, went before the Israelites on their march (Num. x. 33–36; cf. Joshua iii. 3–6). Another constant tradition had it that 'Yahweh went before them by day in a pillar of cloud' (Exod. xiii. 21; cf. Num. xiv. 14; Deut. i. 30–33; Neh. ix. 12; Ps. lxxviii. 14; 1 Cor. x. 1). In Exod. xiv. 19 the theophanic 'Angel of God' is vanguard (cf. xxiii. 20, xxxii. 34; also Isa. lxiii. 9, though the text there is dubious, see LXX and OL). Yet another variant of the tradition (Exod. xxxiii. 14 f.; LXX at Isa. lxiii. 9) had it that Yahweh's 'presence' (*pānîm*, 'face', i.e. Yahweh in person) was to 'go'

(? with, ? before, Israel—there is no prep. in the Heb.): cf. J. H. Newman

> 'God's presence, and His very self
> And essence all-divine'.

For DI there is no circumlocutory shunning of anthropomorphism: lit. '(he who) goes before you is Yahweh'. *rear-guard*] *me'assēp̄*, *Pi'ēl* (cf. lviii. 8, *Qal*, perhaps to be pointed as *Pi'ēl*, though the meaning would be no different). According to Exod. xiv. 19 'the Angel of God' and 'the pillar of cloud' moved from the vanguard to the rear of the Israelites as they came to the Red Sea, to shield them from their pursuers. The meaning of 12*b*, therefore, is that Yahweh himself is to be both guide and protector of his people.

LII. 13–LIII. 12. THE MAN OF SORROWS

No passage in the OT, certainly none of comparable importance, presents more problems than this. Neither the AV nor the RV emends the Hebrew text in a single particular, but a glance at the number of marginal renderings indicates the difficulties in which the translators found themselves. In the period following Duhm textual emendation was freely resorted to: in *BH* a dozen readings involving departure from the MT are marked *legendum* and another four *propositum*. The majority are claimed as having some support from the versions, but some are conjectural. But even before the discovery of the Qumran Scrolls textual critics were becoming more cautious and conservative. Nyberg (1942) was prepared to defend the MT to the last consonant and in a responsible translation like the RSV only two variants from the *textus receptus* are recognized. The prevailing attitude now is that it does not follow that because an LXX reading like ἤχθη εἰς θάνατον (liii. 8) is more easily intelligible than the MT, it is without more ado to be accepted. How should a passage which, by hypothesis, was originally intelligible, even though difficult, have been scrambled into something which is intelligible no longer? The last Song of the Servant is, on any showing, *sui generis*, like Rabbi ben Ezra's

> Thoughts hardly to be packed
> Into a narrow act,
> Fancies that broke through language and escaped.

How should the LXX understand it? It contains no sentence upon which some cardinal doctrine depends. But the evidence of the Scrolls (especially *b*) is sufficient to warrant us in keeping to the MT wherever we can do so with a good academic conscience. It is conceivable that the text as we have it has departed at some points from the original. In that case the principle that a passage 'means what it has come to mean' may be permitted to apply, *to the Hebrew*, though not necessarily to the EVV. In the notes that follow mention is made of the more important emendations that have been proposed. The venturesome reader may make his choice of any that seem convincing to him.

lii. 13. עַבְדִּי] Duhm set a fashion of reading this as an abbreviation for עֶבֶד יהוה ('the servant of Yahweh'), making vv. 13–15 an utterance of the Prophet. Driver ('Abbreviations in the MT', *Textus*, i. 113) gives a number of probable examples of suffixal *yôdh* being originally for יהוה, but this is not one of them. Both Qumran Scrolls agree with MT. יָרוּם] That this verb is unrepresented in the Greek versions and OL is not sufficient evidence for deleting it. The verse may be read as 3:3, whether or not we retain ירום. At the same time two words expressive of the Servant's exaltation would have been sufficient (cf. vi. 1, lvii. 15) and a copyist might be tempted to amplify them.

lii. 14. עָלֶיךָ] Emendation to עָלָיו, 'at him', is general, but when *BH* says that עליו 'should be read with T, P', it is going beyond the evidence. T translated but certainly did not *read* 'him'; neither, it is all but certain, did P. Volz cites one MS. (K. 224 pr. 576) as reading עליו, but this is insufficient authority for emending. The reading עָלֶיךָ, whatever its difficulty, is indubitably early and, as the harder reading, should stand. It is attested by both Qumran Scrolls and by LXX, which has the 2nd person throughout the verse. But how is it to be explained? Nyberg (p. 48) says that change of person occurs in a number of passages in poetry and high style, and he instances Gen. xlix. 4 (the text there is uncertain, see *BH*). 'It is a primitive stylistic device: a passage begins with a purely rhetorical apostrophe, but then the description passes over into the natural 3rd person.' (Examples have been noted above in xlv. 8, 21, li. 7.) *GK*[28] (1909) had already called attention to this peculiarity (144 *p*), citing a number of texts, including the present and lxi. 7. The difference between this passage and other examples adduced is that here the 2nd person occurs in a predominantly 3rd pers. context; usually someone is addressed and the description then passes over to the 3rd person (cf. RSV at lxi. 7). Nyberg puts the case thus: 'We cannot in our language copy the Hebrew usage but must either carry through the apostrophe in the 2nd person or the description in the 3rd.' He therefore translates, without emending: 'As many stood dismayed at him (properly "thee")'. This seems the likeliest solution of the difficulty. The stich (*aa*) has no ‖ and many think that one has been lost. Attempts to restore it, such as 'and princes shuddered at him' (cf. xlix. 7; Ezek. xxxii. 10) are necessarily guesswork. Many transfer the parenthetical 14 *aβb* to the end of liii. 2, where it would fit well and give a fine inversion: מַרְאֵהוּ . . . תֹּאֲרוֹ ‖ תֹּאַר . . . מַרְאֶה. A transfer from liii. 2 to lii. 14 might have been intended to fill the gap after the presumed ‖ to 14*aα* had been lost. But this is, in the nature of the case, conjecture, and on the whole the balance of probability is against it (see below). The overall picture is the same either way. מִשְׁחַת] ἅπ. λεγ. 'a disfiguring from man his appearance'. Many read מָשְׁחָת, *Hoph.* participle, 'disfigured'. But in view of מַסְתֵּר, 'a hiding of face' (liii. 3), the massoretic pointing may stand. There is no difference in meaning.

lii. 15. יַזֶּה] The rendering 'sprinkle' (AV, RV, *Hiph.* נזה, subject the Servant), though supported by the minor Greek versions, is now generally abandoned. This is because the verb never takes accusative of the person or thing sprinkled, but always accusative of blood (or the like) sprinkled, together with עַל (except in Num. xix. 21, though the context there implies it), or a similar prep., of the person or thing sprinkled. Accordingly it is now usual to take יַזֶּה as from a √נזה II (= Arab. *nazā*, 'to leap'), hence 'he shall cause to leap' (in joyful surprise) = 'startle': so RV mg., RSV. To this there are three objections: (i) it imports into Hebrew a √ἅπ. λεγ. and gives it an emotional content it never has in Arabic; (ii) it makes 'many nations' the object of the verb, whereas from the preceding ('many') and following ('kings') ‖s we expect it to be the subject; (iii) 'as many were horrified . . . so shall he startle' gives no progression of thought. Hence such emendations as יִרְגְּזוּ, 'many nations shall tremble because of him' (עָלָיו), based on LXX θαυμάσονται (cf. *BH*). But LXX employs θαυμάζειν for a variety of Hebrew words. Hence a suggestion of Nyberg (p. 47) deserves to be treated with consideration. First, it should be noted that יַזֶּה is closely followed by its pilot עַל, which, if the Servant is the subject of the verb, must be construed with the next stich: so in the massoretic punctuation and EVV. Next, 'many nations' may be the subject of יַזֶּה, notwithstanding that the verb, which stands first, is singular (*GK* 145 *o*). The sentence is therefore patient of a translation 'many nations shall sprinkle (object not specified) upon him'. *Hiph.* נזה is always used in connexion with decontamination or (once or twice) consecration rituals. Nyberg therefore suggests that יזה is used absolutely (i.e. without expressed object) in the meaning 'carry out ritual cleansing' (*utföra rituell stänkning*), i.e. 'perform a purification rite, the principal action in which is cleansing with water and blood'. He does not press the עָלָיו to imply that water or blood will actually be poured on the Servant. He is content that its sense should be 'on his account' and that something of the force of עליו ('as a protection against him') is carried over into the ‖ 'kings shall shut their mouths at him', i.e. to avoid contamination from him (pp. 47 f.). It has already been said that 'many were horrified at him', scared of being infected by him; 14*aβb* may therefore stay where it is. And if what ver. 15 describes seems crude and heathenish, it describes the first reactions of the 'many nations' to the sight of one who seemed altogether revolting. Indeed, as a literary figure 'many nations shall sprinkle upon him' may be quite intentional, though whether we should translate it literally may be a matter of opinion.

liii. 1. עַל] Usually 'on' or 'over'; but can be a more forceful sense of אֶל (see on xl. 2 and cf. 1 Sam. i. 10; 1 Kings xx. 43). But the על here may be intended to picture the arm extended 'over'.

liii. 2. וַיַּעַל] Lit. 'and he shot up'. Heb. *waw consec.* may be used to indicate even a loose connexion with what precedes (*GK* 111 *f–h*), such as in English is expressed by 'for'. לְפָנָיו] EVV take the suffix as referring to Yahweh in the previous verse. Of emendations suggested the commonest is לְפָנֵינוּ, 'before us'. G. R. Driver (*JTS* 38, p. 48) takes the suffix as referring back to the subj., and quotes 1 Sam. v. 3 f., where it is said that Dagon was נֹפֵל לְפָנָיו, 'fallen straight forward'. This is probably right. So 'he shot (straight) up'. וְנִרְאֵהוּ . . . וְנֶחְמְדֵהוּ] Duhm and others delete the first and substitute וְחֶמְדָּה ('and attractiveness', LXX κάλλος) for the second. If it is retained, it is best construed with what precedes and as ‖ ונחמדהו (so RV mg., RSV). This would give a long stich, though it could be read as three beats. Nyberg takes it with what follows (so AV, RV), on account of the paronomasia. Whatever we do, the meaning is much the same.

liii. 4. וּמַכְאֹבֵינוּ] Add הוא with some 20 MSS., P, V.

liii. 5. מְחֹלָל] *Pôʿēl* participle, 'pierced through'. Some prefer to point *Puʿal* מְחֻלָּל ('profaned') after A. βεβηλωμένος. The ‖ favours the massoretic pointing.

liii. 7. וגו׳ נֶאֱלָמָה] Some would delete וְלֹא יִפְתַּח פִּיו as a dittograph. But such repetition is characteristic of DI (cf. Köhler, p. 94 f., who says that this is 'the most beautiful and expressive *Nachklang* in the whole writing'). Köhler himself would delete נאלמה (*Niph.* pf. 3rd pers. sing. fem., subj. רָחֵל), probably *metri causa*. If it is construed with what precedes, the translation must be 'and like a ewe (which) before her shearers is dumb' (4 beats, cf. RSV). Others emend to the masculine נֶאֱלָם, with the Servant as subject. Rowley (*Israel's Mission to the World*, 1939, p. 22 n.) remarks on the 'rhythmical incompleteness of the line', and suggests that this is 'deliberate and impressive', similar to יַעֲמֹד in Job iv. 16.

liii. 8. וְאֶת־דּוֹרוֹ] Can be taken with what follows (so RV, RSV), את being occasionally used, chiefly in later style, with a new subject, to give it definiteness (*GK* 117 *i–m*; *BDB* p. 85*a*, 3). But in Hebrew poetry lines are usually end-stopped (cf. AV, RV mg. here). The meaning 'fate' (acc.) is based on G. R. Driver (*JTS* 36, p. 403), who compares with Akk. *dûrum* ('lasting state', 'permanent condition') and Arab. *daur^un^* ('turn', 'change of fortune'), and quotes Ps. xxiv. 6, which he would render 'this is the state of them that fear him'. Similarly Nyberg (p. 53). The conjectural דְּרָכוֹ for דּוֹרוֹ (*BH*) would give much the same meaning. מִפֶּשַׁע עַמִּי נֶגַע לָמוֹ] Lit. 'on account of the rebellion of my people a stroke to them'. EVV take למו as sing. 'to him'. It has been denied that the suffix can be singular, though it is difficult to see how it can be otherwise in a few passages like Ps. xi. 7; Job xxii. 2 (*GK* 103 *f*., n. 3), unless we emend the text. In Gen. ix. 26 f. we may *translate* לָמוֹ as singular (so EVV), since the reference is to Shem and Japhet, which are collectives (cf. RV mg.). We might do the same here if we could be sure that the Servant is Israel, though 'for the transgression of my people (Israel) he (Israel) was stricken' would make little sense. During the nineteenth century it was not unusual to argue that the collective interpretation (the Servant = Israel) was hinted at by לָמוֹ here and בְּמֹתָיו in ver. 9 (see *SS*, pp. 30, 36, and cf. Ezek. xxviii. 10). It is now usual to emend to יְנֻגַּע לַמָּוֶת 'he was stricken to death', after LXX ἤχθη εἰς θάνατον. This was already noted by Vitringa (*Commentarius in Jesaiam*, *pars II*, Paris, ed. 1724, p. 674, pointing נֻגַּע לָמוּת). But whether LXX read this (how does נגע come to be ἤχθη ?), or was only paraphrasing, it is difficult to say. Another problem is presented by עַמִּי, 'my people'. All the versions agree with MT, but to whom does the pronoun refer? There is no reason to suppose that the Prophet is interjecting a reference to himself. Nor can we assume that Yahweh is now speaking. He is unambiguously the speaker in vv. 11–12, but in 10 he is twice named in the 3rd person. Q^a^ has מפשע עַמּו נוּגַע למו, which could mean 'for the transgression of his people he (?) was stricken'. Of conjectural emendations for מִפֶּשַׁע עַמִּי the commonest is מִפְּשָׁעֵינוּ ('for our transgressions'), which is tied up with the dubious 'stricken to death' of LXX. Torrey, who thinks that the Gentiles are the speakers throughout vv. 1–9, keeps עַמִּי, 'Lit. "for the sin of my people" (said by each of the Gentile rulers)'. This is forced, notwithstanding 1 Sam. xxx. 22, to which he refers. A simple solution to both problems is to point עַמֵּי (construct plural) instead of עַמִּי, and this might have been suggested long ago had it not been for preoccupation with the LXX reading.

The meaning will then be, 'for the transgression of peoples who deserved to be stricken', lit. 'peoples of a striking to them'. This is good idiomatic Hebrew, cf. 1 Kings ii. 26, 'you deserve to die', lit. 'you are a man of death'. It may be significant that the Hebrew is pointed נֶגַע (a noun), not, as we should have expected, נָגַע.

liii. 9. וַיִּתֵּן] Impers. subj., 'and one gave'. עָשִׁיר] 'Rich' is not a natural ‖ to 'wicked'. (Note the alliteration.) Nyberg insists that the words are synonyms and quotes the prophets' denunciations of the rich. So T here, 'rich in possessions they have obtained by violence'. It may be so, but the ungodly rich were buried sumptuously enough. RSV 'a rich man' is pedantic: the Hebrew may be taken as collective, notwithstanding the ‖ רְשָׁעִים, and we cannot assume that the word anticipates the burial of Jesus by the rich Joseph of Arimathea (Matt. xxvii. 57). It is usual to emend (conjecturally) to עֹשֵׂי רָע, 'evil-doers'. Latterly the attractive suggestion has been made that עָשִׁיר is cognate with Arab. *ġuṯrun*, 'rabble', 'refuse of mankind' (A. Guillaume, 'A Contribution to Hebrew Lexicography', *BSOAS* xvi/l, 1954, p. 10). The difference between ع and غ was quite audible in OT times. בְּמֹתָיו] Lit. 'in his deaths'. According to Nyberg an abstract plur., similar to חַיִּים, 'life', by attraction to the preceding context. We expect a ‖ to קֶבֶר, 'grave', but Hebrew had no synonym for it: גָּדִישׁ (Job xxi. 32) is ἅπ. λεγ. and an Arabism. That there was some uncertainty about the spelling is indicated by Qa בומתו, which is unintelligible. Various emendations have been suggested: בְּמוֹתוֹ (sing. cf. LXX ἀντὶ τοῦ θανάτου); בֵּיתוֹ, 'his house' (cf. xiv. 18, where RSV has 'his tomb'); בֵּית מוֹתוֹ, 'his house of death' (cf. Akk. *bît mûti*, and note that בית is occasionally abbreviated to ב); בּוֹרוֹ, 'his pit' (cf. xiv. 19). Very attractive is בָּמָתוֹ, 'his mound' (lit. 'high place'), if it could be substantiated. But in Ezek. xliii. 7 (בָּמוֹתָם, RSV mg. 'monuments') the text is too uncertain to be relied on alone. עַל] For the rare sense 'although', cf. Job. xvi. 17 עַל לֹא־חָמָס בְּכַפָּיו.

liii. 10. וַיהוה חָפֵץ דַּכְּאוֹ הֶחֱלִי] דכאו should mean 'to crush him'. It can mean 'to cleanse him' (LXX καθάρισαι αὐτὸν) if it is an Aramaism, but this is improbable after מְדֻכָּא, 'crushed', in ver. 5. הֶחֱלִי is probably intended as *Hiph.* perfect חלא (lit. 'he made him sick'), a secondary form of חלה (cf. 2 Chron. xvi. 12), the quiescent *āleph* being dropped (*GK* 74 *k*, 75 *ii*). Qa וַיְחַלְלֵהוּ, 'and he de-sacrated him' (see on xliii. 28), gives a tolerable sense but the priority of החלי is attested by both LXX and V. The former has 'The Lord was pleased to cleanse him from sickness' (חֳלִי), the latter 'The Lord was pleased to crush him with sickness'. Nyberg (p. 58) takes החלי as *Hiph.* perfect √חלה II (Arab. *ḥaliya*), 'to appease'. This verb occurs elsewhere only in *Piʿēl*, but an intransitive *Hiph.* (*GK* 53 *de*) is not inconceivable: so 'he was appeased'. Nyberg construes ויהוה חפץ דכאו as a protatic circumstantial clause, 'But as Yahweh was pleased to crush him, so he let himself be appeased'. This leaves a good deal to the imagination of the reader. G. R. Driver (in a private communication) points דִּכְּאוֹ ('him he had crushed'—relative omitted), or דַּכָּאוֹ ('his crushed one'), with slight rearrangement of the following letters: הֶחֱלִים אֶת־שָׂם אָשָׁם נַפְשׁוֹ: 'he accepted as satisfactory him who had made himself a guilt-offering'. An objection to דַּכָּאוֹ, and perhaps also to דִּכְּאוֹ, is that wherever חָפֵץ governs a personal object, the object is preceded by ב: so חָפֵץ בְּדַכָּאוֹ. Further √חלם I is found only twice (Job xxxix. 4; Isa. xxxviii. 16) and Driver employs it in a sense approaching that of its Syriac counterpart. Emendations giving no more clear or convincing sense than MT are precarious. Why should we not point הֶחֳלִי '(with) sickness' (cf. V)? The article is used with words denoting diseases (*Syn.* §22*e*, Rem. 1) and, *a fortiori*, with 'disease'. We then have a sentence exactly similar to Mal. iii. 24, 'I will smite the earth (with) a curse (חֵרֶם).' The verb has two accusatives, the second instrumental, a kind of Latin ablative (cf. also Joshua vii. 25; Ps. lxiv. 7 (*8*); Mic. vii. 2). אִם־תָּשִׂים אָשָׁם נַפְשׁוֹ] AV, RV, 'when thou shalt make his soul an offering', presumably takes 'thou' as addressed to Yahweh. RSV 'when he makes himself an offering', reads יָשִׂים, after V. The right sense is given by AV mg., RV mg., 'when his soul (i.e. he) shall make an offering'. For *śîm*, 'set', in sense 'make', 'constitute', cf. liv. 12. EVV take the words as the protasis of a conditional-temporal sentence. To this it may be objected that the line should be 'end-stopped'. Hence such a slight emendation as אֱמֶת שָׂם אָשָׁם נַפְשׁוֹ 'truly (cf. Ps. cxxxii. 11) he gave himself as an offering'. But in that case what follows ('he shall see . . .') is abrupt, and unrelated to its preceding context. For a free-flowing conditional sentence in poetry, with protasis and apodosis in successive lines, see Deut. xxxii. 41.

liii. 11. There are two obvious difficulties in this verse: (i) the word צַדִּיק; (ii) the massoretic punctuation, which, although it is followed by EVV, is well-nigh impossible to scan (? 4:5:3).

(i) It is generally held that צַדִּיק עַבְדִּי (adj. preceding noun—AV, RV, 'my righteous servant') is grammatically execrable. Hence the usual deletion of צַדִּיק as a dittograph of יַצְדִּיק. But how should such a blunder, if perpetrated, have been perpetuated in the versions and in all but three Hebrew MSS. (cf. *BH*)? We may not delete the word on the authority of three MSS. (Volz, p. 172), which themselves are more likely to have omitted it by homoioteleuton. RSV 'the righteous one, my servant', presumably takes צַדִּיק as standing before its noun for special emphasis, but examples of what is really an appositional relation of adjective and noun are few and dubious (*GK* 132 *b*). We could perhaps justify צַדִּיק עַבְדִּי by taking צַדִּיק as in the construct state, a kind of superlative: e.g. xxxv. 9, 'the (most) savage of beasts'; Job xxx. 6, 'the (most) horrible of ravines', and so 'my (perfectly) righteous servant', somewhat like 'good my page'. The difference between צדיק עבדי and the examples adduced is that עַבְדִּי is sing., while in them the *nomen rectum* is plural. But there are one or two examples of a noun in the abs. sing., with suffix, preceded by an adjective in the construct, as here: so Exod. xv. 16, גְּדוֹל זְרוֹעֲךָ, 'the great of thy arm' = 'thy great arm' (but Ps. lxxix. 11, גֹּדֶל זְרוֹעֲךָ 'the greatness of thy arm', RSV 'thy great power'); 1 Sam. xvi. 7, lit. 'the high of his stature' = his high stature; Ps. xlvi. 4 (5). Such is the flexibility of Hebrew that it is not being facetious to say that one can, with supporting analogies, construe almost anything, if one has a mind to it! What one must not do is to resort to such a contortion as Nyberg's (for בְּדַעְתּוֹ יַצְדִּיק צַדִּיק) 'he who is (i.e. anyone who becomes) righteous shall obtain his righteousness by knowledge of him (the servant—genitive of obj.)'! All things considered it seems prudent to retain צדיק עבדי and to count it as one stress, if we are fastidious about 3:3 metre.

(ii) The massoretic punctuation. This is easily remedied by inserting אוֹר ('light') after יִרְאֶה: lit. 'After his sóul's trávail/ he shall sée líght / (and) be fully sátisfied by his knówledge' (2:2:2). The insertion is supported by LXX and by both Qumran Scrolls, and when the Palestinian and Egyptian traditions are in such accord their testimony is very strong. It should be added that it has been suggested that יִרְאֶה is either an alternative spelling, or a corruption, of יִרְוֶה ('he shall be sated', √רוה), and that בְּדַעְתּוֹ is better understood as 'with his humiliation' (see *below* on ver. 3). There are two varieties of this interpretation: (1) If we keep MT (not inserting אוֹר), the sense will then be 'he will have (had) more than enough of his soul's travail, he will have (had) his full measure of humiliation'. Now that יִרְאֶה could be an alternative spelling of יִרְוֶה, or, it may be, a corruption of it, is not in dispute. We may compare פְּתָאִים/פְּתָיִים, plurals of פֶּתִי, 'simple'. It is also true that רָוָה and שָׂבַע occur together (Jer. xxxi. 14; Lam. iii. 15), and that this ‖ extends to Ps. xci. 16; Job x. 15, where וְאַרְאֵהוּ and וּרְאֵה respectively make better sense if understood as spelling variants of וְאַרְוֵהוּ and וּרְוֵה (see *BH in loc.*). All the same, if satiety (√שבע and saturation (√רוה) are associated together, much more frequently are seeing and knowing (as here). Also, it is something of an anti-climax (after 10*b*) to say that the Servant will have (had) his surfeit of troubles. (2) If we insert אוֹר, the meaning of מֵעֲמַל נַפְשׁוֹ יִרְוֶה אוֹר will be something like 'After his life's labour he will be saturated/drenched with light', an expression which may be English but has no ‖ in the OT. Further, יִשְׂבַּע בְּדַעְתּוֹ, 'he will be sated with humiliation', will be more limp than ever. While if we transpose יַצְדִּיק and צַדִּיק, pointing the latter צֶדֶק, 'through his humiliation he will have abundance of צֶדֶק', we are resorting to a precarious emendation. If we must break up the MT there is as good right, and better reason, to delete the awkward צַדִּיק.

The passage has no obvious connexion with either its preceding or following context. It contains five sections of almost equal length, corresponding to the paragraphs of the RV and RSV. Each of the first three Songs is put into the mouth of a single speaker. Yahweh in the first, the Servant in the second and third. Here the speaker in lii. 13–15 and liii. 11–12 must be Yahweh. Who the speakers ('we') are in liii. 1–6 (? 9) is not indicated and is one of the most vigorously debated questions arising out of the interpretation of the Song. There is no agreement among form-critics as to the category (*Gattung*) to which the 'we' verses most nearly approximate; e.g. whether to a penitential psalm or to a psalm of thanksgiving (see Muilenburg's summary, p. 614). This is hardly surprising for a passage in which such a range of human emotions is evoked. For the moment it is sufficient to say that the Song consists of the words of a human speaker or speakers, set in a framework of pronouncements by Yahweh.

LII. 12–15. THE FUTURE EXALTATION OF THE SERVANT

Yahweh announces that 'my servant' (cf. xlii. 1) is to be greatly exalted. Many had been horrified at his repulsive appearance. To avoid being contaminated by him they will resort to purification rituals. Here is a man and a situation quite outside the range of their experience hitherto, a man who compels their attention.

13. *shall prosper*] So AV mg., RV mg., RSV. AV 'deal prudently', RV 'deal wisely'. Heb. *yaśkîl* (*Hiph. śāḵal*) can have all these meanings, as well as others like 'understand', 'have insight' (xli. 20, xliv. 18). It is a matter of observation that the man who acts prudently becomes prosperous. This is clearly the force of the word in Joshua i. 8 and is recommended by the ‖ verbs here. Nyberg's 'If my servant suffers chastisement, he shall be exalted' (a conditional sentence with *hinnēh* as 'a kind of conditional conjunction' in the protasis) is surely far-fetched. There may be points of similarity between the Song and the Wisdom literature, but it can hardly be closely compared with a typical *Maśkîl* like Ps. xxxii. *high and lifted up*] Note the similarity to Yahweh 'high and lifted up' in vi. 1, lvii. 15. The description of Jesus as 'thy holy servant' (παῖς, Acts iii. 13, 26, iv. 27, 30) who has been exalted (ὑψωθείς Acts ii. 33) is almost certainly reminiscent of this passage (LXX ὑψωθήσεται).

14. *horrified*] Or 'appalled', *šāmᵉmû*: cf. passages like 1 Kings ix. 8; Jer. xviii. 16; Ezek. xxvii. 35. *As . . . so* (ver. 15)] Indicating that the energy with which the many nations act is equal to the measure of their being horrified.

15. *shall . . . guard against contagion by him*] Lit. 'shall sprinkle upon him'. The acc. obj. (unexpressed) of 'sprinkle' is probably blood (see phil. note above). The object of such ritual sprinkling was to neutralize infection or contagion by the person or thing sprinkled (Lev. xiv. 7, 51, xvi. 19; Num. xix .4). Although these decontamination rituals are only described in the P strata of the Pentateuch, they are widespread and ancient (cf. Frazer, *Taboo and the Perils of the Soul*, *passim*). *and kings shut their mouths against him*] The kings act as the representatives of their peoples. The usual interpretation is that their mouths are closed in dumb astonishment (cf. Job v. 16; Ps. cvii. 42, though these passages better describe abject silence). But in the light of the preceding clause the meaning may be that they keep their mouths firmly closed to avoid being infected by the Servant (cf. Frazer, *Taboo*, p. 122). In that case something of the force of *'ālāw* ('upon him') may be carried over into this second stich, in the sense 'against him'. The horrified nations would at first be highly superstitious. *become attentive to*] *hiṯbônānû*, *Hithpô'lēl bîn*. RV, RSV 'understand' credits the heathen with more moral discernment than they so far possess, unless the word is meant to anticipate what they say in liii. 1–6. *Hithpô'lēl bîn* does mean 'understand' in Job xxvi. 14; Ps. cxix. 100, 104; Jer. xxiii. 20, but its usual sense is to give one's attention to something (e.g. 1 Kings iii. 21; Job xxxi. 1). The heathen cannot evade the challenge of this man and they will be obliged to pass some judgement upon him.

LIII. 1–3. THE MAN OF SORROWS

Unnamed speakers declare that what they have heard is something they would have thought incredible. He (the Servant) had been like a sickly plant growing in a barren soil and there had been nothing attractive about him. Afflicted by sorrow and disease, he was shunned by men and himself avoided their society. They (the speakers) had taken the general estimate of him for granted and assumed that he was not worth their notice.

Who are the speakers, the 'we' of vv. 1–6? There are three possibilities: (i) the 'many nations' of lii. 15; (ii) the Israelites; (iii) the

Prophet speaking for his fellow countrymen. The discussion has generally been on partisan lines: those who think the Servant is Israel have always favoured (i); those who think he is an individual have been in favour of (ii) or (iii). But in 1921 Mowinckel, who then thought that the Servant was the Prophet himself, came down on the side of the view that 'the many peoples and kings' are the speakers in liii. 1 ff. (*Der Knecht Jahwäs*, pp. 37 n., 45). Although he has since abandoned that view ('The speakers are Jews', *He that Cometh*, p. 119), he is nevertheless on record as having broken the connexion between the collective theory and the Gentile 'we'. Van Hoonacker also thought that the speakers were the many nations and kings (*Het Boek Isaias*, p. 232). We expect the efficacy of the Servant's work to be confessed by all who were included within the scope of his mission, i.e. the Gentiles (xlii. 1–4, xlix. 1–6), otherwise they are left at the end as mere spectators, with nothing to say. The shutting of the kings' mouths need not mean the dropping of the curtain for them. Their dumb astonishment—if that is what the words are meant to convey—might be temporary, to be followed by voluble speech. If it is argued that the heathen could not possibly give expression to thoughts so deep that they have no parallel in the OT, the same is equally true of the Jews. The interpretation of the Servant's sufferings must be the Prophet's, moved by the Holy Spirit. As such it is, in the universal setting of the passage, as appropriately voiced by Gentiles as by Jews.

1. *Who would have believed . . .?*] Rhetorical question expecting the answer 'No one!' (cf. Gen. xxi. 7). *what we have heard*] Cf. RV mg., RSV. Heb. 'our *šᵉmûʿāh*', meaning 'the report that has reached *us*', as in Jer. xlix. 14, not 'what we have reported', as in AV, RV. As the passage is quoted, from LXX τῇ ἀκοῇ ἡμῶν, in John xii. 38; Rom. x. 16, it is the Prophet who laments that his hearers will not believe what he says. In the Hebrew original it is an exclamation of those who hear the *šᵉmûʿāh* and who say, 'What we have heard is something we should have thought impossible, and yet it is true!' According to Nyberg (p. 48) the *šᵉmûʿāh* here 'can have no other meaning than "the tradition we have received"'. One of the roots of this tradition or μῦθος, 'the myth preserved in the tradition' (p. 61) is the Tammuz-mystery (p. 64). But why all this mystery about a word whose everyday meaning was simply 'something heard', 'news' (1 Sam. ii. 24, iv. 19; 2 Sam. iv. 4)?

2. *he shot up like a sapling*] Engnell, like Nyberg, sees in these words a clear indication that 'we find ourselves in a Tammuz-ideological context clearer than ever. . . . This theme may now be considered so settled that we need not dwell any longer on the subject here'

(*BJRL* 31, p. 31). But when Thetis says of the child Achilles, ὁ δ' ἀνέδραμεν ἔρνεϊ ἶσος (*Iliad* xviii. 437), would Engnell say that Achilles is a Tammuz-figure? The Hebrew and Greek are so alike, even to the double sense of *yônēḳ/ἔρνος* (sapling/suckling) that either could be a translation of the other. It is simply a case of identical similes occurring to Homer and DI. (This is not to deny the 'thesis that Homer and the ancient Near East have a common denominator', C. H. Gordon, *Introduction to OT Times*, Ventnor, N.J., 1953, p. 99.) The parallel between Achilles and the Servant would not, of course, be complete: Achilles was nursed 'as one tends a little plant in a garden bed', and was as vigorous as the Servant was weedy. But in the context he also is a tragic figure, a theme for lamentations. *he shot up*] *Waw consec.* impf. AV 'For he shall grow up' was influenced by the then current view that the passage was messianic prediction. But here and in what follows the sufferings and death of the Servant are described as having already taken place (though see below on ver. 11). This need not mean that he was already dead when the Song was written. The words of the 'we' are set in a framework of divine pronouncements beginning 'my servant shall prosper'. It is in relation to an unspecified future that the sufferings are past. They may, or may not, have been past when the Song was written. *presence . . . dignity . . . beauty*] Heb. *tō'ar . . . hādār . . . mar'ēh*, lit. 'form . . . dignity (RV, RSV Prov. xxxi. 25) . . . appearance'. Beauty of form and appearance are both found in Joseph (Gen. xxxix. 6). David was 'a man of *tō'ar*' (1 Sam. xvi. 18, RSV 'a man of good presence'), likewise Adonijah (1 Kings i. 6). In lii. 14 the two words are used in their literal senses. That the Servant was the very reverse of attractive is indicated by the negative *lô'* (not *'ên*, *GK* 152 *d*).

3. *shunned the company of men*] *ḥ^adal 'îšîm*. The literal meaning of the adjective *ḥādēl*, from the stative verb *ḥādal* (Judges v. 7; 1 Sam. ii. 5) is 'ceasing'; hence 'ceasing from' rather than 'rejected of/by' (EVV). *sorrows . . . sickness*] *maḵ'ôḇôṯ . . . ḥŏlî*. The first of these words (probably intensive plur.) may denote either physical (Job xxxiii. 19) or mental (Ps. xxxii. 10) pain, the second sickness or disease (so RV mg., RSV mg.). *humbled by*] *y^eḏûa'*. This is one of the few examples in which Heb. *yāḏa'* (commonly 'to know') is said to be cognate with Arab. *wadu'a*, 'be still, quiet, humiliated' (D. W. Thomas in *Record and Revelation*, ed. H. W. Robinson, 1938, pp. 393 f.). *yāḏa'*, together with *da'aṯ* ('knowledge') occurs some 1,000 times in OT, say 100:1 as compared with 'be humiliated'. How anyone was to know just when the √ had the rare meaning it is difficult to see. In favour of 'humbled' here is the fact that *y^eḏûa'* is passive ptc. For 'acquainted with grief' we should expect the act. ptc. *yôḏēa'*, which is the reading

of Q[a], though not on that account to be accepted without demur. Perhaps we may make the best of both worlds. Those who meet suffering in the right spirit are humbled or made gentle (not the same thing as humiliated) by it. Suffering is the great cathartic (cf. Prov. xx. 30). This may be the thought behind LXX εἰδὼς φέρειν μαλακίαν. If we take *yᵉḏûaʿ* as 'known', the meaning must be 'known by sickness' (personified), but such personifications are not much at home in Hebrew.

LIII. 4–6. HIS VICARIOUS SUFFERINGS

The 'we' confess that they had been entirely wrong when they assumed that the sufferer mattered nothing to them. Nor was it that he had been the victim of some capricious or inscrutable whim of God (2 Sam. xxiv. 1), or punished by God for his own sins. The sufferings he had borne were sufferings which should have been theirs as the penalty for their own wickedness. They have nothing to say about the way in which this exchange (substitution is perhaps the wrong word for it) of penalties had been effected. It was not that they had been formally tried and sentenced, and their penalty transferred to the Servant. The impression we get is that they found themselves compelled to reflect upon the contrast between what the Servant was and what he had suffered, and what they themselves were and deserved to suffer, until they were moved to repentance and confession. The Servant had wrought in them a change of mind (μετάνοια) which they could never have achieved of themselves. This meant, for them, that 'the LORD brought down on him the iniquity of us all'.

4. *But*] *'āḵēn*, 'assuredly', 'on the contrary', see on xlix. 4. *ours were the sicknesses that he bore . . .*] The pronouns are emphatic throughout this paragraph. Note the repetitions and poetic 'inversions' in vv. 3 f., and cf. xlix. 24 f. To revert to the theme of suffering as the great cathartic: it is arguable that those we call criminals bear penalties which, if justice were strictly meted out, would be shared by those who never come within the punitive reach of the law. Not to speak of corporate or collective 'guilt', there is a deal of bad blood in society. This finds an outlet more especially in the criminal, who may in a measure be said to suffer vicariously. The paradox presented by the Servant, and by Christ in the NT, is that the man who did not deserve to suffer at all was the man who suffered most. *stricken*] *nāḡûaʿ*. This has often been taken to mean that the Servant was a leper: cf. Lev. xiii, which deals with disease described as *negaʿ* (so liii. 8 here) *ṣāraʿaṯ* (RSV 'a leprous disease'). In 2 Kings xv. 5 it is

said that 'Yahweh smote (*way^enagga'*) the king (Azariah) and he became a leper' (*m^eṣōrā'*). But it is going beyond the evidence to say that *nāgûa'* = *m^eṣōrā'*. Even houses could be afflicted with 'leprous disease' (Lev. xiv. 34) and it is doubtful whether true leprosy (*Elephantiasis Graecorum*) was known to the Hebrews. This need not be fatal to the leprosy theory, since there are skin diseases that can kill. The interpretation is as old as the early rabbis and V (*leprosus*). It was strongly urged by Duhm, who maintained that the Servant was not judicially executed but died a natural death, from leprosy. Duhm could hardly have it both ways, since his 'leprous rabbi' (as Peake dubbed him) was not a man likely to be executed as a felon. Moreover, would the death of a leper, however morally perfect he may have been, have excited the consternation expressed in this passage?

5. *pierced*] *m^eḥōlāl* (generally mortally, cf. Deut. xxi. 1, EVV 'slain'). John xix. 37 is a quotation from Zech. xii. 10, where the Hebrew verb (*dāḳar*) is different, though of much the same meaning (cf. Jer. li. 4; Lam. iv. 9). *transgressions*] Heb. 'rebellions', as in xliii. 25, and cf. i. 2, 'they have rebelled against me'. *crushed*] *m^eḏukkā'*, lit. 'broken to pieces'. This was the original sense of EVV 'bruised', which now means injured by a blow that discolours but does not break either skin or bones. In lvii. 15 *dakkā'* (EVV 'contrite') is used with 'of a humble spirit' (*š^ep̄al rûaḥ*), and Ps. li. 17 (*19*) speaks of 'a broken and crushed (*niḏkêh*) heart'. This raises the question whether 'wounded' and 'crushed' are, *in the immediate context*, to be taken literally, any more than 'a sword will pierce through your heart' in Luke ii. 35. Further, may not 'wounded *for* our transgressions . . . bruised *for* our iniquities', again in the immediate context, lay too much stress on transference of penalty? The Hebrew preposition is *min*, 'on account of', 'by reason of', and there are passages where it is best translated 'by' (so RSV at Deut. xxviii. 34; Judges ii. 18). We need not doubt that the Servant died a violent death, though how he died is not as explicit as we could have wished. Nor does it need five or six verses (? 5–10*a*) to keep repeating that he endured the penalties of others, as though he was simply a passive victim. Twice it is said in ver. 7 that 'he did not open his mouth' (so also Jesus at his trial). But before he could be 'pierced' and 'crushed' *for* the sins of others, he had by sympathy (συμπάθεια) to make those sins his own, to be pierced and crushed *by* them, much as we say that the bitterest ingredient in the sufferings of Christ was his identification of himself with man in his sinful plight rather than the physical agony of the cross. *his* (lit. 'upon him') *was the chastisement that brought us weal*] *mûsar š^elômēnû 'ālāw*, lit. as in AV, 'our peace'

being objective genitive. *mûsār*, 'discipline', 'correction', always remedial as distinct from retributive punishment, becomes frequent in Deut. (15) and Jer. (32 times) and is characteristic of Prov. One of the senses of *šālôm* ('peace') is 'weal' (cf. xlv. 7 and 2 Sam. xviii. 32, 'Is it weal with . . . Absalom?'). The sense here is 'the chastisement that brought about our weal-th was upon him and by means of his stripes there is heal-th for us' (for suffixal *-th* see *SOED* ii. 2161*a*). We may compare *P.B.* 'grant her in health and wealth long to live', and *Merchant of Venice* v. 249, 'I once did lend my body for his wealth'. *at the cost of*] The prep. (*bᵉ*) is almost *beth pretii* (*GK* 119 *p*). *wounds*] *ḥᵃḇûrāh*. EVV 'stripes' is now misleading if taken as referring to judicial scourging (Deut. xxv. 3; 2 Cor. xi. 24). The word occurs only five times outside this passage, in four of them with *peṣaʿ*, an open wound which may be 'squeezed out'. Ps. xxxviii. 5 (*6*); Isa. i. 6, picture bleeding and festering wounds. In Gen. iv. 23; Exod. xxi. 25, both words are used of blows received in a physical encounter.

6. *guilt*] *ʿāwôn*, or 'iniquity', or 'penalty' (see on xl. 2).

LIII. 7–9. HIS IGNOMINIOUS DEATH

The meek bearing of the Servant had not saved him from harsh treatment. He had been summarily convicted and executed, and buried without ceremony in a felon's grave. His fate had excited no commiseration; probably few had first-hand knowledge of it. Such grievous ignominy, so utterly undeserved! From what is a restrained summary of the Servant's sufferings, only one comment, apart from his innocence, stands out, viz. that he suffered for the sins of peoples who deserved to be stricken themselves. This is the theme of vv. 4–6, but the passage gives no clear indication who the speaker, or speakers, may be.

7. *He was harshly treated*] *niggaś*, *Niph.* The word implies the use of physical violence, the *Qal* participle being used of the Egyptian task-masters in Exod. iii. 7. *though he submitted humbly*] Or 'the while he submitted . . .', a circumstantial clause with *waw* and ptc. (*GK* 141 *b*, *e*). *as . . . so*] A comparative sentence with simple *waw* in the apodosis (*GK* 161 *a*). It is often suggested that the verse is reminiscent of Jer. xi. 19, though the similarity may be casual: *sheep* (so RSV rightly) is *śêh*, not the *keḇeś* ('lamb') of Jer.

8. *After arrest and sentence*] *mēʿōṣer ûmimmišpāṭ*. The picture is not entirely clear. This is due to the uncertain meaning of *ʿōṣer* and the wide variety of meanings ('away from', 'by reason of', 'without') of the preposition *min*. Three translations are possible: (i) 'From imprisonment (custody, arrest) and from judgement' (judicial sentence); (ii) 'By reason of an oppressive sentence' (lit. 'oppression and sentence'—hendiadys); (iii) 'Without hindrance and without sentence', i.e. no one attempted to secure a fair trial for him. The literal meaning of *'ōṣer* (only four times) is 'restraint', 'coercion', and it has been questioned whether it can be used in the concrete sense of 'prison' or even 'imprisonment'. But the verb *'āṣar* is used of putting in prison in 2 Kings xvii. 4, and Jeremiah is said to have been 'shut up' (*'āṣûr*) in the court of the guard (Jer. xxxiii. 1, xxxix. 15). Perhaps sense (i) is to be preferred, with 'arrest' for the semi-abstract *'ōṣer*. *led away*] I.e. to execution. For this sense of *lāḳaḥ* (in the passive) see Prov. xxiv. 11. Duhm interpreted *luḳḳāḥ* as meaning that the Servant's 'soul' was 'removed', 'taken away' (to God), with reference to Gen. v. 24 (Enoch), 2 Kings ii. 3, 5, 10 (Elijah), and 'the two *Unsterblichkeitspsalmen* xlix and lxxiii'. But he had perforce to admit that his 'body' was buried (ver. 9). It looks as if his exegesis was conditioned by his theory that the Servant died a natural death from leprosy. Anyhow, Enoch and Elijah were 'translated' bodily, and Duhm's distinction between the Servant's body and soul is unhebraic. Everything in the chapter points to his having died a violent death. It is, of course, just possible that he was a leper condemned on a capital charge—though Duhm did his best to avoid this—but it would be making heavy weather of it. *forcibly removed*] Lit. 'cut off'. The implication is that the final tragedy occurred so swiftly that few were aware that it had happened, let alone at leisure to moralize about it. *sin*] Heb. *pešaʿ*, 'transgression' (as in ver. 5). The word is not infrequently ∥ with *ḥaṭṭā'ṯ* ('sin') and *'āwôn* ('iniquity'), and 'sin' gives the right sense here. For the construction of the sentence see phil. note above.

9. *felons*] *reša'îm*. For the 263 occurrences of this word the AV has 'wicked' 252 times. Its usual sense is guilty of *sin* but it can mean guilty of *crime* (e.g. 2 Sam. iv. 11), and that must be the sense here. It was usual for a man to be buried 'with his fathers', and to be denied such burial was a calamity (1 Kings xiii. 22). For those who had no family grave there was the common public burial place (2 Kings xxiii. 6; Jer. xxvi. 23; cf. Matt. xxvii. 7). Whether some part of this was reserved for criminals we do not know, unless it may be inferred from this passage. *wrong*] *ḥāmās*, usually of physical violence, though, from all we are told of him, this is inconceivable for the Servant. Note the position of the negative, before the acc. obj. which itself stands before the verb (*GK* 152 *e*), as if to say 'he did not-violence', the very reverse of violence (cf. Job xvi. 17). The meiosis is similar to that in Luke xxiii. 41, 'this man has done nothing wrong' (οὐδὲν ἄτοπον ἐπράξεν).

LIII. 10–12. HIS RESURRECTION AND REWARD

There is much that is perplexing in this final paragraph. It is clear that the Servant is to live again and be fully rehabilitated and rewarded. But much as in the Tammuz myth the revivification of the god is assumed but never actually described, so it is here. This may be because there is, in the OT, no exact analogy to the triumph of the Servant, and because the Song was composed before the doctrine of a resurrection from the dead became general. Consequently, some features in the description read like anti-climax, notwithstanding that the speaker in the last two verses is Yahweh. The situation is similar to that in Job xlii. 7–17, where also Yahweh is the final disposer. What more could be said after the moving confession and testimony of the 'we'? The Servant is to see his children enjoying long life; he is to see light and to have fulness of 'knowledge'. Having been himself 'righteous' he is to bring 'righteousness' to many, the many being awarded to him as his 'spoil'.

10. *will . . . purpose*] *ḥāpēṣ . . . ḥēpeṣ*. See on xliv. 28. *that he should be broken*] Lit. 'to crush him'. In OT thinking everything that happens is the result of Yahweh's direct action (cf. xlv. 7; Amos iii. 6), but perhaps we may be permitted to soften the impact of this conception by rendering in the passive. *broken by suffering*] Lit. 'to crush him (with) sickness', a violent figure if taken strictly literally. Language breaks down under the strain imposed upon it. Although *ḥ*ᵒ*lî* (see on ver. 3) denotes sickness or disease, it could be caused by violence, and we have seen that the Servant did not die a natural death from disease. So Ahab says, 'Take me out of the battle, for I am wounded' (lit. 'made sick', 1 Kings xxii. 34). And Joram went to Jezreel to be healed of his wounds (*makkîm*), because he was 'sick' (*ḥôlêh*, 2 Kings viii. 29). The nouns in this passage ('sorrows', 'sicknesses', 'wounds'), likewise the participles ('stricken', 'smitten', 'afflicted') are more or less synonyms. Together they give a picture of a man subjected to every conceivable pain and indignity. In the final summing up 'to crush him with sickness' has to suffice. We may perhaps express it *Anglice* 'broken by suffering'. It may be worth noting that although we speak of 'The Suffering Servant', the word 'suffering' is not used in the EVV of lii. 13–liii. 12. Indeed, in the AV OT 'suffering' is nowhere found, and the verb 'suffer' only in its primary sense of 'endure', 'permit'. *If . . . he makes*] A translation 'when . . . he makes' (= has made) is also possible (cf. Num. xxxvi. 4). Either way, the Servant's sufferings appear to be in the future, notwithstanding that in vv. 1–9 they are described as already past (see note above on ver. 2). The same applies to 'and himself bear (*yisbōl*) their iniquities' (ver. 11), with which cf. 'he bore' (*sāḇal*, ver. 4). *restitution for . . . guilt*] *'āšām*. In the priestly legislation, described in Lev. v. 14–vi. 7 (*v. 14–26*) and mentioned a few times elsewhere, notably in Ezek. (xl. 39 and mg. refs.), this word denotes a specific class of offering, the 'guilt-offering' of RV, RSV; so RV mg. here. It is not necessary to assume that it is used here in its full technical meaning, but there is reason to think that the word was chosen deliberately. In Leviticus even the 'burnt-offering' is said to 'make atonement' (*kappēr*, Lev. i. 4; G. B. Gray, *Sacrifice in the OT*, 1925, prefers 'make expiation'), and the same applies naturally to the sin-offering' (*ḥaṭṭā'ṯ*, iv. 20) and guilt-offering (v. 16). At the same time, for deliberate and 'presumptuous' sin (Ps. xix. 13 (*14*)) there was, at least in theory, no remission by sacrifice (Num. xv. 30 f.; Heb. x. 26–31); the only remedy was for the sinner to cast himself upon the divine forgiveness (cf. Ps. xxxii. 5). Even the sin-offering only availed for sins committed in ignorance (Lev. iv. 2, RV, RSV 'unwittingly'). Nevertheless, the guilt-offering is said to cover such deliberate offences as breach of faith and robbery with extortion, and its purpose was to make restitution for injury done (Lev. vi. 1–6 [*v. 20–26*]). These are such crimes as the heathen may have committed and this is probably the reason for the choice of *'āšām* here. *he shall see his children enjoying long life*] Lit. 'he shall see seed (which —relative omitted) shall lengthen days'. An equally valid translation is 'he shall see (his) children, he shall live many days' (so EVV). The meaning is much the same. What is meant by 'seed'? If the Servant is Israel it must mean future generations of Israelites. But if he is an individual, does it mean that the Servant will, after his restoration, beget children, as Job did (Job xlii. 13–17)? Or are we to think of 'spiritual children', as Timothy and Onesimus were 'children' of Paul (1 Tim. i. 2; Philemon 10)? The former is more probable: the word *zera'* is found 228 times, but the only passage in which it can possibly mean 'spiritual seed' is Isa. vi. 13, and that is doubtful. It must suffice that Isa. liii did—supposing that the Servant is an individual—conceive of a man returning from the world of the dead. There were one or two precedents for that in the earlier literature (1 Kings xvii. 22; 2 Kings iv. 35, xiii. 21), but the general expectation of eschatological blessedness was one in which long life was the rule (lxv. 20–23). *purpose*] Here almost 'business', 'affairs' (cf. lviii. 3, 13, RSV mg.). The Servant is thought of as Yahweh's vicegerent, with charge over his affairs. There is a close ‖ in the Joseph story (Gen. xxxix. 3 f.), 'and the LORD made everything he did to prosper in his hand'.

11. *After*] For temporal *min*, indicating the *terminus a quo*, cf. Gen. xxxviii. 24; Judg. xi. 4. *his sorrowful labours*] *ʿᵃmal napšô*, lit. 'the trouble of his soul'. But troubles never come singly, and Heb. *ʿāmāl* is generally used with, or ‖ to, some other word indicating sorrow, toil, or the like: cf. Num. xxiii. 21; Deut. xxvi. 7; Job v. 6, vii. 7; Ps. x. 14. In this final summing up, one word, which has no precise English equivalent, has to suffice. The expression could possibly mean 'his mortal sorrow(s)': cf. Ps. xvii. 9, 'my deadly enemies', lit. 'my enemies against the soul'. *he shall see *light**] For this phrase cf. Job. iii. 16, 'infants that never see the light', i.e. never come to birth; Ps. xlix. 19 (*20*), 'they shall never see light', i.e. this life is the end for them: cf. also Job xxxiii. 30, 'the light of life', contrasted with 'the pit'; Ps. lvi. 13 (*14*), where the psalmist contrasts 'the light of life' with 'death' from which Yahweh has delivered him. *and have fullness of knowledge*] Lit. '(and) be sated with his knowledge'. If 'sated' or 'surfeited' is too strong for Heb. *yiśbaʿ* here, EVV 'satisfied' is too weak if it only means that the Servant will be 'content'. For 'with his knowledge' as the object of the verb preceding, see the minor Greek versions and the textual note above. The verb *śāḇaʿ* usually takes a direct accusative, but the object can be prefixed by 'with' (Ps. lxv. 4 (*5*), lxxxviii. 3 (*4*)). For the asyndetic construction (omission of 'and' before the verb, though Qᵃ has it), see *GK* 120 *g*, *h*, 154 n. 1. *a*. It brings vividness into the picture, as though the Servant's fullness of knowledge is instant with his seeing light. On the content of the Servant's 'knowledge' we are free to meditate, of course within the bounds of the OT connotation of the word. That it is not academic learning goes without saying. That it must be 'knowledge of God' (xi. 2, lviii. 2; Job xxi. 14; Jer. xxii. 16) may be taken for granted. In the Wisdom literature 'knowledge' is an ethical concept associated with wisdom (*ḥoḵmāh*, Prov. xiv. 6) and understanding or discernment (*tᵉḇûnāh*, xliv. 19; Prov. xvii. 27); but even at its most prudential it is never divorced from 'the fear of the LORD' (Prov. i. 7). *shall bring righteousness to many*] *yaṣdîḳ lārabbîm*. AV, RV, 'shall justify many', RSV, 'shall make many to be accounted righteous'. Although Heb. *hiṣdîḳ* (*Hiph.*), like NT δικαιόω, strictly means 'declare righteous', 'acquit', not 'make righteous', there is no need, in this particular context, to invoke the Pauline and Lutheran Protestant doctrine of justification by faith. It is fairly certain that Dan. xii. 3, *maṣdîḳē hārabbîm*, EVV 'turn many to righteousness', is reminiscent of this passage, and that RV mg. 'shall make many righteous' has

caught the intention of the words. *their iniquities*] Or '(the sum total of) their guilt'.

12. 'The strife is o'er, the battle done'. Now follows, in traditional OT language, the division of the spoils of victory. But does this final verse descend to the level of the conventional, with the Servant taking his share with other 'great' and 'mighty' ones (so EVV)? Or is the meaning that he receives the 'many' as his victory award? After all, he has been the sole protagonist. The translation *Therefore I will give him the many as his victory award, and he shall distribute countless spoil*, understands the literal meaning of the Heb. as 'Therefore I will divide for him among (?) the many and he will distribute the numerous as spoil'. It takes *rabbîm* in the sense it has elsewhere in the passage (lii. 14 f., liii. 12*b*) and construes the prepositions *bᵉ* and *'eṯ* differently from EVV. (Prepositions are tricky things in any language, and not least so in Hebrew.) For *rabbîm* ‖ *'ᵃṣûmîm* = 'many' ‖ 'numerous', cf. Prov. vii. 26; Amos v. 12. It should be said that EVV 'I will divide a portion' is only one word (*'ᵃḥallēḳ*) in the Hebrew, not a verb followed by an acc. obj. 'portion', i.e. it is an absolute transitive, with no acc. obj. expressed. Yet nowhere else in the *Pi'ēl*, and only twice in the *Qal* (1 Sam. xxx. 24 and Neh. xiii. 13, where there is no ambiguity) is it used without an acc. obj. This prompts the question whether 'the many' is not some kind of an acc. obj. after 'I will distribute'. There is no question that Heb. *bᵉ* often means 'with', usually instrumental, as in *baḥereḇ*, 'with the sword', but not even in an expression like 'with a large force' (*bᵉ'am kāḇēḏ*, Num. xx. 20) does it mean 'with (somebody else)', as EVV take it here. In the three examples where *ḥallēḳ* = 'divide (with)', the prep. is not *bᵉ* but either *'im* (Joshua xxii. 8; Prov. xxix. 24) or *bᵉṯôḵ* (lit. 'in the midst of', Prov. xvii. 2). The closest ‖ to *'ᵃḥallēḳ bᵉ* in this passage is Job xxxix. 17, *wᵉlô' ḥālaḳ lāh babbînāh*, 'neither has he imparted to her understanding', but the analogy (RSV 'and given her no share in understanding') is not quite exact. Perhaps *'ᵃḥallēḳ bārabbîm* is to be explained as a partitive use of *bᵉ*, as in Exod. xii. 43 ff., where *'āḵal bô* can only mean 'share in eating it', or, with a more directly accusative force, Judges xiii. 16, 'I will not eat (*bᵉ*) your food'. If this will not do, we can take *bᵉ* in one of its common meanings, 'among'. Then 'I will divide for him among the many' can as well mean 'I will give him many of the many' as 'I will give to him along with the many'. It may be added that LXX and V agree substantially with the interpretation here offered: LXX διὰ τοῦτο αὐτὸς κληρονομήσει (? *yᵉḥallēḳ* for *'ᵃḥallēḳ*) πολλούς (V *plurimos*). *he shall distribute countless spoil*] Lit. 'he shall distribute the numerous ones as spoil', taking *'eṯ* as *nota accusativi* (which is used without the article following, as in xli. 7), and *šālāl* as accusative of specification or the like (*Syn.* § 71). The Servant is the arbiter of the spoils accruing from his victory. The figure is not as bellicose as it may sound: cf. ix. 3 (*2*). *he gave himself utterly*] Lit. 'he laid bare (*or* poured out, EVV) his soul': cf. Gen. xxiv. 20, of emptying a jar; 2 Chron. xxiv. 11, similarly of a treasure chest. *by bearing*] Lit. 'and he bore', a circumstantial clause (cf. on ver. 7) conveying the reason why he was counted (*or* counted himself ? *Niph.*) among transgressors. It was because he identified himself with them in their plight. RV, RSV 'yet he bore', fails to make any connexion with the preceding line, but only a contrast. *and standing in the place of*] *yapgîaʿ* (*Hiph.*), the same verb as 'brought down on' (ver. 6). The general sense of the verb is 'meet', 'encounter': so *Qal* 'meet with a request', 'entreat', in Ruth i. 16; Job xxi. 15; Jer. vii. 16, xxvii. 18; and *Hiph.*, Jer. xxxvi. 25. EVV 'made intercession' is therefore quite justified, though in current English usage the main emphasis is on intercessory prayer. More likely, in the present context and in the light of lix. 16, 'there was no one to intervene', the figure is of the Servant placing himself between the transgressors and the punishment they deserved. If, to some moralists, this seems 'unethical', there are situations in which it is true enough.

LIV. 1–10. ZION RESTORED AND REPEOPLED

2. יַטּוּ] *Hiph.* נטה, masc. Impf. (or Jussive?) is difficult to construe. AV, RV, 3rd pers. plur. 'let them stretch forth' translates literally, no doubt taking the form as active (with indef. subj.) for passive, 'let the curtains . . . be stretched out'. Q[a] יַטִּי, a *forma mixta*, is in no better case. The versions construed as *Hiph.* Imper. 2 s.f. הַטִּי, but whether they *read* this, or only assumed it to conform with הַרְחִיבִי תַּחְשֹׂכִי . . ., it is impossible to say. We might essay a pointing יֻטּוּ *Hoph.*, 'let them be stretched out'. To be sure this is a masculine form *after* a preceding fem. subj., but there was some reluctance to use cumbrous feminine forms like תֻּטֶּינָה (cf. *GK* 145 *h*). It matters little how the word is spelled, the sense is not in doubt.

5. בֹּעֲלַיִךְ עֹשַׂיִךְ] The plural forms of the suffix could be *plurales excellentiae* (*GK* 124 *k*), though the *yôdh* in עשיך is better explained as original to the √עשי (*GK* 93 *ss*). Then the suffix in בעליך has been assimilated to it for assonance. The word as pointed is *Qal* ptc. act. בָּעַל and ἅπ. λεγ. The massoretic spelling is artificial, partly to avoid strong anthropomorphism, partly to avoid association with Baal (cf. Hos. ii. 16 (*18*)). This was the easier because בֹּעֲלַיִךְ עֹשַׂיִךְ was too attractive an assonance to be missed. The original spelling would be בַּעְלֵךְ.

6. קָרָאָךְ] For the anomalous pointing קראָךְ see *GK* 58 *g*. יהוה] The verse would scan more easily (3:3/3:3) if this were transferred to precede אֱלֹהָיִךְ at the end of the verse (cf. *BH*). Q[a] has יהוה twice: 'Yahweh called you . . . says Yahweh your God'.

8. שֶׁצֶף] *ἅπ. λεγ.* and not referable to any √ unless it be the rabbinic שסף/שצף, 'to cut off'. The meaning could then approximate to 'in a slash (i.e. momentary fit) of anger', cf. LXX *ἐν θυμῷ μικρῷ*, A *ἐν ἀτομῷ 'οργῆς*, AV, RV mg. This would accord with the context (רֶגַע *bis*). RV and RSV understand the word as = שֶׁטֶף, 'flood' (cf. Job xxxviii. 25; Ps. xxxii. 6; Prov. xxvii. 4), with צ by assimilation to קֶצֶף. On the whole this is to be preferred, since the word would form a bridge to 'the waters of Noah' in ver. 9.

9. כִּימֵי] Can mean either (i) 'like the days of' (RV mg., RSV, following V and T, or (ii) as כִּי־מֵי (*maqqēph* is only a massoretic sign) 'for the waters of' (LXX). AV, RV 'For *as* the waters of' is a conflate rendering. Interpretation (i) is to be preferred (see below) for psychological reasons, not to mention the paronomasia 'the days of Noah . . . the waters of Noah'. אֲשֶׁר] Can be equivalent to כַּאֲשֶׁר, 'when', especially after words denoting time (cf. Gen. vi. 4, xlv. 6; Deut. iv. 10). There is no need to emend to כאשר as in *BH*.

A summons to one who has lately borne no children, to rejoice in expectation of, and to make preparations for, a renewal of her wife- and motherhood. The 'barren one' is Zion, though she is not actually named. In the coming days she will bear more children than she did before her temporary separation from Yahweh her husband. Yahweh lays himself under obligation as solemn as when he declared to Noah that never again would the earth be overwhelmed by flood, that never again will he be severe with his restored and compassionated Zion.

The theme of the passage is similar to that of xliv. 1–5, xlix. 14–21, l. 1, li. 1–3; but the emphasis is upon the increase of Zion's children *in*, rather than upon the return of her exiled children *to*, the homeland. Ver. 1 is quoted in Gal. iv. 27, but allegorically of the heavenly Jerusalem; a striking example of the way in which the NT sometimes interprets the Old. The 'deserted' wife is a figure for Zion during the exile, the 'married' is the city before the exile. In ver. 2 the figure is that of a nomad tent-dweller who must enlarge her tent and lengthen the ropes and strengthen the stakes that keep it erect and taut. The population of the city will spread (*pāraṣ*, lit. 'burst', cf. Gen. xxviii. 14; Exod. i. 12; Job i. 10) outwards to her deserted daughter towns (cf. xl. 9) which during the exile had been occupied by nations (*gôyîm*) like the Edomites (cf. Ezek. xxxv.

1–10). The resettlement will be effected without hindrance. Once more Zion is to 'have no fear' (xli. 10, 13 f., xliii. 1, 5, xliv. 2). She will forget the shameful conduct (cf. Jer. ii. 25 f., iii. 25) of her youth before the exile, and remember no more the disgrace of her 'widowhood' in exile (ver. 4). Her husband is none other than her Maker, Yahweh of hosts (see on xliv. 6), and her Redeemer (see on xli. 14) is the Holy One of Israel (ibid.). The most difficult verse in the passage is 6 (see below). Verses 7 f. convey the suggestion that Yahweh regrets that he had to treat his people so severely (cf. Jer. xxxi. 20). This thought is continued in vv. 9 f. if we read them, as we must, in the light of Gen. viii. 21 f., ix. 14–16. Before the Flood Yahweh was 'sorry' (RSV at Gen. vi. 6) that he had made man; after it his feelings were tinged with regret. Such anthropomorphisms need occasion no misgivings; they even add to the appeal of Scripture. God, in the Bible, is not heartless or unfeeling, as a pure transcendental monotheism could so easily represent him. The passage concludes with the assurance that Yahweh's 'steadfast love' (*ḥeseḏ*, see on xl. 6) and his 'covenanted peace' (*b^e^rîṯ šālôm*, see on xlii. 19, and cf. Num. xxv. 12; Ezek. xxxiv. 25, xxxvii. 26) which is its guarantee, are more enduring than even the mountains and hills. The word 'covenant' is again a link with the sequel to the Flood story (Gen. ix. 8–17).

1. *Rejoice . . . break out into shrill and joyous cries*] *ronnî . . . piṣ^e^ḥî rinnāh w^e^ṣah^a^lî*, lit. 'Shout (for joy) . . . break out into a ringing cry and neigh'. For similar conjunctions of the three vbs. cf. xii. 6, xxiv. 14, xliv. 23, xlix. 13, lii. 9, lv. 12; Jer. xxxi. 7. In some of these passages it is nature that is bidden to shout aloud, in sympathetic acclamation of Yahweh's redeeming work. Perhaps 'shrill' may be allowed to serve as an equivalent of 'neigh': cf. Milton's 'The shrill matin song of birds'. *deserted*] For this sense of *šômēmāh* (also of *n^e^šammôṯ*, ver. 3) cf. xlix. 8, 19; Ezek. xxxiii. 28, xxxvi. 4.

2. *widen*] For the text see above. The primary meaning of the vb. *nāṭāh* is 'stretch out', 'extend' (e.g. the hand), but not in the sense of pulling it out to make it longer. It is used of pitching a tent (xl. 22; Gen. xii. 8, xxvi. 25). To 'pitch' the 'curtains' of a nomad 'dwelling' would be an intelligible figure here. But the other verbs in the description convey the suggestion of making a larger tent, and what we expect is an order to make more ample curtains. When Rizpah spread (*wattaṭṭêh*) sackcloth on the rock (2 Sam. xxi. 10) she did not stretch it to make it bigger. But in Jer. vi. 4 the evening shadows 'stretch themselves out' (*yinnāṭû*), i.e. grow longer. And in Zech. i. 16 the measuring line is stretched out (*yinnāṭêh*) over Jerusalem with a view to a more spacious city (ver. 17). *curtains*] Nomad tent-curtains were generally woven from goats' hair (Exod. xxvi. 7). *dwelling*] Heb. *miškᵉnôṯ*, 'dwellings', plur. of local extension or, perhaps, of amplification (*GK* 124 *b*). So elsewhere with this word (Ps. xliii. 3, lxxxiv. 1 (2), cxxxii. 5). A nomad tent had many separate parts, and more amenities than an igloo. All these instructions are given to the woman Zion, and it is worth noting that all work to do with making and erecting tents was, and still is in Arabia, women's work. *no need to be sparing!*] Cf. lviii. 1.

3. *on every hand*] Heb. 'right and left'; so in English idiom. The words could mean 'south and north'. For Jacob's descendants 'breaking out' to all four points of the compass, see Gen. xxviii. 14. *children*] Or 'descendants'. Heb. 'seed', as in Gen. xii. 7. *succeed to*] Or 'be heirs of'. Notwithstanding DI's universalism (xlv. 20–25) there is a note of nationalism, even of revanchism, in this passage. Heb. 'possess' (*yîrāš*) can also, by implication, mean 'dispossess': so especially in Deut. (e.g. ix. 1, RSV). This irredentism—it was never a dream of world-empire—is a legacy from the (much idealized!) accounts of the conquest of the promised land. But it should not be overlooked that Yahweh's first promise to Abraham to give the land to his descendants, was accompanied by the assurance 'by you all the families of the earth will be blessed' (Gen. xii. 3). *reoccupy*] For this sense of 'make to be inhabited' (AV, RV) see Ezek. xxxvi. 33.

4. *be abashed . . . shame*] *ṯēḇôšî . . . ḇōšeṯ*, from the one √*bôš*, 'be ashamed'. But 'ashamed' does not always give the right nuance in English: e.g. 'they urged him (Elisha) till he was ashamed' (2 Kings ii. 17, cf. viii. 11) can only mean 'till he felt embarrassed' or 'disconcerted'. Either of these words would serve here, but 'abashed' in the sense of 'disconcerted with sudden shame' is better: it links up with 'the shame(ful conduct) of your youth', which Zion would not find it easy to forget. *intimidated . . . embarrassed*] The Hebrew verbs (*kālam* and *ḥāp̄ēr*) are usually ∥ *bôš*, and are equally difficult to render by uniform stock words. So in xli. 11, xlv. 16 f., 'disappointed and mortified'. Their √ meanings are 'be humiliated' and 'be ashamed' (Arab. 'be shy', 'bashful'). All three words imply a feeling of inferiority. *disgrace*] *ḥerpāh*. Note the assonance with 'embarrassed' preceding. Indeed, the whole verse, like so many in DI, is full of delicate alliterations, without being in the least artificial.

6. What the EVV intend to convey by this verse is obscure. Muilenburg's comment is: 'Now the Lord is to restore the ancient marriage relationship, but this time it will be deeper because of the experience of separation and the years of Israel's longing and grief.' If this is a variant of the theme that married bliss is all the greater after the

parties have made up a quarrel, it may be true enough; but is it what the Heb. says? When does, or did, Yahweh 'call' Zion? just now, or in the past? When was Zion 'forsaken' and 'cast off'? It is best to begin with the second half of the verse. *yet who can disown the bride of his youth?*] Lit. 'and a bride of youth, that she should be rejected . . .!?' The sentence is half exclamation, half question, like the serpent's opening gambit to Eve: 'So (it is the case) that Yahweh has said you are not to eat from any tree in the garden!?' By way of reply it needs an emphatic disclaimer. No decent husband would dream of disowning the bride of his youth, much less would Yahweh! (cf. Prov. v. 18; Mal. ii. 14–16). It is true that in such exclamatory questions the *kî* ('that') is usually prefixed by some particle, if only by the interrogative; though see 2 Kings xviii. 34. And if we must have an introduction to *kî* in the present passage, we have it in the emphatic 'a bride of youth'. The foregoing interpretation is substantially that of Duhm, Feldmann, Fischer, and Volz. *For when **he called you, you were a woman outcast and utterly dejected*] Lit. 'For like a woman forsaken and grieved in spirit** he called you'. Does this mean that Yahweh is now *recalling* Israel (the usual interpretation, so EVV) after the temporary separation of the exile? Or does it mean that he *called* her to be his bride (the assumption in Jer. ii; Hos. ii) long ago (so Ewald), though again it goes without saying that Zion has in the meantime disgraced herself and been temporarily banished? This second interpretation seems more probable and is supported by the form *ḳ^{e}rā'āḵ* ('he called you', pf.) and by the undoubted sense of the following context. Although in Hos. xi. 1 the figure is that of the 'child' Israel, not the wife, Yahweh 'called' him out of Egypt. In Hos. ix. 10 he 'found Israel like (wild) grapes in the wilderness', cf. 'outcast and utterly dejected' here. And in Ezek. xvi. a very unprepossessing foundling Jerusalem was brought up by Yahweh and in due course became his bride. Mention should be made of Volz's interpretation of 6*a*: Yahweh 'calls (sc. thinks of) you as a wife forsaken'—for this sense of 'calls' referring to Jer. vi. 30—and for this reason he is moved by compassion, 'for a bride of youth can never be rejected'.

7. *I will gather you home*] Here the thought shifts momentarily from 'taking back' Zion, to the gathering together of her scattered children (cf. xlix. 18), pictured as so many members of Yahweh's flock (xl. 11; Jer. xxxi. 10; Mic. ii. 12).

8. *I will have compassion on you*] *riḥamtîḵ*, Pf. of a divine affirmation, so also the second *nišba'tî* ('now I swear') in ver. 9.

9. *the waters of the flood*] Lit. 'the waters of Noah'.

LIV. 11–17. ZION RESPLENDENT

11. וִיסַּדְתִּיךְ] *Qal* pf. 1st pers. sing., with 2nd pers. sing. fem. sf. and *waw consec.* 'and I will found you', i.e. 'lay your foundations'. The word could be pointed וִיסֹדֹתַיִךְ ('and your foundations') ‖ 'your stones': so Qª ויסודותיך, and cf. Lam. iv. 11. But the vb. can contain its own object, 'lay foundations', and it is better to take it as a verb ‖ with, rather than as a second object to מַרְבִּיץ. The meaning is the same either way.

13. בָּנַיִךְ . . . בָּנָיִךְ] It is unusual for the same word to be used in ‖ stichs. LXX υἱούς . . . τέκνα avoids this, and we might do the same by rendering 'sons . . . children'. Qª has בוניכי ('your builders') for the first, and for the second בניכי ('your sons'), later corrected to 'your builders' by *waw* written above the word. 'Your builders shall be taught (their craft) by Yahweh' is more natural than 'Your sons shall be taught by Yahweh' simply. An objection might be that in this context it is Yahweh himself who is the builder; but see on xlix. 17, where the play on 'your builders'/'your sons' is contained in the one word בָּנָיִךְ.

14. תִּכּוֹנָנִי] For תִּתְכּוֹנָנִי, *Hithpôʿlēl* (*GK* 54 *c*). רַחֲקִי] There is no need to alter to the imperfect תִּרְחֲקִי (so *BH*); the imperative is sometimes used instead of the imperfect to express a distinct assurance or promise: '(you shall) be far from oppression' (*GK* 110 *c*).

15. מֵאוֹתִי] A variant for מֵאִתִּי (ver. 17); so often in Kings and always in Jer., Ezek. There is no need to emend (as *BH*).

17. וְכָל . . . תַּרְשִׁיעִי] The omission of this whole sentence by Qª is only one indication of the general unreliability of the MS.

Yahweh assures inconsolable Zion that his purpose is to make her a city of outstanding beauty (ver. 12 f.). The concluding vv. (15–17) are a promise that the city shall be free from molestation. By comparison they are ragged and inconsequential, but since ver. 14 forms a good bridge to them, there is insufficient reason to deny their genuineness, though see Duhm *in loc.*

The section begins abruptly, without introductory formula. Instead, there is a concluding 'This is the word of the LORD'. It is, for more reasons than one, a passage of remarkable interest. It is obviously the original of the description of the New Jerusalem in the Apocalypse (see especially Rev. xxi. 10–21). Equally obviously, the picture of the city ablaze with precious stones goes back to stories of a mythological paradise in the primeval past, of which a description is still extant in Ezek. xxviii. 13 f. (cf. also Gen. ii. 11 f.). In other words, this passage is a link between the mythical paradise in the primeval past and the equally 'mythological' paradise of the age to come. A difference is that the first paradise was a garden (Gen. ii. 8; Ezek. xxviii. 13), this and the last are cities (Rev. xxi. 2). It was God who planted the garden, Cain, of all men, who built the first city (Gen. iv. 17). 'God made the country, man made the town.' When the sun shines through the morning haze on the towers of Manhattan, it lights them with a glory that seems ethereal. But New York is not the New Jerusalem. It is tempting to sermonize but that is not the business of the commentator. It must suffice to say that the gospel is set for the redemption of all human activity. God will even save the city.

11. *poor*] *ʿaniyyāh*, as in li. 21 ('afflicted'), but here taken as exclamatory. *tempest-driven*] *sōʿarāh*. RSV (cf. AV, RV) 'storm-tossed' is too suggestive of a storm at sea, a meaning which the word can of course carry (Jonah i. 11). For a similar description cf. vii. 2. *Listen!*] *hinnēh*, anacrusis. *black cosmetic*] *pûḵ*, a dark mineral powder (√ 'pulverize'), perhaps sulphide of lead, used as an eye-pigment. Jezebel 'made up' (*wattāśem*) her eyes with it (2 Kings ix. 30); cf. Jer. iv. 30 'you made your eyes wide with *pûḵ*'. It is doubtful whether it was antimony (RV mg., RSV) but it may have been similar to *al-koḥl* (the original of Engl. 'alcohol'), used by Arab women: see Ezek. xxiii. 40, 'you painted (*kāḥalt*, ἅπ. λεγ.) your eyes'. The name Keren-happuch (Job xlii. 14) indicates that it was kept in a 'horn' similar to that containing the anointing oil (1 Sam. xvi. 1; 1 Kings i. 39). The powder would be mixed with a liquid vehicle to make a paste or cement. The only parallel—and that only a partial one—for its use in building is 1 Chron. xxix. 2, which lists 'stones of (i.e. set in) *pûḵ*' among accessory adornments of the Temple. *azure*] *sappîrîm*, 'sapphire(s)' or lapis lazuli (cf. Exod. xxiv. 10). Engl. 'azure' can be a noun and is derived from Pers. *lazhward*, 'lapis lazuli', the *l-* being dropped as supposedly the Arab. def. art. In this verse the profile of Zion, Yahweh's bride, 'made up' with eye-paint, shines through the picture of her as a city (cf. Rev. xxi. 2). Such a figure is so daring, even in an architectural context, that attempts have been made to disguise (AV, RV, 'fair colours') or to emend the text. For *pûḵ* LXX has ἄνθραξ, a word it also employs for *nōp̄eḵ* (? malachite), which is coupled with 'sapphire' in Exod. xxviii. 18, xxxix. 11; Wellhausen, followed, among others, by Volz, would read *nōp̄eḵ* for *pûḵ*. But how should *nōp̄eḵ* have been altered to *pûḵ*? It is questionable if LXX Isa. knew what *pûḵ* was; or, if it did, it may have shrunk from its suggestion of sex-appeal. Sex metaphors can be carried to extravagant lengths by mystical writers. But the OT attitude to sex is frank and healthy. The Bible is never prudish.

12. your *pinnacles*] *šimšôṯayiḵ*, as catching the rays of the sun (*šemeš*): cf. Ps. lxxxiv. 11 (*12*), where, however, the word must mean 'battlement'. Cf. Palgrave *Omar Khayyam*

And Lo! the Hunter of the East has caught
The Sultan's Turret in a Noose of Light!

chalcedony] *kaḏᵉḵōḏ*, elsewhere only Ezek. xxvii. 16. NT χαλκηδών (*NEB* 'chalcedony' at Rev. xxi. 19) must be the same word, though LXX has ἴασπις here. (Jaspers are varieties of chalcedony.) We are to think of some conspicuous fiery-coloured variety. *carbuncle*] Lit. 'firestone', Heb. *'eḵdāḥ*, ἅπ. λεγ. √ 'strike fire'. Precisely what stone is meant is anyone's guess. Even if we knew the exact equivalents of all the precious stones of the Bible, non-experts would be little the wiser. Few can identify all those listed in Rev. xxi. 19. *boundary wall*] LXX περιβολόν, Heb. *gᵉḇûl*, 'boundary', RSV 'wall'; so Volz, who interprets 'the circumvallation (*Umwallung*) of the entire city confines'. The word could be used of the territory of a city, including what we should call its suburbs (Judges i. 18; ? Num. xxxv. 26 f.). These would not usually be walled; but the description here is idealized. *splendid stones*] Lit. 'stones of delight', cf. AV, RV 'delightsome land' at Mal. iii. 12. RSV 'precious stones' is too suggestive of diamonds and emeralds. Even the 'jasper' of Rev. xxi. 18 is not quite in that category.

13. *taught*] Sc. their craft: see on l. 4 and cf. Exod. xxxi. 1–6. *children*] Lit. 'sons'.

14. *you shall be built on a foundation of righteousness*] This is the right order of the sentence *in English*; lit. 'in righteousness you shall be founded', the figure pictured by the preposition 'in' (*bᵉ*) being similar to that in 11*b*. The verb 'founded' (*Hithpô'lēl kûn*) is ∥ 'built' in Prov. xxiv. 3. The only adequate translation of *ṣᵉḏāḳāh* here is 'righteousness'. In the Gerechtigkeitsgasse, Bern, there is a fountain of Justice, but this would be adequately expressed in Hebrew by *mišpāṭ*. It is likely that the present passage is reminiscent of xxviii. 16 f., where Yahweh announces his intention to 'lay in Zion a stone, a tested stone, a precious corner stone for a firm foundation . . . and I will make justice (*mišpāṭ*) your standard of measure, and righteousness (*ṣᵉḏāḳāh*) your standard of weight'. *oppression*] *'ōšeḳ*, generally accompanied by extortion, robbery with violence (cf. Lev. vi. 4 (*v. 23*); Amos iv. 1; Mic. ii. 2).

15. *he shall have no support from me*] Or 'I shall not be the source of it', lit. '(it shall) not (be) from with me': cf. 1 Kings i. 27. lit. 'has this thing come about from with my lord the king?'; Ps. xxii. 25 (*26*). *shall fall because of you*] An equally valid translation would be 'shall fall upon (*'al*) you' (and be broken). Is there any connexion with viii. 14 f. and the firm foundation stone of xxviii. 16 on the one hand, and Luke xx. 17 f. on the other? If so, it gives a more graphic sense to 'he shall fall because of you'. (In Dan. ii. 34 f., 44 it is the stone that strikes the image, cf. Luke xx. 18.)

16. *I it is who have created . . . I, too, have created*] The pronouns, repeated, and separated from the verbs, and the repeated 'created', are most emphatic. For Heb. 'created' (*bārā'*) see on xl. 26, and note here its use for Yahweh's action in contemporary history as well as in the original creation. God creates the smith (xliv. 12) who produces weapons, and also the man who uses them, and he can, at will, nullify the endeavours of both. *weapons of all kinds*] Heb. *k^elî* ('weapon' or 'tool'), though singular here, may be taken as a collective (*GK* 123 *b*); *ma'^aśēhû* is 'for its (RV mg., RSV) use/work', not 'his (the smith's) work', though AV 'his' was probably intended in our sense of 'its'. It was the ravager's part to use the weapon(s).

17. *and if anyone brings an action against you, the verdict shall be yours*] Lit. 'and every tongue that stands up with you in court (*or* for judgement, see on xli. 1) you shall prove wrong'. *This is the inheritance of the servants of the* LORD *and their right guaranteed by me*] Lit. '. . . and their righteousness from with me' (see on ver. 15). There is more in this conclusion than immediately meets the eye. This is the only context in which 'inheritance' (*naḥ^alāh*) is ‖ 'right(eousness)'. In the earlier (especially Deuteronomic) literature Israel's 'inheritance' is the promised land of Canaan (Deut. iv. 21 *et passim*). We may here give to *ṣ^edāḳāh* any content from 'vindication' (RSV) to 'salvation' (see on xlii. 21) and 'righteousness' (ver. 14 above), except perhaps 'victory' (see on xli. 2) in a military sense. Yahweh's guarantee to Zion is of a 'prosperity' (see again on xli. 2) modest enough. Again, no promises of world-empire (see above on ver. 3). 'The servants of the LORD' are not even promised life free from all anxieties. We may compare John xvi. 33 (*NEB*): 'I have told you all this that in me you may find peace. In the world you will have trouble. But courage! The victory is mine'. DI was more concerned with the spiritual than with the material welfare of 'the servants of the LORD' (see Volz *in loc.*).

LV. 1–5. 'COME, EVERYTHING IS NOW READY'

1. This verse contains what look like repetitions and metrical redundancies. The first hand of Hexapla LXX omits וּלְכוּ שִׁבְרוּ, and some MSS. have *πίετε* (= וּשְׁתוּ) instead of *φάγετε* (= וֶאֱכֹלוּ). Q^a omits ואכלו ולכו שברו, which, in view of the LXX evidence, can hardly be due entirely to homoioteleuton. If we keep ולכו שברו we should transfer the *athnaḥ* to the second לכו, even if this gives the same word in ‖ stichs: though see vv. 4 f.

4. *BH* is surely wrong when it says 'read לְעַמִּים with versions' for the first לְאוּמִּים. LXX has ἔθνεσιν (*bis*). For some reason the same words are used in ‖ stichs, perhaps for emphasis in what sounds like a public appeal.

This passage is the OT equivalent of the parable of the Great Supper (Luke xiv. 15–24; cf. also John vii. 37 f.; Rev. xxii. 17). To understand it we should remember that in the East water is still sold in the streets and that a man wishing to be philanthropic will buy up the stock of a water-carrier or baker, and order him to distribute it gratis (so Volz). But the bounty of the divine Donor goes beyond the bare necessities of bread and water, to include the luxuries of wine and milk. All are symbols of the true bread, 'the real bread from heaven' (John vi. 27, 32), as contrasted with the perishable for which men expend toil and money. 'Rich food' (ver. 2, *dešen*, 'fatness') may be used of spiritual food: cf. Ps. xxxvi. 8 (*9*), lit. 'They are saturated with the fatness of thy house and thou givest them drink from the river of thy delights'. The metaphor is in accord with the oriental taste for plenty of oil in cooking and there is nothing, either in Isa. or in the Psalm, to suggest any connexion with sacrificial fat. The sum of the matter is that God offers men spiritual food gratis. This is OT as well as NT doctrine.

Verses 1–2 can be read as an utterance of the Prophet speaking *in propria persona*. The language is of the kind he might use in the bazaar in the name of the God who commissions him. Indeed, it is likely enough that it was a public utterance and that, by the time the words were spoken, he could venture into the open. But it is impossible to disjoin vv. 1–2 from what follows, in which the speaker is Yahweh. This implies that 1–2 are also words of Yahweh. The whole is an example of the way in which a prophet could not only speak *for* God but also *as* God. A similar passage is v. 1–7. The word of the prophet is the word of God, his indignation God's indignation, his sorrow God's sorrow. It is pre-eminently in this that we have in the OT anticipations of the Incarnation, of the Word become flesh.

Opinion is divided on the interpretation of vv. 3*b*–4. Is the meaning that there is to be a revival of the Davidic monarchy (e.g. Duhm, Skinner), or that the covenant with David is now to be transferred to the theocratic community (e.g. Volz, Muilenburg)? Between these views it is difficult to decide. The view taken here is that the second is the right interpretation, but the reasons for it are best deferred until the critical analysis of the disputed verses.

1. *Attend! Attend!*] Probably anacrusis. Heb. *hôy*, though less threatening than *'ôy* ('woe!' vi. 5), more often than not introduces a lamentation (1 Kings xiii. 30) or a declaration of judgement (x. 5). Here, as in xviii. 1; Zech. ii. 6 f. (*10 f.*), it is meant to rouse attention, rather like the (usually) thrice-repeated 'Oyez!' of the medieval town-crier. *money*] *kesep̱*, lit. 'silver'. There were no minted coins until the Persian period. 'Money' in bars was weighed (cf. *tišḳ^elû*, ver. 2; Gen. xxiii. 16). Akk. *kaspu* is a homonym and may mean either 'silver' or '(broken) food'. To translate 'food' here would be wrong, even if it does seem absurd to invite people with no money to 'buy'. (The doctrine of justification by faith is equally paradoxical.) In any case, the end of the verse speaks of 'wine and milk without payment' (*m^eḥîr*, 2 Sam. xxiv. 24). There may nevertheless be a play upon the two meanings of the word. *buy grain*] *šiḇ^erû*. This verb is a denominative and can contain its object (*šeḇer*, 'grain') within itself (cf. Gen. xli. 56 f., xlii. 6; Prov. xi. 26).

2. *your riches*] *y^egî^aḵem*, properly 'your toil'. But just as *p^e'ullāh* ('work') comes to be used of wages earned by work (see on xl. 10), so it is with this word, with some emphasis on its quantity as 'wealth' (cf. Jer. xx. 5; Hos. xii. 8 (*9*)). Such wealth would usually be 'in kind' (cf. Jer. iii. 24), as it still is in farming communities. Or we might translate 'or toil for what does not satisfy?' *taste*] *Or* 'appetite'. For this sense of Heb. *nep̱eš* ('soul') cf. lvi. 11 (some 50 times in all).

3. *that you may have life in its fullness*] Cf. *NEB* at John x. 10. The Hebrew is 'that your soul (*nep̱eš*) may live' (cf. EVV). There is no emphasis on the 'soul' as distinct from the body (see on xlii. 1), though there is probably some intended contrast between *nep̱eš* here and *nep̱eš* (appetite') in the preceding verse. If the Prophet had intended 'that you may live' simply, he could have said so with greater economy of words, omitting 'your soul', which is not so much stuffing to fill out the 3:3 line. *and I will make a lasting covenant with you*] The usual Hebrew idiom was to 'cut' (*kāraṯ*) a covenant (some 80–90 times). In Gen. ix. 12, xvii. 2 (both P) the expression is to 'give' or 'grant' (*nāṯan*) a covenant 'between' (*bên*) God and the second party; this may be to emphasize the fact, which applies to all covenants to which God is a party, that it is he who takes the initiative and even dictates its terms. For a description of what may be the primitive ritual of 'cutting a covenant' see Gen. xv; Jer. xxxiv. 18 f. We may infer from Jer. xxxi. 33 that the terms of a covenant were sometimes embodied in a written agreement, and this is confirmed by Exod. xxxiv. 28: 'And he (Moses; or ? Yahweh, cf. Exod. xxxi. 18; Deut. ix. 10) wrote upon the tablets the words of the covenant, the ten commandments'. The covenant between Jonathan and David (1 Sam. xviii. 3 f.) was 'a gentlemen's agreement', confirmed, not in writing, but by Jonathan's making over to David his princely robe and armour. Nor is there word of any written attestation of the covenant which Yahweh made (*śām*) with David, unless it be the account in 2 Sam. xxiii. 5; but in Deut. xvii. 14–21—though there is no mention of a covenant—the ruling 'David' must make a copy of the Deuteronomic law and be guided by it in the discharge of his royal functions. For Yahweh's covenant with David and his dynasty see further Ps. lxxxix, especially vv. 3, 28, 34, 39 (*4*, *29*, *35*, *40*), which is based on 2 Sam. vii. 8–16; cf. 1 Kings viii. 23–26. *a lasting covenant*] *b*ᵉ*rîṯ* *ʿôlām*, cf. 2 Sam. xxiii. 5. For the meaning of *ʿôlām* see on xl. 28. EVV usually translate it, when it occurs in the genitive after another noun in the construct state, by 'everlasting'. AV has 'lasting (hills)' at Deut. xxxiii. 15, and that is adequate here. *the manifestations of my love for David*] *ḥas*ᵉ*ḏê ḏāwîḏ*, lit. 'the deeds of *ḥeseḏ* to David'. For the meaning of *ḥeseḏ* (usually 'steadfast love' in RSV) and its relation to 'covenant' (*b*ᵉ*rîṯ*) see on xl. 6. The present is one of 15 passages in which the word is used in the plural. RSV has 'steadfast love' (sing.) in all except 2 Chron. xxxii. 32, xxxv. 26; Neh. xiii. 14 ('good deeds'). This may be because it is difficult to render the plural without being clumsy. In Lam. iii. 32 MT could be pointed to read the singular (*ḥasdô*), 'his steadfast love' (so *Qere*), but there is not the slightest doubt that a distinction grew up between the singular *ḥeseḏ* and the plural *ḥ*ᵃ*sāḏîm*, 'deeds (i.e. expressions/evidences/manifestations) of *ḥeseḏ*'. The plural is generally late, though it occurs in Gen. xxxii. 10 (*11*). Ps. lxxxix. 49 (*50*) asks, 'Where, O LORD, are thy former manifestations of *ḥeseḏ* which thou didst swear in thy faithfulness (*'*ᵉ*mûnāh*) to David?' *dependable*] *hanne'*ᵉ*mānîm*, *Niph.* ptc. pl. masc. *'mn*, the √ from which Engl. 'Amen' is derived. The *Niph.* occurs some 50 times, a number of them in the context of the covenant and promises made to David and his dynasty: 1 Sam. xxv. 28; 2 Sam. vii. 16; 1 Kings viii. 23–26; 1 Chron. xvii. 23 f.; 2 Chron. i. 9, vi. 14–17; Ps. lxxxix. 28 (*29*). A peg could be driven into a 'secure' (*ne'*ᵉ*mān*) place (Isa. xxii. 23 f.), a stream be 'perennial' (Jer. xv. 18), a priest 'trustworthy' (1 Sam. ii. 35), Samuel 'vested with authority' as a prophet (1 Sam. iii. 20), Yahweh's declaration 'irrevocable' (Hos. v. 9), and so on. 'Irrevocable' is not the right word here, in the context of the exile, notwithstanding the original assurance to David in 2 Sam. vii. 12–16. There it is said that if David's 'son' acts wickedly, Yahweh will chastise him. 'Him' refers not alone to Solomon, but to any succeeding Davidide, much as 'my servant David' in Ezek. xxxiv. 23, xxxvii. 24 is not David *redivivus*, but any king of David's line,

'David' being perhaps the throne name of the dynasty. The passage concludes (ver. 16): 'But your dynasty and your kingdom shall be enduring (*w^e^ne'man*) for ever before me (with LXX) and your throne shall be established for ever'. In the Deuteronomic prayer of Solomon (1 Kings viii. 23–26), composed (cf. vv. 46–51) under the shadow of impending exile, the promise of the permanence of the dynasty is qualified by the stipulation, 'if only your sons look to their way (of life) and walk before me as you have walked before me'. The late Psalm lxxxix is in two minds—it may be composite. Vv. 19–37 (*20–38*) are related to 2 Sam. vii and 1 Kings viii: 'I will keep my steadfast love for him for ever, and my covenant shall be enduring (*ne'^e^menet*) for him'. But the addition (?) has it: 'Thou hast denounced (*nē'artāh*) the covenant with thy servant' (39 (*40*)), and concludes, 'Where are the ancient proofs of thy love (*ḥ^a^sāḏêḵā*), O Lord, which thou didst swear to David in thy constancy? ('^e^*mûnāh*)', 49 (*50*). The monarchy during the exile was discredited. Since then the only Jewish kings have been Levite Hasmoneans. The text reads as if DI accepted the situation and saw the covenant and its accompanying evidences of Yahweh's love for David transferred from the monarchy to the people. After all, a covenant with Israel was made long before the time of David, and what David and his successors held, they held in trust for the people. It is significant that in 'I will make a covenant with you', the suffix 'you' is in the plural. In many of its aspects the monarchy was an unhappy episode. The final gaze of DI was to the Suffering Servant, not to a revival of the Davidic monarchy, and such attempts as those of Kissane (pp. 179 f.) and Engnell (p. 38) to equate the Servant with the suffering Davidic Messiah are not borne out by the exegesis of Isa. lv. 3 f.

4–5*a*. *As . . . so*] Heb. *hēn . . . hēn*. Not only is there parallelism between the two stichs in 4 and 5*a*, but 4 and 5*a* are in effect ‖ each other. If we take *hēn* in its usual sense 'Behold', the sense is 'Behold, I appointed David . . . behold, you will call . . .'. That is to say, the two stichs are related somewhat as the protasis and apodosis of a kind of concessive conditional sentence. This is even clearer if we take the first *hēn* as 'If' (so in liv. 15; cf. Exod. iv. 1, 'Suppose they do not believe me . . .'.). (The question of the original identity of *hēn* 'if' and *hēn* 'behold', need not concern us; see *GK* 159 *w*.)

4. *I appointed him a witness to the peoples*] For 'the peoples' (*l^e^'ummîm*) see on xlix. 1, where the Servant announces his commission to them. Nowhere outside the present passage is David said to be 'a witness to the peoples', but Ps. xviii. 43 (*44*) says, 'Thou dost make me a head of nations (*rô'š gôyîm*), people (*'am*) I do not know serve me'. The psalm is early and may well be David's, and was certainly regarded

as his by the time of DI. *leader*] *nāgîḏ*, perhaps as 'designated' (cf. vb. *higgîḏ*). David is so called in 1 Sam. xiii. 14, xxv. 30; 2 Sam. v. 2, vi. 21, vii. 8. Saul was the first 'king' to be given the title (1 Sam. ix. 16). The word is also used of Solomon (1 Kings i. 35) and even of the North Israelite kings Jeroboam I (1 Kings xiv. 7) and Baasha (1 Kings xvi. 2). It was probably, in the tentative beginnings of the monarchy, less open to objection than *meleḵ* ('king'). Even if the meaning of the passage is that the Davidic monarchy is to be restored —which is certainly the intention of Jer. xxiii. 3–5; Ezek. xxxiv. 23, xxxvii. 24—the emphasis here is upon spiritual leadership rather than upon political dominion. 'Witness' is used in xliii. 10, xliv. 8 of the spiritual calling of Israel. Nor should any emphasis upon political hegemony be read into the words 'leader and commander', both of which suggest moral leadership rather than military dictatorship.

5. *nations*] The Heb. *gôy* is singular, and if we translate it so, there is no indication what particular 'nation' is meant. The word must have a collective sense (RSV 'nations') as in xlix. 7 (which see). *invested you with honour*] Cf. lx. 9. Heb. *pē'ᵃrāḵ* (*Pi'ēl* pf.). For the associations of the verb and its cognate nouns see on xliv. 23. *and because the Holy One of Israel has invested you with honour*] Lit. 'and because of the Holy One of Israel for (*or* that) he has', &c.

LV. 6–13. HOME-COMING

9. גָּבְהוּ] *Qal* pf. 3rd pers. plur. The normal, and stronger, idiom would be כְּגֹבַהּ ('according to the height of'), especially with כֵּן in the apodosis. This (כְּגוֹבַהּ) is the reading of Qᵃ.

12. תּוּבָלוּן] *Hoph.* Impf. 2nd pers. plur. masc. יבל. This, with the ending *-ûn*, is to be preferred to the prosaic תֵּלְכוּ ('you shall go') of Qᵃ.

These familiar verses, with their emphasis on 'Do not delay!' may well make one poem with the preceding paragraph. Delay in responding to the divine invitation may be fatal. Divine grace is no excuse for human complacency (Ps. xcv. 7–11; Rom. vi. 1 f.; Heb. ii. 3, iii. 7–19). Let the wicked man abandon his way of life and return to the God whose forgiveness is 'abundant' (*yarbêh*), whose thoughts and ways are as much higher than man's ways and thoughts as heaven is higher than the earth. That Yahweh's 'word' will accomplish his purpose is as sure as that the rain makes the earth fruitful. The concluding verses (12 f.) recur to the theme of the second Exodus through the transformed wilderness (xli. 18 f., xliii. 19 f.).

There is, appropriately, an expansiveness about these concluding verses such as we do not often find in Hebrew poetry. It is as if the river, as it finishes its course, broadens into an estuary open to the tides of comprehensive revelation. Vv. 8–9 are tristichs in which words of more than normal length are piled up. There is not a full stop in the four distichs and one tristich—or however we should scan them—of vv. 10–11. Ver. 13 is 4:4/3:3, or if, with Köhler, we scan 2:2/2:2/3:3, it makes no difference; there is nothing staccato about the first half of the verse, such as we have, say, in Nahum iii. 1–3.

6. *Seek . . . call to*] While the temple stood, 'seeking' Yahweh would usually be by the offering of sacrifice: 'I will offer to thee a sacrifice of thank-offering and will call upon the name of the LORD' (Ps. cxvi. 17). In the conditions of the exile, prayer, which in any case would have accompanied a sacrifice, would take the place of sacrifice: see Jeremiah's letter to the exiles (Jer. xxix. 12 f.). Prayer, even private prayer, would in OT times be vocal: *ḳārā'* = 'call aloud'. *while he is to be found*] *b^ehimmāṣ^e'ô*, *Niph. tolerativum*, 'while he lets himself be found' (cf. RSV rightly, at lxv. 1). Man must not presume upon God's patience: cf. Amos viii. 11 f. *turn back*] In repentance. For this sense of *šûḇ* see Hos. vi. 1 and often.

7. *he is always ready to forgive*] Lit. 'does much (*yarbêh*) in respect of forgiving', *rāḇāh* being one of the verbs which serve as an auxiliary to a verb following. The particular verb used for 'forgive' here (*sālaḥ*) is only used with God as subject.

8. *thoughts*] As the context indicates, God has 'thoughts' (*maḥ^ašāḇôṯ*) as well as man. But the noun and its corresponding verb are more often used of man's thoughts and thinking than of God's, and sometimes in the bad sense of 'devices'; e.g. Jer. xi. 19, 'they devised devices' (RSV 'schemes').

10. *but water*] *kî 'im-hirwāh*, lit. 'But (rather) have watered' (properly 'saturated'). The conjunctive particle serves to emphasize the preceding *and do not return there*. Another possible translation is 'unless/until they have watered' (cf. Gen. xxxii. 26 (*27*), but this is ruled out by ver. 11). *give seed*] The grammatical subject is not the earth but 'the rain and the snow', anticipating 'my word' in ver. 11.

11. *that goes out from my mouth*] I.e. 'which I solemnly utter', see on xlviii. 3. *it shall not return to me*] Even a human 'word', uttered as an oath or a last testament, is, in OT thinking, irrevocable (Gen. xxvii. 33–40). The idea is no doubt a survival of heathenism. It is different with 'the word of the LORD' (Heb. iv. 12). The word which God 'swears', and which 'goes forth from his mouth' (xlv. 23), is irrevocable, like an arrow which must find its mark. Having done that, it does not return to God. A word spoken earnestly by a disciple, if it fails of its object, returns to him who speaks it (Matt. x. 12 f.; Luke x. 5 f.; cf. Ps. xxxv. 13). *unfruitful*] *rêḳām*, lit 'empty'. The translation 'unfruitful' is appropriate in view of the preceding context, and the sense is vouched for by the 'empty' ears of corn in Pharaoh's dream (Gen. xli. 27). *instead, it will do . . . succeed*] Lit. 'but (rather) it will have done . . . succeeded'. The verbs are future perfects, with simple *waw* (*wᵉhiṣlîᵃḥ*), not *waw consec.*

12. *led along*] Lit. 'borne along', with some suggestion of a processional march; cf. Ps. xlv. 14 f. (*15 f.*). *safety*] *šālôm* here expresses rather more than absence of physical danger. Something like confident trust in God is meant: cf. Ps. iv. 8 (*9*). *the mountains and the hills shall break out*, &c.] For the 'sympathy' of inanimate nature with God's redemptive activity, cf. xliv. 23.

13. *camel-thorn*] *naʿᵃṣûṣ*, elsewhere only vii. 19, √*nʿṣ*, 'stick into'. *juniper*] *bᵉrôš*, see on xli. 19. *nettle*] *sirpaḏ*, ἅπ. λεγ., V *urtica*. Some such mean and noxious weed is required by the || 'camel-thorn' and the contrasting 'myrtle' (*hᵃḏas*, xli. 19). *come up*] *yaʿᵃlêh* can mean 'grow' (see on xl. 31), but something like the 'beanstalk' growth of the vine in the butler's dream (*ʿālᵉṯāh niṣṣāh*, Gen. xl. 10, RSV 'its blossoms shot forth') is probably intended (see on xli. 19). *memorial*] For this sense of Heb. *šēm* ('name') cf. lvi. 5: 'And I will give to them in my house and within my walls a monument and a name' (*yāḏ wāšēm*, lit. 'a hand and a name'). In 2 Sam. xviii. 18 Absalom is said to have erected a standing stone (*maṣṣeḇeṯ*), 'for he said, "I have no son to carry on my name' (*šēm*); and he called the standing stone by his name, and to this day it is called Absalom's monument' (*yāḏ*), as giving him a kind of posthumous life. *inscription*] *'ôṯ* (usually 'sign'). In Lachish Ostrakon iv. 11 the plural is used of fire-signals. In Isa. xix. 19 f. the standing stone to the LORD on the frontier of Egypt is to serve 'as a sign (*'ôṯ*) and a witness (*ʿēḏ*) to him in Egypt'. In Joshua iv. 1–7 the twelve stones which were taken out of the Jordan—they were sizeable stones, carried on the shoulder, ver. 5—are to be a sign (*'ôṯ*, ver. 6) and a memorial (*zikkārôn*, ver. 7) for ever (*ʿaḏ-ʿôlām*). *lasting*] *ʿôlām*, see above on ver. 3. *effaced*] *yikkārēṯ*, lit. 'cut off': cf. xlviii. 19 ('obliterated'); Ruth iv. 10, 'that the name of the dead man may not be erased from among his kindred and from the gate of his (native) place'.

It might be supposed that once the exiles had completed their journey, the way would revert to its former desert condition; they were not to live there permanently. But no! The transformed desert will be kept in perpetuity as a commemorative park. On the question whether the Prophet intended this quite literally, see Introduction, p. 25. If he did, he was mistaken. But even if he was mistaken, the word of God of which he was the herald will assuredly 'stand for ever' (xl. 8).

INDEX OF SCRIPTURE REFERENCES

(*excluding passages cited in the Introduction*)

OLD TESTAMENT

APOCRYPHA

NEW TESTAMENT

INDEX OF SEMITIC WORDS

(Finite verbs are listed under the roots from which they are derived.)

HEBREW

INDEX OF AUTHORS

INDEX OF SUBJECTS

PRINTED IN GREAT BRITAIN
AT THE UNIVERSITY PRESS, OXFORD
BY VIVIAN RIDLER
PRINTER TO THE UNIVERSITY